MAZE CRAWLER:
A FAMILY IN CRISIS

Susan Christopher
Corraine Conaway

A Conifer Press Book

Conifer Press
An imprint of Conopher, LLC.
P.O. Box 4119
Clifton, NJ 07012

Copyright @ Susan Christopher, Corraine Conaway 2016
All rights reserved

First Published 2016

United States of America

ISBN 978-1-539-94007-4

Cover Art by Jacqueline Kiernan
Cover Design by Susan Christopher

For the brave man who allowed his story to be told so that loving parents and disabled children can find the courage and strength to navigate the bewildering maze of our social system.

S.C.

For my parents, Joan and Soapy, with heartfelt thanks for all the love, support and prayers that helped sustain me through life's difficulties.

C.C.

MAZE CRAWLER:
A FAMILY IN CRISIS

PART ONE

❧

LIVING

Chapter One

The alarm tore through the apartment, shattering the early peace I'd found in the morning kitchen. I gulped another sip of tea, scraped back my chair, and ran down the hall to the bedroom where my husband, Dave, slept peacefully, pillow over his ears, blanket tangled around his feet. I banged my hand on the shut off switch, then decided to let him snore. Maybe I'd be in a better mood after my morning shower.

On my way to the bathroom, I glanced out the hall window. It was early March and the front lawn was spread with a light sprinkling of snow. Winter had been bleak, an endless parade of gray days pierced by sleet. There hadn't been much snow, an occasional dusting quickly washed away by the shadowy curtain of freezing rain, but this morning was clear and bright and the sun was making a belated appearance over the belfry of Holy Family Church across the street. A good omen? The tea had taken effect and I was thawing inside. Now all I needed was a hot shower.

I washed quickly. The questions I had tossed and turned over last night still churned. What would he look like? How would he act? Would I feel anything when I saw him? Would Dave feel the same way I did?

We were about to take a step that would change our lives though I barely suspected how much life would alter by the events that were to take place that morning. If I had known, I would have been far more frightened than I was. There were times in my life when I wished for a guardian angel, someone, anyone, who could tell me what I should do, but I know now that we are not meant to see the future, that if events and their consequences were fully within our control, few of us would choose to perform the difficult tasks life demanded and so much of our learning and growth would be lost in the process.

I put the coffee on to perk and returned to the bedroom. Dave still had the pillow clutched in his arms, the fermented odor of stale liquor rising from his slackened mouth. I grabbed the pillow and shook his shoulder. He rolled over and groaned. I rushed back to the kitchen and grabbed a mug of black coffee. By the time I returned he had struggled to a sitting position and was staring at the clock as if it was about to give him news he didn't want to hear. I handed him the coffee. He grimaced. I took that for a smile and grinned back.

"We still have four hours before we have to leave," he said "I know you have a thing about time, but, come on, Corraine, four hours."

"I couldn't sleep. Aren't you the least bit excited?"

"Sure I am. I just hide it better."

I laughed as I walked back into the kitchen to start breakfast. Dave had a way about him that always made me feel light-hearted. He knew I was nervous and, for my sake, he hid his fears, reassuring me that everything was going to be fine. After all we'd been through it had to be. Sometimes, Dave thought he could use his Irish charm to ward off disaster. Facing problems head on was more my style, but I was grateful for his sense of humor and generosity.

A few minutes later, he staggered into the kitchen, our six- year-old daughter riding his shoulder. Cheryl was a beautiful child, her Canadian Indian heritage imprinted in her high cheekbones, great dark eyes and straight black hair. She was tall for her age and her bare feet dangled as Dave carried her to the table.

"So where is he?" she asked.

"You're as bad as your mother," Dave said. "It's only eight o'clock. We don't meet him until noon."

I scooped out three plates of bacon, eggs, and hash browns, "Look what Mommy made for you. Your favorite breakfast." Cheryl dug into the full plate, but I noticed that Dave wasn't eating.

"Bathroom's free," I said. "Why don't you shower now? You can eat later if you want."

Dave threw me a grateful look and, after a few more sips of coffee, walked down the hall. His stomach was never good in the morning and I should have realized that, after a night like last night, he wouldn't be able to eat. I had made the breakfast more for Cheryl than for us because I didn't want her to feel excluded. I explained to her again that she couldn't go with us, but that next time we would take her. Today, she would visit my parents who lived in the apartment downstairs.

Mom was in her usual place by the sink. She wiped her hands on a dishcloth and turned to look at me. For a moment, neither of us spoke, but a mirror of my own excitement shone in her eyes. I wondered what she saw when she looked at me. Doubt? Fear? Probably both.

"If it's God's will, it will work out," she said before I opened my mouth.

"I'm just nervous," I said. "What if he doesn't like us? What if we don't feel anything for him? It's not like we're shopping for wallpaper."

"If it is meant to be, it will be. If not..." She shrugged her slim shoulders, then hugged me. My Dad stood in the doorway, listening. I gave him the thumbs up sign.

"That's my girl," he said. "You can do anything you set your mind to. And when you set your mind to something, God help us."

I wondered why I always felt better after I spoke to my Dad. It wasn't what he said, but the way he said it, as if he really believed I could do anything if I tried hard enough. I wanted to live up to his confidence in me and I always tried harder after talking with him.

The sharp blast of a horn sent me running to the window. Dave had pulled the car out of the driveway and was waiting in front of the house.

"I guess this is it. Wish me luck," I said. I gave Cheryl a kiss and after a few unnecessary instructions about her care, I walked outside and climbed into the car.

We drove through Nutley in silence. To calm my jumbled thoughts, I stared out the window at the passing scenery. The massive chestnuts and lacy sycamores that lined the streets were still gnarled and naked, their bright new greenery not yet in evidence, though here and there on a front lawn, bunches of blazing yellow or purple crocuses stood up bravely to the March wind. Nutley was a handsome town, its three-story Dutch colonials and the wide porches of its tall Victorians gave it a turn of the century feeling. We had moved here when I was six and I had grown up part of the close knit community. Dave and I had agreed that we wanted to raise our children here, where they would have the advantages of a small town atmosphere within a half-hour bus ride to Manhattan.

When Dave exited the parkway and turned right toward the town of Verona, my chest tightened and I could feel a line of perspiration pop out on my upper lip. I wiped my sweaty hands on the knees of my pants and wrapped my winter coat more closely around my neck

11

and shoulders. Dave backed into a parking space next to Verona Park and glanced at his watch.

"What time is it?" I was so flustered I'd forgotten when we were supposed to arrive.

"Ten minutes before noon. Plenty of time," he said.

Too anxious to sit, but with nowhere to go, I left the car and leaned against the hood, staring at the wide green spaces of Verona Park. I had always loved this park with its well-tended lawns, secluded walks shrouded by rhododendrons and wide lake where in the summer children fished and families rented paddle boats. Now as I stared at the familiar sight I felt as if I were looking through glass, the colors blurred and the edges turned in on themselves.

"Ready?" Dave asked.

He came around to where I was standing and took my arm. My legs stiffened as we walked up the street toward the address we had been given. After nearly half a block, I stopped and clutched Dave's hand. Walking towards us was a middle-aged woman. She was short and thin with a crop of light brown hair pinned beneath a green winter hat. Next to her, holding her hand, a small boy staggered along, his gait awkward and uneven. He was dressed in a warm winter jacket and heavy pants, a knitted cap pulled over his light blond hair. He was not yet aware of our presence and I watched as he struggled to match the pace of the woman holding his hand. He would have fallen several times if the woman had not kept a tight hold. His face was thin and pale. Blue eyes shone from beneath short, stubby lashes. His nose was short and pert and his small mouth had a slight tremble to the lower lip.

They stopped a few steps before us. A younger woman hurried from the opposite direction to make the introductions.

"This is Mrs. Davis, Mark's foster care mother, and, of course, this is Mark," she said. "I'm Marilyn Sagan, Mark's caseworker from the adoption agency."

The little boy raised his eyes at the sound of his name, studied me rather solemnly, but with a sparkle of curiosity, then looked at Dave.

"Mark doesn't speak yet," Marilyn Sagan said. "He's a little over three, but his developmental age is only eighteen months. He's had a rather rough start, I'm afraid. It's affected his development."

I looked at Dave for his reaction, but he wasn't paying attention. He was smiling as he watched Mark grow impatient with the adult conversation and begin to tug on Mrs. Davis's hand.

"He wants to go to the park," she explained. "I promised him he could play while we talked."

"Do you think I could take him?" I asked.

Mrs. Davis bent down and spoke to Mark for a moment. Mark looked up at me with a solemn expression. When I held out my hand, he took it trustingly. I slowed my steps to match his. Once again, I looked at Mrs. Davis.

"I'll tell you all about it when we get to the park," she said.

Dave took Mark's other hand and we swung him along as we walked. He giggled and garbled sounds we took for talking. Over the top of his head we looked at each other and, for a moment, everything seemed to switch to slow motion, giving me time to imprint the scene in my mind and heart.

At the park, Dave took Mark to the play area while I sat on the bench with Mrs. Davis and Marilyn Sagan. I watched Mark and Dave run from the slide to the swings to the jungle gym. I knew how much Dave wanted a son. We had always planned a large family, but things didn't work out that way. When we adopted Cheryl, she had brought a deep fulfillment to our lives. There was no question that we wanted another child. But there were still some unanswered questions. I turned to Mrs. Davis

"Why does he walk so awkwardly?" I asked.

"Inner ear infections," she said. "A few months ago he had such a bad infection that he had to have surgery to relieve the pressure in both ears. They inserted tubes at the same time to help with the fluid build-up, but the infection affected his balance. The doctors assured us that it would right itself in time and he would walk perfectly."

"How about his language? Shouldn't he be talking?"

Mrs. Davis looked at Marilyn Sagan as if uncertain how much she should say.

Dave and Mark were playing in the sand box, Mark digging up sand and throwing it. Dave spoke to him quietly. One of things I loved most about Dave was his sympathy for and affinity with children. He adored them, simply and without reservation. Mark stood up and ran to the edge of the sandbox. He tripped and fell, picked himself up without a sound and toddled down the path towards the lake. Dave followed at a rapid walk.

"He's very active," Mrs. Davis said. "That's something you should consider."

"We're very active, too," I said. "No problem there."

"Mark's had a difficult start," Marilyn Sagan said quietly. "He's been in quite a number of foster placements, but never in one long enough to form any attachments. That alone could account for his delayed development. Except for Mrs. Davis, I don't think anyone has ever taken the time to teach him anything. He is toilet trained, but that's about it. He has no vocabulary that we know of though he does make sounds and gestures to express some of his needs. You should also know that his biological mother neglected him if not worse and his biological father most likely committed suicide. Mark will not inherit anything from his father's estate. "

"We're not adopting Mark for money," I said. "After what he's been through, he deserves to be loved and we have plenty to give."

Marilyn Sagan did not seem put off in the least. "All I'm saying is that Mark might need extra help in the years to come which means extra expense for you. No money will be coming to you to cover those needs."

"If we adopt Mark, he will be our son. We'll find a way to provide for him."

"I think your husband's getting tired," Mrs. Davis said. "Would you like to come back to the house for a cup of coffee?"

She was obviously uncomfortable with the turn of the conversation and kept looking back and forth between us.

I called Dave. He bent down, scooped Mark up in his arms and, pretending to be a horse, trotted back to us. When he tried to put him down, Mark protested, so with a pleased grin, Dave carried him back to the house.

Once inside, I removed his hat and coat and took him to the bathroom. He wasn't the least bit shy with me. I kept up a light chatter, asking him whether he'd like to come live with us. I told him about Cheryl and described the apartment. Since he could not respond, I wasn't sure how much of what I was saying got through to him. He grew impatient, wiggled around and, as soon as he was finished in the bathroom, shot off to the kitchen where Mrs. Davis fed him a snack of milk and cookies. When Mark ran off to play, Mrs. Davis served us our coffee. She didn't sit with us and I noticed that she wandered frequently to the connecting door to check on Mark.

"He's rather fearless," she said. "He gets into everything with no thought of the consequences. But then, most three year olds don't, think of the consequences, I mean."

I wondered why she was so nervous. Wanting to make a good impression maybe? I gulped down my drink and walked back into the living room where Mark was moving blocks around on a large cocktail table. Beside the blocks was a collection of miniature plastic cars and trucks and other vehicles he could slide between the rows he was forming. I sat down to watch. Dave stood beside my chair, his hand resting lightly on my shoulder. Now and then, Mark would look up at us as if making sure we were still there.

"How does he get along with your other children?" I asked Mrs. Davis.

She was about to answer when, with a loud cry, Mark crashed all the toys onto the floor. I jumped. Mrs. Davis didn't seem the least surprised.

"He doesn't know any better," she said. "He thinks this is the right way to play. Nobody's bothered to correct him."

I noticed that she didn't correct him either.

"He must be getting tired." I stood up to leave.

Mrs. Davis looked up from the toys she was collecting and shook her head. "One thing you'll learn about Mark," she said. "He never gets tired."

Marilyn Sagan walked us back to our car. "I think you should spend more time with Mark before you make your final decision," she said. "Perhaps you can come back in a week with Cheryl and then contact the adoption agency if you're still interested."

I didn't want to wait that long and neither did Dave. We asked her to arrange for another visit on Saturday, two days from today. We would bring Cheryl with us then and, if everything went well, we would go to the adoption agency and fill out the final papers.

As we drove away from Verona Park, I looked at Dave. He sensed my excitement and reached out to hold my hand.

"Do you want to keep the name Mark or do you think we should change it?" Dave asked.

"Mark Graham sounds great to me."

"Why don't we go out somewhere and celebrate?" he suggested.

I hesitated only half a second. "This is such a wonderful moment I want it to go on forever. But don't you think we should share it with Cheryl and my parents?"

"They can wait a few minutes. It's not every day a man gets a son."

He drove to a small pub in a neighboring town. We had been there before, but not at three o'clock in the afternoon and the large, dimly lit room was practically deserted. The hostess led us past the few stragglers at the bar to a secluded table in the back. I treated myself to a Vodka and Tonic. Dave drank his vodka neat and ordered another. On the second round, he lifted his glass. "To my lovely wife, Corraine, my daughter, Cheryl, and my new son, Mark."

"Through God's grace," I said. I was a little uncomfortable about Dave's certainty that Mark was ours. We still had to earn the approval of the adoption agency and I wanted to make certain that Cheryl liked Mark and did not feel jealous or anxious about having a little brother. I had explained to her there was a strong possibility that we would adopt Mark. She acted excited about becoming a big sister, but she was only six years old and had been a member of our family for a little over a year.

"You haven't changed your mind, have you?" Dave was on his third drink and had just ordered his fourth.

"Not at all," I smiled at him. "I'm just not looking forward to all the hassle with the adoption agency. Remember how awful it was when we adopted Cheryl. A criminal interrogation would be a piece of cake compared to what we went through."

Dave pinched up his face to look like the disapproving prune of a social worker. "And just why do *you* think *you'll* make good parents?" he mimicked.

I laughed and pushed the painful memories away. This was supposed to be a celebration and I would not allow anything to come between me and the joy I felt on realizing I was going to have another child. This time I raised my glass. "To the family we always wanted and are lucky enough to have."

When the after-work crowd filed in, we left. Our news wasn't the kind we wanted to share with strangers. I drove since Dave was in no shape to get behind the wheel and by the time we arrived home, he was snoring loudly.

"Instant replay," I thought, remembering the difficult time I had rousing him this morning. With his head thrown back and his mouth open wide, he looked like a dead shark and was just as difficult to move. When I finally managed to rouse him, he said, "I'm going upstairs for a nap. Do you mind telling your folks the good news? I'll be down in a little while."

"Can't you wait a few minutes? It's a big moment in their lives, too. We should all be together."

"I'll be down soon. I promise."

I wanted Dave to be with me when I told them, but what did it matter. I was too excited to let anything bother me. I rushed into the house and ran to the kitchen. Cheryl was at the table cutting out paper dolls and my mother was putting the finishing touches to the lasagna we were having for dinner. She spun around as I ran into the room. My dad hurried in from the parlor, leaving the TV blaring.

"Well?" he asked. "Do I have a grandson or don't I?"

"Congratulations Grandpa and Nana," I said. "Grandchild number two is on the way."

I swooped down and hugged Cheryl. "And you're going to be a big sister. What do you think of that?"

"Neat," she said. She let me hug her for a few seconds, then squirmed to get down.

"Where's Dave?" My father looked over my shoulder toward the door. I shrugged.

"He's upstairs already. It's been a long day and he wanted a nap before dinner. He loved Mark as much as I did. No problems there."

"He's a lucky man. First Cheryl. Now Mark."

"And don't forget me," I laughed. "I'm the best of the bargain."

"That you are, honey, that you are. I only hope Dave realizes it."

"I won't let him forget," I promised.

I grabbed my Dad's arm and we waltzed around the kitchen. "Ain't life grand?" I said and at that moment, it was.

Chapter Two

Marilyn Sagan called to tell us if we wanted to take Mark home after our next visit we could. Since we had already been approved because of Cheryl's adoption, we didn't need to go through the initial formalities, but she suggested we come in anyway because there were a few things she wanted to discuss. What was there to talk about, I wondered. Children were children. Of course, you had to contend with different temperaments and different abilities, but wouldn't the enjoyment be the same? With a year of parenting behind us, we were ready for another child. I called Dave at work and asked him to come home early because Marilyn had said she would be at the agency until five o'clock this afternoon.

"If that old battle axe is still there, I'll ask her some questions she won't want to answer this time," Dave said, referring to the woman who had handled Cheryl's adoption. In the bright afternoon sun, I noticed how careworn he looked. He was still handsome, with that rugged Irish charm, but his skin showed red blotches and there were lines dug in around his mouth and fanning out from his eyes. Dave had been working two jobs for the last few months. He was making a good income, but I realized that we had had little time away from our responsibilities. Now, with another child on the way, we would have even less.

"Why don't we go out to dinner after we're done here," I said. "Just the two of us. We won't have many more chances after Mark comes."

Dave gave me a crooked smile. "Sorry, Mom," he said. "I have to get back to work. I've got a family to support."

Dave had always been a social person. It was rare he would refuse to go out in favor of work and I knew he had taken the rest of the day off so we could arrange for the adoption. I decided to let it go, but I promised myself I would sit down with him soon and have a long talk. We had discussed the adoption, but I couldn't remember the last time we had just been together and talked as husband and wife.

A pleasant woman I didn't remember greeted us at the reception desk and ushered us without waiting into Marilyn Sagan's office. How different from the last time we had been here! Marilyn had decorated her office in soft shades of blue, with comfortable modern chairs. Spread across the walls were candid photos of children. Everything about the office was calculated to make perspective parents feel appreciated. I smiled my approval. She poured us each a cup of coffee, then sat behind her desk and reviewed the file. I tried not to worry. Hadn't she said Mark was ours? My hands started to shake and I set my coffee cup down quickly.

"Everything seems to be in order," she said after a long silence. "I requested this meeting because there are a few things you should know before you make your final decision about Mark." I started to interrupt, anxious to reassure her about our intentions, but she shook her head. "I know you've pretty well made up your minds, but you should be aware that Mark has had a tough start. This might affect the ease with which he adjusts to your family. When a child's been bounced around as much as Mark has it's difficult for that child to bond with others." When I looked confused, she explained. "Bonding is a term we use for the ability to form an emotional attachment. It depends not only on love, but trust as well. Mark has not had a chance to build that trust with anyone. Just the opposite." She consulted the file.

"We don't know a great deal about Mark's biological family except that his father was killed in a railroad accident. Probable suicide. The newspaper article states that he ignored the flashing red warning lights and drove around two stopped cars and onto the tracks. Mark's birthmother cared for him for the first three weeks of his life. After that he was in twelve different placements with friends and relatives until he came into foster care." She looked up. "See what I mean about the bonding." I started to speak, but she interrupted me again. "There's more. You should hear it all before you decide.

"Mark was brought to Passaic General Hospital several times with burns on his face and severe bruises on his arms, thighs and back," she continued. "Child abuse was suspected, but it was never confirmed. The hospital records also showed that the back of Mark's head was flattened, a condition usually caused when a child lies on his back for long periods of time without being lifted.

Mark's birthmother requested foster placement and he was evaluated by Dr. Nagel," she consulted the file again. "That was done this past December. The news was mixed. He was found to be of low but trainable mental potential with an IQ in the mid-70's. At the time he had poor impulse control and was acting out which isn't surprising. Twelve placements in the first three years of his life caused him to feel an enormous amount of rejection. Dr. Nagel felt that Mark was a little boy who needed a great deal of loving discipline and structure. What this means is that even though he is very young, he is likely to be distrustful until he understands that this is to be his permanent home with parents who will not neglect nor abandon him. He may act out or he might just be very careless. In all conscience, I have to tell you that his initial placement for adoption was disrupted. Mark had been playing with a cake box which caught fire when he turned on the stove. The family felt they could not handle him after that and asked for his immediate removal. Mark is not mean or malicious, but he does have behavioral problems and he's into everything. He may also be hyperactive."

She had thrown out so much information that it didn't occur to me to question what she meant by hyperactive. To me, it just meant that Mark had a whole lot of energy, a normal state of affairs for a small boy. That was no problem because I was always on the go. Fine, I thought, my son will just go with me.

"Everything you've told us has strengthened my conviction that we're the right parents for Mark," I said. "There's no question of changing my mind or thinking anything over. Dave and I decided when we first saw Mark that he is ours. If we have to work a little harder to get him to trust us, then we will." I looked over at Dave for reassurance. He was fiddling with his coffee cup, his eyes on the carpet. He said nothing.

We set up a meeting for the following Saturday to visit with Mark and his foster parents once more. The social worker told us that if Cheryl had no problems, we could take Mark with us that same day. I was sure Cheryl would adore him. She had been talking about her little brother ever since I had spoken to her about the possibility of having another child in our family. Cheryl was neither outgoing nor shy. She had a remarkable ability to accept things as they came. We agreed to meet again in Verona Park so the children would have a chance to play together.

Dave dropped me off at our apartment. He said he didn't have time to come in because he didn't want to be docked another hour's pay. On the way home, we had talked about Mark. Dave assured me he was looking forward to having a son. We still wanted a large family and felt that at last we were making strides towards fulfilling our dream.

I ran inside to tell my parents and to collect Cheryl so I could tell her about Saturday. She wanted Mark to stay in her room, but I told her he was still small and that, at first, I wanted to put him in a crib in our room. That way, if he woke up scared at night, I would be right there to reassure him. Throughout the rest of the afternoon I answered her questions about Mark and made a point of telling her how much I would need her help caring for him.

I had already fallen asleep when Dave returned home from his second job and I didn't hear him come in. The next morning he was again difficult to rouse and the fetid smell of alcohol on his breath was so strong I gagged. I finally got him up and on his feet, but I had to help him to the shower.

By the time we were to leave for Verona Park, he was sober and looking forward to being with Mark again. It was a beautiful day, the air carried a hint of early spring, and the sun was warm on our shoulders as we left the car and walked to the park. I spotted Mark in the sandbox, sunshine glinting off his hair. I squatted down beside him and told him that there was someone special I wanted him to meet. He listened, then jumped up and shot off. I caught him by the back of his coat and brought him over to where Cheryl was waiting with Dave.

"Cheryl, this is your new brother, Mark," I said.

I waited to see if my words had any impact on Mark. I wasn't sure if he knew what the word brother meant. He looked at Cheryl. She looked back at him. Cheryl was only six and Mark was developmentally a young toddler. I wasn't sure if they were supposed to kiss or tear each other's hair out. Dave suggested that we take them over to the playground equipment. I was surprised when he took Cheryl's hand instead of Mark's, although Mark was perfectly willing to come with me. Cheryl looked back over her shoulder, watching us. I talked to her as we walked along. I didn't want her to feel left out, but she was happy with Dave.

Cheryl wanted to go on the slide so I brought her over and stood there as she climbed the ladder. I was watching Dave talking to Marilyn Sagan while he pushed Mark in the swing. Cheryl sang out for me to watch her as she slid down. I glanced up, but my attention was on Mark. I was soon to have a son and the wonder of it had caught my imagination. I loved that my family was growing and I loved the challenge of a new life within my guardianship.

A loud wail cut my reverie short. Cheryl was lying on the ground at the end of the slide, holding her leg and crying. The skin on her right knee was torn and bloody and dirt had smeared into the cut from where she had landed on the ground. I dabbed at the cut with a clean tissue from my purse.

"You weren't watching," she accused me.

"You're right," I said. "I'll have to grow two sets of eyes now that there are going to be two of you."

I thought she would laugh. She didn't. She looked over to where Dave was lifting Mark from the swings.

"Can we go home now?" she asked.

"Just as soon as we pick up Mark's things. I want to wash out your cut first and put a Band-Aid on the sore."

The idea of the Band-Aid brightened her up. I made sure I walked with her to Mark's foster mother's house. I remembered to ask about a security blanket or stuffed animal. She said there was nothing he was especially attached to. She had packed his toys and clothes. He had nothing from his biological parents. I took Cheryl into the bathroom and patched up her knee.

"Ready?" I asked her.

"Is Mark coming with us?" she asked.

I nodded. "Is that okay?"

"I guess," she said, but she didn't sound happy.

"How would you like to sit in the front seat with Daddy? We can stop for ice cream on the way home and you can order for all of us."

"I guess," she said again.

Better than nothing, I thought. I put Mark in the car seat that Cheryl had outgrown and climbed into the back beside him. He had come with us easily. Too easily. I couldn't help thinking about what the social worker had said about Mark being bounced around so often, he hadn't been able to bond with anyone. His foster mother had been a lovely person and yet, when she hugged him good-bye, he had squirmed to get down and showed no sadness in leaving. Maybe he's just too young to understand that he won't see her again, I thought.

By the time we ate our ice cream, Cheryl had recovered her good humor and chatted to Mark all the way home in the car. She told him about his grandparents and how he would have to stay in the room with Mommy and Daddy until he wasn't scared of being in a new place anymore. She told him about her dolls and toys and how he would have lots of things to play with and how we could go to the store and pick out something he liked. While she talked, I watched Mark. He made a few small grunting noises and wiggled around in the car seat, but I couldn't tell whether he understood her or whether he was just excited. I made a mental note to schedule an appointment with my pediatrician as soon as possible. Mark's foster mother and the social worker had assured me there was nothing wrong with his hearing, but I wanted to have it checked myself. He was my son. I felt that my responsibility to him started now.

Dave had been strangely silent throughout the visit and when we pulled up at the door, I couldn't help thinking how different it was when we had brought Cheryl home. The next day had been Thanksgiving. My Aunt Sis and Uncle Al had all the relatives over for dinner and, of course, to meet Cheryl. What a fuss! I had taken several rolls of pictures that day. My favorite was of Cheryl sitting at the dining room table, very coy and shy, wearing a huge carnation corsage my Uncle Al had bought her. Everyone had showered her with attention and my little niece, Michelle, had presented her with a baby doll she had saved her allowance to buy.

Mark, I knew, would be as welcome and as loved, but it was almost as if he had been expected and no one would be surprised by his coming. I wasn't sure whether I was happy or saddened by it. I finally decided it was better for Mark to get to know the family gradually. All of us together could be rather overwhelming and I wasn't certain how he would react. Meeting my parents would be enough for the first day.

When I unbuckled the safety strap from the car seat, Mark bounded out and took off up the front walk. I ran after him, calling his name and managed to catch him before he fell up the steps. His gait was still unbalanced and I was afraid he would trip on the steep brick stairs leading up to the front door. I grabbed his hand and helped him up the steps.

My Mom bent down to give Mark a hug. He tolerated it for a moment, and then squirmed to get away. The minute she released him he zoomed past her into the house. I wished I had remembered to warn my mom to child-proof the living room. Cheryl had always been a quiet child, easily distracted and able to entertain herself. We had never felt it necessary to put away knickknacks and breakable items because Cheryl had never grabbed for them. Mark was not in the house more than ten minutes when he knocked over a lamp and pulled down one of the candy dishes my mother had on the living room end table. Fortunately, it landed on the rug and didn't break.

I took out the box of Legos I had bought him and scattered them on the rug. He sat down and started feeling them, turning them over curiously. Cheryl curled up some distance away, but close enough to be near him, and picked up her Barbie doll. I watched them for a few seconds, and when it seemed they were settled, I went into the kitchen to have a cup of tea with my parents.

"The social worker warned me he was very active," I said. "But I think he's over-excited as well. A new house, new family. He's been bumped around a lot. I'm sure that makes a difference."

"Don't worry about it." My mother handed me a cup and patted my shoulder. "Some children are just more active than others. You'll get used to it."

"And boys are usually more physical than girls at this age," my father said. "I was a holy terror growing up."

I smiled at him. "I'm not sure if that's reassuring or frightening."

"How can you say that?" he laughed. "Look how wonderful I turned out."

Cries from the living room had us on our feet. I sprinted into the room, tripping over traps of scattered Legos. Cheryl was crying so hard she couldn't talk. She pointed to where Mark was running around the room. He had Cheryl's doll by the hair and was waving it wildly as he picked up speed. Round and round the room he ran, dodging Cheryl as she reached out to snatch her Barbie back from him. Each time he shook the doll at her she cried harder.

For a little guy unsteady on his feet he was not that easy to catch. It took me three tries before I finally grabbed him. I wrapped my arms around him and carried him to the over-stuffed armchair. He was still clutching the doll. I quietly explained to him that the Legos were his, but the doll belonged to Cheryl and that he couldn't play with it unless he asked. I talked to him in a quiet tone until he calmed down. Cheryl came over to take her Barbie and Mark let it go without a fuss. I realized then that raising two children was a whole different experience than raising one.

"Let me take the little guy outside," Dad said. "You and your mother relax a bit. It's been a big day for everyone. Mark can run around the yard and work off some of that energy."

I smiled my relief. I realized I was pent up and that a few quiet moments would restore my balance. I helped button Mark's jacket and told my Dad to watch him on the stairs because his walking was still unsteady. Cheryl dried her tears, gulped some water and went back to playing with her doll in the living room. I kicked off my shoes, fell into the kitchen chair and sipped the fresh cup of hot tea my Mom set before me. I looked at her across the table. We both started to laugh.

"Remember those poor Moms I used to pity in the Mall," I said. "You know the type, one screaming kid going one way, the second running off in the opposite direction. The mothers always looked so frazzled. I have a feeling I'm in for a lot of frazzled days. Are you ready for this, Mom?"

"The question is, are you?" she said.

I shrugged. "How bad could it be?"

I remembered that conversation often in the years to come. At good moments I was able to laugh at the irony of it. At bad moments I wondered at my carefree self so certain that my love could conquer whatever problems life had in store. And life had a storehouse of problems, the door of which I had just opened. But that afternoon, sitting quietly in my mother's kitchen, life was filled with blessings and I was grateful for each of them.

Since Dave was going straight to his second job that evening, I decided to stay downstairs and have dinner with my parents. My Mom suggested we go out for pizza, but something told me that Mark in a restaurant would be too much for me to handle. We decided on

25

spaghetti and meatballs, messy but fun. Cheryl loved helping make the meatballs so while she was mushing the ingredients together, I checked out the window to see what my Dad and Mark were doing.

"Calm down," my mother laughed. "Dad knows what he's doing. I remember so many spring days when you and your father worked outside together. You used to dig holes and then, when you weren't looking, he would cover them up again. Do you remember all the peach pits you planted outside? Didn't you ever wonder why none of the peach trees grew?"

"Don't tell me he used to take them out of the holes?" I laughed.

My mother nodded. "If he didn't we would have had a peach orchard for a backyard." She stirred the pasta in the pot. "You'd better call them now. This is almost done."

I didn't feel like putting my jacket on so I leaned out the back door and yelled, "Dinner's ready."

My Dad and Mark came back in a few minutes later. They were holding hands and my Dad was shaking his head and smiling.

"You're not going to believe this," he said. "We found a colony of ants out under the old maple. Mark stood there and watched them going in and out of their anthill almost the whole time we were outside. I tried to get him away to play something that might wear him out a bit, but he kept going back to the ants. He didn't stomp on them or anything, just stood around and watched."

Mark wiggled his grubby fingers to show me how the ants moved. I felt a tremendous wave of relief. Because of his ear infections and his delayed language, I had been afraid he did not understand what I had been telling him. Now I knew he could communicate. I gave him an extra big hug and carried him into the bathroom to wash his hands. He wiggled his fingers under the water and giggled. I was overwhelmed by my feelings of love and I was determined that my devotion would make up for all that Mark had endured during the first three years of his life. From now on his days would be filled with the happiness a secure home and a supportive family could provide.

I lifted Mark into the high chair my parents had bought for him. I had a plastic fork and spoon that Cheryl had never used because she was past that stage when she came to live with us. I unearthed them from the back of my mother's junk drawer and handed them to Mark along with a plate of cut-up meatballs and spaghetti. I didn't try to guide him at first because I wanted to know whether he could use them himself. He showed no recognition of the utensils and, after playing with them for a while, he threw them on the floor and turned his attention to the food. He pushed the meatball around with his finger, then looked up at me with a confused frown.

"Obviously not Italian," my Dad said.

I gave up on my dinner and moved my chair next to Mark's. Taking his hand in mine, I twirled a small amount of pasta onto the fork and lifted it to his mouth. He squirmed in the high chair, no longer interested in the food or what I was trying to show him. I managed to feed him a few forkfuls before he lost interest completely and refused to open his mouth.

"Now we know why he's so thin," I said, returning to my cold dinner. "He isn't interested in food."

My Mom got up from the table rather quickly and removed the remains of Mark's dinner from the high chair tray. He had started to take the strands from the bowl and throw them over the side onto the floor. His behavior was typical of a younger child, but I knew he was developmentally below his age. All children at some point throw their food on the floor. Perhaps Mark would have to go through certain phases in order to catch up. I had never gone through those phases with Cheryl, but I had read enough books on child care to know they were normal. Mark's slow start put him back to the two year old stage.

After dinner, I took the children upstairs and got them ready for bed. As I ran Mark's bath, Cheryl showed him her room and the crib where he would sleep in my room. I could hear her talking to him, explaining about bedtime and lights out. When I went to find them, Mark was crying, not loud or noisy sobs, just a steady stream of tears flowing down his cheeks.

"What happened, Cheryl?" I asked.

She shook her head, her eyes wide and frightened. I picked Mark up and carried him into the bathroom. Cheryl wanted to help bathe him but, for this first night, I asked her to go play in her room. She looked hurt.

"I didn't do anything to him," she said.

"I know you didn't, sweetheart." I hugged her with one arm. "I just think it would be better if I spent a few minutes alone with Mark. He's probably pretty confused by all the changes he went through today. A nice calm bath will help him settle down. Get your PJs on and, when I've put Mark to bed, I'll come in and read you a bedtime story."

As soon as I laid Mark in the warm water of the bath, I felt his body relax. He leaned back on my arm while I soaped him up and seemed to fall into a half sleep. Great, I thought, getting him to bed will be easy. I'll just dry him off and lay him down in the crib. Then I could read to Cheryl and relax myself.

When I lifted Mark from the water, he was still drowsy. I wrapped him in a fluffy bath towel and carried him into my bedroom. I diapered him, just in case he was still a night wetter, then picked him up to carry him to the crib. Not halfway there, I felt his body tense and, when I looked down, tears were running down his cheeks again in a steady stream and his skinny little chest heaved.

"It's all right, Mark," I soothed. "You'll be fine. Look over there. Mommy and Daddy will be sleeping right near you. We won't leave you. We'll never leave you."

Slowly, I lifted him up to put him in the crib. He clung to me and wouldn't let go. His fingers clenched, his nails dug painfully into my arms. I cuddled him close to me again and walked with him around the room, singing to him softly, but when I tried to put him in the crib, he started thrashing and screaming, his arms and legs flying wildly. The screams turned into howls. His head snapped around and he tried to bite my hands. I ran with him to the bed, laid him down and captured his hands in mine. I kept talking to him in a soothing voice, telling him that I loved him and that I wasn't going to leave him alone in the dark. When he quieted enough for me to hold him, I lifted him onto my lap and held him tightly. His screams subsided into sobs. I held him for a long time, singing and talking to him until he wore himself out and fell asleep in my arms. He did not wake when I laid him in the crib and covered him with the quilt. His pale face was tear-streaked and occasionally he hiccupped as he breathed. When I was certain he wasn't about to wake up, I tiptoed out of the bedroom.

I found Cheryl curled up asleep on the carpet outside my door. I had forgotten my promise to read her a story. I carried her to bed and tucked her under the covers. She moaned and I hoped she would not have nightmares from what had just happened. Nightmares! What horrors Mark must have lived through in his short life to experience such terror. I could only hope that in time, the fears from his early life would fade, their memories replaced with all the happy times I planned to share with him.

I flopped onto the couch utterly spent. I wanted to stay up and wait for Dave, but within a minute, my eyelids began to droop. Before I fell asleep, I prayed that I would find the patience I needed to replace Mark's terror with peace. Tomorrow I would begin the slow, steady work of building a bond between us that not even the worst nightmare could threaten.

Chapter Three

"Corraine, get in here now!"

"It was six thirty Saturday morning and I had just gotten up to fix Mark breakfast. He was an early riser, on the go at sunrise. It amazed me how he could be so energetic when the nighttime routine was so traumatic. The screaming and crying had persisted though Mark had now been with us for a month. Often it took me an hour of rocking and cuddling and even holding him down to get him to sleep. What had happened that caused him such terror at the thought of being put to bed? Likely I would never know. All I did know was that I was worn out by the routine and by the early starts

Dave was still working his second job, coming in late and going straight to bed. After my struggles with Mark, I often fell asleep on the couch where I had laid down to watch television and unwind. Sometimes Dave would wake me, but more often than not, he would let me sleep. We were both up at dawn. Dave would drink a quick cup of coffee with me before work, then we would both take up the duties of the day. But today was Saturday and from the sound of it, Dave had no intention of getting up early and playing Daddy.

"Corraine!" dropped the banana I was peeling, wiped my hands on a dish towel and ran into the bedroom. Dave was huddled up half-asleep near the edge of the bed while Mark jumped wildly in the middle of the mattress.

"Oh no you don't!" I said. I caught him in mid-leap and carried him off to the kitchen where I plunked him down in the high chair. I ran a belt around his waist and snapped on the serving tray. Mark had already found a way to slip under the tray and run off. To keep him in his seat long enough to eat I had fashioned a soft belt which threaded through the spokes of the chair and tied in back. Mark was still not interested in eating. It was a daily battle to get food into him. I had given up trying to get him to use utensils.

"Don't do that while Daddy's sleeping," I told him as I spooned cereal into his mouth. "When he tells you to stop, you stop!" Mark waved his arms around, accidentally knocking the spoon from my hand. Cereal and bananas splattered across the linoleum.

While I wiped up the floor I listened for sounds of awakening from the other bedrooms. I tried to keep Mark occupied in the early morning so Cheryl would have a chance to sleep. She had started first grade the previous September and was doing well in school. I wanted it to continue that way. Having Mark around had proven a bit of an adjustment for her because he was on the go from early morning till he wore himself out crying at night. Mark loved Cheryl. Sometimes he was content to play with his Legos while she talked to him or played with her dolls. But other times, he would bother her, grab her things and run away with them or push her, trying to make her get up and run around with him.

I detected no noise from her bedroom and Dave was snoring peacefully so I decided to let Mark play in the bathtub for a while. It was the one place where he seemed able to relax and focus on what he was doing. Every morning I would fill the tub with warm water, bubbles, and toys and let him play in it as long as he liked.

"Not too long in the tub this morning, young man. We have a busy day ahead of us. First we have to go to Dr. Patterson's, then Miss Sagan is coming for a visit. You remember her. She's the lady who used to go to the park with us when I first met you."

I often spoke to Mark in this way, hoping he might pick up a few words and throw them back to me. Mark's speech had not improved in the month he had been with us and I was concerned that his hearing had been affected by the operation to drain the fluid in his ears. Also, his constant activity and the difficulty in getting him to sleep were beginning to concern me more than I was willing to admit. All of that and his size as well. I looked at him playing happily in the tub and noted all of the things I was worried about, his little stick arms and legs, the way his ribs protruded from his skin, the knobby line of his backbone. It was obvious that even after a month of fighting to get food in him, he wasn't gaining. I checked my watch. I had an hour to get ready. Mark was beginning to look sleepy so I plucked him up, wrapped him in a towel and took him into my room to get dressed.

"Shhh now! We don't want to wake Daddy," I said, though Dave was snoring so loudly a four-alarm fire wouldn't wake him. I dressed Mark quickly, then took him into the living room where I called my mother. She was an early riser so I knew I wouldn't be disturbing her. I nearly dropped the receiver, as Mark took a belly flop off the couch onto his face. I righted him, checked for damage and let him go. Some mornings there was no stopping him.

"Sorry about that," I said. "Typical morning. Do you think you could come upstairs while I take Mark to the doctor? No, nothing special. Just a routine exam, but I have a lot of questions I want to ask him." I checked my watch. "How's fifteen minutes? Cheryl's still sleeping and so is Dave. He needs to sleep and I don't want Cheryl to wake him. Thanks Mom."

I collected the records the adoption agency had given me and the psychological report that had been done in April. I wanted my pediatrician to look over the reports just in case there was something there that could account for Mark's developmental difficulties. I had no basis to compare Mark with other children except Cheryl and she had come to us when she was older. I wanted Dr. Patterson's assurance that, although Mark had had a difficult start, after a few months he would be fine. I waited until my mom came up, then bundled Mark into the car seat and drove off. The town was just waking and there were few cars on the road. May was a beautiful month in Nutley, the tree lined streets trimmed in green, the lawns sprinkled with violets, daffodils and tulips. The morning air, warm but retaining a hint of crispness, poured in through the car windows. I turned on the radio and hummed along, enjoying the ride.

In the doctor's waiting room, I noticed that Mark's hands were fluttering and fidgeting, his movement more awkward than usual. He clung to me when the nurse called for us to enter the examining room. When I asked him to sit on the table so I could undress him, he co-operated, but he kept watching the door. I picked him up, then walked around the room to show him the different pictures on the wall. His head kept arching back to the door and, when it opened, he threw his arms around my neck and held on tight.

Dr. Patterson patted Mark on the back, then ignored him as he turned to me and took the folder I had in my outstretched hand. He sat down at the desk and quietly looked through the papers, making a notation here and there. Mark watched suspiciously, then calmed down enough to squirm out of my arms and wander around the examining room though he kept an eye on me all the time. Dr. Patterson looked up from the papers he was examining, watched Mark walk, then checked the charts again.

"Has he complained about his ears since he's been with you?" he asked.

I shook my head. "He just doesn't seem to respond properly when I talk to him. I'm not sure whether he can't hear me or he doesn't understand what I'm saying to him. I'd like you to check his hearing if he'll let you."

Doctor Patterson looked at me inquiringly, encouraging me to go on. I wasn't quite sure how to express my concerns. I just had the vague feeling that something wasn't right though I couldn't pinpoint it. I floundered for a moment, then said, "Mark's had a pretty rough start so I don't expect him to be the same as other kids his age. I guess what I'm asking is whether he'll catch up and what I can do to help him?"

Dr. Patterson looked back at the records. "Twelve placements in the first three years of life would leave anyone confused. It might be nothing more than that, which is still quite a lot to overcome. Did you read Dr. Nagel's report? His IQ was reported to be on the low side with a score of 75, poor impulse control and little speech." He turned a page. "The neurological exam that was done a month later shows no specific abnormalities. Dr. Hudson notes that he came from a chaotic and rejecting background and that he requires structure and limits to develop appropriately. What this little guy needs is a lot of patience and appropriate discipline. Now, let's take a look at his ears, shall we?"

Mark had been wandering around the examining room, touching the crinkly paper on the table and ripping at the edges. I didn't think he had been listening to our conversation but, as soon as he heard "ears", he flew into my lap and covered the sides of his head with his hands.

"I don't think you need to worry about his hearing," Dr. Patterson said. "He certainly heard that I was going to examine his ears and he also understood what it meant."

He leaned over and spoke to Mark in a quiet but firm voice. Mark watched him and, after a while, he let me take his hands in mine. Dr. Patterson kept talking to him as he looked first into one ear, then the other.

"Good boy," he said, when the ear exam was finished. "Now, if you let me weigh and measure you, I'll have my nurse give you a sticker and a lollypop." Mark looked up at me. I bent down, gave him a kiss and took him by the hand over to the scale. He allowed me to weigh and measure him though he stiffened up whenever Dr. Patterson came near. His height and weight were well below the percentile for his age, but his overall physical condition was fine.

Dr. Patterson left the room for a few minutes. I dressed Mark and told him what a good boy he was and how proud I was of him. He seemed his normal active self now that the exam was over and jumped off the table as soon as I finished dressing him. By the time Dr. Patterson returned, he was racing around the examining room, cooing his excited little noises.

Dr. Patterson asked his nurse to take Mark into the waiting room and give him a lollipop. Mark was perfectly willing to go. Dr. Patterson sat behind his desk and I sank down into the chair I had been sitting in before.

"So, Doctor, what's the verdict?" I asked.

He smiled. "Nothing quite so serious as that, Corraine. Mark's ears have healed well from the procedure and there doesn't appear to be any hearing loss. His speech is delayed, but I think that's more the effect of his never having been encouraged to talk. Children learn by hearing conversation and being allowed to participate in it. Mark hasn't had much encouragement to do anything. You've only had him for a month. Be patient. He is also underweight, but that too will take time to correct. Don't fight with him at mealtime. Just encourage him to eat when he's hungry. Some of what you've noticed may be part of the neglect he suffered in the early years. With the proper attention and discipline, there's every hope that Mark will soon be a healthy little boy." I so wanted to believe him that I told the little voice still nagging inside me to shut -up. After all, what did I know? I drove home, relaxed and reassured.

At home, Dave was awake. He, Cheryl and my mom were sitting at the kitchen table finishing up the remains of a light breakfast. They looked up at me with a "so-what's-the-news" expression. I repeated everything Dr. Patterson had said.

"Any questions?" I said, looking at him.

He shrugged and downing the last of the coffee in his mug, got up and went into the bathroom.

"What's with him?" I asked.

My Mom stood up. "Isn't the social worker coming this afternoon?"

34

I looked at the clock, a moon-shaped contraption hanging over the refrigerator. Twelve o'clock. Marilyn Sagan was due to arrive at one. Foolishly, I had invited her for lunch, forgetting that I had also invited our friends Marie and Bob for dinner that evening.

"Mom, could you run to the Italian deli for me and pick up a few meatball and sausage sandwiches," I said, reaching for my purse. I had planned to make a fancy lunch to impress Marilyn, but that was clearly impossible. "Pick up some salads while you're at it. And, of course, you and Dad are welcome to join us for lunch. Actually, I'd appreciate it if you would come." I looked toward the bathroom. "It would take some of the pressure off me, especially if Dave's in a bad mood."

My mom hesitated a moment. "I'll be back in a half hour with the food. We'll fix it so Miss Sagan won't even notice it's not home-cooked."

After she left, I turned the TV on in the living room, set the kids up with toys, then walked down the hall to the bathroom. The water was running in the sink, but I could tell the shower wasn't on. I knocked on the door, waited a few minutes and knocked again.

"Dave, Miss Sagan will be here in a little while. I don't mean to rush you, but I need to get in there if you're done"

The door flew open, the handle cracking against the plaster wall. Dave stood in the doorway, shirt open, hands on his hips. I looked closely at him for the first time that morning. His eyes were bloodshot; his skin mottled and grey. He hadn't bothered to shower or shave and a strong odor of liquor hung about him. A sudden recognition amounting to fear shot through my chest. Maybe he was seriously ill and I had been so caught up in my concerns with the children that I hadn't noticed or given him a chance to tell me. I stared at him helplessly. I couldn't deal with this right now. The social worker from the agency was on her way to evaluate our fitness as parents. If she walked in and saw Dave like this, we might lose Mark. I willed myself to calmness though my heart was racing and my hands felt moist.

"Dave, you've got to shower and get dressed," I said in my most matter-of-fact voice. "If Marilyn sees you looking like the wrath of God and me all nervous and upset, she might just understand, but I wouldn't count on it. You know how important this is to us and to

Mark. If you want, we can talk after she leaves, but for God sake, please fix yourself up."

I turned on my heel and walked off down the hall without giving him a chance to reply. With the mood he was in, he might want to pick a fight and that was the last thing I needed now.

In the living room, Mark had turned the TV up full blast and was climbing the shelves of the entertainment unit. At the third shelf I picked him off and carried him into the bedroom to change his suit which he had somehow managed to get filthy. I tried to keep my mind focused on the home visit and the dinner I was going to cook later in the evening for Marie and Bob, anything to keep my mind off Dave. I could hear the shower running and I prayed he would recognize how important this afternoon was to all of us. I had just finished buttoning Mark's shirt when the doorbell rang. I jumped, then ran to answer it.

"Just me," my mom said as she came in, her arms filled with bundles. "I couldn't reach my purse to fish out my keys." She laid the parcels on the counter and turned around to ask me something, then stopped dead.

"I won't ask you what's wrong because you look like you're about to burst into tears. Get dressed and fix your face, Corraine. Your father's coming up to watch the kids and I'll take care of the lunch. I know where everything is. Just take a few minutes for yourself."

I ran back into the bedroom and, by the time the doorbell rang again, I looked calm and collected though I was feeling anything but. The apartment was spotless, Mark's suit, by some miracle was still clean, and my mother had laid out a feast fit for a queen. Dave had still not emerged from the bathroom, but I could hear the sounds of the razor scraping against his stubbly cheek and I assumed he was sobering up. I cast one quick look around the scrubbed up kitchen and opened the door. Marilyn Sagan gave me a quick smile as she walked in. I was surprised, but delighted by her warmth.

"I've got something for Mark," she said after first admiring the arrangement of food laid out on the counter. "Where is he?"

I ushered her into the living room where my Dad and Mark were playing. Mark had just knocked down a tall tower of blocks and was squealing with delight. My Dad was laughing.

"Thank you, God," I whispered. She could not have walked in at a better time. She sat down in the overstuffed chair and watched Mark help my Dad build another tower. Mark was now able to balance one block on top of another and with some help to build a tower of four or five blocks. I was proud of his achievement and glad Marilyn noticed it as well. After a little while, Mark tired of the game and started looking around for something to do.

"Miss Sagan has a present for you," I said and took his hand to lead him over to her. From a bag, Marilyn drew a soft, spongy tugboat.

"It's for your bath," she said.

Mark looked at it a moment. "Tub," he said happily.

Marilyn looked at me, a smile lighting up her face. "He's talking? How marvelous!" I didn't have the courage to tell her that he had never said anything before so I ignored it as if it was an everyday occurrence.

"You must be hungry," I said, lifting Mark up for a quick hug and marching with him into the kitchen. Dave joined us for lunch, his appearance much improved by a shower and shave. He put himself out to be charming and between us and my parents, the lunch was a pleasant experience.

"I'd love to stay," Marilyn said after we had finished our cheesecake and coffee, "but I'm late for another home visit. It was a wonderful afternoon and I think Mark's a lucky boy to have such a fine family."

As soon as she left, I sank down on one of the kitchen chairs and cradled my head on my arms. "Wasn't that something though? I think she was really impressed. Don't you?"

When no-one answered I looked up, surprised. Dave and my parents were sitting in silence, a strained look on their faces. Could my perceptions have been that far off? I started to ask what was wrong when Dave interrupted me.

"Mom, would you and Dad mind taking the kids downstairs for about an hour? I'd like to talk to Corraine in private."

My mother shot me a look and scooped Mark off the top of the cocktail table where he had managed to climb in the short time we were talking. Cheryl calmly collected her coloring books and crayons and the four of them went downstairs.

At a loss for words, I put the kettle on and busied myself at the counter making tea. Dave sipped his coffee in a silence that stretched on for several unbearable minutes. Since I had known him, I had never been afraid to talk to Dave about anything. Now I felt as if I was searching for a subject of conversation with a stranger. I didn't know how to begin the discussion. I didn't know what the discussion was about. I stirred sugar into my tea and carried it to the table. Dave seemed sunk into some reverie of his own. I sat down beside him and took a sip of tea. I wanted to reach out and put my hand in his, but he seemed so remote, so withdrawn. I gathered up the shreds of my courage.

"Dave, what's wrong?" My voice came out shaky, but that was how I was feeling. I made no attempt to pretend otherwise.

He looked at me and shook his head. "Corraine. I'm not sure I can do this anymore. I'm not sure I want to."

The panic within me grew stronger, pressing on my chest until I had trouble breathing out the words. "Do what?"

"Work two jobs, be a father and a husband, live here with your parents and your family. I thought this is what I wanted, but now I'm not sure. I don't know anything anymore." He reached into his pocket and pulled out a bottle of pills. "It's gotten so bad lately that I went to the company doctor and got these."

"What are they?" I asked.

"Antidepressants."

I stared at him. I could feel my mind beginning to shut off. What he was saying was so threatening, so shocking, I couldn't think straight.

"Why didn't you tell me how you were feeling? I'm your wife, for God's sake. If you're so damn depressed you need medication, don't you think I have a right to know?"

"I just figured it was my problem. You were so wrapped up with the kid's problems..."

"Oh no you don't." I jumped up, knocking over my chair and started to pace. "Whatever's wrong, you're not going to blame this on me. If you wanted to talk to me you could have at any time. I've never once put the kids ahead of our relationship. I may have had to deal with them more immediately, but as their father, I figured you understood that. It isn't me that's had no time for you. It's you that hasn't been around enough to have time to talk to me."

"Maybe you're right. I don't know," Dave watched me as I paced. "All I know is that I'm confused and unhappy. Nothing seems to be working for me anymore."

"So what are you saying, Dave? That you want to end the relationship? That you want to move out on me and the kids?" I didn't want to hear the answer. I still couldn't believe we were having this discussion.

Dave dropped his head in his hands. "I don't know. I honestly don't. I love you and I love the kids. But something's got to change. I can't live like this." He looked up. "I didn't mean to blurt this out. I'm sorry. What I really wanted to talk about was Mark. He's out of control. I know what the doctor said. I know he needs love and patience, but I think he needs more discipline. He doesn't listen and he's wild. If he's not jumping or climbing on the furniture, he's bothering Cheryl or breaking things."

"That's great, Dave. Just great. First you talk about moving out and abandoning your son. Then you tell me, he needs more discipline. Are you going to be around to administer that discipline? Are you?" Suddenly, I didn't want to talk. I could feel the tears pricking my eyes. I wanted to get away somewhere quiet and sort out my thoughts. "I need to get out of here for a while," I said. "I'm going downstairs."

I walked into my mother's kitchen and burst into tears. She was sitting alone at the kitchen table. "I sent your father and the kids to the park. If you want to talk about it, I'll listen. If you just want to cry, I'll sit with you," she said.

"I don't know what I want to do?" I sniffed. "Yes, I do. I want to scream at the top of my lungs for a long, long time, but I don't think I've got the strength. I can't seem to get my thoughts in order. I feel so scrambled up. How could I not have seen this coming? Why didn't he say anything to me?"

"What did he say now?" she asked.

"That he was miserable and he didn't know whether he wanted to go on with the marriage."

"Oh, Corraine. I'm so sorry." My mom's eyes filled with tears. "Did the two of you decide anything?"

I shook my head. I had stopped crying for a moment, but a fresh torrent came on and I gave myself up to the luxury of indulging my grief. "He's taking antidepressants. I didn't even know things had gotten to that point. He never told me. He never told me anything."

"Corraine, my dear. As hard as it is, it's time you faced certain facts. Your father and I have debated talking to you. We never wanted to interfere with your marriage, but we've been very worried. Dave is a really good guy when he's sober. He's a good father and a generous man when he's not drinking. But darling, he's almost always drinking now. We've noticed the deterioration over the last two years. Corraine, Dave's an alcoholic."

I felt like my mother had slapped me right across the face. I stared at her with the same stunned expression I'd worn just a few minutes ago. Had everyone gone mad or was it me? My mother looked like she was about to cry, but oddly enough my tears dried up. Scenes from our early marriage flashed into my mind. I could see the difference in Dave just as my mother had said. He was sick, but with an illness I knew nothing about and one that was eating away at him slowly and with devastating effect.

"What do I do?" I asked helplessly.

"You can go talk to Father Blake. Why don't I call and make an appointment for Monday? Even if Dave won't go, maybe Father can tell you where to get help."

I shook my head. "Everything is moving too fast. I need time to think. Bob and Marie are coming for dinner and it's too late to cancel. I need to get some groceries. I'm going to ride around for a little while, then stop at the store. I need to do something normal or... or... I don't know what I'll do."

"Are you sure you want to be alone?" I could tell my mother was frightened for me. I leaned over and patted her cheek.

"I've been a whole hell of a lot better," I said. "But I'm certainly not desperate. I just need time to think. I'll be home in less than an hour, I promise."

I walked out the front door in a daze. My father had taken the children to the park in my car because I had been the last to pull into the driveway. Dave's car was next in line. I often drove it on the weekends and I thought nothing of taking it now. Too bad if he wanted to go out. For once, he could sit at home and wait for me. I slid into the driver's seat and reached underneath for the lever to adjust the length. As I pushed the seat up, I felt a piece of paper sticking out from the side. I gently pulled it out, careful not to rip it in case it was something important. It was a greeting card, the design and words on the cover decidedly romantic. With trembling hands I flipped it open and read the hand-written note inside. It was to Dave from a woman, a woman who was certainly no stranger. I laid my head down on the steering wheel and did not lift it again until I had gathered enough strength to perform that simple motion.

Chapter Four

Dave's misery haunted me even in my waking hours. In the evening, after the children were asleep, I'd lay alone on the couch remembering the days of our courtship, the tender words, the late night phone calls. I pulled out our wedding album and cried over the young girl I was then, the one with the innocent face and dreamy eyes. I tore apart Dave's expression. Was that look of love a pretense for the photographer or had it been real, even for a moment? Why had he married me? Was it simply to replace the mother he had lost and when he had to share that mother with his children, did he lose interest? Dave had always told me how much he wanted a family and now that we had one I couldn't understand why he didn't want us anymore.

A thousand times I replayed the major events of our life together, looking for clues I had missed. I went over every action, every gesture, every conversation, every fight I could remember, but I couldn't find anything so terrible that Dave would want to give it all up. We had shared so many good times together, so much fun and laughter. True, Dave had been drinking through much of the fun. When had his drinking turned from a social amenity to a disease? Was he really too ill to recover? Anger towards Dave and anxiety for myself and the children spilled into my every thought, my every action. The home I had built so lovingly and with so much faith now felt like an armed camp, my relationship with my husband an uneasy truce.

To mask my anxiety from the children, I kept them on the run. I dragged them from the library to the mall, to the movies and out to eat at McDonald's. Cheryl, as always, fell in with my schemes, and Mark raced through them without noticing much of anything.

One Saturday, at loose ends and not wanting to spend the day tearing myself apart with unanswered questions, I called my Dad and asked if he wanted to have a picnic with us.

"Sure," he said. "Just so long as I don't have to sit on the ground to eat. Once I get down I may never get up again."

I packed a hamper with cold chicken, potato salad, pickles, lemonade and cupcakes for the children. My Dad was waiting for me on the front porch.

"Walk or ride?" he asked.

"Let's walk. The fresh air and exercise will do us good. We were cooped up in the house yesterday because of the rain. The kids need to run."

"And you need to run away. Is that it?" The question was gently asked, but I chose to ignore it and grabbing Mark's hand, I marched on ahead.

Nutley is a town of parks, a wide strip of green grass, trees and streams running through the center of the town. At this time of day, only a handful of people idled there, mostly mothers with small children who paid no attention to us as they watched their kids on the playground equipment. We decided to stop at Yantacaw Park where there was a playground and a fishing stream. There was also a collection of rough wooden picnic tables scattered about. I set the hamper down on one of the tables and told the kids they could run off and play. They raced each other to the slide.

"You've got to watch this," I said. "It's hysterical."

Cheryl climbed the ladder, sat down and slid to the bottom, then ran around to get on line behind the other children. Mark started his climb to the top, and although it took him longer, he made it with no trouble.

"Now watch," I whispered.

Mark stood up on top, waved his arms above his head and babbled unintelligible sounds as loudly as he could, looking for all the world like a pint-sized Tarzan about to swing across the jungle on a vine. The other children shouted for him to slide down, but the louder they shouted, the louder Mark babbled and gestured. My dad and I looked at one another and burst out laughing. I suddenly realized I hadn't laughed in a long time. It felt good.

Mark finally slid down, then ran to the back of the line. After three or four times the other children began to get impatient, one little boy threatening to push him down if he didn't go himself. I jumped up from the bench. My dad caught my hand and gestured for me to wait while he calmly walked over to handle the situation.

"Time to eat," I said when he returned with both kids in tow. Cheryl wiggled onto the bench and waited while I loaded her plate with a drumstick and salad. Mark was too wound up to sit still. He spun away and took off for the swings.

"We'll eat in shifts," Dad called over his shoulder. By the time I had finished eating, Mark had run to the swings, then to the wooden horses, back to the slide and was starting on the swings again. I gulped the last of my lunch, captured Mark and brought him back to the table. I wanted him to eat something, anything. Mealtime was such a struggle. He nibbled on a few cut-up pieces of chicken, then wanted to play again.

"I know just the thing to calm him down," Dad swallowed a forkful of potato salad, searching the ground near the table as he chewed. When he straightened up, he had a thin willow switch in his hand.

"What are you going to do?" I asked. I had occasionally screamed at Mark, more to get his attention than to punish him, but I did not believe that hitting children taught them anything but how to use violence to solve their problems, something I did not approve of.

My father laughed at the expression on my face and from his left pocket he drew out a long string with a hook on the end. He tied the string to the branch and brought Mark over to where the rolling bank sloped down to the stream. There were fish in the water and Mark was instantly mesmerized. My dad explained that the fish would swim away if he made noise or jumped around. Mark sat down quietly and held the fishing pole out over the water the way his grandfather showed him. I couldn't believe he was able to sit so quietly. It seemed a miracle, one for which I was tremendously grateful.

After watching Mark for a few minutes, my father returned to the table. Cheryl had finished eating and had run off to play with the other children. My dad looked at me and without preamble asked, "So what are you going to do?"

It wasn't an unreasonable question and one perhaps, I should have expected, but it took me by surprise and left me speechless. I thought I had been dealing with the situation in my own way, but I suddenly realized I had just been pretending that everything was normal and that I didn't need to make any decisions. I shook my head.

"You can't keep going the way you are. You have to face it and make some plans," he said.

"I don't believe in divorce, Dad. I married Dave for better or for worse. I want to make my marriage work."

"Then talk to Dave. Avoiding one another only makes things worse. You can't work it out if you don't talk to him."

Suddenly, I wanted to lash out, to hurt someone as I had been hurt. I wanted to scream and cry and make someone understand that I didn't deserve this. After all I had been through trying to do what other women did so easily, women who did not even want their children, women who got pregnant accidentally and threw their children into garbage cans, women like Mark's mother who neglected, then gave their babies away and never thought about them. All the painful tests, the fertility drugs, the disappointments, the operations, the humiliations of the adoption process, all this and now, the terrible pain and loss of divorce. I didn't do anything wrong. I didn't deserve it. All I wanted was a loving husband and healthy children that I could love in return. Was that so bad? I felt like I was being punished for something I had never done, that I was living someone else's life. I jumped to my feet and for once, I didn't care who heard me.

"What do you know about anything?" I screamed. "You and mother have been married over twenty-five years. Did she ever drink herself into forgetting you exist? Did she threaten to leave you and your child? Did she cheat on you? How can you possibly know how I'm feeling? Tell me what I did to deserve this? Tell me, I want to know."

I knew I was making a scene. The people in the park were watching me, probably thinking I had gone mad, but I didn't care what people thought. I didn't care about my dignity or about being a good girl. I stood there with my fists clenched, glaring down at my father.

"You're right, Corraine. I can't know how you feel," he said. "But I can tell you how I feel. The father in me wants to beat the daylights out of the man who hurt my little girl, but the man in me recognizes that you are no longer my little girl. You are a woman and a wife and mother. You have to make your own decisions. You're the one who has to face the truth and, with that truth, no matter how hard it is, you have to choose what you are going to do not only for yourself but for your children."

"And what about Dave? Doesn't he have to face up to what he's done? Doesn't he have to take responsibility for the hurt he's caused me?"

"Can you make him do that? Isn't that something he has to do for himself?" he asked.

"But will he?"

"Honestly, honey, I don't think so. Alcoholics come to a stage where the alcohol means more to them than anything else in the world. It becomes their mother, father, lover and best friend, or so they think. Dave may have reached that stage. And if he has, there's nothing you can do to change that."

"I can't accept that. Dave loves us. I know he does. I only need to remind him somehow and he'll stop drinking."

My Dad shook his head, but he didn't argue.

"Then you've made your decision?" he asked.

I nodded. "I'm going to fight for this marriage even if that means fighting Dave to save it."

"Then I think you should talk to Father Blake or a counselor from Alcoholics Anonymous. They can tell you what you're likely to face in the months to come," he said.

"I'll think about it," I promised.

All I did was think about it. I decided that the first step towards our recovery was to put aside my anger and inject some romance in our lives. I thought about going to our favorite restaurant, a scene reminiscent of happier times, but Dave's hours were so irregular and his condition so sloppy when he came home, that I didn't know whether we would ever get there. Instead I bought the fixings for a romantic dinner at home. I thought of buying champagne, but changed my mind. Dave would drink regardless of what I said, but I wasn't going to encourage it. I wasn't going to say anything about Dave's drinking tonight. I needed us to be together in the old way. I wanted Dave to remember the love that had brought us together in the first place. I no longer denied that the drinking was a central part of our problem, perhaps the most important part, but I didn't understand alcoholism. To me, drinking was still just drinking.

I occasionally had wine or a mixed drink when I went out to eat with friends and had gotten a bit tipsy, ending up flushed and silly that night and sick the next morning. But I could go for months without drinking or even thinking about having a drink. It was not a part of my life and, although I knew what fun drinking could be as well as the dangers of it, alcoholism was as foreign to me as leprosy. I had no idea what I was dealing with and, at the time, I knew no one who could tell me. Innocently, I believed that if I loved Dave enough, he would realize he didn't need to drink and he would turn off the alcohol like you turned off a faucet.

My parents agreed to keep the children downstairs for the night. I called Dave at work and asked him to please come home as soon as his shift ended. He didn't agree, but he didn't disagree so I assumed he understood how important this was to me.

At eight o'clock I put the potatoes on to bake and ran my shower. I dressed with care in a sunny yellow skirt and sweater outfit that Dave had always said made me look young as a new buttercup. I brushed my hair till it shone and applied a light mist of perfume. I felt feminine and attractive for the first time in a while and wondered if, in taking care of the kids and the house, I had begun to neglect myself. I vowed that no matter what the outcome, I wouldn't allow that to happen again.

When I was satisfied that there was nothing more I could do to make Dave notice my charms, I went back into the kitchen to start dinner. The London broil had been marinating for an hour. I stuck it under the broiler for a few minutes and washed and tossed the greens for a salad. I set the table with our wedding china and stemware and put out the carnations, rose buds and baby's breath I had bought at the florist. I stood back and surveyed my work and I began to feel again the way I had felt when Dave and I had been dating, that warm wonderful feeling of anticipation waiting for your lover. I hummed as I put last minute touches to the arrangement, then glanced up at the clock. If Dave left right after his shift ended, he would be home in fifteen minutes. I checked my appearance in the mirror once more, laughing at the pleasant butterflies in my stomach.

Fifteen minutes passed. A half hour. An hour. I called Sel-Rex to see if Dave had left yet. No one knew where he was. I tried to distract myself with a book. I turned the television on and stared at the screen. Two hours passed. The juices surrounding the London Broil congealed into globules of white fat, the potatoes shriveled in their jackets and the salad wilted, the lettuce browning soggily in the salad bowl. At eleven thirty I swept everything up and dumped it in the sink, meat and all. I would deal with the mess in the morning. I didn't cry. I couldn't feel. I was beyond that.

A wave of exhaustion hit me and I had just changed into my nightgown when I heard the key turn in the lock. I walked out of the bedroom and sat silently on the couch. Dave stumbled through the door, his eyes fiery red in the dim glow of the foyer light. He headed for the bathroom, but some instinct made him glance over to where I was sitting. Surprised to see me, he stood motionless, a hunted animal in the sights of my rifle.

"Where were you?" I asked calmly, my words cold in the silence of the night.

"I stopped off for a beer or two," Dave said. His words were slurred and his face looked ready to dissolve, as if one good washing would melt all the features away.

"Are you in any shape to talk?" I was determined to make him understand what he had done tonight, but I didn't want him so drunk he wouldn't remember what I said tomorrow morning.

"I'm tired. Very tired, Corraine. Can't we put this off till later?" he mumbled and started to walk past me to the bedroom.

I took a deep breath and remembered that this was my life as well as his and that I had a right to make it the best life I could. I had to pin him down before he slipped away forever. I took a deep breath and blurted out, "We can't go on like this, Dave. You can't continue to ignore me and I can't live in a dream that everything is going to be all right. We have to face the truth and work out our problems step by step."

He turned around and the dead look on his face frightened me into silence. He shrugged his shoulders as if anything I said would make very little difference to him. "What do you want to do, Corraine?" he asked.

"I want to try again," I said. "We're husband and wife, Dave, and the parents of two children. To me that's worth fighting for. I know it's not always easy. I know there are burdens and pressures on you, but there are burdens and pressures on me too. That's life. If we have each other to lean on, we can make it through. It's a good life and I'm not willing to throw it away without a fight."

48

I waited for him to answer. Under my hurt, my heart was still filled with hope and a sincere willingness to forgive. Dave stood near the doorway, his head bowed, his arms hanging loosely at his sides. His bloodshot eyes were half closed and his breathing was labored and heavy. He looked defeated. I would have gone to him, but I read all over him warning signs that said, "Keep Out."

I hadn't broken through to him, but words were beginning to fail me. If he had gotten mad, shouted at me, even blamed me for whatever had gone wrong, I would at least have known how he felt. I would have had the opportunity to tell him how I felt, but he was shut down, closed up and I was a stranger who wasn't allowed in the door.

"Don't you care, not even a little bit?" I asked.

"Corraine, I'll do anything you want," he said. His eyes did not meet mine and for once I was glad. I was afraid to see the blankness there, the complete lack of interest I knew I might find if I looked.

"I want you to help me," I said. "I want you to help us. I want to put this family back together so we can live out the dreams we had talked about not so long ago, not the rose colored ones, but the real dreams we both shared."

"You can't live on dreams, Corraine."

"No, but we can make the dreams reality. You and I working together. I need you. I need your help."

"What do you want to do?" he asked without enthusiasm. "I'll do whatever you say."

I was unprepared for the concrete quality of his question. I had thought about what we would say to each other, how we would sit side by side and rekindle the warmth that had blessed our earlier relationship. I had planned to talk about our dreams and to plan what steps we would take together to make those dreams come true. I hadn't once thought that he would dump all the responsibility for the relationship in my lap. Frantically, I searched for something that would startle him into another way of thinking, something that would allow us to work together to start recovering control of our lives.

"We have some money saved," I blurted out, thinking off the cuff. "Why don't we start shopping for that house we always talked about buying some day?"

Dave looked at me as if I was crazy, but, at least, I had caught his attention. "We don't have nearly enough money for a house, Corraine. It would take years to save that kind of money."

"Maybe not," I said. "Maybe... maybe we could pick up something at a sheriff's sale. That's possible, isn't it? We'll go through the papers every night and see what's available. Dave, come on. At least it's a start."

He shook his head. "I'm going to bed, Corraine. If you want to look through the papers, go ahead. I don't care one way or the other."

Once I had fixed on the idea, I was sure it was the answer to our problems. Early the next morning I ran out to the corner store and bought the local and county papers. We had not discussed whether we could afford to stay in Nutley or move to a neighboring town, but right now it didn't matter. More than anything, I wanted to get him interested in doing something that would draw him back into the family.

I poured through the papers and circled in red all the announcements that looked interesting or even possible. There were several sheriff's sales in town and some real estate ads that might grab his attention. I was determined to stay up that night and show them to him, whatever time he came in. I didn't mention anything to my parents or the children because I was still so uncertain about the outcome of my action. Dave had not said anything about buying a house or even looking at the ads. But he had not said he wouldn't either. He had just gone to bed and fallen asleep. I wasn't sure he would even remember our discussion.

He did. He came home at ten o'clock, earlier than usual and when I showed him what I had done, he didn't seem surprised. We sat together on the couch and looked over the ads, canceling out those we weren't interested in and discussing the merits of those we liked. My heart was still sore from the beating it had taken and, although I was certain I wanted to fight for my marriage, I found I resented Dave for making a fight necessary.

On Saturday, Dave suggested we look at some of the houses we considered real possibilities. We both wanted to stay in town, but we agreed to look at surrounding neighborhoods as well. Dave wanted a two story house, with the living area separate from the bedrooms so there would be some privacy when he wanted it. My biggest need was a backyard where the children could play safely. Few of the houses fulfilled both conditions and were within a price range we could afford. We drove around for several hours, marveling at the expensive Victorians with their gingerbread trim and wide wrap-around porches and bemoaning the few dumps that we would never consider buying.

"Back to the drawing board," I said as we headed home. "I'll get the paper again tomorrow. Something's bound to come up."

After a few weeks of searching I began to feel discouraged and I could tell that Dave was losing interest. He had been coming home early for the first two weeks, but now the night hours were stretching into early morning. Soon I knew my discouragement would turn into desperation and I searched the papers like a bloodhound tracking a fugitive. When the house on Brookdale Avenue appeared in the Estate Sale Column, I didn't wait to show Dave. I ran over myself to see it.

I knew the block the house was on because a childhood friend had lived nearby. The houses on Brookdale Avenue were post World War Two Colonials, two floors with large yards. When I drove up to the number listed, I had my fingers crossed on the steering wheel. "God, just give me a chance to make things work," I prayed out loud.

The house was halfway down the block and my first look revealed that it was not exactly the answer to a prayer. The outside was aluminum-sided in a faded shade of pink and the front porch looked like it would peel away from the house if I walked up the broken steps. Bricks were missing from the stoop and the yard was little more than a weed patch. I didn't know how structurally sound it was or how old-fashioned the inside might be, but I was willing to work and if Dave and the children would chip in, we could make it home. Right there, sitting in the car staring at that old house, I made my decision. Somehow I would convince Dave that this house was worth saving. Somehow I would convince him that we were worth saving. I didn't know how, but I would figure it out one step at a time.

That night I waited up for him to come home from wherever it was he spent his late night hours. I tried not to think about it, but to stay focused on the future. The past was dead and nothing there could hurt me if I didn't let it. Bringing my family back together was all that mattered. I would have time to heal my wounds when I was no longer in the fight of my life.

I kept all the lights on in the living room and blasted the television. Anything to stay awake. When Dave walked in at 2:00 a.m., he took one look at me and groaned.

"Don't tell me," he said. "You found a house."

"I sure did and it's just right for us, a two story Colonial with a big backyard. It needs a little work. It belonged to an old couple with no family. She died and he's in a nursing home. That's why it's up for sale. But the best thing is, it's right here in town. It will be a wonderful project for us to work on. You don't have to say yes now, but promise me you'll look at it."

Dave threw up his hands, "I'll look at it. I promise. Now can I get some sleep?"

As I expected, Dave was less than enthusiastic. He was right, the house really did need a lot of work but, after some wheedling, he agreed to go with me to the real estate office to find out how to put in a bid. Dave flinched when they told us what the minimum acceptable bid would be.

"Well, that's that," he said as we drove away." We can't even make the minimum, no less outbid someone else."

"We'll sell my car," I said. I was getting better at making spur of the moment decisions. "The money we get from that and what we can borrow from my parents will put us over the top and leave some for lawyers' expenses as well. Who knows, maybe no one else will bid on the house. Maybe we'll get it for the minimum bid. All we can do is try."

"I don't want to borrow from your parents, Corraine. If we can't make it on our own, then we can't make it."

I didn't argue with him. I just went ahead and made the arrangements. I wanted this with all my heart and I knew that once everything was accomplished, Dave would go along. The drink was slowly sapping his will and, for once, this was to my advantage. True, I was nervous about leaving my parents when my marriage was so unstable, but once I had made up my mind, I pursued my course with great determination. I was elated when our lawyer called to say that our bid had been accepted and the house was ours.

Ten minutes after I heard the news, I drove the kids over and showed them the house. Mark made his usual unintelligible sounds, but Cheryl wanted to know why we had to leave our apartment and Nana and Grandpa. I explained to her as gently as I could how nice it would be to have our own special place and that Nana and Grandpa would be only a few blocks away and could come over whenever they wanted. "Think how much fun it will be to go visit them," I said. "And they can come visit us anytime they want. We can have a pool in the backyard and you can decorate your new room."

I chatted on about the work we would do on the new house and how she could help Daddy make things and fix it up. She cheered up a little, and wanted to wait up for Dave so she could talk to him about her ideas for her new room. Of course, Dave didn't come in before midnight and Cheryl was fast asleep, but I waited up and when I told him the house was ours, he shrugged and stumbled off to bed. Not much of a beginning, but a beginning, none-the-less. As I sat in the dark, sipping a glass of wine alone, I couldn't help wondering if it was the beginning of the end.

Chapter Five

I clutched Mark's hand tightly as we rushed across the icy, windswept Montclair College campus, already late for our ten o'clock appointment. Cheryl had gone off to Holy Family School at the usual time, but not a half hour later, one of the Sisters had called to say she was running a fever. Mark had not been cooperative about getting dressed, galloping around the house and throwing toys every which way in his excitement. By the time I wrestled him into his jacket, picked up Cheryl at school, brought her to my parents' house and raced up to Montclair State College, I was nervous and exhausted.

I hurried across the campus, dragging Mark in my wake, not sure where I was going since none of the buildings had names. I was headed for the Department of Communication Sciences and Disorders, but where that was I had no idea. Finally, my overworked brain clicked on and I asked a passing student where the Communications Department was. She pointed to a building close by. I scooped Mark up in my arms and ran into the building where another student directed me downstairs and through a door into a large, bright area divided by partitions into colorful sections. Pre-school children played on the plush carpet and tacked up to the walls were posters of Barbar the Elephant and The Cat In The Hat.

"Mrs. Graham?" A young woman, neatly dressed in a skirt and sweater, looking very young, threaded her way towards me.

I nodded, still winded from my wild trip across campus. Mark wiggled wanting to get down and play, but I didn't have the strength to chase him around so I settled him more firmly in my arms.

The girl watched our momentary power struggle, then gestured for me to follow her into one of the larger cubicles. She sat down at a table over the top of which were scattered various cows, pigs, horses, sheep and roosters. Mark's eyes lit up when he saw the figures. He reached out both arms, making his usual squeaks and grunts and tried to grab the farm animals.

"Can he play with them?" I asked.

"Sure," the girl said, then when I let Mark down, she stuck out her hand. "I'm Carol. Madeline and I will be testing Mark today." She referred to a folder of papers I had filled out at home and sent in a few days ago. "Mark's four years old now and you're concerned about his language development. Is that correct, Mrs. Graham?"

I nodded. I was breathing easier now, but I needed a few minutes to collect my thoughts. "When we adopted him he was only three and because of all the different placements and changes in his living conditions, I wasn't especially worried. I thought he would naturally pick up on language skills by being around people who spoke to him directly. But now he's four and has been with us almost a year. As far as I can tell, his language has improved a little, a very little, and I'm beginning to get concerned," I rushed on. "His speech is so garbled. At first, he didn't speak at all, just used gestures. Now he uses one and two word sentences with his gestures, but even those words are hard to understand. He gets so frustrated. When he has difficulty being understood, he forgets about talking and goes back to gestures. He wants to communicate so badly and it's hard for him to stay calm when everyone keeps saying, "What? What?"

She jotted down a few notes, then asked, "How does he react when no one understands what he's saying?"

"Sometimes he gives up and runs off to do something alone. Lately, he's gotten more aggressive though and that concerns me, too. He hits, bites and grabs things away from his sister and other children on the block."

She nodded. "Is there anything else you'd like to tell me before we begin the tests?" she asked.

I hesitated, but decided not to tell her about the incidents that had been happening in the neighborhood. I wanted an objective evaluation and I was afraid that if I said too much, it might prejudice her judgment.

"No, that's it," I said, not quite making eye contact. She stood up and walked me toward an area where other parents were waiting. "The evaluation will take about an hour and a half, but if at any time, you want to see how Mark is doing, we'll be in one of the cubicles or next door in the play area. Feel free to look in. The reason we don't have the parents with the children during the tests is that we find they act out more trying to get Mom or Dad's attention."

When Carol left, I wandered over to the coffee maker and poured myself a cup. I would have preferred tea, but since none was offered I settled for the coffee, sweet and light. I took a seat somewhat distant from the other parents, not because I was feeling unfriendly, but because I had a lot on my mind and very little free time to sort it through. I wanted to use this opportunity to look some of my problems in the face. I hunched down in the chair, balanced my coffee on the arm and closed my eyes, hoping the other parents would respect my "Keep Out" signals. Always organized, I decided to deal with my difficulties in terms of my priorities.

First on the list was my marriage. I no longer fooled myself that things were going to work out there. Since we had moved, Dave's drinking had become noticeably worse and his behavior more abusive. I loved the house, but Dave saw it as one more burden added to his already too heavy load. My attempts to involve him in fixing up the house and building a home had only made him resentful. I was grateful now when he didn't come home and there had been a few recent occasions when he had actually frightened me, stumbling around and yelling and accusing me of God knows what. The man I loved and had married no longer existed, his kindness and generosity drained like the last drops of the hundreds of liquor bottles he had consumed. I was living with a stranger and I knew that it was only a matter of time before this stranger and I parted company.

I had spoken with Father Blake and I now understood that Dave would probably have to hit bottom before he decided to seek help. Nothing I could do or say would hasten that process and there were no guarantees that he would ever seek help. Although some part of me would always love him, I had two children to think of and protect. After months of soul searching, I'd had to accept the inevitable and had already begun to emotionally detach myself from Dave. Sad days and lonely nights had given way to acceptance and the need to plan for the future. I still cried over cherished memories and broken dreams, still berated myself for my blind faith that love could heal all, but I no longer expected miracles.

On to the children! Cheryl was still doing well at Holy Family School and had made friends with several girls in the neighborhood. Mark's behavior had grown steadily worse. I could not get him to stay still. If he wasn't running, he was jumping. If he wasn't jumping, he was climbing, or falling or throwing things or grabbing toys from other kids. But what had happened last week had really upset me.

I had become friendly with several of our neighbors on Brookdale Avenue, especially the family that lived next door. Judy was my age and her three children were close in ages to my own. They were good kids, respectful and always willing to lend a hand if I needed help. I was thrilled for myself that I had a good friend next door and thrilled for the kids that they had buddies to play with.

But this day was different. It was early afternoon and Cheryl and Mark had been playing in the backyard with a few of their friends from the neighborhood, including our next door neighbors. The backyard was covered with snow from a recent storm and the children were building a snowman. While I fixed dinner, I checked on them occasionally through the kitchen window, bright red snowsuits and knitted hats and mittens made them easy to spot. Mark was racing around the yard, picking up handfuls of snow and throwing it over his head. He didn't appear to be paying attention to the other kids who were busy packing snow around the neck of the snowman. I had turned away for a few minutes to peel the potatoes and cut up some carrots when Cheryl raced into the house. She grabbed my hand and pulled me toward the door.

"Wait a minute, honey." I wiped my other hand on a dishcloth and tried to steer her toward the front hall where my coat was hanging.

She tugged my hand hard. "Hurry up, Mommy! Hurry up! They're hurting Mark."

I dropped her hand and threw open the back door. A circle of children surrounded Mark and another bigger boy as they rolled on top of each other in the snow. I heard shouts but paid no attention while I grabbed Mark and pushed the other child away with my outstretched hand.

"What happened here?" I asked. My voice was calm, but inside I was shaking like a leaf. Blood was pouring from a cut over Mark's eye, his nose was red and squashed looking and his lower lip was already swelling.

All the kids shouted at once. "He did it. He ruined our snowman. He ruins everything. We don't want to play with him anymore."

"Okay, it's time to go home now," I said, taking Mark firmly by one hand and Cheryl by the other and marching them back into the house. Once there I leaned against the door and took several deep breaths. Slightly calmer, I surveyed the damage. Mark's face was covered with blood and for once, he was standing still and quiet. Cheryl had started to remove her snowsuit, her expression sullen.

"Finish undressing," I said. "I'll talk to you later."

I left Mark's snowsuit on while I collected a wash cloth, soap, disinfectant and bandages. There was no sense asking him what happened. Cheryl would tell me. I bathed his face and examined the cut. It was large but not especially deep, the blood only a trickle now. I decided he didn't need stitches. I bandaged it, removed his snowsuit and set him before the TV to distract him. He hadn't cried once throughout the whole incident and now seemed to have forgotten it altogether. I was far from forgetting it. As soon as Mark was settled, I called Cheryl into the kitchen.

"Tell me everything!" I said.

"It was Mark's fault," she said. "He always messes things up. Our snowman was great. You saw it. We were almost done when Mark ran into it and smashed it. On purpose. The head fell off. We tried to save it but Mark kept bumping into it until the whole thing fell apart. That's when Thomas pushed him down and sat on him. All the kids were cheering for Tom. They really wanted him to beat up Mark."

"Why didn't you stop them?" I asked.

Cheryl started to cry. "Mark ruins everything and.. and.. I'm not going to have any friends because of that little monster."

I wanted to yell at her, to tell her she was supposed to defend her little brother, that was what family was all about, but I didn't. She was too upset to listen and I was too upset to make much sense.

"It's all right, honey," I smoothed her long straight hair and kissed her on the top of the head. "Start your homework now. Dinner will be ready in half an hour."

I reached for the phone, called Dr. Patterson's office and made an appointment for the following week.

I waited up that night for Dave to return. My usual routine was to go to bed hours before he came in, but tonight I wanted to talk to him about Mark. Dave usually slept on the couch; he was not especially happy to see me sitting there when he came home.

"Now what?" he asked, throwing his coat in a heap on the floor and sinking into the armchair across the room. The distance might

58

have been a mile we had grown so far apart. In the harsh light of the lamp that shone directly on his face, he looked ghastly, his eyes red rimmed and sunken, his cheeks puffy and his jowls and neck pouchy and lined. I looked away, saddened by the change in the man I had once loved.

"Mark got into a fight with one of the neighborhood kids today," I said.

Dave shrugged, "So what? Boys fight all the time. What's the big deal? You don't want him to be a sissy."

"He's only four years old, for God sake. But that wasn't the worst part. All of the other kids were standing around cheering for Tom, who was much bigger than Mark. Even Cheryl seemed to think it was Mark's fault."

"Maybe it was his fault. I've told you a hundred times that he's out of control. If he wants to act that way, he has to pay the penalty for it. That's life. Except for saints like you who never do anything wrong. For the rest of us mortals, life is tough. Now I'm tired. Get off my couch and let me get some sleep."

"That's your final word on it," I asked.

He must have recognized something in my tone of voice because he looked directly at me for the first time. There was nothing left for me in his eyes.

I stood up, walked past him into the bedroom and closed the door and with that, I closed the door on my marriage. From now on I was alone. I cried myself to sleep that night and for many nights after and in the mornings, bleary eyed, I got my daughter ready for school and took care of my son. But along with my sadness, I felt a tremendous sense of relief. I hadn't realized how much the constant worry about my marriage had drained me. I knew there would be lonely times to come, but I had my children and I was willing to face the obstacles and overcome them with my own strength rather than waiting for support that was just not there for me. Anger and illusion had been eating away at my confidence for over a year. Now, at least, I was no longer afraid of the worst. It had already come.

The following week, I took Mark to see Dr. Patterson. He greeted us warmly and, after examining Mark's cut, sat down with me and listened to my tale of woe.

"There are two things I can suggest," he said. "There is a fairly effective drug, Ritalin, they are using for children with hyperactivity. I'm not saying Mark is hyper-active, but he might be. It's a difficult diagnosis to make. Often the only way to tell is if the medication eases the condition. We can try him on Ritalin and monitor the results."

I interrupted him. "What exactly is hyperactivity? That's the third time I've heard that term regarding Mark and I have no idea what it really means."

"That's not surprising," Dr. Patterson reassured me. "As I said, hyperactivity is very difficult to diagnose. In a nutshell, hyperactive kids have a hard time staying focused. They can't slow down enough to think ahead and plan the next step. Children with hyperactivity are unable to inhibit behavior like squirming or chattering or fidgeting and are constantly running or climbing or talking non-stop. Their brakes don't work. The everyday clamor of stimuli on their nervous system puts them into overload and they just can't seem to sort out what's important and what's not. They attend to everything and this causes them to switch their attention rapidly from one stimulus to another and never finish anything."

"That definitely sounds like Mark. But what causes it?"

"We don't know what causes it and we don't have any medical tests to diagnose it. It's one of those conditions that fall between the cracks. Is it a chemical imbalance or a neurological condition? So far, we simply don't know. But we do know that in some cases, we can treat it with medication."

"Is that the only option?" I asked, my discomfort evident in my tone.

"Not at all. If you want to hold off the Ritalin for a while, I would suggest you have him tested for speech and hearing disorders. He may just be terribly frustrated because he can't communicate properly. There's an excellent program at Montclair State College. They'll evaluate him and if they find he qualifies, they have a program where they work with the children to improve their communication skills."

I opted immediately for the evaluation program. Mark clearly had a communication problem and the thought of putting him on a powerful medication at four years old did not appeal to me. Now I could only wait and hope they could help him.

I had just finished my second cup of coffee when Carol stuck her head in the waiting room door.

"Mrs. Graham, will you please come with me?" she said. I noticed she wasn't smiling and immediately my heart began to pound.

"Is Mark all right?" I asked.

"He's fine. I wanted to discuss a few things with you before you picked him up. He's with Madeline in the playroom. You'll see him in just a minute."

I followed her into yet another office and sat down on a comfortable couch while she sat in the chair facing me.

"Of course, all the results aren't in and we need to evaluate the tests more thoroughly, but from our initial observations, we feel that Mark is a candidate for our program. I must warn you though that we could not complete the formal language tests because Mark refused to do many of the tasks. Most of our attempts to elicit specific language concepts failed because Mark would not cooperate. He refused to take his coat off, did not stay seated in his chair even after many reminders, and manipulated the farm animals as he wanted not as we asked him to. His hearing tests proved normal so that was not the problem though you might want to have him evaluated by a specialist. He does have a severe articulation problem which makes him a candidate for our program. We feel we can help him with this and provide him with the proper structure he needs to learn. He is very easily distracted and too much stimulation frustrates him."

She smiled. "I know I'm giving you a lot of information all at once, but don't worry. Everything I am telling you and more will be in the written report along with suggestions for helping Mark at home. Now would you like to see him?"

I nodded, experiencing that overwhelming sense of relief for the second time this week. Problems don't throw me. I believe in facing them head on, but it is the difficulty in finding solutions that frustrates me. Now I was on the right track. Mark would get the help he needed here and his frustration level would decrease when he was able to get his needs across.

When I entered the playroom I noticed immediately that Mark was separated from the other children playing there. A young woman who must have been Madeline was sitting on the floor beside him, showing him large, colorful photos of vegetables. At the moment, she was holding up a bright orange carrot. Mark pretended he had a carrot in his hand and said, "Up doc. Up doc."

"Pretty creative solution, no?" I said. Carol nodded.

"Why isn't he with the other children?" I hung back, out of Mark's sight so she could answer before he interrupted us.

"We had a little problem," she explained. "He started grabbing toys away and pushing so we thought it best to keep him occupied where he wouldn't get frustrated and act out. But we have every confidence that he will improve as he is able to make others understand his needs and preferences."

I walked towards my son, who, when he saw me came running and gave me a big hug and kiss, his smile like sun breaking through clouds. He was beautiful and he was mine and whatever problems the future held we would face them together. Love couldn't fix my marriage but, at the time, I still believed it could fix my son.

Chapter Six

I grabbed Mark under the arms and lifted him into the chair. He squirmed and tried to wriggle out, but I pinned him with my hip, then practically sat on him while I tried to balance the phone between my ear and shoulder and not lose my grip on him. I could hear breathing on the other end of the connection, but the person refused to speak or hang up.

I threw the phone on the floor and slid the high chair tray into place. Although Mark was four, he was still small and I found it easier to keep him in the high chair, especially when he refused to eat and wanted to run around during mealtime.

Cheryl climbed into her seat and looked at me strangely. I was not in the habit of yelling or throwing the telephone on the floor.

"Nobody on the other end." I stirred the stew and whisked hot garlic bread out of the oven. "Can you hang the phone up for me, honey?"

"Pone," Mark repeated.

"Phone," I corrected. "Phone."

His language had improved in the few months he had been enrolled in the Montclair College program. He still had difficulty articulating the more complex sounds, but he was less frustrated and better able to make himself understood.

"Phone?" he said.

"That's right, sweetie," I encouraged though not with my usual enthusiasm. My thoughts were still on the abortive phone call. These silent connections had become more frequent lately. The phone rang and when I picked it up, no response, but I knew someone waited on the other end, someone who wanted to hear my voice, but didn't want to reveal their identity. At first, I didn't think much of it, but lately, the calls came at all times of the day and had increased to more than once in a while. The phone company referred me to the police, but I had taken no action because I wasn't sure I wanted to get the police involved. Not yet. The calls were annoying, even frightening, but they weren't obscene or threatening. In the back of my mind I thought the caller might be Dave, needing help, but too ashamed to ask.

I ladled out the stew into plastic bowls and set them in front of the children. Cheryl waited for me to bring my bowl to the table, but I didn't bother. No appetite. The phone call had upset me more than I realized. That and the difficulty Mark was having getting along with the children, both in the neighborhood and at Montclair State College. Although his language had improved, his behavior had not. He had gotten into a fight with another child in the backyard and bitten a little girl in his speech therapy workshop. At home, he was aggressive and wild one minute, loving and affectionate the next. I had come in from hanging the wash in the yard one day last week to find the white walls of the living room "decorated" with crayon scribbles. Was this normal behavior for a four year old or was there something seriously wrong here? The reassurances of Mark's pediatrician were wearing thin, but he did suggest I take Mark to a neurologist in Manhattan just for my own peace of mind. I was considering the possibility.

"Mom, he's eating like a pig again. Make him stop." I snapped out of my reverie and turned to see Mark's hands and face covered with stew, a small puddle of it oozing its way down his shirt.

I took a deep breath. "Mark, remember what we were practicing. Good table manners. I want you to use your spoon now. Catch a little of the food on your spoon, then put it in your mouth and chew. Then catch a little more on your spoon and bring it to your mouth again."

Mark ate a bite, then put down his spoon and wiggled to get down.

"Not yet. You have to eat more than that to grow big and strong. Now pick up your spoon."

Mark picked up his spoon and splashed in his bowl, but refused to eat any more until I covered his hand with mine and guided the motion from the bowl to his mouth. I had noticed from the beginning that Mark held tightly to his dish and wolfed down a spoonful or two before anyone noticed what he was doing. I wondered if, at one of his foster placements, he had had to fight for his food or if he had been severely neglected, possibly starved as an infant. I had no way of knowing, but teaching Mark to eat was a daily struggle.

I let go of his hand, hoping he would continue the motion, but as soon as I stopped guiding him, he stopped eating. This time he threw the spoon on the floor.

I washed it off and stuck it back in his hand.

"Eat," I said.

"No!"

This was fast becoming a power struggle, something I knew better than to engage in, but I was tired and worried and for once I wanted to win. I grabbed his hand and forced him to feed himself, but each time I let go he threw the spoon on the floor. He was so thin, his cheeks were sunken rather than rosy, his arms toothpicks and his knees were knobby above little stick legs. He had to eat to thrive.

"Eat!" I yelled. "Eat!"

The phone rang again. I ignored it. If it was important the person would call back; if not, I could avoid the annoyance of the harassment. It diverted me enough to regain my perspective though. I cleaned Mark's face and hands and wiped as much of the stew as I could from his shirt, then gave him a cookie and some milk to drink. He had eaten so little that I resorted to sweets just to get something in him.

I watched him eat his cookie and prayed he wouldn't spill his milk, but my prayers weren't answered. Over went the plastic glass. Milk flew across the table and dripped over the flowered tablecloth onto the floor. I had learned to keep the mop and bucket next to the table and the paper towels within arm's reach. Cheryl wiped the table as I did my usual routine with the mop on the floor. No sooner had I started mopping than the phone rang.

"Cheryl, can you get that?" I called. "If no one answers just hang up."

Cheryl threw the dripping towels into the sink and grabbed the phone. After a few minutes conversation, she held out the receiver, "It's Nana."

I breathed a sigh of relief and stood the mop up in the pail. I left Mark in the high chair and sat down across from him at the table.

"What's wrong?" my mother asked as soon as I said hello.

"Nothing but the usual. I practically had to wrestle food into Mark and when I gave up on that, he spilled his milk all over Cheryl, the table and the floor. I just finished mopping it up. Why? Do I sound worse than all the other times you called?" My laugh had a bitter edge to it. I couldn't help it. I was sick of life's constant challenges.

She didn't answer my question. Instead, she asked if I wanted to take the kids to Newark Airport to watch the planes and perhaps get some dessert. Tired as I was I needed to get out and the kids needed some fun. I still loved going to the airport and watching the jets take off and land. More than once I had fantasized about getting on a plane and flying somewhere, anywhere just to get away. I would change my name, change my life and all my troubles would magically disappear. I returned to reality, all tied up and nowhere to run.

"How soon can you be ready?" she asked.

"How's an hour ago?" I answered.

I whisked Mark out of his chair, scrubbed his face and changed his pants and shirt. Cheryl had already put on a new outfit since her pants had been soaked by the spilled milk. When I told her we were going to the airport she forgot her distress over her ruined pants and stood by the front door until Nana and Grandpa arrived. Mark ran from the front door to the back door. I'm not sure he knew what was happening, but he was wound up and I let him run, hoping he would dissipate some of his energy before they pulled up.

We arrived at the airport just as the sun was beginning to set. I stood outside the entrance and looked up at the colors of the evening sky, the regal red and purple robe spreading royally across the wide horizon. In the presence of such transcendent beauty, I was able to release some the concerns of the day.

I turned Mark over to my Dad who had the most calming effect on him and walked beside my mother and Cheryl through the electric glass doors. Mark took off down one of the long corridors, running as fast as his legs would carry him, my Dad in hot pursuit. I looked at my Mom and suddenly we burst into guilty laughter.

"Poor Dad. What a night he's going to have!"

"Should we go after them or head in the opposite direction?" Mom asked. She had Cheryl by the hand as we strolled along at a leisurely pace. Cheryl enjoyed watching the passengers on their hurried way toward the terminals and I was glad to see her happy. She needed time away from Mark. "I suppose we'll have to go after them eventually, but I think Dad can handle him for a little while. It will give me a break and Cheryl, too."

"Mark's a pain," Cheryl said. "He never stops bothering me. Never!"

"But you love him, right!"

She didn't reply and I didn't force her. She was a patient child, but she had her limits and I had to permit her to complain once in a while.

We took the escalator down to the terminal area and walked to the wide windows where we could look out at the runways. Cheryl knelt down on one of the chairs and pressed her nose to the glass. I knelt beside her, pointing out which planes were taking off and searching the sky for planes about to land. We made up stories about where we thought they might be going and I explained to her where different cities and countries were. She listened, then asked about Canada. I was surprised. She had never asked about the country of her birth before and I had assumed she had forgotten about it. Her interest sparked me to a promise that we would buy some maps in the gift shop and I would show her where she had lived before she came to us.

After a while she got bored and I began to wonder what had happened to my dad and Mark. I turned around and sat down in the chair next to my mom.

"Shall we go in search of them?" I asked.

"They've probably headed toward the ice-cream shop expecting we'll meet them there."

"To the ice cream shop it is then," I said. "And remind me next Christmas to buy him a Dad of the Year award."

"Have you decided whether to take Mark to New York for the neurological exam Dr. Patterson suggested?"

"I'm still thinking about it. Sometimes I think there's really something wrong. Other times I'm convinced he's just a very active little boy and all this worry is for nothing. Right now I have other, more pressing, problems to take care of first."

My Mom didn't ask me any other questions and sure enough, when we arrived at the ice cream shop, my dad and Mark were already seated at the table, a big sloppy Sunday running chocolate puddles down the side of Mark's dish. I pulled over another chair and we all sat down. My Dad looked weary, but he smiled at me and shrugged.

"Thanks, Dad. You're a life saver," I whispered.

I was suddenly hungry and ordered a hot fudge Sunday complete with whipped cream. For the first time in a while I was enjoying myself and when I was finished, I leaned back in my chair with a satisfied sigh. My children were a mess, their faces smeared with chocolate and yet, at that moment, they looked beautiful to me. Yes, it was all worth it - every difficult moment because they were happy and healthy and they were mine.

When they had finished playing with their bowls I cleaned them up as best as I could with a napkin dipped in a glass of water and we started toward the exit.

"Hang on a minute," I said, coming to a quick stop. "I want to dart into the gift shop to buy the maps I promised Cheryl. I'll be out in a jiffy."

Since it was a quick stop I didn't bring the kids in with me. I looked around the small store, found the maps on the counter and selected a few. When I came out, my parents were waiting with Cheryl near the gift shop entrance.

"Where's Mark?" I asked, looking around.

"Isn't he with you?" my dad asked.

I shook my head.

"I assumed you took him with you," he said. My heart started its slow steady pound.

"Don't panic. He can't have gone far. He was just here." My mother started back into the gift shop.

I looked around frantically, focusing on nothing and everything at once. A quick movement between the crowds caught my eye.

"Mark!" I screamed and started to run. I don't know if he heard me. It didn't matter. He never turned around. He swerved to avoid running into a woman carrying a heavy suitcase and flew into the metal guard rail on one side of the automatic entrance doors. His head, colliding with the heavy metal, sounded like a gunshot and he fell backwards onto the floor. I pushed through the crowd and knelt beside him. His face was stained with blood and he wasn't moving.

"Someone call Emergency!" I shouted.

I pulled out a handkerchief and wiped the blood from his face, but it kept flowing. I grabbed his hand and patted it. Still no reaction. I told myself head injuries bled a lot and it didn't mean it was serious, but I didn't breathe again until Mark opened his eyes. He lay quietly

68

on his back, his eyes wide, but unfocused. I waved my hand before his face, talking to him in a normal tone and asking him to blink if he could see me. His eyes remained blank. The airport security guards arrived, but all they could do was keep the crowd moving. I continued to wipe away the blood and kept up a steady stream of one -sided reassuring conversation. Meanwhile, my father brought the car up to the entrance.

"Maybe you shouldn't move him," one of the guards said. "A head injury is nothing to fool around with."

I asked Mark if he could hear me. This time he nodded yes and tried to sit up. I asked him to wiggle his fingers and toes, then his hands and arms. When he did, I tucked my jacket around him and scooped him up. No emergency vehicle had arrived so I pushed past the guards and, with my mother and Cheryl trailing behind, I got into the back seat of the car and laid Mark on my lap. My Dad drove through the airport traffic at a steady determined pace and once on the highway sped to Clara Maass Hospital in Belleville.

Mark was still bleeding heavily, his face drained of color, his lips a bruised blue. When he looked like he was about to fall asleep, I sat him up and talked to him about the animals we would see when I took him to the zoo. For once, he stayed perfectly still and that scared me more than anything.

At the emergency room entrance, I jumped out and ran with Mark into the hospital. I prayed that I wouldn't have to go through the usual endless paperwork before they would see him. I left my mother at the desk giving information and stepped boldly past the formidable looking matron without a second glance.

A bearded, dark-haired young man whom I assumed was a resident led me into a cubicle and pulled the curtain. I laid Mark on the bed. My hands and slacks were covered with blood. Quickly, the doctor cleaned Mark's wound and examined it, then gently felt his head and looked into both eyes with a pencil-thin flashlight.

"Is he all right?" I asked.

The doctor looked at me for the first time. "Do you want to wait for your pediatrician? He may be on duty at the hospital. I'll page him now."

I gave him Dr. Patterson's name. He signaled for a nurse to call the page. When he was finished I touched his arm to get his attention. As light as my touch was it left a bloody fingerprint.

"If Dr. Patterson arrives right away, fine. If not, do what you need to do."

The doctor checked Mark's vital signs. "He's doing fine," he said. "There doesn't appear to be any skull fracture though I'd like to take an X-ray to be sure. First, though, I'll need to close the cut on his forehead. Why don't you go clean up and if Dr. Patterson hasn't arrived when you come back, I'll stitch him up, okay?"

I rushed off to the ladies room and scrubbed my hands as hard as I could. The blood, mixed with water, flowed in a red river down the drain. I stared at it in sick fascination. The shock was beginning to wear off and fear took its place. If I didn't get back to the Emergency Room right away, I might not make it at all.

I held Mark's hand as the young doctor carefully closed the wound, cleaned it again with disinfectant and bandaged it with gauze and tape. Mark was half-awake, but dazed and made no sound during the procedure.

"What about concussion?" I asked. "He was very groggy on the way here and he's definitely not himself. He's barely moved the whole time we've been here and Mark's always on the move."

"Concussion is always a possibility. If the X-rays show no fracture, I'll let you take him home. Just watch him for any unusual symptoms and wake him up a few times during the night. Now, I'm afraid I have to ask you how this happened?"

At first I didn't understand what he was getting at, but when I did, I blushed. "I don't abuse my children, Doctor," I said stiffly. "He ran into a metal guardrail at Newark Airport."

The doctor smiled sympathetically. "We're required to ask when there is an injury to a child. I'm sorry."

He signaled an orderly to transfer Mark to a wheeled stretcher and then to X-ray. I ran out to see how my parents and Cheryl were doing and to tell them where I would be. Cheryl was curled up on one of the plastic waiting room couches asleep. I quickly relieved my parents' anxiety, then raced after the orderly who was disappearing down the corridor. It was after midnight before we had the results and were able to leave the hospital. I carried Mark. My Dad carried

Cheryl and if someone was left to carry my mom they would have, she was so worn out with worry.

The house was ablaze with lights when I stuck the key in the front door. Dave was sitting fully dressed on the couch. He jumped up as I walked in, his face contorted with rage.

"Where the hell have you been?"

He walked towards me and was about to grab my shoulders when he saw Mark, bandaged and hanging limp in my arms. It took him a few seconds to react, but when he did the anger left him and he looked at me anxiously. I explained what had happened and, for a moment, I saw the old Dave return as he took Mark in his arms and carry him to bed. My parents had come in and now stood hesitantly at the door. I took Cheryl from my father who seemed reluctant to leave.

"It's okay," I said. "I can handle it."

"Are you sure?" he asked.

"I'm sure."

"If you need us, just call." He patted me on the back, then he and my mom left.

I helped Cheryl undress and tucked her into bed. She was exhausted and drifted right back to sleep. I tiptoed into Mark's room. He was also asleep and breathing normally, but Dave was no longer in the room. I heard the front door slam as I tucked the covers around Mark. The car engine revved and the Buick sped out of the driveway before I had left the bedroom. I threw my bloody clothes in the corner and fell into bed, but my concern for Mark kept me awake. I woke him several times that night to check for signs of concussion. Nothing unusual. I finally fell into a fitful sleep at daybreak. Dave had not returned and when I woke in the late morning I could tell that he had not come back last night. I didn't expect to see him the next evening either because I was so exhausted I planned to go to bed as soon as the kids went to sleep .When he stepped through the door at six o'clock, I was shocked.

"How's Mark?" he asked. "I meant to call during the day, but work was so busy I didn't get a break."

"He's fine. I took him to see Dr. Patterson. He had the X-rays from the hospital. No fractures or concussion. Just a good, hard clunk on the head."

"That's great news."

Dave headed past me to the bathroom. I could hear the sounds of his shower and then the scrape of the razor. He came out looking spruce though his eyes were fiery, the whites shot through with blood vessels.

"Where are you going?" I asked. "Certainly not to your night job looking like that."

Deep in my heart, I knew what he was going to say, but I needed to hear it from his lips to believe it was true.

He looked directly at me. "I've got a hot date, Corraine. She's waiting and I don't want to be late."

"Please ask her to stop calling me or I'll report her to the police," I said. For the second time in two days that false serenity overtook me and I spoke in a calm matter-of-fact voice.

Dave looked momentarily surprised, but not in the least guilty. The alcohol had taken over his conscience. He shrugged. "I'll give her the message. Now can I go?"

The moment had come and we both knew it. No hysterics. No screaming or foot stomping. No tears or accusations. Just nothing.

"When you leave tonight, I'd like you to take your things with you. I don't want you back in this house ever," I said.

"Fine with me," he shrugged. He stepped into the bedroom and shut the door. I sat in the kitchen drinking tea while he packed his clothes. Thoughts flitted through my head like trapped birds, then flew out again before I could capture them. I had known this was coming for a long time. Now I just wanted it over. I was doing the right thing. My mind knew that, but my heart had not quite caught up. When the front door slammed shut, I laid my head on the table and wept.

PART TWO

❧

LOVING

Chapter Seven

I crossed Park Avenue and ran up the steps to the Ambassador Apartments, a stately four-storied brick building with wide lawns and gray stone lions guarding the front walks. The late winter winds whipped around me, stinging my eyes and setting my nose on fire. Good, I thought, the super will think my inflamed eyes are from the cold, not from crying half the night. I reached into the pocket of my new coat, blew my nose and hunched down deeper into the wide shawl collar.

The coat was a Christmas gift from my parents. It was made of hunter green wool, came mid-calf with a wide collar and cuffs. I felt comforted and warm with it wrapped around me, almost as if I had brought a blanket from home. Right now, I needed all the comfort I could get. I found the bell with the name tag of the superintendent and rang it several times to make certain I wouldn't have to stand out in the icy wind any longer than necessary.

My bell ringing was hardly effective. Winter makes waiting impossible and it seemed like spring would come before anyone answered the door. After a wait of at least ten minutes, an old man wearing a brown sweater and a pair of bedroom slippers pressed his face against the large panes of the leaded glass door. He fumbled with the lock, then jumped back as the wind ripped the open door from his hand. I grabbed the handle and pulled it hard, slamming the door behind me. If I had been expecting a polite thank you, I would have been seriously disappointed, but I had taken the man's measure and passed off gratitude as a constitutional impossibility on his part.

"Here to see the apartment, are you?" he asked.

I nodded, trying to breathe in the suffocating heat of the interior. I looked around as the old man shuffled down a fairly spacious hall and wheezed his way up a flight of stairs. The building was old, circa nineteen twenties, but the hall rugs were vacuumed and the plaster walls sported a fresh coat of beige paint. Cooking smells and faint sounds of television sets behind closed doors reminded me of old movies. I had lived here when Dave and I first married, before we had moved into my parent's upstairs apartment, but that seemed a lifetime ago, and the apartment building felt confining after the spaciousness of my house.

The old man stopped before a door on the second floor at the rear of the building. I was surprised to find the apartment unlocked, but he assured me the former tenants had moved all their things out and there was no need to keep the apartment secured. None of the neighbors were interested in poking around where they had no place being. Properly chastised, I walked into the apartment.

Empty rooms always have an eerie atmosphere and I felt like an intruder on someone else's memories. I certainly had no connection to the blank white walls and large staring windowpanes. Keep a business-like attitude, I told myself. This old man isn't interested in your troubles.

Luckily, he stayed by the door and allowed me to wander through the apartment alone. The one large bedroom would do nicely for Cheryl and Mark. There was also a good sized pantry off the kitchen that could hold a twin bed when Mark grew too old to share Cheryl's room. The living space was open and light and there was a huge eat-in kitchen rather than a kitchenette.

Decorating came naturally to me and I saw the possibilities right away. Besides, what choice did I have? I had already put the house on the market. Dave was paying no child support and the mortgage was too much for me to handle alone. Mark had started kindergarten in the fall and I had gone back to work. My salary paid for the necessities, but the house payments were too much. No, I told myself, I wouldn't think about that now. I loved that house and it was breaking my heart to leave it. But leave it I must!

"I'll take the apartment," I said. We had already talked about the rent over the phone. It was within my budget and I was anxious to secure a place for the kids and myself because the real estate agent who was handling the house sale already had a serious client. If the house sold quickly I would have to move in with my parents and I didn't feel that was fair. As it was, they were taking care of the kids after school.

I followed the old man down to his basement apartment and tried not to look too closely at the dirty kitchen where we signed the papers. I paid him a month's rent and a security deposit. He gave me the front door key and the key to the apartment. He made no effort to escort me out. I was now a tenant and, as such, deserved no special attention.

When I walked out the door, I looked once behind me, trying to to picture the Ambassador Apartments as home. The building was in a safe neighborhood and I felt comfortable knowing we would be secure from harm. But in the merciless clarity of a biting winter day, it looked pretty bleak.

I drove to Roth's Deli to pick up a sandwich before heading back to work. I had missed my lunch hour and I was surprised to discover that I was actually hungry. My appetite had been irregular at best and I hadn't been eating properly. I had lost weight and my nights were constantly interrupted with one or the other of the children climbing into bed with me. Cheryl had taken the separation calmly, at least on the surface. At first, she had acted like Dave was away on a business trip, asking me, at least once a day, when he was coming home and ignoring my answer as if I hadn't spoken. This had gone on for weeks, wearing my nerves to a frazzle. Then had come my tears. I tried to limit my crying to the nighttime, after the kids had gone to bed. I wanted them to feel they had a strong parent they could count on to be there for them whenever they needed me. If I dissolved into tears in front of them, I was afraid they would feel like they had to parent me. I did not want to become an adult child. But Cheryl's uncomplaining acceptance of the situation and her attempts to help me with my responsibilities often brought me to the verge of tears. I still had a lot of healing to do.

By the time I reached my desk at Suburban Finance I had myself pretty well under control. I set down my roast beef sandwich and my soda with what I hoped was an efficient air and reached over to pick up my messages. The two from my mother were marked urgent. Now what? I plunked down in my chair feeling defeated and no longer caring what impression I made. There were no clients in the office and I had received enough urgent messages from my mother so that my personal affairs were no secret from anyone who had worked there more than a few weeks. My co-worker Jean looked over at me.

"Sorry," she said. "But your Mom said it was important and that you should call her right away."

"So what else is new?" I shrugged. "If I didn't get an urgent message I'd think something was wrong. This way I'm reassured Mark is still alive and kicking."

I unwrapped my sandwich and took a bite before picking up phone. My mother answered on the second ring and I washed my food with a gulp of soda so I could speak. I didn't bother to hello

"What's wrong, Mom?" I asked.

"Mark's teacher called. She wants to schedule a conference with you right away. She said ..."

"I know. I know. She said it was urgent. Did she happen to mention what exactly it was he did?"

"No, she just requested that you come in as soon as possible."

"Requested?"

"In no uncertain terms. She left a number where you can contact her after school today."

I took another bite of my sandwich and another gulp of soda while my mother went to locate the number Mark's teacher had given her. I wondered whether I had the strength to face this conference today and decided I didn't. I would schedule it for tomorrow during my lunch break. No wonder I was losing weight. Thinking about it, I couldn't remember the last meal I had sat down peacefully to eat. I was always doing something else when I was supposed to be eating.

My mom finally came back on the line and I made the call to the school as soon as she hung up. The secretary assured me that tomorrow at 12:30 would be convenient for Mark's teacher to meet with me. She sounded as anxious for me to come in as I was reluctant to oblige her. If I could have avoided this meeting I would have, but there was no escape. I knew she wasn't calling me in to congratulate me on Mark's progress. Although his speech had improved, his behavior had not. I had hoped the structure and discipline of the daily school routine would ease some of his anxiety and constant movement, but I could see no improvement so far.

Mark's first weeks in school had brought back all the terrors of his younger years. Although I had explained to him that he would be going to kindergarten like all the other children his age, he hadn't paid attention to my explanations. He had been going to the Montclair Speech Program twice a week so I had assumed that he understood about school. Wrong! He had marched into class brave as lion, but refused to let go of my hand. When it came time for me to leave, he clung to me and cried. His teacher assured me that this was perfectly normal and that he would stop as soon as I left. His sobs shook me as they had always done because he cried so rarely. I had to tear myself away and run out the door before I picked him up and carried him home with me.

I had also enrolled him in the Jack and Jill Nursery School in the afternoons because I had to work full-time and wouldn't be home until after five. Mark was such a handful I didn't want my mother to have to sit for him all afternoon Monday through Friday. I thought the afternoon nursery school program would give Mark the structure and supervision he needed and not burden my mother with his constant care.

Before enrolling Mark in the pre-school program, I had gone for an interview with the director of the nursery school. I had explained Mark's unique difficulties, including his speech problems and his distractibility. She had responded with enthusiasm.

"That's what we're here for," she said, "to help children develop the skills they need to do well in school and, we hope, to do well in life. Our classes are small, only seven or so children in each and we provide them with a lot of individual attention. I'm sure we can help Mark catch up with the other children his age."

When I picked Mark up at kindergarten that first day, I could see by his face it had not been the positive experience I had hoped it would be. His cheeks were still tear- stained and his hair stood up in spikes as if he had been pulling it up by the roots.

"How was your first day at school?" I asked brightly as I turned out of the parking lot.

"Want to go home!" Mark stuck out his lip. It quivered a bit, but he clamped down on it and looked at me defiantly.

"You know that Mommy has to work, Mark. But I'm going to take you someplace where you can play with other children. It'll be lots of fun. You'll see."

"Want to go home!"

Guilt reached out its icy tentacles and wrapped them around my chest. What to do? I knew he had had a terrible day at kindergarten and here I was driving him to another situation where he had to face another separation and another set of strangers. But I had to work and Mark had to be somewhere structured and safe. He needed to learn how to interact with other children if he was to succeed in school and he needed to learn that I was not going to abandon him. By picking him up each day, he would learn that I was reliable and that the world was safe to venture out into. He would not know this if he stayed wrapped around my leg.

Although more than anything I wanted to turn around and take him home, I drove straight to the Jack and Jill Nursery School. On the way I chatted about how nice the teachers were and how much fun he would have learning to do puzzles and playing with the other children. I described how bright the rooms were and how the walls were decorated with colorful artwork the children had made themselves and how great he would feel when he saw his own pictures hanging on the walls. I waited for him to ask questions, but he remained quiet during the ten minute trip.

"Here we are," I said as we pulled into the parking lot beside the nursery school. "Don't worry, Mark. You'll have lots of fun playing with the other kids."

Except for an unusual pallor to his skin, he didn't look particularly upset. I breathed a sigh of relief. He's probably scared, I thought, but he likes to play with other kids so he'll be all right. No fight getting out of the car either. I began to feel more confident, less guilty. Thank you, God, for small favors.

But at the door, he refused to go in. He planted his feet on the steps, pulled back and would not budge. I tried to take his hand, but he broke away from me, grabbed the stair rail and wouldn't let go. Other parents passed us, their sympathetic smiles made my blood boil. Why didn't anything ever go smoothly?

"Why don't we sit down on the steps and watch the other children go in?" I suggested. "We don't have to go in until you're ready."

"No!"

"Mark. Don't make me yell at you. I know you're scared and I won't leave you until you're more comfortable. But Mark, you're going in!"

After a half hour, he let me take his hand and lead him up the steps, but once we were inside he clung to me and began to wail so loudly one of the teachers came out into the hall to see what was going on. She introduced herself to Mark and invited him into her classroom so he could see what the other children were doing. I disentangled him from my leg and led him by the hand into the room. He quieted down, but he kept my hand in a death grip. My fingers were numb. I must have had the typical stricken parent look on my face because the teacher looked at me more sympathetically than she looked at Mark.

"Don't worry, Mrs. Graham," she reassured me. "Mark's behavior is not at all unusual. Some children take a little longer to adjust than others. Why don't you stay for a while then take him home? Next time you can stay with him for the whole afternoon. After that, I'm sure he'll be just fine."

"I can't. I've got to get back to work. I'm already late as it is." I shook my head. "I just don't know what to do."

She took Mark's hand and firmly guided him to where some children were sitting at a table working with finger paints. Mark kept looking over his shoulder, his lower lip puckered, not quite certain whether to cry. The teacher placed a large sheet of paper on the table and tucked Mark into a munchkin-sized chair. While she was showing him how to use the finger paints, I slipped away. I felt like a thief in the night, but what else could I do. I assured myself he would be fine. He was with trained professionals who dealt with this sort of thing every day. Other kids had difficult first school days and it hadn't traumatized them for life.

For the rest of the day, whenever the phone rang, I felt my shoulders tensing up and my maternal instincts going into overdrive. I just knew the school was going to call and ask me to come pick him up, but five o'clock came without a call. I breathed a sigh of relief. Maybe this was going to work out after all. I approached the school entrance in a much better frame of mind than when I had dropped him off.

He was waiting for me at the door, his little plaid jacket buttoned up to his neck and his face pale and smeared with tears. He looked as exhausted as I felt. He flung himself into my arms and held onto me as if he was never going to let go. His sobs were shuddering and breathless.

"Was he like this the whole time?" I asked.

The teacher smiled sympathetically. "Pretty much so," she said. "I couldn't get him interested in anything. He kept running to the door every few minutes. He started some of the other kids crying, too, so all in all, it was a pretty rough afternoon. I requested an aide for tomorrow so Mark can have some individual attention. Maybe that will help him feel safer." She shrugged. "It's worth a try."

After two weeks, she was not quite so willing to try and neither was I. Mark was miserable in kindergarten, but he was horrible in nursery school. He screamed when I left him and did not stop crying or running to the door until I came to pick him up. Nothing worked, the teacher explained, and she had other children to care for. Mark's behavior was disrupting to them as well.

My mother graciously volunteered to care for him after school, but her very graciousness made me feel guilty. What other choice did I have? I had to work to support myself and my children and Mark couldn't be left in day care. I went to work every day with a load of guilt that would have buried a lesser person. This was certainly not the life I had dreamed of in those girlish hours waiting for Dave to call me from the naval base.

I had already attended several conferences with Mark's kindergarten teacher, but for some reason I felt pessimistic about this one. Last time, she had sent a note home pinned to his shirt. It had been non-committal, just a request for me to come in to talk. I had figured that all the parents had received such a note. I asked Mark if the other little children in his class had gone home with notes pinned to their shirts. He didn't seem to know what I was talking about. I placed my hands on his shoulders and looked directly into his face.

"Notes. Pieces of paper like this one," I said. "Did the other children have them pinned to their shirts like you did?"

He looked past me to the kitchen counter where I kept the cookie jar.

"Cookies," he said. "Want cookies."

In his eyes I saw no recognition, no recollection of anything I was asking him. He was not being defiant. He did not understand or remember what I was talking about.

"Calm down," I told myself. "Remember, developmentally he's only three and what can you expect from a three year old. You're over-reacting" But a warning light flashed in my brain, a neon sign I could not turn off.

On the morning of the interview I dressed carefully, needing the confidence looking neat and professional always gave me. As we drove to school, I tried to keep an open mind, not anticipating bad news before it came.

"Sufficient unto the day is the trouble thereof," I thought. "And Lord, spare me today's trouble."

Mark cried as usual, clinging to my leg as I climbed the stairs and making a scene before I practically shoved him into the classroom. I hid behind the door for a few minutes watching. After a little while, Mark stopped crying, but did not sit down when the teacher asked him to take his seat at the little blue painted table. He refused to remove his jacket when she asked him to and wandered aimlessly about the room. His teacher let him walk from the kitchen corner to the library section, then when he seemed less agitated she led him firmly to his table. She had not gotten very far into her morning routine when Mark was up again, wandering around. He bumped into a puzzle she had set up for the children to work on during free time. With a crash, the pieces scattered everywhere. I had seen enough. I knew that when it came time for the conference, I was not going to hear her sing Mark's praises.

Somehow, I made it through the morning without snapping at clients or making clerical errors it would take me the whole next day to unscramble. Once again, I would be missing lunch, but the way my stomach felt, food was the last thing on my mind. I wanted to be calm for this conference. I needed to assess what steps to take to help Mark through this difficult transition. His behavior, I knew, was not improving.

I needed help for him. I was fully aware of that but I wasn't sure, with all that I had been going through, that I could sit and listen to his teacher tell me more bad news. Don't be defensive, I told myself many times that morning. Listen and learn. But my good intentions were at war with my emotions.

At 12:30 precisely, I reported to the principal's office on the first floor of the Holy Family School. The secretary gestured me to a seat and I instantly flashed back on my memories of the adoption agency waiting room. Not a good beginning, I thought, as I tried to banish the feeling that rose up in me so strongly. There was something about those particular situations that made me feel like a child, helpless against forces that knew, or pretended to know, more than me. I had only been waiting a few minutes in this uncomfortable state when Mark's teacher entered. She gave me a tight smile and preceded me into an empty office next to the principal's. Thankfully, she did not sit behind the desk, but chose a comfortable leather chair opposite to the one I had perched on.

She was silent as if collecting her thoughts and choosing appropriate ways to phrase them. I felt my body tense more with each wordless moment, the stiffness in my shoulders screaming pain to my brain. I knew I was tense, but I hadn't realized how tense until I felt my right arm twitch spasmodically when she cleared her throat.

"We are very concerned about Mark's behavior in the classroom," she began. I wondered if she was talking in the royal "we" or if everyone in the school was concerned, but I didn't ask her to clarify the point. "He can't focus on any task more than a minute or two before becoming restless and popping out of his seat. If there are several materials on the table, like paper, crayons, scissors and glue, he gets terribly confused and cannot figure out what to do first. Sometimes, when he gets particularly frustrated, he will sweep all the materials onto the floor including the other children's artwork. As you can well imagine, that upsets everyone and soon we have a whole table of crying children. This isn't good for Mark or the others because none of the children want Mark to sit with them. They have started to tease him and call him names. No one wants to play with him."

I felt my heart sink to the bottom of my chest, but she wasn't finished.

"Mark is so easily distracted we can't get him to attend to the social cues the other children are giving him or to the skills we need to teach him so he can successfully complete the work he'll be getting in first grade. He can't follow two step directions, he forgets what I tell him a few minutes after I've given instructions, he distracts and bothers the other children. To tell you the truth, Mrs. Graham, in all my twenty-five years of teaching, I've never had a more difficult child than Mark."

She finished in a rush, her face slightly flushed and I had the odd feeling that she was angry at me though she had spoken no words of blame or censure. I wanted to rush in and defend myself and my child-rearing practices. I wanted to shout at her that I was a good mother, that I disciplined my child and tried to teach him what he needed to do well in school.

I felt angry, agitated, and too confused to ask questions, but I needed to know what she intended to do. She was the professional. She had to supply the answers. As steadily as I could, I asked, "What can we do, working together, to improve this situation?"

She nodded her head and steepled her fingers thoughtfully. "Mark is still very young. You could withdraw him for the rest of this year and start him again next year. He may have matured enough to settle into the routine of school by then."

I shook my head. "I work full time and can't afford home care for him. Also, I don't believe that's the solution. Isolating him from other children won't help him learn the social cues he needs for his growth and development."

She sighed as if she had been afraid I was going to say that. "Have you spoken with Mark's pediatrician about his difficulties? Perhaps he can suggest possible reasons for his hyperactivity or prescribe a mild dose of a child safe medication that might calm Mark down enough for him to perform better in the classroom. But what Mark really needs is one-on-one attention, something we can't provide him with."

On the drive back to work I thought of all the things I should have said to her. Why is it that when you're in the midst of a situation you can never come back with the brilliant responses, but at home or in the car or in the shower, they all come to you and you redo the conversation victoriously. What I had wanted to say to her was it was her job to teach my son, not throw up her hands and say was too difficult to handle. She had twenty-five years' Didn't that count for something? Hadn't she encountered very active children before or was my son the first in her vast experience? I found that difficult to believe. I needed help from her as an expert in children's behavior and all I got was a subliminal message of blame. I wanted to turn around, drive back and give her a piece of my mind, which was much clearer now than when I was on the carpet a few minutes ago. But I knew what the response would be. 'You're just being defensive and not dealing with the problem.' Why is it teachers are never defensive, but parents always are?

I took the children to Burger King for dinner because we all needed a treat. I planned to tell them about their new home and to ride past the building so they could begin to recognize it before the big move. But as I sat across from Mark and watched him shovel in french fries with both hands, guarding his food as if I would steal it from him, I felt the panic rise in me again. No, Mark was not making progress. He couldn't dress himself, sit at a table for more than a few minutes, follow directions no matter how many times I repeated them, he wasn't making friends and his language was still below his chronological age. But along with the panic was the unwavering determination to guide my son through any difficulties he might experience. I was certain his problems stemmed from a traumatic start in life and I vowed that he would never suffer any of those traumas again. With enough love, we could conquer anything. I plucked Mark up from his chair, gave him a fierce hug and, exhausted but renewed, I took my children home where, for at least a little while, they would be protected from the harsher realities of life.

Chapter Eight

"What have you what decided to do?" Mom asked.

"Run away from home?" I suggested.

She smiled patiently. If she only knew how serious I was. I wanted to get away from everything for a few days, go to a quiet place where I could think, somewhere I might regain my perspective and some small appreciation of life. I was losing the little things, the feeling of renewal a quiet snowfall, a clear winter day, a good book or a long chat with a friend could bring. Too often now I looked inward at the bleak landscape of my battered emotions and that could hardly be counted on to bring laughter back into my life.

"I think Mark's teacher was over-reacting," I said. "God knows, Mark's not easy to handle, but he certainly isn't the devil incarnate and that's how she made him seem. I understand that in a classroom full of children, you can't give special attention to one, but on the other hand, it's her job to help him adjust. That's what she's being paid for. To help him, not to make things worse. You should have heard her 'In all my twenty-five years of teaching I have never had a student like Mark.' Give me a break. You mean to tell me, she's never had an active little boy or girl who had trouble focusing on art work or letters. Come on, how bad could it be?"

My Mom got up, refilled my cup with hot water, then looked out the window into the backyard where Mark was making snow balls and tossing them against the trunk of an oak tree.

"Did you talk to Mark about his behavior at school?" she asked. She returned to the table slowly. For the first time I noticed how tired she looked.

"I tried, but he didn't seem to understand what I was talking about. It's like he forgets what he's done from one minute to the next. I asked him why his teacher said he wandered around the room. He didn't know. I asked him why he threw the paper and glue on the floor. He didn't know. Maybe I'm being naïve, but I don't think he remembered any of the things he'd done."

"Was he lying, do you think?"

"I don't think so. I just don't think he is mature enough to know the difference between his own perception of things and reality."

My mother laughed. "Do you remember the fish? How awful they looked all belly-up in the tank."

The situation hadn't been funny at the time but, in retrospect, it did take on an absurd quality. A few months ago I had confronted Mark about breaking one of Cheryl's toys. He had lied to me and so to teach him a lesson, I had put a bar of Ivory soap in his mouth. The old "liar, liar, tongue's on fire" idea. Anyway, I came back into the kitchen a while later. Mark was standing in front of the fish tank and all the fish were floating belly up.

"What did you do?" I screamed.

"Liars." He pointed to the fish. In his hand he was still holding the box of soap flakes.

Exhaustion and the memory of those poor fish was too much for me. I started laughing and couldn't stop. Hours of taking care of Mark after school had put my mother in the same giddy state and she laughed along with me.

"God, that felt good. I thought I had forgotten how to laugh," I said.

I jumped up and looked out the window. It had become a necessary habit to check on Mark every few minutes. He was so active and so restless he could be up to anything.

"What's he doing?" Mom asked.

"Still chucking snowballs at the tree. We're safe for a few minutes, I hope"

"What are you going to do, Corraine?"

"I've already made an appointment with Dr. Patterson. I hate the thought of putting Mark on long-term medication. He's only five, for heaven sake, but I can't think of any alternative. I have to work and even if I was home full-time, I don't think it would make a difference. I'm hoping a small dose will calm him down and help him focus. Maybe, if he does better in school and isn't always being yelled at by the teacher or rejected by the other kids, he'll feel better about himself. It could start a chain reaction. He'll do better, get better feedback and feel better about himself."

My feelings were actually more mixed than I was telling her. It was almost as if I was trying to talk myself into it. I hated the idea of my child becoming dependent on a drug in order to function. Dr. Patterson had mentioned Ritalin, but I didn't know much about it.

What were the side effects? What were the long term effects? Would his height be affected, his already bird-like appetite diminish? Would he look like a drugged out zombie? I had asked Dr. Patterson all these questions before. All he could tell me was that studies had shown that the drug helped a percentage of children who showed symptoms similar to Mark's.

My mother nodded, "We'll support you whatever you do. You never know. Ritalin may be just the miracle you're praying for. And if it's not, it may help him enough to get things back under control."

"Speaking of under control," I said. "I have another favor to ask you. Do you think you and Daddy can watch the kids for me Saturday night? I need to get out and have some fun or my controls will really snap."

"Sure we can watch them. Are you going to do anything special?" she asked, trying to hide her curiosity.

"Actually, I have a date. Cousin Joann introduced me to a nice guy, her boss, who works at the Stop and Shop in Clifton. He recently went through a separation and he's just looking for someone to go out to dinner or a movie with. "

My mother's face grew serious. "Are you sure you're ready to go out with someone? You're only recently separated."

"I'm not "going out with someone". Just dinner with a nice guy. And yes, I'm ready. Boy, am I ready! After months and months of feeling like a dish rag, I need to feel like a woman again."

Bang! A shattering crash against the side of the house had us up and running for the back door. Tired of throwing the snowballs against the tree, Mark had changed his target to the house. The snowball had banged into the window of the backdoor, but thankfully he had not thrown it hard enough to break the glass.

I shrugged into my coat and gathered my purse and the bag with the groceries I had bought after work. "Time to go," I said. "Thanks Mom. See you tomorrow."

I picked up Cheryl at her friend's house and drove home. While I started on dinner, Cheryl did her homework and Mark began his usual routine of annoying his sister while she worked. He only wanted her to play with him because he was bored, and explaining to him that she had to do her homework made no impact on his annoying behavior. Out of patience, I pulled him into the living room, turned on the TV and set him up with blocks and Legos.

"Don't you come into the kitchen until I call you for dinner," I said, shaking my finger at him.

He looked up at me, his bright blue eyes clouded with confusion, uncertain what it was he had done wrong this time. He was so forgiving, so affectionate, so confused about other people's anger with him, I felt myself melting and reached down to ruffle his hair. He smiled and snuggled into my arms, but only for a moment before he was off and running again. I returned to the kitchen, feeling the exhaustion racing down my back making my arms weak and tingly.

Dinner was its usual struggle. Mark alternately guarded his food or messed it all over his face in a perfect imitation of a pig eating slops. Cheryl made a face, but I shook my head. I knew I should correct him every time he did it, but I had corrected him at least a hundred times already and tonight I was too tired to make it one hundred and one.

I had just finished washing the dishes and scrubbing the mess off the table when the phone rang. After Dave had moved out, the mysterious phone calls had stopped. Thank God! But for some reason I didn't want to answer the call tonight. I let it ring three or four times, but the caller was persistent.

"All right! All right!" I said aloud and reached for the receiver on the sixth ring.

"Good news!" A cheery voice boomed from the other end. "I definitely have a buyer for the house. He's made a fair offer and if you agree, we can start the paper work tomorrow." My agent, Barbara, told me the offer and she was right. It was fair, although I would be losing some of the money we put into fixing up the house. Tears welled in my eyes and I could barely speak.

"Corraine. Are you still there?"

"I'm still here," I said. "And yes, the offer is acceptable. Write up the contract or whatever it is you have to do and I'll come in tomorrow to sign it."

Saturday morning I ran to the realtors, signed the contract, then drove straight to Dr. Patterson's office. Because he hadn't needed a check-up and because I wanted to talk to Dr. Patterson, I left Mark and Cheryl with my parents. I told Dr. Patterson everything Mark's teacher had told me about his behavior in school.

"I'm still uncertain about the Ritalin," I said. "Can't you tell me anything else about it?"

Dr. Patterson motioned me into a chair and came around his desk to sit down beside me. "Physicians have been treating symptoms like Mark's with medication since the 1930's and follow up studies of adults who took medication as kids show no long term side effects. Ritalin is of the class of drug we call stimulants. We don't know why a stimulant has the opposite effect of calming down a hyperactive child, but we do know that in the majority of cases it works. It makes them less active and consequently helps them to concentrate. They tend to be able to plan their activities better and are able to blot out many of the unfiltered messages from their senses and bodies that overstimulate them. The drug doesn't sedate them or make them behave like Zombies. Any questions so far?"

I had a million questions, but once again, they packed themselves so closely into a solid mass of confusion that I couldn't separate a single one into a coherent line of inquiry. I dumbly shook my head.

"You will probably see a remarkable improvement in his ability to focus and in his behavior. The drug begins to work almost immediately, but it leaves the body very quickly and only works for the prescribed time period. When it begins to wear off, Mark's behavior may seem all the more severe for having been under control. After the first three weeks we will need to re-examine the dosage until we have him stabilized."

"You mean we'll need to increase the dosage?" I asked.

"Possibly or we may need to change the times of day he receives it. Some children can go all day on a single dose, others may need to take a certain amount in the morning, another at noon and another in the evening. We have to work with it for a while until we set up the right regimen for Mark."

I felt trapped. I didn't want to do this. But what were my options? Things couldn't go on the way they were. My mom was exhausted watching him. He was doing poorly in school and I was running myself into the ground trying to do what we needed to survive.

"When do we start?" I asked.

Dr. Patterson consulted Mark's height and weight from the last visit and wrote out the prescription with a detailed set of instructions for me. We were to begin tomorrow morning. Sunday. That would give me a chance to look for any allergies or unusual side effects before he had to go back to school on Monday. I drove to the pharmacy, picked up the prescription and was about to get the kids at my mother's house when on the spur of the moment I dropped into the jewelry store on the corner of Franklin Avenue, Nutley's main street.

After the usual "Can I help you" and "No, just browsing" I peeked into the subtly lit cases of diamond earrings and gem set rings. I wasn't shopping for anything special. I wasn't even sure why I was there. Perhaps the elegantly dressed windows and the thickly carpeted floors that shut out the noise from outside had looked like a calm haven from the chaos I was living with. The lavender velvet of the draped cases and the sparkling radiance of the jewels cast a hypnotic spell over my jangled nerves, a serenity that I knew was only momentary, but that I welcomed all the same. I longed to load down my earlobes and fingers with the heavy weight of the gold and the sparkling iridescence of the diamonds, not from any sense of greed, but from a desire to bring the beauty of them into the drab reality of my life.

One piece caught my eye and I returned to the case several times to stare at it with longing. It was a thin gold chain suspended from which was a charm that in tiny gold letters admonished me to LIVE, LOVE and LAUGH. The living I had covered, the laughter and love I had to work on.

"Excuse me. Can you tell me how much this necklace is?"

The somewhat bored sales lady, dressed in a cream silk suit and matching silk high heels, opened the back of the glass case and with long, red lacquered nails withdrew the pendant and handed it to me. A tiny white tag fixed to the underside whispered a price I could barely afford. I thought of my date tonight and my impulse shouted WHY NOT!

Before I had time to think about it, I wrote out the check. The sales lady looked up at me, her eyebrows raised as if she thought I would be the last person she would expect to buy anything. She wrote out the slip and arranged the pendant in an elegant black leather jewelry box. I felt my spirits soar. I had actually acknowledged myself as someone worthy of an expensive gift. One giant leap for womankind. Or at least for this woman.

I raced home, called my mother and asked her if she and Dad could take the kids to the movies for the afternoon so I could get ready for my date. She asked about the doctor's visit and whether I had gotten the Ritalin.

"We start tomorrow," I said. "And right now, at this very moment, I'm feeling great. So can you keep them a few extra hours?"

"I suppose so. Your father took Mark to the park and Cheryl is playing with her cousins. No need for you to rush back."

I rang off and headed for the bathroom. I turned the taps on so the water ran almost hot and dumped in a bottle of bath salts. I had been out with a few men since Dave had left and, although the experience was mildly pleasant, I had not been in any frame of mind to enjoy myself. Tonight I wanted to let go. I thought of the pendant I had bought. Yes, tonight I was ready to Live, Laugh and if not Love, at least flirt a little. I lingered in the tub until my skin wrinkled like a dried cranberry, then stepped out and vigorously toweled myself dry.

Wrapped in a terry cloth robe, a towel turbaned around my head, I searched my wardrobe for something to wear. Before I had gone back to work I had lived in pants and easy to care for shirts and sweaters. I had been adding to my collection with business suits and conservative dresses for the job, but conservative just didn't do it for me tonight. Trouble was - I didn't have anything but conservative. The best I could manage was a print dress with a dark background and small rose and white flowers sprinkled around the bodice and hem.

"Well, maybe he's a conservative kind of a guy!" I told myself as I sprayed on cologne and fastened my new pendant around my neck. I didn't know very much about my date except that we had attended the same high school. He had graduated a year before me and I couldn't remember ever having met him at Nutley High. So what? At least, we could talk about the teachers and coaches as an ice breaker.

The bell rang just as I was putting the finishing touches to my hair. My heart began to pound and I could feel the heat rising up my neck into my face. Suddenly, I felt like a teenager again and I wasn't sure I liked the sensation. I walked to the door calmly and opened it as if I had been doing this for the past year or two.

"Come on in, Doug," I said with what I hoped was a sophisticated smile. "I'm just finishing up and I'll be ready in a few minutes. Would you like a drink before we go?"

I remembered I had no liquor in the house. When Dave left I had searched out all the hidden bottles and dumped the contents down the toilet. Silently, I prayed Doug would say no.

He consulted his watch. "No thank you," he said politely and I breathed a sigh of relief.

"What time is our reservation?" I collected my coat from the hall closet and was about to swing it over my shoulders when he reached for it and helped me slip it on. It had been a long time since a man had helped me on with my coat. I had no doubts about my competence to put on my own coat or to do anything else I needed, but the attention felt good and the courtesy helped put me at ease.

"Dinner's at seven-thirty. We can have cocktails there. Is that all right?"

"Actually, I have a confession to make." I had locked the door and was walking with Doug down the front steps of the house. The slight pressure of his hand on the small of my back was intimate enough to be exciting, but did not feel the least bit intrusive.

"Already," he laughed. "I hardly know you."

"Shall I be a woman of mystery then, and keep all my secrets to myself?"

"Now that you've started you have to finish. What were you going to tell me?"

"I didn't have any liquor in the house anyway. But I only remembered that after I had asked if you wanted a drink," I said.

He laughed again, his voice a rich baritone in the quiet confines of the car. We had pulled out of the driveway and, for once, I was content to let someone else take control of my time. I didn't even bother to ask where we were going.

"Tell me what's new in your life?" he said. "Since I don't know anything about you, we can start at the present and work backwards."

"Fair enough." I settled back against the upholstery and thought about what I wanted to tell him. "I guess the biggest thing in my life right now is selling my house. I signed the papers this morning."

"Because of your separation?" he asked.

"I'd stay if I could. I have mostly good memories of living there in spite of the problems with Dave. I just can't afford the payments on my salary."

He didn't waste time on false sympathy which I liked. "So what are you going to do?" he asked.

"I've already signed the lease on a three room apartment in town. It's a large space so I think we'll be comfortable."

"Good for you. It's difficult after a separation. I know. But the trick is to get on with things, which is exactly what you're doing. So let's make a deal. Tonight neither of us can talk about our children or our ex's. Tonight we kick back and enjoy ourselves."

We had just turned into the parking lot of a large, well-lit restaurant, one I had never been to before. Doug parked the car and came around my side to help me out. I put my hand in his large one and felt suddenly that I had made a friend. I looked up at him from the front seat and was surprised at how tall he was. For some reason I hadn't noticed before, perhaps because I had been too worried about how I looked. Yes, he was definitely tall with broad shoulders and chest. His face was handsome, his smile warm and sincere. There was in his expression the simple regard of one person for another. I felt myself warming towards him.

The restaurant he had chosen had three stories, the bottom floor a dark, smoky cocktail lounge, the second a spacious dining room and the third a dance floor surrounded by tables. We decided to eat first, then go upstairs to dance. At the table Doug helped me off with my coat and smiled his appreciation at my flowered dress.

"I'm not much with compliments, but you really do look nice," he said

The shy sincerity pleased me more than effusive flattery ever could and I blushed. I buried my face in the menu until I regained my composure. We ordered cocktails and discussed the various merits of the dishes offered. Once the waitress had taken our orders and brought out drinks, I looked across the table at Doug and said,

"Your turn?"

"My turn for what?" he asked.

"Your turn to tell me something about your life."

He hesitated, then looked somewhat uncomfortable. "I know we aren't supposed to talk about kids or ex's, but I really am just settling in after my separation. Everything turns upside down as I'm sure you know. All the plans you made, the whole future you've mapped out for yourself is suddenly blank. For the moment, I'm trying to get used to being alone after nine years of being a husband and father."

"It's difficult on both ends, I guess. Being a single parent with two children to support and raise is no piece of cake but, at least, I have my children with me. My parents live close by and I have aunts and uncles and cousins galore to keep me from loneliness."

"So you never feel lonely?" he asked.

"Of course, I do. But it's not the kind of loneliness that comes from being alone. It's... it's... the loneliness of being abandoned, I guess. Of waking up at night and knowing there is no one to hold you against the fears or to comfort you against life's many sorrows. It's the loneliness of having no mate."

For the second time that evening, my face turned bright red and I was grateful when the waitress arrived and started moving things around the table to make room for the laden dishes. He probably thinks I want to get married, I thought, staring down at my side dish of linguine. I can't believe I said that and on a first date. I wanted to explain, to tell him I was not looking for a husband, but I knew that if I brought the topic up again I would only make matters worse. I cut a slice of veal and placed it in my mouth to keep myself from talking. When I looked up again, Doug was smiling at me.

"Relax." he said, raising his glass. "Remember our promise. No heavy conversation tonight."

We lingered over our food, keeping the conversation light and ranging over topics from work to local politics. I had ordered a cream pie for dessert and was rather stuffed when Doug suggested we go upstairs and dance.

"But only slow dances," he said as he took my arm to guide me up the stairs.

"Why is that?" I asked. "I need to work off some of that dinner or I'll probably gain two pounds by tomorrow."

"I never really got into dancing much and I'm not very coordinated. I'm basically a watcher, but I can manage to enjoy a waltz."

I laughed. "Slow dances it is, then."

The band was too loud to allow for much conversation, but we found a table and watched the other couples dancing quickly to the rock beat. The crowd was mixed, both young and old mingling on the floor, the music reflecting the tastes of all ages. Soon after we arrived, the band played a slow sentimental tune. Doug led me out onto the floor and I was surprised how graceful he was for such a big guy. He held me at a respectful distance for which I was grateful. I was not yet ready for a tight clinch. I wanted to dance, to enjoy myself and not have to worry about sexual overtures. His lead was easy to follow. I relaxed and allowed myself to flow with the music. We stayed until one when I reluctantly suggested that we leave.

"Time for Cinderella to turn back into a drudge," I said as we walked out to the car. "This truly was an evening out of time, but now I have to pick up the kids and tomorrow, pick up the burdens of reality again."

"Tell you what," he said. "Would you like to do this next Saturday? I could use a break from the reality of my everyday life, too. We can make Saturday night our night to get away from it all. That is if you ..."

"Yes, I enjoyed the evening very much and yes, I'd love to go out with you again next Saturday."

We smiled at one another in relief, having gotten past an awkward moment easily. I liked Doug, I enjoyed his company and it was nice to have another Saturday evening to look forward to.

Chapter Nine

On my last night in the house on Brookdale Avenue, after the children had fallen asleep, I walked around the silent rooms touching the walls with trembling fingers. My house, my wallpaper, my kitchen, my carpet. I had worked so hard to reach this goal, suffered so much to keep it, and I had tried so hard to make it a home. Another pipe dream up in smoke.

After midnight I crawled under the covers and lay awake, listening to the steady clicking of the steam heat coming up through the pipes and thinking about moving day tomorrow. Doug had helped me bring some boxes to the apartment on his days off, but there were plenty left to go. I had scrubbed down the bathroom and kitchen, lined the drawers and put away a few odds and ends I didn't need for daily living. Tomorrow I'd turn over the key and the house would belong to strangers. Never again would I open the backdoor to let in the sunlight or play Candyland with the children on the living room rug or cook another dinner for my family here.

What does any of this means? I wondered. I had been in contact with Dave over the sale of the house. He was still drinking heavily and was in no condition to have any relationship with the children. I wondered for the hundredth time if any of the feelings I had had for Dave were real and what had happened to them. Was love simply an illusion of youth, a biological signal for mating and nothing more? I had to believe that all I had been through was meaningful even if I couldn't understand that meaning just yet. I drifted off to sleep wondering how to end this chapter of my life and begin again.

The insistent buzz of the doorbell jolted me awake, and I lay in bed, my heart pounding, trying to figure out what was going on. I took several breaths and looked around at my box strewn bedroom, the sun streaming through my curtainless windows. The movers couldn't be here already! I threw on my robe and rushed to the front door. Two large uniformed men stood outlined against the bright light, their truck parked and ready with the doors flung open at the curb.

"Sorry. Overslept," I mumbled as I let them in. I didn't even try to tidy my hair. Grief stricken and with just a few hours' sleep, I knew I looked like hell.

"Where do you want us to start, Ma'am?"

I hadn't cooked the kids' breakfast or finished packing up my bedroom. Where were the kids anyway? They hadn't made an appearance and it was past their usual wake-up time.

"Living room, I guess. Excuse me."

I dashed past them into the bathroom, brushed my teeth, washed my face, and ran a comb through my hair. In record time, I threw on my clothes and dumped my nightgown, robe and a few stray belongings into an overnight bag. The sheets, blankets and pillow I stuffed into a half empty box. As I dressed I could hear the sound of the men grunting as they lifted the heavy furniture and carried it out the door. I wanted to scream STOP, that it was all a mistake and would they please bring my belongings right back into the house where I belonged. I took a deep breath and stumbled the few steps to the children's bedroom.

"Up and at 'em, guys," I said. I could have gagged at the hypocrisy of my own cheerfulness. "The moving men are already here. We've got to get breakfast going and pack the rest of your stuff."

When there was no answer, I opened Cheryl's bedroom door and poked in my head. She was sitting up in bed, the covers bunched to her chin, her face unnaturally pale. Mark sat next to her, quiet for once, his eyes wide with fear. I took another deep breath and prayed for the right words.

"I know you're feeling bad. So am I. It's hard to leave our house, but like I told you, a house isn't a home. Home is any place we choose to make it. As long as we're together, any place we live will be home. You'll see. You'll get used to the apartment in no time. We'll have lots of fun there and before you know it, you'll forget about this old place."

I stopped. Nothing like a flood of tears to spoil the effect of a good pep talk. I swallowed down the lump in my throat, bent over the side of the bed and gave each of them a hug.

"Cheryl, do your teeth, face and hair. I'll lay out an outfit for you on the bed. And leave your PJ's in the bathroom. I'll pack them when I clean out the rest of the stuff in there. Now scoot."

I was grateful when she said nothing, just did as I asked her. After she closed the bathroom door, I lifted Mark off the bed and holding his hand, walked with him to the kitchen where I took his bottle of Ritalin from the cabinet and poured him a glass of water. He made a face and I thought I would have to battle him to take the medication, but after a minute's mutiny, he swallowed it down.

"Good boy," I said. Even though he was unusually subdued this morning, I prayed that the medication would take effect quickly. I needed him to be able to focus enough to wash up and get dressed without having to remind him what he was supposed to be doing every two minutes. The Ritalin had the startling effect of changing my son from a whirlwind to a quickening breeze in a matter of minutes. It did suppress his appetite somewhat and he still talked incessantly, but he was able to focus much better and the time he needed to complete simple tasks was greatly reduced.

While Mark dashed off to the bathroom, I pulled some bowls and spoons out of an already packed box, poured out the Cheerios and milk and set them down on the table.

"Excuse me, Ma'am, but we're done with the downstairs furniture. Where do you want us to pack up next?"

I showed them the way to my bedroom and checked to make sure Cheryl was finished in the other bedroom. She was dressed and sitting on the side of the bed.

"Come get your breakfast, Cheryl," I said as matter-of-factly as I could. "The moving men have to pack up your room." I hesitated a moment, then said, "I know how hard all of this is on you and I promise, we'll talk about it tonight. But right now, we've got to go."

I walked with her into the kitchen, settled her at the table, then ran back to strip the beds and stuff her night clothes into her little suitcase. Mark was still dawdling in the bathroom, an everyday occurrence. I opened the door and instead of insisting he complete the tasks himself, I washed his face, brushed his hair and quickly popped him into a polo shirt and pants. Mark did not do well with change and this was a major one. I was worried about what the consequences would be, but right now I was thankful that he wasn't being difficult. He ate a few spoonfuls of cereal, hunched over and guarding his bowl, then lost interest and ran off to see what the moving men were doing. Within three hours the house was stripped and the moving men, equipped with our new address, were ready to leave.

While the children stood huddled by the front door, I wandered the empty rooms alone, saying good-bye to the ghosts of memories that lingered there, the good times and the bad times that had woven the fabric of my days and the dreams that had kept those days from unraveling. When I turned the lights off for the last time, I realized that I was leaving more than the house behind, I was also leaving my memories of Dave. I had finally broken my connection to him. It was time to move on. Time to start a new life for myself and my children.

I had driven past the apartment house with the children many times, but had never taken them upstairs. The unfamiliar building and the empty apartment were more likely to give them nightmares than to reassure them. I wanted them to see it first filled with our furniture and all the familiar things from home. A new start for all of us. I resolved not to let bitterness from the past spoil this moment for me or them.

When I pulled into our numbered parking space behind the Ambassador Apartments, a wave of confidence washed over me and I no longer needed to pretend an excitement I didn't feel. "Come on, guys," I said, bundling them out of the car. "Let's go explore our new home."

While we walked to the front of the building, I pointed out the big grassy park across the street and I promised them that as soon as the weather brightened, we would play and have Saturday afternoon picnics and baseball games there. Mark wanted to go right away, and took off up the street. I caught him by the hand, and marched him up the steps to the Ambassador Apartments. Cheryl had not said a word in the car and would not answer when I asked her if she was ready to go up. She was eight years old, more mature and more capable of understanding what was happening than Mark, at five, who thought we were on an adventure. I promised myself I would have a heart-to-heart talk with her as soon as we settled in.

I hurried the kids upstairs so I could direct the moving men where to put the furniture. We had not taken everything from the house, of course. I had bought a hide -a- bed for the living room where I would sleep and a few other new odds and ends, but I wanted to keep as much of the familiar as I could. Now, as I looked around the cluttered space, I wondered where I was going to put all the stuff I had taken. The three large rooms suddenly looked like a child's playhouse.

The moving men tromped up and down the stairs, carrying the furniture and placing it where I asked, then moving it again because it didn't fit properly or because I didn't like where it was. The living room took the longest, but I finally arranged it to my satisfaction. The children's bedroom and the kitchen filled quickly with boxes and then it was over. The men left and the kids and I looked around our new home, utterly at a loss what to do or how to feel. One look at their pinched faces and I said, "Tell you what. Let's swing by Nana and Grandpa's, pick them up and go to McDonald's for lunch. We need a good lunch before we tackle all these boxes. Is it a deal?"

I whisked them out and into the car before they had a chance to think about what was going on. I felt overwhelmed by the strangeness of it all and I hoped that by doing something normal, I could ease myself into acceptance and give the kids a treat as well. A treat or a bribe not to disturb my somewhat fragile balance. I couldn't tell which and didn't care.

My parents had been waiting to hear from us and fell into my plan without explanation. As we waited on line to collect our burgers and fries, Mom said quietly, "Things happen for a reason, even though we don't always know what that reason is. Something good will come of this."

"I sure hope so, Mom," I said. "I really could use a break."

I finished unpacking the boxes around ten o'clock that night. I had started in the kids' room, filling their dressers with clothes and arranging toys on the shelves I had put up earlier. I had kept their same curtains and comforters, hoping to ease the bedtime anxiety in a new place. I hadn't found time to talk to Cheryl about her father, but tomorrow was Sunday and I promised myself I would discuss it with her then.

Bone tired, I dropped into bed, then lay awake, my scrambled thoughts flying in all directions. I couldn't get comfortable, the hide-a-bed unfamiliar, the car noises from Park Avenue intruding on what were left of my thoughts. Thank God the children were sleeping soundly. Mark had been strangely subdued all day, not bothering anyone and keeping pretty much to himself. Funny, I thought, as I drifted off to sleep, now I'm worrying when he reacts like a healthy, well-adjusted child.

I fell into an uneasy doze until a strange sound burned into the depth of my dreams, forcing me to the edge of consciousness. I threw off the covers and sat up, shaking my head to clear it. The strange sound had ceased and the unfamiliar dimensions of the apartment came into focus. I must have had a bad dream, I thought, and swung my cold feet back onto the bed when a scream sent me running for the children's bedroom.

Cheryl was sitting up in bed, the blankets pulled to her chin, her large dark eyes round and unblinking in the light from the hall. She lifted her hand and pointed to the bed where Mark was thrashing and screaming, uttering piercing cries as if he were fighting something and being wounded by it. I knelt by the side of the bed, but he was kicking and punching so wildly I couldn't come near him. I finally succeeded in capturing one of his fists in my hands.

"Mark. Mark. It's me. It's Mommy. Wake up now. You're having a bad dream. Can you hear me? Mark. It's just a dream. Wake up now."

I held his hand and gradually he relaxed, his body soaked with sweat, his mouth open as if gasping for air. I smoothed back his hair and dried his face with the edge of the blanket. He turned on his side, away from me, and I continued to stare at the back of his head for a long time. What was happening inside my little boy that kept him in such a constant state of anxiety? What impulses prompted him to beat against the walls that would hold him in safety? Anger, fear, blind panic, a memory of abuse or abandonment. What? Something was not as it should be within his being, but what? Rising from my knees on the cold floor, exhausted and emotionally spent, I silently promised my son that we would search out the answers together, that I would do everything I could to help him live a normal healthy life.

I tucked the covers securely around him, listened to his breathing for another minute, then tiptoed over to Cheryl's bed to make sure she was asleep. She wasn't. She stared up at me, her eyes wide open and scared. With a sigh I tried to stifle, I sat down on the edge of her bed.

"Do you remember when Mark first came to live with us, how he used to scream and fight when I tried to put him in the crib? Remember how I used to hold him and rock him for a long time before he'd fall asleep?"

She snuggled up next to me and nodded.

"He was frightened though we never knew why. He was too little to tell us and even if he was talking at the time, he probably wouldn't have known why he was so terrified. Well, some of that fear came back tonight. Maybe he was afraid we would leave him and go back to the old house without him. Or maybe the change made him remember something that happened to him before he became part of our family. But, after he gets used to the apartment, he won't have these nightmares any more. Okay?"

She looked up at me and I could see from the light of the hall lamp that tears were glistening in her eyes. I slipped under the covers and put my arms around her.

"What is it, Cheryl?" I asked. "I understand you're upset. Sometimes it really helps to talk about it. I know I've been very busy, but I'll always make time if you want to talk to me. Can you tell me what you're upset about?"

She was only eight years old. I wasn't sure she could tell me what she was feeling. Not that I didn't know, of course, but I wanted her to tell me in her own words so she could get it out. I waited while she cried, not loud noisy sobs but silent tears that dripped down her face and into my heart.

"Will Daddy ever live with us again?" she finally asked.

I took a deep breath and tried to marshal my tired thoughts. I wanted to tell her the truth, but in a way that would not frighten her.

"Daddy will always be your Daddy. He will always love you. But, right now, Daddy is sick and can't be with us. He has a kind of sickness that we can't help him with and until he does find help, no honey, he won't be living with us."

"I'm glad," she whispered. "I don't want him to come home."

I was shocked, but tried not to show it. I wanted her to tell me her true feelings, and I knew that the wrong response would make her feel that she had to protect me. The guilt I felt for having relied on her acceptance and help during these vulnerable months threatened to break through my reserve. I swallowed the menacing tears and asked her in a calm voice why she felt the way she did.

"It was scary when he was around," she said. "I like it better when it's just you and me and Mark."

I pulled her close and felt her relax against me. "You don't need to be scared any more. Daddy will not be living with us again, but if he gets better, you might want to see him more than you do now. But only when he gets better. Okay?"

I knew there was more on her mind, but the fears and the late hour took its toll and she fell asleep nestled in my arms. I settled myself more comfortably on the narrow bed and closed my eyes. In the early hours of the morning I must have fallen asleep because I awoke to the sound of church bells pealing through a sunny spring sky.

Chapter Ten

I put down the pot of soup I had been ladling into bowls for dinner and listened, uncertain what had given me such an eerie feeling, chills shivering down my spine for no reason. Everything was quiet. The background music of my life had become the sounds of Mark running around the apartment or something crashing as he accidentally hit into it or Cheryl complaining about him bothering her. Except for the louder crashes, I had learned to put the noise aside, always listening, but rarely giving it my full attention.

Mark had had a particularly bad day at school. Nothing could keep him focused and the principal had called to request an update on his medication level, a couched indication that perhaps I should have the dosage upped again. Mark had been on Ritalin since February and it was early May now. Dr. Patterson and I had been monitoring the drug effects very carefully, but even so, I had noticed that in the last few weeks, Mark's activity level had increased and his ability to concentrate had decreased again. My feelings about raising the dosage were so mixed I had put off taking Mark to the doctor, just in case there might be some other cause for his agitation. But today, when I had picked him up from my mom's, she had shown me a large bruise on his knee and scrapes on both his elbows.

I had learned not to overreact to Mark's mishaps because they happened so frequently. Actually, I was thankful the bruises were superficial and I didn't have to take another trip to the Emergency Room.

"He was so wild today," my mother said. "I thought he would be better outside where he could run around. You know how I hate it when he collects those bees, but I gave him a bottle and sent him out to find his bugs. I had clothes on the line. I just turned my back to collect them when he shot off on his two wheeler. I yelled for him to stop, but that doesn't mean anything to Mark, as you well know. He was pedaling down the block at break neck speed and then he was up in the air. I don't know if he hit a rock or what happened. The bike crashed and he landed, thank God, on the grass, but he came down hard and skidded on his knees and elbows.

"No crack on the head?"

"Not that I could tell. He was shaken for a few minutes, but then he was up and running. I brought him in to clean up his cuts and then sat in the yard while he collected bees. You know what I do with those bees he catches. When he's not looking, I unscrew the lid of the jar, blast the bees with hair spray and close the jar back up again. The creatures are out of their misery and they can't get loose in the house."

I stayed and chatted a few minutes more, then left for the apartment. By the time we arrived home, Mark was wound up again and five minutes in the small apartment was all I could take of his bouncing off walls. I marched him into the bathroom, filled the tub with warm water, threw in a few bathtub toys and lifted him in. I handed him his little tugboat and watched as the water had its magical, soothing effect. In a few minutes, he was playing calmly and I told him he could stay in the tub a little while longer while I checked on dinner. The bath routine usually gave me time to prepare dinner in peace. I'd call Mark every minute or two to check on him or pop in and out of the bathroom to see if he was okay.

But tonight something was wrong. Mark was too quiet and, when I called his name, he didn't answer. I raced into the bathroom, slipped on the damp floor and banged my knees into the porcelain tub. Mark was lying face up in the bottom of the tub, the water lapping at his nose and mouth. The skin around his lips was blue, but I could still see his chest rise and fall with each breath. Praying madly, I pulled him out and with one hand, reached for a towel. I wrapped him up and held him close to me, gently shaking him and calling his name. I watched his face as he struggled up from a deep sleep. His eyelids fluttered open. I said a quick prayer of thanksgiving and was about to yell at him for falling asleep in the tub when I saw that his eyes, filled with fear, were fixed on my face.

"Do you love Mark?" he asked. "Is Mark a bad boy?"

"I love Mark very much," I said. "Sometimes Mark does things that upset people, but that doesn't make him a bad boy."

His thin arms came around my neck and he pulled my head down for a rare kiss. I held him, rocking back and forth on the damp bathroom floor till the fear in his eyes was replaced by a confidence that everything was alright.

I didn't want him to know how badly I was shaken, how worried I was about what had just happened. I knew he hadn't done it on purpose. I knew he could not help so many of the irresponsible actions that formed my everyday fears. But with each day that passed he was becoming more wild, more irresponsible, his behavior less controllable even with the medication. He was neither mean nor malicious, but he was troubled. Surely, somewhere there were answers to his problems, solutions that would help him overcome his difficulties and ease my constant anxiety. Maybe the reason I wasn't getting the right answers was because I was asking the wrong questions. I just didn't know who to turn to for help.

After supper, I called Dr. Patterson, who listened without interruption as I described Mark's continuing difficulty in school, his unwillingness or inability to listen and the events of today from the bike accident to falling asleep and nearly drowning in the bath.

"We may need to alter the dosage of the Ritalin again," he said without hesitation. "Every patient is different and, as I had warned you, it may take time to find the dose that works best for Mark."

"I understand that," I said, "but medicating him isn't enough. I need to know why he's behaving the way he is. What are we talking about here? Is it physical, emotional, environmental, psychological? What?"

"I wish I could answer you, Corraine, but I can't," he said. "Bring him tomorrow for a blood test and we'll see about increasing the medication. Then, if you like, I'll give you the name of the neurologist we had discussed a few months ago. He might be able to answer some of the questions I can't."

The neurologist Dr. Patterson recommended was the Director of Child Neurology at the Mount Sinai School of Medicine in Manhattan. The soonest he was able to see Mark was July twenty sixth, two months from now. Of course, once determined on this course I was impatient to get going, but Dr. Patterson assured me that it was worth waiting to see Dr. Avery because he was a top specialist in the field. In the meantime, he increased Mark's prescription and decreased the time between morning and afternoon doses. It was enough to get Mark through the last two months of school. He completed kindergarten to the great relief of his teacher. He could recognize some of his letters and numbers, tie his shoelaces and zip and unzip his coat when he felt like it. Not much, but more than he had accomplished before he went to school.

A few weeks into summer vacation, I decided to take him off the Ritalin. I discussed it with my mom who would now be watching both the children full time during the week. I knew it would be harder for her to handle Mark, but I felt it was justified because I did not want him dependent on medication for daily living. I wanted him to have the chance to learn the coping skills he would need to function normally. How would I know what was the medication effect and what was Mark's natural development if I had him on medication all the time?

My folks agreed to try it with the proviso that if Mark's behavior deteriorated we would go back to the dosage he was on at school. Ritalin is unusual because it takes effect almost immediately after it is introduced into the body and it does not stay in the body long. We began to see the difference immediately. Mark was into everything, unable to focus on anything, a constant blur of movement and non-stop talking. His language had improved and he made up for the past with a vengeance, talking about everything and nothing all at once. He was also beginning to talk back, to question simple requests. When I asked him to get me a cup, he would ask me why he had to do it, why couldn't I? After a long day at work, my patience was not equal to constant challenges and I began losing my temper and yelling more.

As summer wore on and my mom wore out, I decided we all needed to get away. What better place than the Jersey Shore, I thought. As a child I had loved the white sand beaches, the burning summer blue of the skies and the hot dog and pizza smells of the Boardwalk. I wanted to share that with my children, to take a vacation from the mundane tasks of daily life and just have fun, something I believed in and rarely indulged. I asked my parents if they would like to accompany us. They were delighted even though summer days at the shore meant hours of traffic and very little room to lay out your blanket on the beach. I hadn't missed a full day of work in ages and I had a few sick days coming to me.

So in the heat of a July morning we packed up the blankets, striped beach umbrella, bathing suits, coolers, pails and shovels, a jug of lemonade and a few sandwiches and started down to the shore.

The kids sat in the back with me, Mom and Dad in the front trying to ignore the constant "when will we get there" which went on for the full hour and fifteen minute ride. But it was a beautiful bright day, not too hot, and I was in a wonderful mood. Dad zipped into a parking space right near the Boardwalk entrance and unloaded the trunk.

"Mark, can you be my helper and carry the bag of sandwiches and the jug?" I asked. The rest of us were already loaded down with the other seaside paraphernalia.

"Can't Cheryl do it?"

"No, Cheryl's already carrying the beach bag and her towel," I explained patiently.

"Give it to Nana."

"Nana's loaded up and so am I. You can see that. Please take the bag and the jug so we can get to the beach, Mark."

Reluctantly, he grabbed what I held out to him and without waiting ran up the wooden steps leading to the Boardwalk. It was nine o'clock in the morning and the regular beach throng hadn't yet arrived. I spotted him standing before one of the barker's stalls. He was staring at a display of pink elephants and mint-striped fuzzy zebras. For a split second I wanted to leave him there, to walk past and pretend he wasn't mine. I needed a day to relax and my sixth sense told me this wasn't going to be it.

"Come on, Mark, " I called to him as I breezed past, ignoring whatever impulse it was that had made him run away from me. "We need to buy our badges so we can get onto the beach."

I grabbed Mark's hand as we moved to the wooden steps leading onto the beach. The white sand gleamed as I paid for the badges and the roar of the surf set my heart pounding. I did not look out at the ocean immediately. I wanted a serene moment alone for my first glimpse of the sea. I had always had a strong affinity for the ocean, its constancy and eternality a healing force in my life. But to feel the spirituality of the sea, I needed to be alone and free, unburdened by beach blankets and striped umbrellas and greasy sandwich bags, relieved for the moment of the responsibilities of child care. I needed to be the child and let the sea nurture me with its hope and promise of peace.

There were plenty of good spots to choose from and I laid our blankets down on a crest of the sand, far enough away so they wouldn't be caught by the incoming tide, but close enough to see the ocean. We had worn our bathing suits under our clothes. Mark had already ripped off his shirt and was heading down to the waves when I grabbed his arm and hauled him back.

"Not so fast, young man. I want to put suntan lotion on you." I slathered on the Coppertone while lecturing him about how he had to stay close to me, and that he could not go into the water by himself.

"Sit down on the blanket and wait until I get undressed." I kept one eye on him while I pulled off my shorts and tank top. He squirmed, but stayed put for the few minutes it took me to disrobe. As soon as I was down to my bathing suit, he jumped up, ready to go. So much for my need to see the ocean alone.

Hand in hand, we ran down the white sands to the water's edge. The hot sun felt good on my shoulders, the heat penetrating to relieve some of the tension there. I smiled down at Mark who was still clinging to my hand. With the vastness of the ocean as a backdrop, he suddenly looked pitifully small. Still undersized, his ribs stuck out through his skin and his arms and legs looked like toothpicks stuck on a pale clay figurine. He looked about four though he was now almost six and a half. I bent down and kissed the top of his gleaming white-blond hair.

"Ready to take the plunge?" I asked.

He hesitated. "I'll hold your hand the whole time," I said. "If you don't like it, we'll come out and you can play in the sand. Okay?"

He tugged on my hand and together we walked to where the waves were rolling into the shore. The water was chilly and Mark stood shivering as the water splashed onto his bare legs.

"It'll feel warmer once you get used to it," I promised. I splashed myself to wet my arms and legs, then splashed him. I expected him to laugh, but he looked at the water seriously, then turned and ran back onto the shore.

"Do you want to go in again?" I asked. I was puzzled by his response because he was usually so reckless. He shook his head, then ran back to where my parents were sitting under an umbrella. Cheryl was playing in the sand. My mom opened one eye and looked up at me. I shrugged. I handed Mark a pail and shovel and set him up beside me on the blanket.

More people were arriving, kicking past us on their way to find places for themselves on the sand. The beach often reminded me of a refugee camp, escapees from a stressful world setting up temporary shelter in a restful haven. I watched the young parents dragging diaper bags, inflatable tubes, beach chairs and babies across the hot sands, lovers already locked in gritty embraces, old folk holding hands as they helped one another negotiate the holes dug by kids. I felt myself, at long last, begin to relax.

"Mark, don't throw the sand, honey. Scoop it up and put it in your pail like this," I showed him how to avoid flinging the sand so the wind wouldn't carry it into people's faces. Perfectly content, he shoveled up the sand, uncovering shells and reburying them in his pail. Some people had already begun to eat and seagulls flocked to the food, circling overhead or landing boldly on the beach to stare at the diners and hope for scraps. Mark pointed excitedly at the birds.

"Can we feed them, Mommy? Can we? Can we?"

"If you feed them, Mark, they don't leave you alone. I don't want them around us for the rest of the afternoon." I turned to my father. "Throw me the Coppertone, Dad. I'm starting to burn already." My legs and the top of my feet hadn't seen much of the sun all summer and were already a darker pink than was good for them. I concentrated for a few minutes, giving them a good slathering of the protective cream, then covered my arms, face and neck. The special smell of the suntan lotion brought back memories of younger days spent happily dreaming in the warm salt air.

Before laying down, I turned to see how Mark was doing with his digging. His bright orange pail and shovel sat only an inch from my hand. Mark no longer sat beside them. I twisted around quickly, searching the immediate area around our blanket. I didn't see him. I stood up and scanned as much of the beach as I could. There were plenty of children running about. I zeroed in on the blondes, hoping Mark had found a playmate and had gone a little ways in some game or other. I would scold him for not telling me and be thankful it was no worse. I spotted several blond boys, but no Mark. My parents, sensing my movements, sat up.

"What is it, Corraine?" Mom asked.

I tried to keep my voice calm. "I can't find Mark."

She didn't question me. She didn't need to. "I'll take Cheryl and we'll search the beach to the right. You go to the left. Your Dad will go further down. We'll report it to the lifeguards and meet back here in half an hour, sooner if we find him."

My first thought was that he had gone in search of the gulls, but they were now feeding out at sea. 'He didn't like the water. He wouldn't go out there, I told myself over and over, as I walked first along the wet sands, then higher up on the beach, stopping to peer intently into the faces of skinny blond boys. Tears kept forming in my eyes at each disappointment and my heart was drumming so hard I thought I might faint. I made it to the lifeguard's chair and, in a breathless voice caught by the wind, hollered up to him that I had lost my son. He could not leave his post, but he did relay the information via a walky-talky to the rescue station on the Boardwalk.

"They want you to go up there and give a complete description. Meanwhile, they'll radio all the lifeguards and tell them to keep a look out. Don't worry, Ma'am. We'll find him."

I walked off in a daze. My mind, protecting me from the worst possibilities, shut off. It took me a few minutes to realize I was wandering aimlessly. I had to return to the lifeguard for directions to the rescue station. He patiently repeated them twice more. I stumbled toward the wooden steps and almost bumped into my mom and Cheryl, barely recognizing them in the grip of the panic that was now shaking me. I didn't need to ask whether they found him. They were alone.

"We have to go to the rescue station," I said. "They need a description, then they'll start a search."

We walked quickly and in silence. Miraculously, I remembered the directions though I felt like I was walking on some alien planet where the sights and sounds were familiar, but I just couldn't place them somehow. Their meanings had all changed. Now there was something sinister and menacing in the dark interiors of ice-cream parlors and pizza stands and the raucous music of the carnival atmosphere stretched my nerves to the breaking point.

Two men at the desk looked at me sympathetically when we walked in. One of the men came around and took my arm, leading me to a chair. He handed me a glass of water. I took a few sips and, for a minute, my head seemed to clear.

"Can you answer a few questions?" he asked. "It won't take long because we want to start the search right away. We've called the local police. They should be here any minute, but let's get the description out now. How long has your son been missing?"

I looked at my watch. "About an hour, I guess. We arrived here around nine, settled on the beach, I took him down to the water around ten. He didn't like it so we came back and he played with his pail and shovel for a while. When I looked to see how he was doing, he was gone. That was around ten thirty. It's nearly twelve now." I knew I was babbling, but I couldn't help it.

He wrote something on his pad. "Okay, now what's the little guy's name, how old is he and what does he look like?"

"His name is Mark. He's six and a half, but he looks like he's four. He's very thin, he's got blue eyes, pale skin, light blond hair and he's wearing orange and green swim trunks and ... and .. no shirt or shoes." I held up his polo shirt and sneakers. I hadn't even realized until then that I was clutching them.

Two police officers entered the small room which now felt crowded and claustrophobic. I didn't want to be there. I wanted to be out searching for Mark and I stood up, signaling my impatience. The officers conversed with the rescue squad workers and then, with a nod in my direction, left.

"They're going to sweep the Boardwalk. My men will search the beach. We'll find him, Ma'am. You're welcome to stay here as long as you like. When we find him we'll bring him back here so if you decide to leave, check in every once in a while."

"I want to look for him myself," I said. I glanced at my mom and, for the first time, noticed that Cheryl was crying. I went over and put my arms around her. "We'll find him. Mommy's worried, but she isn't mad at you or anything. When Mark comes back, I'll get you the biggest ice cream cone you've ever seen. I promise."

I walked out, the adrenaline pumping through my veins. At each of the open stands I asked if anyone had seen a little boy answering to Mark's description and to please keep him at the stand if he should show up. Some of them had already spoken with the police, but I didn't care. Maybe if they saw how distraught I was they would take it more seriously and help find my son.

My first check back at the rescue station was disappointing. There was no news either from the beach or the Boardwalk. The man behind the desk assured me that none of the lifeguards had seen him in the water so I was sure he hadn't drowned and I refused to believe he was kidnapped. He was lost. He would be found. I knew if I didn't believe that I couldn't go on.

I told Dad and Mom to get Cheryl a piece of pizza and a cold drink and wait for me on the shady bench next to the rescue station. I was going to hit a few more places further down the Boardwalk and maybe one or two of the cottages near where we had parked the car in case he had wandered there looking for us.

All along the Boardwalk families gathered at picnic tables, laughing and enjoying hamburgers and greasy fries or spooning gobs of ice cream from paper cups. The crowds had grown, clustered around stalls where kids were banging hammers on pop-up frogs or throwing hoops around bottles in vain attempts to win stuffed bears and zebras. I wandered along the edges, wild-eyed, staring angrily at families having fun. It seemed to me that everyone had what I had wanted so badly – a few hours of simple pleasure without heartbreak. I knew I wasn't thinking rationally. What did I know about their lives and what they had suffered? All I knew was that they weren't suffering now. Envy added to fear stole most of my strength, but I struggled on keeping hope ahead of me as my goal. By the time I reached the end of the Boardwalk even hope had disappeared.

An hour later, in tears, I slowly made my way back to the bench. My legs shook under me, a sudden weakness from the adrenaline loss. I intended to stay at the beach all day and evening, hoping it would be easier to search when the crowds thinned out.

I spotted Cheryl and my parents patiently waiting on the bench. At that same second, I saw coming towards them a police officer and skipping along next to him, holding his hand and chattering non-stop, was Mark. I stood, rooted to the spot, unable to move. I wanted to run to him, to grab him, hug him, hold him close to me, yell at him, smack him, but a terrible paralysis came over me. I couldn't move. The officer stopped to talk to my mom, then they all came to where I was standing. With a superhuman effort, I managed to hold out my arms. Mark ran to me for a hug, chatting about getting some crumbs for the birds. His sun-burned face was glowing with excitement and when I looked into his eyes, I knew that he had not given a single thought to what he had done. I tried to ask him where he had been for so long, but no words came out. I held him tight, unwilling to let go.

The officer explained that he had found him begging for food from one of the hamburger stands. The boy behind the counter kept him there while another worker went in search of the police officer who had stopped there only a short time ago. My parents took charge and thanked the officer, then went with him to file the report. I still couldn't talk. I clung to Mark's hand and wouldn't let go until we were safely in the car again. The rescue squad had been kind enough to collect our things from the beach and stow them in the trunk for us. My Dad drove while I sat silent in the backseat. The little voice in the back of my mind, the voice that had tried to catch my attention since my first days with Mark, screamed aloud. I tried to argue with myself that it was not unusual for little boys to wander off oblivious to their surroundings and that I was certainly not the first mother such a thing had happened to, but my intuition urged me to look beyond that to the larger picture that was forming. Taken individually, each of the events that had happened in the last three years could be explained away as "boys will be boys" behavior, but put together they revealed a shadowy pattern of disturbing design that left unaltered could lead to disaster.

On the way back to the car, my mother spoke sternly to Mark about running away without telling anyone where he was going, how badly he had frightened us, and how he might have been hurt or lost forever. She told him to apologize to me for all the worry he had caused. At first, he had looked up at me with his usual lack of comprehension, but when she insisted, I saw his expression change to one of defiance. Not only was he not aware of having done anything wrong, but he was not willing or able to understand the consequences of his behavior for others concerned. As frightened as I still felt about the recklessness of his having run away, deep down I was more frightened by his inability to feel remorse for having caused pain to those who cared about him. For the first time, I wondered if my love and care could reach the core of damage done to this little boy and, if I did reach it, would my love make any difference to his life.

Chapter Eleven

I had written down a list of questions to ask the neurologist, Dr. Avery, and I had them safely tucked away in my purse as I drove into Manhattan with Mark. It was a muggy July day, a dirty gray haze visible over the skyline of the city. As we neared the Lincoln Tunnel, I kept up a steady stream of observations pointing out the Empire State Building to Mark and guessing at the other skyscrapers to distract him.

Earlier that morning I had explained to him that we were going to visit another doctor who might tell us why he wasn't doing as well in school as he might be and why he was having trouble with his classmates and the neighborhood children. Mark wanted friends. He was old enough to feel hurt about the fights and about not being allowed to play with other kids. He didn't understand that it was his wild behavior that was to blame for this. He was just doing what came naturally to him. He had no idea that what came naturally to him did not come naturally to other six year olds and that his behavior was strange or different.

As we walked through the impressive lobby of Mt. Sinai Hospital, I looked down at Mark and my heart clenched in my chest. He looked so small and scared. I asked God to help us through this, to provide some answer to the puzzle of this little boy. I wanted Mark to be able to put behind him all the unhappiness he had suffered in his young life and to replace that unhappiness with a bright future. If I knew the answers to what was wrong, I would know what to do.

We took the elevator to Dr. Avery's office and after a brief wait, we followed his nurse into a comfortable examining room. Dr. Avery joined us a few minutes later. I liked him immediately. His manner with Mark was natural and friendly, but not overly solicitous. He told Mark what he was going to do, then explained that it would be better if Mommy left the room for a few minutes. We both reassured Mark that I would be right outside and that if he needed me the nurse would come and get me right away. Mark seemed okay with this so I followed another nurse into a small office to fill out the papers. But before I left, I told Dr. Avery I wanted to ask him a few questions when he was finished examining Mark. He agreed without the defensiveness or arrogance I half expected.

The nurse took an extensive medical history, from the time we had first brought Mark home, to the present. She asked me questions about his life before he had come to us, questions that I could not answer, but that made me wonder whether the problems I was dealing with were specters of his infancy about which I knew so little. She asked me about the Ritalin and his school progress before and after the medication and whether I had noticed any medication effects. I answered as thoroughly as I could. I wanted Dr. Avery to know everything there was to know about Mark and more. I told her about the bullying by other kids and his inability to make friends, his hyperactivity, his impulsiveness and whatever else I could think of. When we were finished, she led me to a pleasantly decorated room where other anxious parents waited for their children. I took a cup of coffee and walked over to the huge, hermetically-sealed windows. Manhattan with its millions of people lay stretched out before me. I didn't see it. All I could see was one small boy with many problems. Problems that I still believed were my responsibility to solve.

Time drags endlessly in hospital waiting rooms, the air of tension so thick you feel like everything is happening in slow motion. I must have glanced at the clock ten times. Not an hour had passed. I reassured myself that Mark must be doing okay because they had not called me to go in. After another half hour, the nurse came for me.

Mark was wandering around the room, looking at brightly colored pictures of the nervous system plastered up on two of the four walls.

"Please sit down, Mrs. Graham." Dr. Avery gestured me into a chair. "Before I answer your questions I want to tell you the results of my examination. Of course, further tests can be done if you wish, but on the basis of what has been done so far, I found no pathological reflexes, no sensory abnormalities and no cranial nerve deficits. In other words, there is nothing here that makes me feel Mark has any organic central nervous system damage. He was able to accomplish most of the specific tasks I set for him - copying shapes, recognizing some of his numbers and some of his capital letters. His speech is immature, but shows no specific pathology associated with various nervous system disorders. I will write up for you the tests done and the specific evaluation for each. But I can reasonably assure you, Mark does not have a deteriorative disease."

"But what does he have then?" I asked. My voice revealed my desperation for answers and he looked at me sharply. I guess he had expected me to jump for joy at the news he had given me and, although I was thrilled that Mark was healthy, I was frustrated because again I had received no answer and no direction that could help Mark with his problems.

"The information you have given me and the results of the exam support the impression of minimal cerebral dysfunction. This is based on a behavioral pattern of hyperkinesis, and immaturity in his fine motor skills, hand-eye coordination and cognitive delays."

"Is this something he'll outgrow when he masters some of the skills you said are immature?" I asked hopefully.

"It's hard to tell. I expect him to show progress, but for now I would keep him on the Ritalin for the hyperkenesis. I would also enroll Mark in an educational program where there is a reduced student-to-teacher ratio with a teacher geared towards special needs children. Most school districts offer such a program. You might also think about counseling for you and Mark so you can learn techniques for handling your son's behavioral difficulties."

"What you're saying then is that you don't know what's causing Mark's problems?" I felt like someone had shoved me into a maze I could not see around, over, under or through.

"It's not that simple, Mrs. Graham." His eyes conveyed his sympathy. "We are seeing more and more of these children. Hyperactive, unable to pay attention, frustrated, angry, unfocused, with a variety of hearing and speech problems. A pattern, yes. But a definite organic cause, no. We can speculate on the reasons but, for now, the best we can do is treat the symptoms."

Armed with Dr. Avery's neurological report, I enrolled Mark in the first grade at Holy Family School where he had attended kindergarten. I had expected some opposition to my application and I was not surprised when, during the second week of school, Mark came home with a note requesting that I attend a conference with the principal. I was not dismayed by the note as I had been last year. I wanted to talk to the principal. I wanted to find out what the school intended to do to help him improve his behavioral and academic difficulties. I walked into school far more determined than I had ever been before. I was Mark's advocate now, not his apologetic mother.

I sat in the same chair, in the same office, as the principal pulled out a manila folder with Mark's name on it. She reviewed the pages for a moment, then closed the folder and looked at me over the top of her glasses.

"I'm afraid Mark cannot remain here with us any longer," she said. "We are a small school and we're not equipped to handle Mark's problems. He obviously needs to be in a class with a teacher trained to teach children with learning and behavioral difficulties. Our budget does not stretch to special education."

I was amazed. I had expected her to tell me what Mark was doing wrong in the classroom. I had not expected her to tell me that he was being thrown out.

"Just what do you base this judgment on?" I demanded.

"Please don't view this as a punishment for Mark," she said. "By remaining here he will not get the special help he needs, the help that could mean all the difference between success and failure in his school career."

"Please tell me what he has done that he can't remain at your school?" I asked again.

She consulted the manila folder. "Mark does not have the fundamentals to go on to reading and arithmetic. He cannot identify all his letters, he can't write his letters legibly, he doesn't know what sounds the letters make, he can't identify more than a few single numbers nor does he have the readiness for adding or subtracting.

Behaviorally, he talks when the teacher is talking; he cannot focus on his papers so he bothers the other children when they are doing theirs; he wanders around the classroom; he turns off the phonograph in the middle of a song; he can't sit still during Mass; he doesn't listen or respond to discipline. I'm sorry, Mrs. Graham. We have our standards for first grade and we cannot make an exception in Mark's case. It would be setting him up for failure. It's not fair to him or to the other children. We will keep him here while you make arrangements for alternative education."

I was dismissed. There was to be no further discussion. I left the school and walked across the street to my parents' house.

"He needs to be transferred to another school," I said to my mom the minute she opened the door. "She said they can't meet his needs there."

She walked with me into the kitchen and put the kettle on for tea.

I explained to her what had been said. Wisely, she gave no advice and when I had worn myself out, I regained some perspective.

"In some ways, what she said confirmed the report from Dr. Avery. Mark isn't ready to read yet and forcing him into the first grade won't to do him any good. I think the best thing to do is to put him back into kindergarten in public school. He's small for his age and it will be a new school where no one will make fun of him for staying back. It will give him a chance to catch up. He might even be ahead of some of the other kids because he's been through kindergarten already. That should boost his self- esteem. What do you think, Mom?"

"I think you should make an appointment with the principal of Washington School right now. The sooner you get Mark enrolled there the better."

I phoned the Nutley Board of Education offices, found out what paperwork I needed to fill out and arranged to meet with the school principal on my lunch hour the next day. I didn't tell Mark because I didn't want him to worry. I did tell Cheryl. She was relieved because she had been teased about her "bad boy" brother. Cheryl's progress in school had been excellent and I did not want her to slip because of Mark.

My meeting with the principal of Washington School went off without a hitch. I spoke with her concerning Mark's difficulties and his previous school history. She assured me that the kindergarten teacher was a veteran and had her classroom well under control. She would be able to work with Mark on his socialization skills as well as his readiness for first grade work. Mark would be able to start the next day if I wished, but I explained to her that he had difficulty with change and that I wanted to prepare him. We agreed that he would begin on the following Monday.

To my surprise, Mark made no fuss when I told him he would be going to a different school. He had no friends at Holy Family he would miss and his kindergarten experience hadn't been a pleasant one. I crossed my fingers that we were on our way to a positive school experience and I conveyed this to him in the tone of my voice and the enthusiasm with which I extolled the virtues of his new school. He also liked that I would pick him up at lunchtime every day and take him to Nana's house myself. Kindergarten was only a half day.

I realized that Mark was never going to have an easy time of it in school. His early traumas had caused scars that would take a long time to heal, but he was a warm, affectionate child who held no grudges against those who had hurt him in the past. I believed that with extra help and guidance he could eventually make up for his slow start and that, once he was accepted by his peers, he would adjust to the discipline he needed to succeed.

Over the next few months I kept in close contact with Mark's teacher. He improved in the skills Dr. Avery had identified as trouble areas and, as I had suspected, his previous year in kindergarten had given him enough of a boost to allow him to stay with the rest of the class. He still had difficulties getting along with the other children and I still received the urgent phone calls from my mom after school. But compared to last year, things were definitely looking up and I was able to breathe more easily as the days went on.

My father was traveling now for the insurance agency he worked for in Manhattan and he would often take my mother and the kids with him on short trips after school or on school vacations. The short breathers away from the children allowed me time to heal and I began to feel more myself again. Dave and I were now divorced and I was learning to adjust to my status as a single parent and the sole financial support of my family. Although Dave was supposed to pay child support, his condition was desperate and he could no longer keep a job. He had not seen the children since we separated and they no longer asked about him. For that, I was grateful. I was also grateful that my anger toward him had turned to pity and I no longer carried the same burden of hurt I had in the beginning.

In April, I was called in for a conference. As I had seen regular reports during the school year, I was not alarmed. I assumed that Mark's teacher wanted to give me an update on his progress as she had been doing every several months. I sat with her in the pleasant atmosphere of the kindergarten class, the walls around us decorated with shiny starred papers and bright flowers to welcome Spring. She hesitated slightly and I was quick to notice it.

"Is something wrong?" I asked.

"I'm not sure." She shook her head. "We've been getting into more difficult material in readiness for reading and Mark is definitely falling behind. Behaviorally, he is moving between hyperactivity and lethargy. First thing in the morning, he's very lethargic. Then as the day moves on and he gets frustrated with the work we're doing, he becomes more restless and his behavior becomes more inappropriate. I'd like to suggest that we bring in the child study team. They can do a complete evaluation on him and maybe then we can see how much his skills have or have not improved over the year. Also, if he needs special help next year, the report of the child study team will help you get that aid."

I agreed. I wanted Mark to get all the help he needed and I also wanted to see the improvement he had made over the year. The principal scheduled an appointment for the following week. I was optimistic. Mark had certainly had fewer problems this year and I could see the improvement in his letter and number identification, matching, his ability to color inside the lines and, in general, the readiness skills for harder tasks.

After the testing was completed, I was again called in for a conference. The four members of the child study team were seated around a table along with Mark's teacher and the principal. It flashed through my mind that I was facing a tribunal, but I quickly dismissed the errant thought and sat down, eager to hear the results of the tests. Several reports were passed to me and I was given a small amount of time to review them. The language was technical and I didn't have the opportunity to study them well before one of the members began to speak. I was suddenly nervous, as if I was somehow to blame for all this. I couldn't explain what "all this" meant, but I felt at a distinct disadvantage. No one was being mean, just impersonal and professional.

The results of the report were inconclusive. There was a definite gap between Mark's chronological age and his developmental age. Developmentally, he was functioning on the level of a four year six months old child. His scores on reading readiness, math readiness, general information were below those of other children at this age, but not so far below that he needed immediate intervention. Hyperactivity and an inability to concentrate on tasks were noted.

I was given a sheet of paper with a set of tasks to practice at home, the same tasks his teacher was encouraged to use with him in the classroom. Any questions, I was asked.

"What does all this mean?" I tried hard not to sound defensive, but it was the same jargon I had heard before. The report held nothing I didn't know already. I was anxious for answers. I wanted a prognosis. I wanted solutions for Mark's problems and, again, I was being handed shadows, vague possibilities and maybe suggestions. Come on, guys, tell me something I don't already know, I wanted to say, but I didn't. I still believed they knew something I didn't and I didn't want them to leave without telling me.

"We would like to test him again at the beginning of next year before we make a final evaluation. Mark may mature enough to stay in a regular classroom with remedial help in the areas where he's weak or he may need special help in which case, we would recommend alternatives. Right now, he can remain in his regular classroom where every effort will be made to implement the additional exercises we've recommended for Mark."

End of conference. I walked out knowing nothing more than I had when I walked in. I tried to take what they had said as an encouraging sign. Help was available if he needed it and perhaps he would never need it. Perhaps he would outgrow his difficulties. I wanted to believe that. This year had gone reasonably well. Next year would be better. I asked Dr. Patterson to reduce his medication so he wouldn't be so lethargic in the morning. Maybe there are no solutions because there is no major problem, I thought. Yes, he is having developmental difficulties, but as he develops better skills maybe those difficulties will dissipate. But that neon sign, somewhere in my subconscious, just wouldn't stop flashing.

Chapter Twelve

In September, Mark went on to the first grade and I started a new job. My responsibilities increased and so did my salary, but the one thing about work that didn't change was the number of phone calls from my mother. Mark was always in trouble and, because he was now being bullied constantly, he was becoming belligerent. I knew my mom was having a hard time handling him, but what choice did I have? I had to work to support myself and the kids.

This afternoon, the phone rang non-stop. Every customer had a complaint and every complaint needed to be handled immediately. I made a face at Rose who shared the office with me and she smiled back, then quickly ducked out of the room, her arms loaded with files.

"Metropolitan Maintenance," I said into the phone one more time, vowing it would be my last for the day.

"Corraine, it's Mom. You'd better come home right away."

I could tell by the tone of her voice that she was holding it together by a shoe string. I glanced at the clock. Ten minutes to five. Just a few more minutes and I would have gotten through the day without an emergency phone call. My co-workers were used to my zipping in and out during lunch hour or at the end of the day to handle some catastrophe and even covered for me sometimes when I had to leave early. I was dealing with a daily barrage of situations, but somehow, I managed to get my work done well and on time.

"I'm on my way. Hang on a few minutes longer." I didn't bother to ask her what Mark had done this time. Every day, it was something different, fights with the neighborhood kids, bike accidents, trips to the Emergency Room for stitches, complaints from neighbors that he was picking their flowers or breaking their shrubs or playing with their animals without permission. He often brought home "strays" whose owners were not thrilled with Mark's attentions to their pets.

I tidied up my desk, put the work I needed to finish in a separate file and left the office, all within five minutes. I was getting good at this. I'd certainly had enough practice.

During my last conference at Washington School, the principal had asked me if I could bring Mark home during the lunch hour because there had been too many incidents on the playground where he had been hurt, had caused minor injuries to other children or refused to listen to the teachers. The request had upset me enough that I had called Dr. Patterson to ask his advice. No way, he had said. It is the school's responsibility to care for him during school hours. The principal did back off, but I knew she would have loved to be free of the problems he was causing. Not that I blamed her. But I had my hands full, raising two children, working full time and dealing with Mark's difficulties simply coping with the normal skills involved in daily living. I needed my lunch hour to run errands so that when I picked Mark up at five o'clock, I could provide him with the attention and structure he needed in the evening.

When I pulled up at my parents' house, my mother was at the front door waiting. I could see the tension in her face even before I got out of the car. I had learned to read her body language and facial expressions. She was not wearing a worried look, thank goodness. That meant Mark had not been beaten up or involved in an accident of any sort. Nor had he gotten lost on his way home from school. On the days when neither my mother nor I were able to pick him up, he walked. He knew the way home. We had been over the route many times, but he had gotten lost or wandered away so often that I had written on his black bookbag in bright red nail polish, "If I am not home from school by 4:00, please call..." and I had put my work number and my parents phone number where they could clearly be seen. I was always afraid of losing him. Even on days when I could get away at 3:15 to pick him up, he was already gone, wandering somewhere on his way home from school.

Today was not one of those days. Today was a discipline day and I felt myself relaxing. I had gotten to a point where I would rather he do something wrong, although I did not condone it, then be afraid that he had gotten hurt or lost. I shrugged my shoulders at my mother and gave her a "now what did he do" look at the front door. Without a word she led me down the basement stairs.

Mark stood in the middle of the floor, a large brown bucket of soapy water at his side, a scrub brush in his hand. His sneakers squished when he came over to show me the dripping brush, his face creased in a smile. I did not give him a hug or kiss because I wanted him to know he was being punished although I did ask him what he had done to make Nana so mad.

"I painted the cellar for her," he said.

I followed my mother to the side of the basement that had just been remodeled. Swathes of red paint festooned the freshly plastered walls, the storm window, the new porcelain sink and even the floor and ceiling. I threw up my hands. Mark walked over to me before I called him. I had wanted a few minutes to get myself under control. I was not furious with him, just tired after a long day's work and I was not looking forward to the hours it would take me to scrape the dried paint off the new sink and wall. I grabbed his shoulders and looked into his eyes.

"You know that it was wrong to paint Nana's new basement. Tell me why you did it?"

He looked at me with that blank stare I was becoming used to, but that still had the power to frighten me. It was like staring at the glass eyes of a baby doll on the shelf of a toy store - no reaction, no recognition. I still did not know whether he was tuning me out when I reprimanded him or whether he was unable to connect his actions with their consequences.

"Mark, do you understand that painting Nana's new sink has made her very angry and unhappy. It was the wrong thing to do. Understand? The wrong thing. Now apologize to her and we'll clean up this mess."

He stood looking at me as if I had never spoken, as if he had constructed a wall around himself that no-one could penetrate. His face was not defiant, only strangely still, no puzzlement, no comprehension showed in his expression.

I took his hand and led him over to my mother. "Tell Nana you're very sorry for painting her new sink and window," I said. "Tell her you're sorry for making her angry."

Mark parroted what I had said, his words an exact mimic of mine. He sounded more like a tape recorder than a little boy, but at least he had said it and maybe the words would sink in.

From a cabinet I took out turpentine and a rag and started scrubbing the sink. Mark climbed up on a chair and went to work with more goodwill than skill on the walls, happily splashing in the soapy water and dripping it all over the floor. My mother had gone upstairs to start dinner and I listened to Mark's incessant chatter with only half an ear.

By seven o'clock, I had finished the job. Mark had long since gotten distracted and, when my Dad came home, I suggested he take Mark to the park. I had developed a throbbing headache, born of equal parts exhaustion and turpentine and Mark's constant babble only made it worse. My Mom offered to finish the job and, although I was tempted to take her up on the offer, my conscience pained me worse than my head. My mother was fifty-five years old and had raised her child. Now she was watching my children and trying to cope with one who was nearly impossible to control. I still had not discovered exactly what his difficulties were, what this pattern of behaviors meant, but I believed it was only a matter of time before I connected with the right doctor or educator who could tell me how to turn Mark's problems around. Mark was scheduled for re-testing by the child study team at Washington School later this month and I was optimistic that a clearer pattern would emerge, one that would be recognizable to the experts on the team, one they would know how to correct.

Once he had entered the first grade, his academic difficulties had become more noticeable. He still could not identify the sounds that letters made or put those sounds together to form a word and, although he knew all his numbers, the idea that you could add those numbers together never penetrated his consciousness.

He was falling farther behind the children in the first grade and, with the unerring instincts of the barely socialized, they had spotted his differences and were beginning to exclude and bully him. Because he could not understand his work, he could not attend to it for long and, bored and restless, he bothered the other children while they were working. His first grade teacher had requested a re-examination to see how far behind he had really fallen and what kind of special help was needed to get him back on track. I was waiting for an appointment for Mark to take the tests, then another appointment for them to discuss and review the results with me.

When I walked into the apartment later that evening, the phone was ringing. I was tempted not to answer it. After a full day of jangling phones, all I wanted was to be left alone, to pretend for five minutes that life had no problems and, even if it did, that I did not have to provide solutions. I wanted to stand under the shower and sing at the top of my lungs, drowning out the rest of the world. But before I could do that I had to check the children's homework, make sure they had clean clothes for tomorrow, run their baths and get them to bed. We had eaten at my parents' house, one less of the usual chores I had to perform when I got home from work. Reluctantly, I picked up the receiver.

"Corraine. It's Doug. I tried to reach you earlier, but no-one was home. Everything okay?"

I had continued my relationship with Doug Conaway, slowly forging bonds that had led to a comfortable friendship. Neither of us were in a hurry for a deeply romantic relationship. The wounds from our marriages were taking time to heal. I occasionally dated other men with Doug's knowledge, enjoying myself while keeping clear of the emotional entanglements I wasn't ready to handle. Doug had a daughter, Karen, from his previous marriage and sometimes, on weekends, Doug and his daughter and the kids and I would go out together. It satisfied my need for a family, but I still craved the independence of a single life. I needed time to come to grips with the mistakes in my marriage and to learn from them. I did not want to bring old baggage into a new relationship and, for the time being, Doug seemed satisfied with what I was able to give.

"Mark had a problem again," I said. "But what else is new? Want to guess what I've been doing for the last two hours. Scrubbing red paint off the basement walls. That's why you weren't able to get in touch with me."

"I know you must be exhausted, but I wouldn't get too upset by what Mark did. It sounds like a typical boy thing."

"It's not what he does that upsets me so. I know there are worse things he could be doing, much worse. It's just that something happens every day. He never seems to think first before he does anything and he never learns from the consequences of what he does. He wants so badly to fit in, to have friends and he's so forgiving when other kids hurt him, but his unpredictability frightens them. It frightens me sometimes and I'm aware of his problems. But I don't want to talk about Mark any more. I've had it with him for today. Tell me some good news. I could use a lift."

Doug hesitated a trifle too long and, when he did speak, his voice held a false note of heartiness. "I'm not sure if you'll consider this good news or bad news. I just learned that I'm being transferred."

"Transferred. Where?" I asked.

"Upstate New York. I'm going to manage one of the stores there. But I'll be coming to New Jersey on week-ends and I'll be here for the holidays. We can still see each other then."

I felt tears start to my eyes and quickly blinked them away. It wasn't Doug's fault he was being transferred, but coming on top of an exhausting day, I wasn't sure I could cope with more depressing news. The silence grew uncomfortably long and I knew I had to say something. I covered the receiver, took a long, shuddering breath and said as cheerfully as I could manage,

"Of course we can. It's not like you're moving to Paris or the wilds of Borneo. Is there still such a place as Borneo?" My attempts at flippancy fell slightly flat, but Doug played along and we joked for a while until I excused myself to check on the children's homework. Mark's was a disaster as usual and even though I had promised myself I would not scream at him, my patience snapped when, for the fifth time, I explained that one red ball and one red ball makes two red balls. I drew pictures for him with red crayon. I hunted in the toy box and pulled out two red rubber balls. I did everything but stand on my head. And still nothing. Not a glimmer of understanding. I finished the arithmetic paper myself.

After the kids were bathed and in bed, I curled up on the couch with a cup of tea and the latest best seller and tried to read, but my mind kept slipping to Doug. Why did he have to leave now? We were becoming close and I was beginning to rely on him more. He was calm and dependable and, slowly, I had healed enough to let him get past some of my barriers. We were in the "less than lovers, more than friends" stage and I realized that someday I might want more. Fat chance, I told myself. Why was it that whenever something good came into my life it slipped right away again? I shook my head. No, I was not going to do this to myself. I would wait and see what life brought. Worrying never changed anything and only doubled the misery. I had to learn to live one day at a time and allow the future to unfold as it would. I rinsed out my tea cup and went to bed.

Three days later, when my desk phone jangled around four o'clock, I said a quick prayer that it wasn't my mother. Sometimes she would call me at work just to report that Mark and Cheryl were home safe, but that was always around three thirty. If she called later it was because something had gone wrong.

"Metropolitan Maintenance. Can I help you?"

"Corraine. You've got to come home this minute. I'm sorry. I know how difficult it is for you to leave work again, but this can't wait." I couldn't see her face, but I could tell by the sound of her voice that this time it was something serious. I felt the sweat moisten my palms and my upper lip.

"He's not hurt, is he?" I asked.

"No, he's not hurt, but he could have been killed. Come home now, please."

"I'm on my way, Mom. Stay calm."

I dropped the receiver back into the cradle, picked up my suit jacket from the hook near my desk and slid my purse over my arm. I told my office mate, Rose, that I had to leave on an emergency. She looked at me, her eyes round with sympathy and concern.

"Serious this time, huh?" she asked.

I nodded, not trusting myself to speak, and ran past her, out to the parking lot. On the short drive home, I tried to imagine what he could have done that would have upset my mother so. She had been angered by the red paint and upset by his many accidents around the house, but she had never sounded like this before.

My mother, my Aunt Sis, Mark and Cheryl were standing in front of the house when I pulled up to the curb and scrambled out of the car. My mother's face was ashen. I looked from her to my aunt and then to Cheryl and Mark. No-one spoke. I had expected a babble of accusing voices and recriminations, not this sudden silence. I slowly stepped away from the car.

"So, is someone going to tell me what he's done or am I supposed to guess?" I said. I heard the nasty tone of my voice, but I didn't care. My nerves were screaming up and down my spine, into my stomach and out my fingertips.

My Aunt Sis looked at my mother, but before either of them spoke, Mark pulled on my sleeve.

131

"I made a big fire, Mommy. Nana got mad, but I was just playing."

'Don't over-react,' I told myself. I wanted to grab him by his skinny little shoulders and shake him until his head rattled, but I knew it would do no good. Looking down into Mark's face, it was clear to me that he was not defending himself against the consequences of his action. He simply did not understand that his "playing" might have caused serious damage to himself, his sister and his grandmother.

"Show me where you made the fire," I said. I took his hand and he led me around the back where a large circle of soggy ashes lay against the rear wall of the house. I flinched at the size of the fire and looked at my Aunt Sis who had followed me into the yard.

"What happened?" I asked.

"I don't know the full story," she said. "All I know is that when I pulled into the driveway, Mark had a good size blaze going in the backyard. The flames had climbed as high as the top of the first story and he was running back and forth feeding leaves and twigs into the flame. Your mother must have realized what was happening at the same time because she came running out of the house with Cheryl and yelled, "Call the Fire Department." She was about to go back in when I grabbed the garden hose and sprayed the fire full blast. The flame went out quickly and it didn't spread. I don't think there's any major damage to the house. The firemen checked between the siding. No sparks or smoldering embers."

I looked up at the sooty back wall and without a word, I grabbed Mark's arm and marched him back into the house. He came willingly enough, twisting around once to look back at the destructive mess he had made. I plunked him down in the kitchen chair and stood in front of him, hands on hips, not trying to hide my anger.

"I want you to apologize to Nana for setting the fire in the backyard," I said, my voice shaking.

Mark looked at my mother and smiled, his blue eyes crinkling up appealingly at the corners. "I'm sorry, Nana," he said.

"You're sorry for what? Tell her what you're sorry for," I insisted.

When he turned to me, his expression was utterly blank, but this time I wasn't going to stand for it. I was going to make him understand the consequences of his actions if it took both of us the rest of the night.

"Tell her you're sorry you set the fire in the backyard," I repeated.

"I'm sorry I set the fire in the backyard, Nana."

"Why are you sorry you set the fire in the backyard, Mark?"

Mark looked up at me, then down again, wiggling his fingers and kicking his feet against the chair leg. I repeated the question. He didn't answer.

"Mark, why are you sorry you set the fire in the backyard?"

He jumped out of the chair, heading for the living room. I grabbed his arm and pushed him roughly into the chair. I didn't want this to turn into a power struggle, but I had to make him see, make him understand that he was responsible for his actions, that there were consequences to these actions for himself and other people.

"ANSWER ME!" I yelled at him. "Why are you sorry?"

"I'm sorry because you told me to say I'm sorry. But I won't say it again. I won't. I won't."

I remembered the day when Mark had gotten lost at the beach and the first hint of defiance he had shown then. I remembered, too, my fear that he was unable to take responsibility for his actions. I found myself trembling and knew that if he kept this up I would snap and do him some damage, but I had to make him see.

"The reason you are sorry is because you could have hurt Nana and Cheryl by setting that fire. You're sorry because you did the wrong thing, because you could have hurt your family, burned down Nana's house and because you upset us all by your thoughtless action. And because you did the wrong thing, you're going to be punished. When we go home, you are to stay in your room for the rest of the night. Every day for the next two weeks you cannot go outside and play or go to the park with Grandpa. No cookies, no ice cream, no cake. Do you understand that?"

"I don't care. You're mean and I don't love you anymore." Mark jumped off the chair and ran into the living room where a few seconds later I heard the television blasting. I fell into the kitchen chair opposite my mother and lowered my head into my hands.

"What can I say, Mom. I'm really sorry. And the worst thing is, I can't promise you he'll never do it again. He's upset now because he got yelled at, but an hour from now, he'll forget about his anger and the fire and everything else I've said. He cannot understand cause and effect. He does not realize the consequences of his actions. I tell him over and over. I discipline him and still, nothing."

"What about the child study team at school?" she asked. "Have you told them all of this?"

"I told them. They're going to test him again and then we'll sit down and discuss the results. I pray they come up with something that will help."

I met with the child study team a month later. As usual, I dressed in my conservative best, a man tailored business suit, white blouse and black pumps. I wanted them to know that although I was divorced, Mark came from a stable family with a mother who was able and willing to provide him with the best care possible. The impression I wanted to give was that of an interested, concerned parent who would take what they had to tell me seriously and work with them to insure that Mark had the best chance to achieve successfully in school.

When I arrived, the secretary showed me into a small consulting room just inside the main entrance where the child study team awaited me. I sat down in the one empty chair left at the table. I found myself not wanting to hear what they were going to say. Yes, I wanted to help Mark, but I was still grappling with the fact that he had a problem, the extent and nature of which I did not comprehend. The three people who faced me across the table were about to tell me what exactly it was I was facing.

The school psychologist led off with his evaluation. He explained that because of Mark's distractibility, testing had been difficult and extended. On the Wechsler Intelligence Scale For Children , Mark had scored a 74 in the verbal section and a 69 in overall performance, placing his cognitive functioning in the "borderline" range. For the most part, the tests showed that Mark was functioning about two years below his grade level and that this gap had widened since the preliminary testing in kindergarten. Besides the low test scores, the evaluation indicated that Mark's behavior allowed minimal conformity toward his environment inhibiting him from acquiring general information and understanding from it. He was impulse ridden, with superficial expressive skills, his idea formation was weak and he didn't understand cause and effect relationships. His overall emotional development was less mature than his peers and his self-concept was low.

As I was struggling to take in what the psychologist had said, the learning consultant presented her findings. On the tests she had given Mark, she had found deficits in visual memory, auditory sequencing of letter and number form, auditory memory, auditory/verbal sequencing, fine motor skills and expressive language development. The Peabody Achievement Test showed Mark to be functioning well below his grade level. The social worker simply gave a history of facts that might account for some of Mark's difficulties.

I listened, stunned, as they recommended that Mark be classified as Neurologically Impaired, and outlined the advantages of such a classification for "children like Mark." The Nutley School District did not have a special education program though they did have a co-operative program with other communities that did. What this meant was that if I wanted to enroll Mark in a school for the neurologically impaired, the Nutley School System would have to evaluate his difficulties and, if needed, pay for his tuition there as well as transportation to and from the school. If I rather Mark remain at Washington School, then certain recommended measures would be implemented in the classroom. He would get special help in reading and speech therapy as well as an IEP, individualized education plan, which would help the classroom teacher structure his activities to make maximum use of his classroom time. He would need a great deal of structure and a minimum of external stimulation. I was told that children like Mark could make progress in the classroom with the proper IEP.

"What do you mean by children like Mark?" I asked. "What exactly is his problem? I had him evaluated by a top neurologist who said he was not neurologically impaired. Is he brain damaged then? Is it a medical condition that can be corrected? Is it a psychological problem? Will therapy help? What? Someone tell me what I'm dealing with here!" My voice rose on the question, but I couldn't help it. I didn't want to help it. Again, I was getting nothing concrete, no real answers. I wanted to help my son. I needed to know what was wrong. Sitting there I felt like I was in one of those terrible dreams where a thick fog blankets the vision and although there is something menacing out there, it can neither be seen nor felt nor heard.

I was asked to make a decision about transferring Mark to a different school or keeping him at Washington where an IEP would be developed for him and his progress monitored on a regular basis. I asked for more time to evaluate what I had been told today and to look over the copies of the test results they had given me. I walked out through the fog of my nightmare, got into my car and somehow made it through the rest of the work day.

Chapter Thirteen

I enrolled Mark in the Wyoming School in Millburn in a class for the neurologically impaired. After I had calmed down from my last interview with the child study team, I realized that Mark was not yet capable of achieving what he should in a regular classroom. He was too easily distracted by the other children. It was in his best interest and mine to have him transferred to a smaller class where the teacher would have both the knowledge and the time to work with him on the areas where he was weak. I was also increasingly fearful that he would be seriously injured.

A few days after I met with the child study team Mark came home with cuts on his face and bruises on his legs. He would not speak about it, but I learned from a neighbor that a gang of older boys had waited for him on the corner near the house and had pushed him around for bothering their younger siblings. I knew then that he could not stay at Washington School. He started Wyoming School in the middle of first grade and so far I was pleased with the results, although our mornings could hardly be separated from our nightmares.

Besides getting myself ready for work, I needed to get Cheryl off to Holy Family School and Mark dressed and outside on the stoop before the bus came to pick him up. I had developed a routine of breakfast and bathroom time that would have worked if Mark had been able to co-operate. He never complained about going to school. He simply wouldn't get dressed in the morning. He dawdled in the bathroom, constantly distracted by one thing or another, so that he forgot to brush his teeth or wash his face. He didn't like the clothes I laid out for him and insisted on picking out his own outfit. At breakfast he ate like a pig shoveling a few spoonfuls of food into his mouth and playing with the rest. As for actually putting on his clothes, that seemed as alien a request as asking him to solve a problem in quantum mechanics.

While I waited for his Ritalin to kick in, I pushed him out the door of the apartment in his underwear, his clothes piled at his feet and told him if he didn't put them on quickly, the neighbors would catch him undressed. It was the only thing that worked. Somehow I managed to get him on that bus in the morning, and myself off to work. Some mornings I felt guilty about Cheryl and how little attention I paid her. She was so quiet, so self-sufficient that I assumed she understood. I hoped so. I planned to take her shopping and out to eat to thank her. One day when I had the time. One day when Mark's problems were under control. One mythical, magical day in a future where all our problems were solved.

In the meantime, the barrage of phone calls to work continued. Mark had set another fire. My Aunt Betty had been visiting at the time and smelled smoke on Mark's clothes when he came up from the basement. She asked him what he had been doing. He didn't answer. She ran downstairs and through the haze of smoke discovered something in the downstairs stove aflame. She and my Mom managed to smother the fire and open the windows, but it had frightened them both badly.

Fire became an obsession with Mark. My mother frequently found matches in his pockets though he could not tell her where he had gotten them. He also "found" candles and lit them whenever he could. My mother was worn out with the constant watching. She handled the fights with the neighborhood kids and returned the dogs and cats he constantly brought home. My father took him fishing and tried to work with him on his academics, but his hyperactivity kept him from focusing on anything long enough to master a single skill.

Mark was eight years old, still undersized, but no longer a baby. Family friends and relatives no longer made excuses for him and their treatment of him changed. Subtly at first, then with greater exasperation, they tried to discipline him through shaming him or ridiculing him and when that, too, did not work, recommended that physical punishment was the only thing that would get through to him. No matter how much I explained that he had a neurological handicap, they did not understand. He looked normal to them. He was just spoiled. All he needed was a good beating and that would solve the problem once and for all they told me. Sometimes, I was tempted. I wanted a quick fix to the problem, but I had talked with doctors, psychologists, learning specialists, and teachers. I knew that a good beating was not going to repair what was wrong with my son. I had finally accepted the fact that whatever disability Mark had was not going to disappear as he matured, but I still did not know the exact nature of that disability.

I had been told that he was learning disabled, immature, neurologically impaired, hyperactive, but I was not told what all these problems added up to or what effect they would have on his ability to function as he grew up. In the few spare moments that I had, I began to research the problem on my own. Although I found piles of information on learning disabilities, I was surprised to discover that there was still relatively little known about ADHD, attention deficit hyper-activity disorder.

I often shared my discoveries with Doug when he came home on weekends. We had been seeing one another whenever he came to New Jersey and our mutual respect and affection had grown steadily during that time. I had come to rely on his practical advice where my children were concerned and I had grown closer to his daughter, Karen. I was overjoyed when he told me they were transferring him back to New Jersey. I helped him find an apartment in the Lincoln Building, an apartment complex adjacent to the Ambassador where I was still living.

One afternoon several months earlier, I had come home from work to find the super from the Lincoln Apartments lying in wait. He informed me that someone had taken red paint and written across all the screens on the first floor windows of his building. Mark was often scapegoated for incidents that occurred around the neighborhood. Immediately defensive, I demanded how he knew it was Mark who had ruined the screens. He gestured for me to follow him. I stalked across the lawn in his wake, ready to give him a piece of my mind, when he stopped and pointed out the problem. There, scrawled in blood red letters that seemed to stand ten feet high, was MARK, MARK, MARK. I quickly apologized, offered to scrub the screens and ran back to the apartment. Mark readily admitted he had done it. When I asked him why he had written his name on someone else's property he said he wanted to. I explained to him that what he had done was wrong and that he must scrub the screens which he did without protest, but still without any recognition that this was a consequence of his wrong action.

That night, snuggled up on the couch next to Doug, I discussed with him something I had found in an article on attention deficit hyperactivity disorder and impulsivity.

"It described Mark to perfection - the child who has difficulty taking turns, interrupting everyone and everything, who can't slow down in order to think or plan ahead, who's always squirming or chattering and who can't wait for anything. You know how Mark will ask over and over for something and can't wait a minute until he gets it. In the article, the author called the disorder ADHD, Predominantly Hyperactive Impulsive Type. So far, it's the closest definition to Mark's behaviors that I've discovered. I'm going to ask Dr. Patterson if there's anything in the medical literature I can read about it. I do remember that the article theorized that it is caused by immature brain development and this shows itself in uncoordinated, random, unthinking, excessive movement. What Mark did today, painting the screens like that, wasn't because he wanted to do something destructive. It just occurred to him to do it, so he did. Though where he got the paint from I don't know. He's very resourceful when he needs to be."

"Did the article mention ways to control his behavior or medication that might be more effective than Ritalin?" Doug asked.

"That's my next line of research. I think this weekend I'll go to the Montclair College library and see what I can find there. I know they have a special education major and so they must have the latest research for their students."

Doug moved closer to me and took my hand in his. "Maybe what he needs is a good male role model. Someone who would be around all the time and can teach him ways of handling himself that his mom can't."

I felt my heart leap and, when I looked into his eyes, I didn't have to ask what he meant. Love had crept up on me more cautiously this time. I had loved my first husband, Dave, with all the passion of youth and dreams yet to be realized. Doug I loved with the maturity of a woman who understood that life was a journey filled with mountains to climb and valleys to fall into. I vowed that as long as Doug was willing to be my partner and my friend on this journey, I would work my hardest to be his partner and friend as well.

We were married the following September in a private ceremony with a small family reception at the San Carlo Restaurant in Lyndhurst, a neighboring town. We understood that we were marrying not just one another, but that we were joining our families for better or for worse.

We bought a house in Clifton on a quiet residential street where the children could ride their bikes and play safely. The closing date was in October just shortly after the start of the next school year. Cheryl would be attending Woodrow Wilson Junior High School in Clifton. She was unhappy about the move. She had done well in Holy Family and wanted to move on with her friends to Nutley High School. We had already had several emotional scenes where she had ended up crying and I had ended up screaming, but there was no hope for it. She had to come with us. Mark would continue at the Wyoming School in Millburn.

The morning we left for the new house I breathed a sigh of relief. Our lives would be more settled now. I loved the house and looked forward to the good times we would have there. Doug still needed to get used to the large Italian family he had married into. I had warned him that I planned to do a lot of entertaining because I hadn't been able to do so in such a long time and I liked having my family around on the holidays. The first Christmas Doug had spent with us had almost scared him off , so many people and so much food and drink had flowed through my parents' house that he had been overwhelmed. But he laughingly said that he would put up with it for my sake or find some excuse to absent himself if he couldn't.

The house was a new two story center hall colonial, very different from the old home I had so lovingly fixed up for my first marriage. This house was all light and open spaces with the living room, dining room, kitchen and family room connected by wide archways on the first floor. Upstairs there were three big bedrooms and a bath. Cheryl was getting older and needed her own room and Mark's was close enough to mine so that I could hear him if he needed me during the night. Outside, we had a large, grassy yard for barbecues. I felt safe in that house and secure in my marriage. Life was beginning anew and I was full of confidence that everything was going to work out for the best.

The moving men tromped in and out, placing the furniture where I thought I wanted it and unloading the boxes from the truck. I was busy in the house and I could hear Doug calling out occasional instructions from somewhere outside. I had set Cheryl the task of watching Mark and keeping him out of the movers' way and I assumed that they were in the backyard playing. Now and then I would look out the kitchen window, but I couldn't see much of the yard so when I didn't spot them I wasn't especially worried. Cheryl was almost a teenager and Mark had turned nine on his last birthday and, although he was a handful, he was no longer a baby. I had to give him some freedom. Or so I thought until I heard Doug shout for me from the yard.

I ran past the movers, rushed by the urgency of his voice. On the ground before the trunk of the large tree in our front yard sat Mark, his face dripping blood from an open cut on his forehead. Next to him was a hammer, the head dyed red. I took one look and didn't have to ask what had happened.

"It wasn't my fault," Cheryl said. "I told him not to play with the hammer. He ran away from me and banged the tree with all his might. The hammer jumped back and hit him in the head."

I knelt down and examined the cut. Yes, he would need stitches. The moving men were standing around watching us, uncertain what to do. I looked into the truck as I headed toward the kitchen to run some cold water on a towel I grabbed from one of the boxes. There was no furniture in the truck and only a few cartons left to unload.

"Please finish," I said calmly. They looked surprised. How could they know that I had been through this many times before. Luckily I knew what box the towels were in, having systematically labeled the contents of each carton. I dumped a tray of ice cubes into the cloth and ran back outside. Doug had pulled the car around and I helped Mark in, then climbed in beside him. Cheryl jumped onto the front seat, the movers left and we pulled out behind them. We spent the evening in the Emergency Room where Mark eventually received ten stitches. Not exactly the way I had planned our first night in our new home, but I had learned not to count too much on my own plans. Somehow God always had an alternate plan for me. On the way home that night, I quietly asked, "This is neither the first time nor the last time something like this is going to happen. Are you sure you're willing to take it on?"

Doug laughed, the warm sound filling the small dark space inside the car. "You should have asked me that before we got married," he teased.

"And what would you have answered then?"

"The same as now, Corraine. I would have said, Yes."

Settling in wasn't easy, but Doug and I tried hard to accommodate one another's habits and lifestyles. We were both working full time and the quiet evenings newlyweds usually spent together were filled with children, chores and homework. Cheryl's unhappiness over losing her friends and adjusting to a public school overlapped Mark's difficulties with his homework and the new behavioral problems he had developed at school.

Doug accompanied me this time when Mark brought a note home requesting a conference. With Doug by my side I felt less vulnerable than I had at other school conferences. Together we could figure out what was going wrong and how we could best assess and change the situation. I had had other conferences with Mrs. Archer, Mark's teacher, and had been favorably impressed. She was a caring person and she was willing to work with us and with Mark to help improve his academic and behavioral difficulties. Once she had invited us to her home to talk to us on an equal footing about Mark's progress. She felt he was making strides and, although it was somewhat slow going, he was moving forward.

Mark's annual report from the previous year concluded that he had made excellent progress and would be ready to move into the intermediate level N.I. class. I was greatly encouraged. We were finally traveling in the right direction. I had great hopes that by the end of this year, Mark would be reading and adding and subtracting on his own. Maybe, if he continued to progress as he had been, he would be able to take his place in a regular classroom. His IQ made it certain that he would never be a scholar, but that was fine with me. I just wanted him to be able to function competently and to feel good about himself.

When we pulled up in front of the school, I reached over and took Doug's hand. He looked over at me, his eyebrows raised slightly.

"You're not nervous about this, are you?"

"I'm always nervous about these conferences. I never know what I'm going to hear. I try to be optimistic but, so far, few of them have been filled with good news. What if they can't handle him anymore and want us to take him out of school. Just when he's beginning to progress."

"That's not likely, is it?" Doug said. "If he was in serious trouble, we would have heard something by now."

I nodded, but continued holding his hand until we reached the door of the school. I could not expect him to understand what it was like to go to these conferences and hear how badly your child was doing. I used to watch the other parents at Washington School leave the classrooms beaming and thanking the teachers for telling them how wonderfully their children were progressing. How I had longed for just one of those conferences!

We were shown immediately to the office of the Director of Special Services. He was seated behind a large desk strewn with papers, but he rose and offered us each a friendly handshake. I looked around for Mrs. Archer, but she was not yet in the room. He must have noticed my action because he nodded at me and said, "Mrs. Archer will be in to see you in a few minutes, but I wanted to talk to you first because we have something of an administrative problem. I understand that you have recently moved to Clifton. Is that right?"

I looked at Doug and smiled. "We were recently married and we just bought a new house in Clifton."

"Congratulations. I'm sure everything will work out for the best. The problem, though, is that you are no longer a Nutley resident and, therefore, not entitled to the special education benefits you are now receiving through the Nutley School System."

"In other words, Nutley won't pay for Mark to go to Wyoming School any longer. Is that it?" I said.

"In a nutshell."

"Can we go through the Clifton School System?" Doug asked.

He shook his head. "School districts have cooperating programs with different out-of-district schools. Clifton is not one of the districts we're hooked up with."

I could feel the frustration creeping up the back of my neck, making my shoulders tense. Just when Mark was beginning to make progress, just when I was beginning to believe we had actually found

144

the right place for him, this had to happen. For what seemed like the hundredth time, I told myself not to over- react.

"I'd like to discuss this with my husband," I said. "I'm pleased with the progress Mark is making here and I would like him to continue if possible. There have been enough disruptions in his life with the marriage and moving and changing schools and whatever. How soon do I have before Mark has to leave Wyoming School?"

The Director looked at me. His sherry brown eyes were kind and sympathetic. "I'd like to be able to say that we could keep Mark here regardless of what the Nutley Board decides, but I can't. We need the funds to pay our teachers and buy the equipment our children need. I'm sorry. Why don't you see what you can do and get back to me as soon as possible?" He looked over our heads and nodded. "I see Mrs. Archer is out in the hall waiting to talk to you. Shall I tell her to come in?"

Why not, I thought. Maybe she'll have something good to tell us and we'll end the conference on a happier note.

I was always impressed by Mrs. Archer's calm, competent persona. She had the type of manner that made you feel energized and relaxed at the same time. I wondered if she had the same effect on her students and if that was why she was such a fine teacher. She congratulated us on our marriage, then took the seat beside Doug. I looked at her hopefully and she smiled back as if she really could empathize with how I was feeling.

"I wanted to reassure you that Mark is doing well in the intermediate class. The work this year is more difficult, but with help he is moving forward though slowly. Mark's learning pattern frustrates him because he takes two steps forward and one step backward. Things he did well yesterday, he often forgets today. But his progress is steady. He is now reading and spelling on a first grade level and his math skills have improved as well. I have okayed him to join the music and art classes which he hadn't been involved in last year. But what I wanted to mention to you is a new behavioral problem he's developed. When he becomes frustrated or feels he's not receiving the attention he wants he starts acting out, pretending he is a cat or dog. He crawls around on all fours, meows or barks or paws at my skirt when he wants me. Has he been doing anything like this at home?"

145

"Mark loves animals. He's always bringing home frogs or lizards, even stray cats or dogs. He's not allowed to keep most of them and that makes him angry sometimes, but no, I can't remember him pretending to be any of the animals."

Her eyes crinkled with humor. I was once again struck by the difference between her attitude toward her pupils and the other teachers Mark had previously had. It strengthened my resolve to keep Mark in Wyoming School for as long as possible.

"You can imagine how disruptive it can become if one of the students is allowed to act like an animal. The other kids will want to try it and soon I'll be running a menagerie rather than a classroom. If Mark shows the same behavior at home, explain to him that he will not get what he wants by acting this way. Reward his good behavior and ignore the inappropriate. This way he'll be getting the message that good behavior will gain him positive attention at school and at home."

Doug and I assured her we would co-operate and she left us with a cheerful reminder that Mark really was making strides both academically and getting along with his peers.

"See what I mean," I said to Doug as soon as we left the building. "Don't you feel as if all the wind had left your sails even though nothing terrible was said?"

Doug nodded. "I'm trying to sort out the good from the bad and see what we need to do. I like Mrs. Archer and she seems good for Mark academically and in her approach to his behavior problems. He's moving ahead and he doesn't react well to change. The difficulty is keeping him there. The Nutley School Board is not going to pay for a child who is no longer a resident of their town. That's not something we considered when we moved."

"I agree. Our next step will be to see what we can do to keep him there. Even with our combined salaries, I don't think we can pay to keep him as a private student."

Doug looked over at me, his face suddenly serious. "I'll support you in whatever you want to do, you know that, but I can't do anything officially because Mark is not my adopted son."

I reached over and squeezed his hand. "Thanks for coming with me today. And thanks for your support. It helps more than you know."

The next day I called the Nutley Board of Education and talked to the Director of Special Services who told me there was nothing they could do to help me because I was no longer a resident of Nutley. I was told that Mark's problem was now within the jurisdiction of the Clifton School System and that I should take the matter up with them. The phone call ended abruptly.

"Same to you," I said, slamming the phone down. I had often felt frustrated by the lack of understanding I had encountered because of Mark's problems, but this time I felt the flickering of an anger that would remain with me a long time. I was not the enemy. I was not an annoyance to be summarily dismissed. I was a concerned parent trying to get help for my disabled son. I understood the economics, but I was just beginning to realize that economics took precedence over child welfare. I had been told that this was not personal, that it was just the way the system worked. But it was personal. My son was a person and I was not about to let him get lost in the maze of an impersonal system. I called back and made an appointment to see the Director of Special Services a week from that Monday. That gave me five days to come up with a plan.

I called Doug and told him the result of my phone call and that I would be late coming home from work. Since Mark was still being bussed to my mother's house from Wyoming School I would pick him up there on my way home. Cheryl would be alone for a little while, but Doug would go straight home from work so she wouldn't be alone long. The beginnings of a plan were forming in my mind, but I would need my parent's cooperation for it to work.

I waited until my Dad came home from his job in New York and over dinner I presented my parents with my half-formed idea. I explained what had been said during the interview at Wyoming School and then related the details of the conversation with the Director of Special Services in Nutley. My dad had often worked with Mark on his math and spelling and he had seen the progress from last year to this.

"I think it would be a mistake to move him from Wyoming School now, don't you?" I asked him.

"Yes," he said, drawing the word out slowly. "But what choice do you have?"

I took a deep breath. "What if I turn legal guardianship of Mark over to you for the rest of the school year and he could live here. Nutley would then legally be his place of residence and they could have no case against continuing his education." The words tumbled out rapidly. I knew what I was asking and it was a great deal, but it was the only way I could see of solving the problem.

My parents looked at one another, their distress clearly visible. Mark was almost too much for my mother to handle for a few hours after school. How was she going to cope with him all night long. I promised her I would take him with me as often as possible and that I would be responsible for his homework, doctor's appointments and visits to Nutley Family Services where he was now going for psychological counseling on the recommendation of the child study team. They had felt that counseling would help him curb some of his more aggressive tendencies and would help him get along better with his classmates. I was willing to try anything especially if it would build my case to keep him moving forward.

"How long do we have to think about it?" Dad asked.

"I have an appointment a week from this Monday. If we're going to fight this, I have to go to my lawyer and get the legal guardianship papers drawn up before that," I said. "I also need time to get Mark prepared for the move."

My dad sighed and my mom looked pinch-faced. I felt sorry for them, but I could see no other way out. I knew that I would have to fight for every precious inch of Mark's development. He was crawling forward. I could not afford for him to fall back. It was already the beginning of December. Mark would be off for almost two weeks at the Christmas break which meant he would not start living with my parents until January.

"We'll need to talk this over," Dad said. "We'll let you know."

"Tomorrow?" I asked.

"All right, tomorrow."

I knew better than to push it any further and beat a hasty retreat. The next day, my mother called me at work with the go ahead and by Monday I had the guardianship papers ready. I picked up my Mom, ignored her long suffering look, and drove determinedly to the Board of Education Offices where we discovered that an early

Christmas party was in progress. Mom looked at me and shrugged, ready to leave.

"Oh, no," I said. "I'm getting this resolved if I have to wait all night."

I dragged the secretary away from her merry-making and insisted she honor the appointment she had made. She looked doubtful, but I was not to be put off. She returned to the room where the party was in progress and came back with the Director of Special Services.

"Can I help you?" he asked, clearly annoyed.

"Sorry for interrupting your party, but this is rather urgent and needs your immediate attention." I handed him the guardianship papers, already signed and sealed, and assured him that my mother was willing to sign any other papers he might need right then and there. No longer smiling, he showed us into his office and removed Mark's file from his cabinet. After a prolonged review of the file, he informed us that what we meant to do was highly irregular and, by that, I inferred that he was annoyed by the request, although he did call his secretary in to witness the signing of the necessary papers. He could not guarantee that our request would be honored. We would be informed of the decision after the Christmas break. He talked about how the budget could only accommodate so many special education students, but I knew from his demeanor that there was nothing he could do to deny my son a proper education as long as he was a legal citizen of Nutley.

Chapter Fourteen

Mark was becoming more difficult to manage and Doug and I often argued about how to control his behavior. Doug believed that a stricter form of discipline was necessary. Through my on-going research, I had learned that strictness or leniency made little difference. Mark was impulse-ridden and did not understand cause and effect. Punishing him for one offense did not translate into caution or self-discipline in the next case. If Mark felt like doing something, he did it without thought or understanding of the consequence.

The dinner table was our battlefield. Mark's table manners had continued to worsen as he had gotten older. I had hoped that over time he would realize that no one was going to take his food away and that there would always be plenty when he wanted it. Now, almost six years later, he still didn't get the message. He continued to wolf down his food, hunched over and protecting his plate. He was painfully thin and rarely finished a meal.

After a long day at work, Doug wanted a pleasant dinner and could not watch Mark eating like an animal without attempting to correct his manners. I had tried for so many years to do so and knew it was a losing battle, but Doug had to learn for himself. Bites of food were interspersed with Doug telling Mark to "sit still, stop eating like a pig, take small bites, slow down, chew your food, wipe your mouth." Sometimes, livid with frustration, Doug reached over the table and pulled Mark's plate away, simply reinforcing his childhood fear and making the next meal more of a hell than the last. Cheryl and Karen would sit quietly, their faces twisted with anxiety, afraid to eat.

After the children went to bed, Doug and I sat over cups of tea and discussed calmly what could be done. I suggested eating in shifts, but Doug felt that Mark's dinner manners could and should be changed. I no longer believed it possible. The dinner war went on, but, despite the problems, Doug and I were united in our love for the children and in our desire to give them as happy a childhood as we were able.

One warm May week-end, we planned a trip to Terrace Lake. On Saturday morning I woke up early, eager to get under way. The morning sky was pink with only a few wispy clouds to give interest to its startling clarity. From my kitchen window I could hear the birds chirping and on the back lawn a fat robin dug for worms. I had planted impatiens and geraniums in pots on the back patio and their bright blooms made me smile as I cooked chicken, potato salad, biscuits and packed other condiments into the picnic basket. By the time I was done, the children were up and wanting breakfast. Doug and I had agreed that the children were not allowed to take food and drinks into their rooms because it was too much of an extra burden on me to have to clean that up as well as cooking, cleaning, vacuuming, laundry and all the other tasks involved in running a household.

Cheryl and Karen were showered, dressed and seated at the kitchen table when Mark, still in his pajamas, came down for breakfast. I decided not to say anything because, for once, I wanted a day free of controversy. I set bowls of cold cereal and fruit on the table and poured out glasses of juice. Mark bolted his food while Doug was still in the shower, and ran back upstairs to his room. I finished my breakfast, then went upstairs to hurry Mark along. Rarely did he get dressed or remember to brush his teeth without some prompting from me. I knocked on the door and, after receiving no answer, turned the knob. Mark was hunched over, doing something in the closet and I could tell he was unaware of my presence. I walked over to see what was going on. Mark was holding a large container of iced tea to his mouth and was drinking thirstily. I waited until he hid the container under some clothes before asking him where he had gotten the iced tea. He jumped back startled and, seeing that I was angry, mumbled, "It just showed up there."

"Where did you get the iced tea?" I asked again.

"It was just there," he answered.

"Iced tea just doesn't appear in someone's closet. Where did it come from, Mark?"

Doug had finished his shower and, hearing my voice, had come into the room. Mark's startled look was replaced now by a defiant one.

"I don't know where it came from," he said.

"Do you remember that we said no food or drink in the bedrooms?"

"No"

"No what?" I asked.

"No, I don't remember."

"We told you many times before."

"Well, I don't remember."

I could feel myself slowly losing patience. I was annoyed by his defiance, but more than that, I needed to find out where he had gotten the container from. I had not bought it and Mark was not given money because too often it had been stolen from him or he had given it away. He had no idea of the value of money. I had to know if he had stolen the bottle from somewhere. This was a far more serious problem and one I could not allow to develop.

"Where did you get the iced tea?" I asked again.

"Grandpa bought it for me," he said.

I knew this wasn't true because when I had picked Mark up from my parents on Friday, he was empty handed.

"Enough of this," Doug said. "Mark knows he's lying and so do we. Mark, come with me."

When Doug spoke in that tone of voice, Mark listened. He followed Doug to the bathroom where he had to stand with soap in his mouth for a few minutes as a punishment for lying.

"I will not allow the incident to ruin my day," I vowed as I ran downstairs. Karen and Cheryl were still sitting at the table, their eyes following me anxiously as I swept the breakfast dishes into the sink and cleaned the crumbs off the counter tops.

"What's over is over," I said, smiling at them. "Run upstairs and get your beach things. We might even be able to swim at the lake if the weather stays this warm all day."

When Mark had finished his time in the bathroom, we packed up the car and headed off. The promise of the morning held true and we rolled down the car windows and turned up the radio. I closed my eyes and let the soft breeze brush my cobwebs away. We were going to have a wonderful family outing after all. I covered Doug's hand with mine where it lay on the seat beside me. He had inherited a lot when he took on Mark's problems and I was grateful to him for his steady support. He turned to me briefly and smiled before returning his attention to the road.

152

Spring shone in bright wildflowers and blooming dogwood trees that lined the sides of the road. Yellow green leaves hung gracefully from the weeping willows and in between the trees I could see glimmers of sparkling blue water. Mark was unusually quiet and I hoped that the morning events had subdued him enough so that he could get along without the usual back seat complications. I didn't want to break the peace by turning around to check on him but, after we had been on the road for ten minutes and he had not made a sound, the temptation was too great. I sneaked a look over my shoulder.

"Oh my God. Doug, pull over right now."

Doug scooted through two lanes of traffic to pull over onto the shoulder of the road. I hauled Mark out from the back of the car and sat him down on a grassy bank. His face, distorted and blotchy, was blown up to nearly twice its normal size and his ears had all but disappeared. His eyes were squinted shut, his eyelids so swollen they covered the iris completely. His lips were twisted and grossly distorted and his breathing was labored. I could hear the girls crying from the car.

"We've got to get him to a hospital right away," I said. "We don't have time to wait for help."

Fortunately, Doug knew where the nearest hospital was. I sat with Mark in the backseat, holding his head in my hands, making sure his breathing was clear. The girls were still crying and I spoke to them softly, trying to reassure them that everything was going to be fine and that Daddy would get us to the hospital in plenty of time. They kept turning around from the front seat to look at Mark who couldn't see them or respond to their concern. He continued to swell and his breathing grew more labored. I was afraid he was having an asthma attack. I wanted to shout at Doug to drive faster though I knew he was well over the speed limit as it was.

We rushed into the Emergency Room where, for once, we were not kept waiting. Doug stayed outside the treatment room with the girls and filled out the forms. The doctor on duty identified it as a severe allergy attack and asked if Mark was allergic to any medications. I told him he was on Ritalin. He nodded and ordered a series of injections which were administered immediately. I watched anxiously as Mark's breathing eased though the swelling was still so severe his features had practically disappeared.

"It's the breathing that's always a scare in cases of allergic reaction," the doctor told me." The tissue inside the throat can swell and close off the trachea, but Mark responded well to the treatment so I don't think you need to worry. Did Mark eat or drink anything unusual that you think set off the reaction?"

I tried to think what he had eaten this morning. Mark was such a poor eater that I rarely knew what or how much he had consumed. I remembered the argument over the iced tea and was about to mention that when suddenly, I felt my face flame.

"Soap," I said.

The Doctor looked up from his chart. "Excuse me?"

"Soap," I repeated. "He lied this morning so my husband and I made him stand in the bathroom with soap in his mouth."

I was so embarrassed I wished the floor would open up and swallow me forever. How could I explain to a stranger all of Mark's neurological and behavioral difficulties and all we had been through in trying to teach him right from wrong? How could I explain the blank look in his eyes and the total incomprehension of cause and effect or the impulsivity, hyperactivity and all the rest? I decided I couldn't. He would never understand.

"Has he ever had an allergic reaction to the soap before?" he asked.

"Of course not." I was stung by his assumption that we would recklessly endanger Mark's health by disciplining him in a way that we knew would cause an allergic reaction.

The doctor looked at me coldly. "I suggest you find another form of discipline next time," he said. "Mark obviously does not respond well to this kind of treatment."

I looked at Mark and, for one moment, I thought, I can't handle this. I simply cannot take any more, but I knew that I could and that I would. I prayed for the strength to carry me through my difficulties.

It took most of the day for the swelling to go down enough for us to take him home. Doug had taken the girls out for lunch. I thought of the spoiled chicken and potato salad in the trunk. Was it only this morning that I had fixed it with such hope?

As the day wore on I felt anger tear through the hope I had held for so long. What was there left to hope for? An endless succession of days where happiness turned to misery, peace to accusation and humiliation. Nights where I would cry myself to sleep and fight the morning for renewed belief that today somehow everything was going to be fine. In the face of countless incidents where nothing was fine my optimism felt like willful blindness that hid a future I couldn't face. I bent my head and allowed the darkness to wash over me. I would find a way out. I had to but for now I no longer wanted to try.

No one said anything on the way home. Mark was worn out by his ordeal and slept the whole way home. I sat in the front seat with my eyes closed and, after I had tucked Mark in for the night, went straight to bed. I wanted the day to be over.

Several times during the night, I woke to check Mark and make sure his breathing was normal. Around two in the morning, no longer sleepy, I fixed myself a cup of tea and a buttered roll and took it into the living room to relax. I had been having cramps on and off during the night. Stress? Hunger? They were no better after I had eaten and I was certain it was not my time of the month. On my way back to bed, I stopped off in the bathroom. As I began to undress, my legs felt sticky and hot. I looked down and realized my thighs were covered with blood.

It took all my willpower not to scream. The children were sleeping and I did not want to frighten them after the ordeal they had gone through. I willed myself to take several deep breaths so I would not faint, then fixing myself up as best as I could, I stumbled into the bedroom, woke Doug and told him what had happened. He suggested I call my parents to come stay with the children while we go to the Emergency Room. I convinced him to wait up with me for a while to see if the bleeding lessened. I did not think I was hemorrhaging and I did not want to go back to the Emergency Room. I was badly frightened, but I wanted to see my own gynecologist, not some intern who would push and prod and tell me to come back when my doctor was on duty. Doug sat with me through the night and in the morning, I made an emergency appointment with Dr. DiGiacomo. Hope felt as far away as Heaven.

Chapter Fifteen

"So what's the verdict?" Doug asked as I walked back into Dr. DiGiacomo's waiting room. He kept his voice light, but I could see in the quick glance he gave me that he had been sitting on the edge of his chair for the last forty-five minutes.

"Fibroid tumor," I said. "I have to have it removed. Dr. DiGiacomo wants to do a partial hysterectomy."

"How soon?" Doug put his arm around my shoulder. Not a demonstrative man, his unusual gesture reminded me how often I had leaned on him for emotional support and how often he had been there to give that support. I lay back against his shoulder and relaxed for a moment, although I was still quaking inside. I had never lost my dislike of medical procedures and more gynecological troubles reminded me of all I had endured trying to get pregnant. I had stuffed all those operations and medications and painful procedures away in a "Life Before Doug" file and had assumed that I would never have to reopen that file again.

"The tumor is most likely benign so there's no big rush, but the bleeding hasn't stopped. It's more annoying than scary like it was at first," I said. "I told Dr. DiGiacomo I would call him and let him know when I was ready. I want to get Mark's school situation solved before I have this operation. Who knows what shape I'll be in afterwards and if there's all kinds of aggravation, I probably won't feel like coping with it. It's not fair to ask you to take time off from work to deal with Mark's school problems. So I'll do that, then schedule the operation. Agreed?"

Doug threw me a raised eyebrow look. "Are you sure you're not just putting the operation off? Your health is more important than the school difficulties. I can deal with them if I have to."

Earlier in the month I had tried to persuade the Clifton Board of Education to fund Mark's next year at Wyoming School, but they would have none of it. There was a public school in town that had classes for the neurologically impaired and they had assured me that Mark would do well there. I wasn't so sure. I had learned that neurologically impaired was one of those catch-all phrases for children who had a wide variety of problems. Some children classified as neurologically impaired were academically advanced, but had other nervous system disorders, others were learning disabled, but had no hyperactivity or behavioral difficulties and others, like Mark had attention deficit disorders with hyperactivity and impulse control problems. My intuition told me that in such a mixed class, Mark would have trouble adjusting. I refused to accept that there were no other options than this one class for my son. I knew they wanted to try him there because they did not want to pay out-of-district costs, but I also knew I didn't have the legal or financial ammunition to combat them effectively.

By mid-summer, the battle was lost. I was given no other option. It was unfair to expect my parents to keep Mark at their home for another year. He was my son and my responsibility, but I could not afford to send Mark to a private school on my own. I enrolled him in the neurologically impaired class in School Sixteen and I scheduled my operation for mid-August, hoping that, if there were any school situations to deal with, they wouldn't begin until later in the first marking period and I would be fully recovered by then.

The night before I was to go into the hospital, I lay in bed listening to the quiet surrounding me. Through the buzz of the cicadas outside my open window I could hear the faint hum of cars going past and the occasional music and laughter of teenagers out joyriding on a warm summer night. Inside, the children were tucked up safely in their beds. I had checked on them a half-hour ago, an old habit from when they were younger, but one I still indulged in. I loved to see their sleep flushed cheeks and their arms flung back on the pillow, limp and soft like the arms of rag dolls. In the winter, I would tuck their arms beneath the blankets and bend down to give them a soft kiss before climbing wearily into my own bed. This night I stood a little longer by their bedsides. I could not help wondering whether I would see them again. What if something went wrong with the operation? What if I remained in a coma? What if... what if...? I gave myself a mental slap, gave each of the kids a kiss and climbed into bed, but after a half hour tossing and turning I knew I wasn't going to sleep. I turned on my side and looked at Doug through the haze of darkness.

"Worried about the operation?" he asked, startling me so I jumped.

"Can't sleep either?" I asked.

"Not with you pulling the blanket off me every five minutes," he chuckled. "You might as well tell me what's on your mind or neither of us will get any sleep. Is it pre-op jitters?"

"Partly. You know how I hate all this medical stuff. But it's not just that. Doug, do you think Mark's going to be all right? I don't mean tomorrow, but down the road. Nothing we've done so far seems to help him. I've believed in doctors and medication, psychologists and teachers and learning specialists and nothing so far has seemed to make any difference. He's on my mind all the time, wondering what to do, where to bring him, how to handle him. I have a bad feeling about this N.I. class we've enrolled him in. I just don't know what else to do."

Doug pulled me over into the warmth of his arms. "We're doing everything we can, Corraine. Mark may outgrow some of his problems when he reaches puberty. I doubt he'll ever be a brain surgeon, but he'll find his way. He's a good hearted kid. He'll be okay. And besides, what's the alternative? I can't tell you how to think or feel, but for myself, I'd rather build my life on a solid foundation of action than a slippery bog of confusion, misery and hopelessness. And," he tugged on a lock of my hair, "guess who taught me to think that way?"

I smiled though I knew he couldn't see me in the dark. "So you do listen to me every once in a while. It's nice to know not everything goes in one ear and out the other. One more thing..."

"I know. I know," Doug's voice sounded amused in the dark. "If anything should happen to you, I have my list of instructions. I wrote them down and I carry them with me wherever I go."

I reached down and gave him a gentle punch in the ribs. "Don't make fun of me. I'm scared."

Doug held me a little closer. "Nothing's going to happen," he said.

Nothing disastrous did happen, but it was difficult to tell my recuperating body that. I felt like someone had taken a knife and sliced up my insides, which was exactly what they did do. The problem was, no-one had told me that afterward, I would feel every slice of that knife. I stayed in the hospital four days, fighting a fever, and drifting in and out of that delightfully detached state that pain killers provide. But I knew I needed to return to reality quickly. I had two children to look after. When the pain killers wore off, I worried how Mark was reacting to my absence. I didn't want him to think I had abandoned him. Doug would not tell me about any problems. They're under control, he'd say, and I let it go at that, especially after I had just swallowed a pill.

I pushed myself to get back in shape, but it was slow going. After the first week, I was able to move slowly about the house, performing light chores, but not much more. Gradually the soreness began to ease and I was able to go up and down the stairs.

On the first day of school in September, I hobbled from the front door to the special bus for handicapped students that stopped in front of the house. Mark wasn't crying, but I had a feeling that if he wasn't a ten year old tough guy, he would have been. I put a brave face on it for both of our sakes. "You'll be just fine and so will I," I said. "And Mark, do your best. That's all Daddy and I expect of you, okay." I waved as the bus pulled away and limped slowly back up the stoop, praying that everything would work out fine and knowing that it would not.

I was right. I was called in for my first conference two weeks after the start of school. When Mark handed me the note, I was not surprised. I had been expecting this. Mark did not tell me he was unhappy in school and he did not cry when he had to get on the bus each morning, but his behavior at home had changed for the worst. He often ignored Doug and me when we spoke to him and, although he did not mouth off to us, he simply refused to do what we asked him to do. If we insisted he complied with our request, he would perform the task for a minute then return to what he had been doing before. His mood wavered between sullen and sad and he began isolating himself more and more from the family. I knew something had to be done, but I was hoping for a few more weeks to recover from the surgery.

Still sore and tired, I climbed the steps to the front door of School Sixteen chanting to myself what had become almost a prayer. Don't over react. Don't over react. But this time, unlike before, I was angry rather than conciliatory. I had told them prior to Mark's placement that this was not going to work. Mark's unhappiness, my frustration and physical condition and the teacher's obvious discomfort with the situation was a stew that could easily boil over if I didn't keep my temper.

When I walked into the school, it was clear they were ready for me. Seated around a conference table were the principal, Mark's teacher and two members of the child study team. After a round of hand-shaking, I eased myself into my seat and folded my hands on the table. I was prepared to listen, but not with the openness I had previously shown. Mark's teacher looked down at her notes.

"Mrs. Conaway. I'm sorry we have to meet for the first time under these conditions, but I wanted to make you aware of certain things that are happening and to deal with these problems as promptly as possible. I have never had to call in a parent this early in the school year, but Mark is behaving in a way that calls for immediate attention." She quickly consulted her notes and read in a nervous choppy voice.

"From the first day of school Mark has been extremely disruptive. He runs around the class, sometimes crawling on all fours, pretending he is a dog or cat. While he's doing this, he growls or barks if he is pretending to be a dog. If it's a cat, he meows loudly or yowls. At snack time, he puts his cup on the floor and laps at it. As you can guess, it often spills and I have to take time to get towels and clean it up. If I ask Mark to wipe it up, he pretends he doesn't understand me and barks or meows in a questioning tone. At first, the other children thought this was funny, but now they are becoming frightened or annoyed and their school work is suffering for it. He refuses to do any class work and, if I try to discipline him in any way, he runs out of the classroom and has to be caught and brought back. I sincerely believe I could work with Mark in a one-on-one situation, but we do not have the resources for me to do this. I have to consider the comfort and academic welfare of my other students. And frankly, Mark is violating their rights to a quality education. Several students have been very upset by Mark's behavior."

When she paused for breath, red-faced and agitated, the principal took over. "On September 11th, Mark grabbed a younger classmate, ripped his shirt sleeve off and bruised his arm. In music class, he stabbed a different classmate with a pen and slightly injured him as well. On Friday afternoon, Mark had to be restrained from punching a student and, in doing so, a staff member suffered a bruise to her right leg. I could have suspended him for that which would have been recorded on his permanent record, but I chose not to until we had the opportunity of discussing this problem with you."

I looked up to see the deep blue eyes of one of the child study team members boring into mine. I felt violated, as if he was trying to expose me for crimes I hadn't committed. Hot words rose to my tongue and I was about to fire them across the table when my "Don't over react" prayer came to my rescue. I still wanted to shout at them that Mark should never have been placed in this class, that he was frustrated and frightened and that as professionals they should recognize this, but I did not.

"As you know from the intake reports, I did not want Mark placed in this class," I said with admirable control. "He was doing well in Wyoming School in Millburn and I wanted him to continue there. As you have pointed out, Mark's teacher is a specialist in educating the neurologically impaired and, therefore, should know how difficult change is for someone with Mark's particular impairment. Also, he has become increasingly aware of his learning disabilities and in a class where even the younger children are more academically advanced, it seems logical that he would refuse to publicly display his disabilities. His acting out behavior seems to me to be less of a desire to hurt anyone and more of a cry for help. A special education class is a place to address a child's special needs. My son's needs are not being met by this class. Don't you agree?"

I knew my tone was cold, even sarcastic, but I no longer cared what anyone thought of me. Mark was my son and I was going to do what I thought best for him. If I could get him out of this class and into a learning environment where he would be able to achieve, I was going to do it. While I awaited an answer, I realized I had jumped a hurdle I hadn't even seen on the track. No longer was I going to let anyone blame Mark or me for his handicap, especially people who claimed, by virtue of education or profession, to be experts in dealing with just those handicaps. If they didn't know what to do, that was not the fault of a ten year old handicapped child. I would no longer accept the blame and let it go at that. My taxes were paying their salaries. I was determined they would work for their money. I sat back and waited for their solution to Mark's problem.

After a long pause, the principal cleared his throat. "We would like to suggest an updated evaluation and a more current neurological and psychiatric examination before we make any determination in Mark's case. His teacher has agreed to continue to work with Mark until we can re-evaluate and possibly re-classify him as having multiple handicaps. He would then have a different placement, hopefully more suited to his problems. But that determination cannot be made before we have him retested. We have set up a tentative appointment with a neurologist for the end of September. Is this acceptable to you?"

I nodded, shifting in my chair. The twinges in my side had grown to stabs of pain. I looked at the principal, then at the teacher, and knew they had no solutions to offer. I stood up, carefully. "I'm sorry any of this was necessary, but I'd just like to repeat that I was against this placement from the start, however, I was given no other option. My concern is for my son and I will do whatever is needed to make sure he is placed where he can benefit most."

"So how'd the interview go?" Doug asked later that evening. We had waited to discuss it until the children had finished their homework, then gone to bed. I plopped down on the couch in the living room and rested my head against the back.

"Could you get me a glass of wine?" I asked without opening my eyes. I had stopped taking Tylenol a few days ago and a glass of wine sounded like a small sip of heaven right now.

Doug handed me my glass and sat down beside me on the couch. I took a sip and let myself relax for the first time that day.

"I've replayed that conversation ten times in my head since it happened and I still come to the same conclusions. At first, I thought maybe I did over react and read things into the interview that weren't there. You know, the old I'm just Mark's mother, not an expert, and all that breast-beating I usually do. But no, Doug, I'm not going to do that anymore. We both know that Mark is not a vicious child. If he's acting this way in class, then something is wrong and I want to know what it is. Are the other children making fun of him? Are they bullying him again? Is the work so far over his head he doesn't understand any of it? What? But the worst part about it was they seemed to be blaming Mark for his behavior and blaming me for not being able to control him. He's disabled, for heaven sake. That's why he's in this class. Surely, they have ways of helping disabled children. We're not living in the 1880's where they locked people who were different away somewhere and forgot about them."

"What did they suggest we do?" Doug asked.

"They made an appointment with a neurologist and they want Mark to have a psychiatric evaluation after the neurological results come in. After that, they are going to make some kind of determination. They seem to want to classify him as having multiple handicaps and, from what I understand, that will get him into another program. I think that's the agenda."

"Did they tell you what they meant by multiple handicaps?"

"No and I forgot to ask."

"Do you want to go through with all this testing again?" Doug asked.

I took another sip of the wine. "If it's going to help, I'm willing to try it. Mark's particular combination of problems makes a diagnosis difficult to pinpoint exactly. I know he has a lower than average IQ. I know he's hyperactive and impulsive, but I want more than that. I want to know why and if there is anything medically we can do to improve his condition. If there's not, I want to know that, too. Then we can explore an educational or psychological approach geared towards his special needs. So far all I've heard is veiled criticism and most of it not very constructive."

I pointed to the desk at the far end of the room. "In the top drawer is an information packet my Dad picked up from the New York Institute for Child Development. I didn't have much of a chance to look it over, but from what I remember, they have a more holistic approach to hyperactivity and attention deficit problems."

Doug stayed where he was sitting. I could tell from the stubborn set of his jaw that he had something on his mind. I finished my wine and set the stemmed glass on the cocktail table.

"Have you talked to Mark about all this?" he asked.

I knew what was behind that question. We had talked and fought about disciplining Mark and how much responsibility we believed Mark had to take for his actions. Doug still felt that Mark had more control over his behavior than he was displaying. I was never so sure. If he was brain damaged as the reports indicated, the extent of that brain damage was as yet unknown and might never be known.

Perhaps the impulse control center of the brain was dysfunctional. Could someone without the proper physiological equipment perform the same as people who did? Or was I grasping at straws? His earlier test results had indicated a major glitch in his operating system, but where it was located, what exactly was wrong and how to fix it, no one had yet been able to tell me. For my son's sake, I'd continue to look for answers. But with Doug , I decided not to repeat the same old arguments.

"Of course I spoke to him. I spoke to him till I was blue in the face. Did it do any good? No! Does it ever do any good? No! I grounded him. I took away his bike. I yelled at him. I explained to him that he was wrong to do what he did. I asked him why he was behaving this way..."

"And what did he say?" Doug's calmness irritated me. He accepted the situation. I wanted it changed.

"He turned sullen, said he didn't know why and he didn't care. He hates it there and he blames me for putting him there."

Doug got up and took the brochure for the New York Institute from the desk. We read the brochure in silence, then looked at one another and started to laugh. I, of course, wanted to try it. Doug was skeptical. Our typical approach to things.

"Shall I make an appointment?" I asked.

"Do you need to ask?" He smiled and I knew that even if he didn't agree he would back me up all the way.

I leaned over and kissed him on the cheek. "What would I do without you?" I whispered.

"Exactly as you damn well please," he grumbled, but I knew he wasn't angry.

We tried the program at the New York Institute for Child Development, but Mark wouldn't stay on the diet and vitamin regime. For a few weeks, he had enjoyed the attention the new program caused as we tried to encourage him to stay with the schedule and to eat the natural foods that were an essential part of the therapy. But in a short while, I began finding food wrappers for cookies and chips stuffed behind furniture and under the bed in his room. His behavior both at home and at school was a mixture of sullenness and defiance. Doug and I were both worn out by the frequent trips to Manhattan and the nightly battles over diet and homework. I had also returned to work and the strain of that coupled with Mark's constant problems in school was delaying my recovery from the surgery and making all our lives more difficult than we could cope with.

When the principal called me for the third time in two weeks to pick up Mark because they couldn't handle him, I snapped. I promised my boss that this would not happen again, took off from work and stormed into the principal's office.

"I refuse to pick Mark up again," I said. "I work full time and your inability to do your job is jeopardizing mine. This problem needs to be solved now. The neurological report you ordered showed that Mark has neurological impairment and dyslexia, but no emotional disturbance. I was led to believe that your program here is geared for exactly those problems. If Mark is acting out, then it must be because you are not providing him with what he needs to succeed."

His brow furrowed and his face drew into a frown, but when he spoke, his voice was professional and cool. "I agree that this problem has to be solved both for Mark's sake and for the welfare of the children in his class. I do not agree though that Mark is not displaying strong problems of an emotional nature. Quite simply, Mrs. Conaway, Mark is uncontrollable. I'd like to read you part of a report filed last week by Mark's teacher." He removed a typed paper from the file on his desk, settled his glasses more comfortably on the bridge of his nose and after searching the closely typed sheet for the paragraph he wanted began reading,

"I would like to know why an N.I. class with severe problems in distractibility, attention span, emotional overlay, and negative self-image would be exposed to a situation where the teacher has to spend most of the school day physically controlling a child who attacks without provocation, makes animal noises, runs uncontrollably around the classroom, swears, refuses to do any individual work or partake in any group activity. As you are well aware, I have been injured. My entire day from admission to dismissal is spent trying to keep children from getting hurt. My class is regressing academically, behaviorally, and manifesting all sorts of physical complaints just to get a few minutes of peace in the nurse's office. I am well aware that Mark is crying for help, but I can't give him the constant attention and control he needs at the expense of the rest of the class. It is impossible to take him to art, music or swimming without his attempting to hurt or upset another child. Will someone please help me take the necessary steps to avoid a disaster? Medication does not help. My class can't wait any longer."

He finished reading and looked at me over the top of his glasses. If he expected me to feel guilty or intimidated, he had mistaken my reaction. I looked back at him calmly,

"Your teacher seems a bit dramatic and she has certainly lost control of her classroom. That is not my problem. It's yours. My question remains the same as it had been before you read me that. What are you going to do for my son?"

He closed the folder with a snap. "You're correct in assuming that something has to be done, but I need to consider my teacher and the other children as well as Mark in my decision. I have scheduled a psychiatric evaluation for tomorrow afternoon if that's convenient."

"For what purpose?" I asked.

"To determine whether Mark's acting out behaviors are the result of emotional disturbances that are independent of the classroom situation."

"I see. And if they are, then what?"

"Then he'll be classified as multiple handicapped and he will be eligible for another placement."

How convenient, I thought. They can get him out of here and not have to admit that there was anything amiss in their treatment of him. I said nothing. There was no point.

"I can't take another day off of work for this, but luckily, my husband will be home and he can take him to the psychiatrist."

After the usual battle at dinner over Mark's deplorable table manners, I explained to him that his behavior could not continue the way it had been and that the school had ordered him to go to another doctor for an evaluation.

"I won't go," he said. "I'm not answering any more questions."

"Okay, but they won't let you go back to school if you don't," I said.

"Good. I'm never going back there anyway."

166

I cautioned myself to remain calm. "What are you going to do then? Daddy and I have to work and your sister has to go to school. What do you plan to do all day?"

"I don't know .... stay home, I guess."

"That's against the law for someone your age."

"Enough," Doug said. "You're going to the psychiatrist tomorrow. Understood!"

The last week in October, I was called in for another conference. The same two members of the child study team were already in the conference room. I noticed that Mark's teacher was missing and, when I questioned her absence, I was told that she was unable to attend. As soon as I was seated, I was handed a copy of the psychiatric evaluation. It was very short, less than one typewritten page. The first paragraph detailed age and past history. I skimmed that until I came to the line "Severe behavior problems, aggressive and belligerent attitudes towards various teachers as well as other students necessitates re-evaluation and assignment to an E.D. Class." I was about to question the fact that the conclusion came before the evaluation when I decided to hold my peace and read further.

During the interview Mark appeared uncommunicative and tense, refusing to answer questions that he found "not important" - i.e. when he did not want to be confronted with behavior problems that he referred to as 'just fights.' He was negativistic and responded like a much younger individual. He used denial and projection, although I informed him about the anecdotal information from his school. His extreme hyperactivity, short attention span and his poor impulse control are obviously related to his neurological impairment. His considerable perceptual deficit causes his lowered intellectual and academic functioning." I skipped down to the summary. "Mark is a 10 year 10 month old boy, suffering from severe perceptual difficulties and emotional problems necessitating transfer to a class for Emotionally Disturbed students."

When I looked up into the faces of the men assembled around the table, my heart was pounding. I tried to speak, but nothing came out and it took me several minutes before I was able to control my voice. "I wanted to read this report carefully before I answered, but I think it is obvious to us all what has happened here. You wanted my son declared emotionally disturbed and so he was. May I quote from the report, "severe behavior problems, aggressive and belligerent attitudes towards teachers and other students necessitated re-evaluation and assignment in an E.D. class." It's a wonder to me why you even bothered to have him go to the psychiatrist's office."

When one of the members of the team seemed about to interrupt, I waved him to silence. "It's here in black and white and if you intend to tell me I'm being defensive and misinterpreting what's written, don't bother. We all know the truth. This evaluation was a foregone conclusion. It clearly states that anecdotal information from the school was used in the determination of the diagnosis. There is nothing objective about that, is there? I do agree with one thing, though. Mark does not belong in this class, but I argued that before he entered it in September. What I need to know now are my options, or rather, Mark's options."

The principal did not try to dispute my statement for which I was grateful. He pushed back his glasses, pinched his lower lip and looked at me, his expression guarded. "As a multiply handicapped child, Mark qualifies for our program for emotionally disturbed youngsters. This program is at School Fourteen and the teacher is Mrs. Bechtold. We can schedule an appointment for you to talk with her any time you'd like. The other possibility, of course, is for you to find a good private school you and your husband could afford to send Mark to. "

"Meaning, of course, that the Board of Education will not pay for Mark to go to an out-of-district school."

No one answered but the meaning was clear in their silence.

I stood up signaling an end to the meeting. The principal came around the table to escort me to the door. "Please let me know your decision as soon as possible. As I said before, I can make an appointment for you with Mrs. Bechtold whenever you wish."

I took my leave, but did not thank him for his time or his cooperation. It seemed obvious to me that he wanted Mark removed from his charge. I was disappointed, but I did not blame him as much for his decision as for his seeming lack of concern for a child who so clearly needed help. I tried to tell myself that this environment was as wrong for Mark as Mark was wrong for it. In special needs cases, it was becoming clear that a certain amount of "shopping around" was necessary before the environment fit properly. When I looked at it that way, it made more sense. Perhaps the School Sixteen environment worked for academically advanced special needs children. But as much as I tried to give the teacher and principal the benefit of the doubt, in my heart I knew that Mark had been classified emotionally disturbed for their benefit, not his, even if it was an appropriate diagnosis. The tears started to flow even before I pulled into the driveway.

Mark was barely eleven years old. How would this label affect him? He was beginning to be aware that he was different from other children and the knowledge was hurting him, making him angry. Now another label had been added, one that society frowned upon more than they frowned on neurologically impaired. Children with emotional difficulties were treated as if they were somehow responsible for their problems. I had run into this attitude in my own family and Mark had suffered for it. How much more would he suffer from the censure of the outside world.

On Doug's next day off, we went to visit Mrs. Bechtold at School Fourteen. We had discussed both of the options the principal had presented to me. We had looked into private schools for the neurologically impaired and were shocked by the expense. There was no way we could afford the tuition for an expensive private school for children with disabilities and we were given no other options.

Mrs. Bechtold greeted us at the door to her classroom which was currently empty. My first impression of her was that she was a no-nonsense sort of person. Her manner toward us was pleasant, but strictly professional. Her explanation of the program was clear and concise, a strict behavioral modification approach in which good behavior was rewarded and noncompliant behavior punished. She also handed us charts which we were expected to use at home to reinforce the school program and emphasized how important it was for us to stick determinately to this course of discipline. As she shook hands with us at parting she said she felt strongly that she could help Mark both behaviorally and academically.

"So what do you think?" I asked the moment we got into the car. Doug backed out of the parking space and started the car towards home before he answered.

"What other option do we have, Corraine? You know that I feel strongly that he needs discipline and this system of rewards and punishments is consistent and fair. Maybe he'll finally learn that there are consequences to his behavior by having the same rewards and punishments associated with the same behaviors. It's worth a try."

On October 23rd, I went to Clifton High School to sign the Individual Education Program (IEP) that had been designed by the child study team for Mark. Special needs children are given these plans which are supposed to target their needs and provide strategies for addressing those needs. The plan I was handed had not yet been finalized and, with my input, certain changes were made. I had to swallow the lump in my throat when they asked me to sign the final version. My hand trembled and I felt as if I was condemning my child to a future in which he would never be considered normal again. Mark was now classified in black and white as a child who was emotionally disturbed, neurologically impaired, intellectually challenged, hyperactive and dyslexic. I could only pray that this classification would lead Mark to someone who could help him overcome his difficulties. My belief that one day my child would look back on this from a safe distance and say, "I won" was still strong.

Chapter Sixteen

Dear Mrs. Conaway,

[Mark] should be able to do his assignment in his Social Studies workbook with someone just reading the questions to him. However, I will send whatever books are necessary to complete the assignment. In class, we have discussed both the concepts of the assignments and have done the actual page. [Mark] has it for homework because he did not participate in class.

[Mark] received the punishment assignment when, for the second time within a week, his actions during lunch had caused physical injury to a teacher. Thankfully, the injury was minor, but the concept of striking a teacher or anyone else is totally unacceptable. The punishment was agreed to by [Mark] and the teacher involved. The alternative would be to have the matter referred to Mr. Vogel for further action.

Mrs. L. Bechtold

I read the note quickly, picked up my purse from the bed and locked my bedroom door, dropping the skeleton key in my handbag as I left. Doug and I had installed locks on the bedroom doors and dead bolts on the outside doors and windows as well as the garage and basement doors. At this point, I wasn't sure whether they were to keep Mark in or out. During the months that Mark had been going to the Institute for Child Development he had begun climbing out the upstairs windows and running off to buy snacks from the corner store. While I believed he was in his room doing his homework, he was sliding down the chimney and running to the store. Doug and I had found a way to limit the opening allowed on the old wooden sashes so he couldn't get out.

Then, several months ago, I had found him in my room, opening bureau drawers, and "borrowing" things that did not belong to him. After talking to him about my right to privacy, I had found him in Cheryl's room doing the same thing. He claimed he wasn't hurting anything or doing anything wrong, that he was just bored, but he would not stop regardless of the rewards when he wasn't doing it and the punishments when he was. Nothing ever seemed to remain in Mark's mind more than a few minutes. Just as when he was younger, he would look at me blankly, stop for the time I was yelling at him, then go right back to what he had been doing five minutes later.

"Mark, get moving. It's time for your doctor's appointment," I called as I checked the lock on Cheryl's door. It was still fastened so I felt certain Mark had not been in there today. Cheryl was not home yet. She had been spending a lot of time with her girlfriends from Nutley lately and I was glad. I didn't want her to feel neglected, but the amount of time I needed to spend with Mark had continued to increase. I now carried a notebook with me just to keep track of the dates and times of Mark's appointments. This week alone there were scheduled visits to his pediatrician, his case worker at the offices of Clifton Mental Health, a parent-teacher conference and right now, we were off to Dr. Ramsey, who ran a bio-feedback clinic in Elizabeth.

"Come on, Mark!" I yelled on my way down the stairs. I had to start calling for him a full fifteen minutes before it was time to leave. I still had to remind him every morning to brush his teeth and wash his face and to hurry him through his dressing so he could make the bus on time. Although School Fourteen was only a few blocks from the house, I insisted he was bussed there and back. I worried enough. I did not need the added aggravation of sitting in work worrying about whether he got to school or not. He was entitled to the transportation and I was going to make sure he received all the services he was entitled to.

"Mark, I'm not kidding. I want you here now."

From the kitchen, I heard his footsteps pounding down the stairs. Mark never walked when he could run or jump. I looked up at him as I locked the back door and picked up my keys. He was still so thin and the paleness of his skin over his sharp cheekbones gave him a lean and hungry look that was in contrast to his eleven year old immaturity.

"How is your head feeling today?" I asked as I pulled out of the driveway. "Any more headaches?"

"Yeah,"

"Yeah what?"

"Yeah, I had a headache and a stomachache again. All afternoon," he said.

"Did you go to the school nurse?"

"Yeah!"

"Mark, please try to tell me a little more. I've scheduled another appointment with Dr. Patterson, but I don't know what to tell him. What did the school nurse say?"

"She told me to go back to the classroom. She said I can't keep coming there every day."

When Mark first started complaining about his head throbbing and his stomach hurting, the nurse had called me and asked me to make an appointment at Mark's regular doctor. Dr. Patterson had felt that Mark's dosage of Ritalin might need to be readjusted because his afternoons in school were so much worse than his mornings. He had increased the lunch time amount, but the headaches had continued and the stomach aches seemed to be getting worse.

Mark changed the subject and talked all the way to Dr. Ramsey's office about the rabbits he was going to raise in a hutch in the back yard. I let him talk. Sometimes he would get obsessed with some notion or other, usually about animals, and I found that if I let him talk them out for a few days, he would forget about one idea in the excitement of another. He still loved animals and often brought home frogs and fish, lizards and birds which he kept in the backyard. Dogs and cats were forbidden, but that didn't stop Mark from bringing them home. The dogs went back to their owners or to the pound. The cats came and went, but were never allowed in the house. I tuned out the latest obsession and tried to relax with the car radio as I drove to Elizabeth.

When we had ended Mark's treatment with The New York Institute for Child Development, I began looking for an alternative form of treatment. I had never been comfortable with Ritalin because it was a stimulant and because I was never sure which of Mark's behaviors were a result of the medication or his disability. A more natural remedy that could help him calm down and improve his ability to focus would be infinitely preferable to medicating him.

My father had read about a doctor in a nearby town that had developed bio-feedback techniques to help children with learning disabilities. When I called and described Mark's particular pattern, Dr. Ramsey had assured me that Mark was a perfect candidate for the program. Wow! I thought. A must try! One of these days I would find exactly what I was looking for, a program that would fit Mark's needs and we would finally be on our way to solving his problems. I would never find that program if I didn't keep looking. So off to Dr. Ramsey's we went once a week.

We had been going to Dr. Ramsey's for over a month now and I was still waiting to see results. He had warned us that the process would take some time because Mark would need to learn how to recognize and manipulate his own physiological reactions.

We walked into the office and sat in the waiting room. Mark was still talking about the animals. I tuned in for a few minutes and was amazed at how much he knew about the habits of fish and frogs.

"How did you learn all this?" I asked. "Have you been reading books about this?"

He didn't answer. He just went on talking about the breeding habits of frogs. I was about to question him further when the inner door opened and Dr. Ramsey stepped forward.

"Okay Mark. We're all ready for you."

Mark stood up and followed the doctor into the examining room. For the first few weeks, I had joined them because I wanted to see what biofeedback was all about. I watched as they attached wires to Mark's right and left temples and plugged the wires into a machine. Dr. Ramsey assured me that Mark would experience no discomfort. He was hooked up to other monitors and the doctor explained to him what he would be seeing and what it meant. Mark fidgeted a bit, but I could tell he was interested. He watched the monitors as the technician took over, listening to the explanations and doing what he was asked to do. The purpose of the biofeedback was to co-ordinate the left and right brain activity and bring them into a better balance. After the first few sessions, Mark lost interest and often fell asleep during the session. On his way out, the nurse always gave him a small blue Smerf as a reward. A reward for what, I thought, eighty dollars' worth of sleep?

As I waited for Mark to finish his session, I checked my notebook to see what we needed to do next. No more today, but tomorrow I had a parent-teacher conference with Mrs. Bechtold, a therapy session for Mark and a meeting with Father Jim about Mark's Confirmation. Another full day. I also needed to schedule another appointment with Dr. Patterson to have Mark's medication reviewed. I decided to do that on Saturday so I could spend time with Cheryl after work. Doug had off tomorrow. I would take Cheryl out to dinner, just the two of us.

The next day was sunny and unusually warm for the middle of March. I found myself hoping this was a good omen as I walked up the steps of School Fourteen for my parent teacher conference. I was getting to be a pro at these conferences and I no longer had to gear myself up to face what I would hear. I knew it wouldn't be good. I had kept in close communication with Mrs. Bechtold throughout the past months, following closely Mark's academic and behavioral ups and downs. He had made some gains in certain academic areas though math and science still eluded him. His reading and writing were now on a second grade level, his behavior still very immature. He had taken to bringing little toys to class and playing with them at his desk, match box cars, paperclips, army soldiers, anything he could shove in his pockets. I tried to be as vigilant as I could in the mornings, but he was quick. As soon as my back was turned he grabbed something and hid it. I didn't have time to search every pocket every day.

In class, he would take out his toys and try to involve other children in playing with them. When he couldn't get them to play, he would play himself, making noises and gestures that disrupted the lesson and bothered the other children. If disciplined he either ignored the teacher or became angry and told the teacher off. For this he would be punished and the cycle of testing and punishment continued. Mrs. Bechtold was very strict with him, insisting that he receive the necessary punishment for the offense.

She had been keeping me apprised of Mark's progress in phone conversations and through letters sent home, but this time, she had asked if I could come in for a conference. I was prepared to hear bad news. I knew that Mark's behavior had changed very little and that she was not satisfied with the advances he had made. I stepped into the classroom and looked around before walking up to the desk where she was working on some papers. The children had decorated the walls of the class with pictures of spring and colored cut-outs of flowers and birds. Perfect papers were hung up in the front of the classroom, their bright red A+ grades a badge of pride. I did not look for Mark's paper there. I rejoiced when he got even half the assignment correct.

Mrs. Bechtold must have heard me enter though she did not look up immediately. When she did stand up to greet me, her face was stern and unsmiling. My internal radar could now detect the difference between bad news and awful tidings. Mrs. Bechtold's face told me this conference was somewhere between the two. We shook hands and I took a seat in one of the small chairs neatly tucked beneath a small table. Thankfully, Mrs. Bechtold did not sit at her desk, but folded herself into one of the small seats across from me. For the first time, she smiled, an apologetic gesture for the discomfort of the accommodations. She hesitated a moment as if choosing her words then shrugged her slim shoulders.

"I don't know if Mark told you what happened a few days ago, but I wanted to be sure you knew. As I have written to you before, Mark often teases the other children unmercifully. He makes faces, obscene gestures, antagonistic comments, and pokes or pushes his peers. During lunch, he is especially disruptive. He does not obey the teachers or the aides either in the lunchroom and on the playground. He had been fined every day and he has been kept inside since last Friday. On Monday of this week, he started a fight with a classmate and he would not stop when I told him to. The only way to insure the safety of the other student was for me to grab Mark and restrain him. I pushed him up against a wall and held him there while another teacher took care of the other student. Since the incident, Mark has been wary but compliant. I just wanted you to know."

I looked at her, my thoughts whirling and my face a complete blank. I didn't know whether to apologize or protest. Although I did not like the idea of Mark being thrown up against a wall, I also knew that if he was really wound up, there was probably no other way of making him stop what he had been doing. There were plenty of times, at home, when I would have to grab his hair or push him down into a chair to get his attention.

I looked up to find her watching me, her face concerned. I wondered if she was afraid I would report the incident to higher authorities and jeopardize her job. I hastened to reassure her that I understood the necessity of the action and asked if there was anything more I should be doing to help Mark make a better adjustment to the classroom environment.

"Mark's a very angry young man and he's likely to become more so as his frustration level builds. Although I am working hard to keep him interested in learning, I can see that I am losing him as often as I am able to teach him something. He wants to learn, he wants to have friends, but his behavior is too extreme to permit it."

"Mark goes for counseling once a week at the Clifton Mental Health Center and he receives biofeedback therapy once a week as well. He's on Ritalin and we use the behavioral modification techniques you recommend at home. I don't know what more we can do to help him."

She shook her head. "The only thing I could suggest is to speak to his doctor about changing the level of his medication or perhaps trying a new medication that might be more effective. The Ritalin just doesn't seem to be doing the trick. Mark can be such a likable child at times. It's such a shame that he acts out to sabotage his own best interests."

As I left the conference I felt the same old depression welling up, forcing the tears into my eyes. I loved my son. I wanted to help him and I did not know where to turn for that help. So far we had tried counseling, medication, diet and vitamin therapy, behavioral modification, special education classes and biofeedback. We disciplined him with loving firmness and consistency. So far none of it had made the least bit of difference. Mark was on a downhill slide and I needed to stop it. But how? Tears of frustration rolled down my cheeks as I drove home. I was not angry at Mark. He had not chosen his problems. I was angry because I could not find the way to relieve him of the burden he was carrying.

I decided to stop off at St. Andrew's Church and speak with Father Jim about Mark's Confirmation. He was supposed to be confirmed in May and I wanted to make sure he would be ready. Father Jim had been giving Mark private instruction because Mark had been unable to settle into the Confirmation classes. I was planning a big party for his Confirmation. Cheryl had always had parties for the important events of her life and I wanted to do the same for Mark. I wanted him to know that, regardless of the constant problems, my feelings of love for him were unchanged. When I told him about the party, he was pleased. "Mom, I want a moped just like Cheryl's," he'd said, but when I asked him if he understood how special it was that he was receiving a Holy Sacrament, he'd looked at me blankly and run off. Now, I needed to make sure that Mark was going to be able to be confirmed.

While I walked up to the rectory I said a little prayer that he would not be denied this affirmation of his being accepted into the church. Religion had little meaning for Mark though I had taken him to church every Sunday and had made sure he received Holy Communion. Mark lived on the impulse level, moment to moment as the mood struck him. Abstract concepts of another world populated by unseen beings had no meaning for him. After much prayer I had accepted that, but I still believed that if he could grasp some of the moral foundations, some of the more earthly teachings of love and compassion for one's fellow being, he might use this to stop himself from his heedless, hurtful actions.

Father Jim answered the door, his face creasing into a slight smile at my greeting. He took my elbow and led me into the living room and seated me in a comfortable, though somewhat shabby, armchair.

"So, is it Mark you've been crying about?" he asked in his usual forthright manner.

"You can tell?" I asked.

"Red eyes and mascara stains are a good give away."

I rubbed my hand across my cheeks and looked at the black smudges ruefully. "I just had another interview with his teacher. It seems she had to push him against the wall to keep him from bothering a classmate. Sometimes it gets to be too much and I can't help crying. I don't know how to help him. That's the worst thing of all. But I didn't come to cry on your shoulder though I appreciate your listening. I came to find out if you think Mark has learned enough to be confirmed this May."

Father Jim looked out the window where the bright sun streamed through in colored designs on the floor. "I don't know how to answer that, Corraine. Has he learned enough? No. He's not disruptive when he comes here. He listens, but when I ask him questions he has no idea what I'm talking about. If I tell him the answers and ask him to repeat after me, he will. But the information is lost five minutes later. If I try to engage him in a conversation about his commitment to the church or what confirmation means, he talks to me about animals. But Mark is as God made him and in all conscience, I cannot and will not withhold from him the sacraments. I thought about postponing his Confirmation until next year when he might be more mature, but I don't think it will make that much of a difference."

"Meaning that you don't think Mark will improve in his behavior and understanding," I asked.

"That is in God's hands," he said.

From the rectory I drove straight to Dr. Patterson's office. Although my appointment was not until Saturday, I knew he would see me for a few minutes between patients. I needed to know what I could do. I needed to have some direction to go. Every door was slamming in my face. Somewhere a window needed to open.

After a ten minute wait, Dr. Patterson waved me into his office. I apologized for bursting in on him and explained what Mrs. Bechtold and Father Jim had said.

"I refuse to believe there is no way of helping him. There has to be something we can do, a new medication we can try. The Ritalin isn't working as well as it should be or he wouldn't be so impulse-driven, so unable to focus. What's left that we haven't tried?"

"There are other medications that might have a better result, but all medications have side effects and I know you've been worried about that. You also said on the phone that he's been having severe headaches and stomach aches. Until I examine him I can't know the cause and I don't want to change his meds until I can see him. But there is one thing you and your husband might consider. You might think about putting Mark in Arthur Brisbane Hospital for a time. It might be the best alternative."

I left worrying about Mark's physical health. I had not thought the headaches and stomach aches were that severe. It was not until a long time afterward that I learned that Arthur Brisbane was an institution for mentally ill and emotionally disturbed adolescents.

Chapter Seventeen

"Corraine, you'd better call Mark. He's been in the bathroom a long time and I still need to shower and shave. We only have an hour until we have to be at the church."

I wondered why Doug didn't call Mark himself. I had been running around all yesterday and early this morning getting things ready for Mark's Confirmation party. I was expecting close to thirty people and, although I had catered the food, there was still so much to do. Doug had never really gotten comfortable with the size of my family and, although he enjoyed the get-togethers, he had made it clear that he did not want to get involved in the preparations for the parties. I loved having the whole family together, but the amount of work involved did turn me into a whirlwind with feet.

"Mark," I called up the stairs. "Mark, get out of the bathroom. Your father has to shower now."

No answer. What did I expect? I ran up the stairs and knocked on the bathroom door.

"Mark, come on. Other people have to get in there. We don't want to be late for church."

Still no answer. I laid my ear near the crack of the door. The water wasn't running and I couldn't hear him rustling around in there. My mind flashed back to the time he had fallen asleep during a bath, but he was much older now and besides, I was certain he had taken a shower because I'd heard the water running the last time I had run up the stairs to get fresh towels for the downstairs bathroom.

Doug came out on the landing. I looked at him over my shoulder.

"Maybe you should try the door. I don't want to because he's bigger now and I don't think it's quite the thing for a mother to walk in on her eleven year old son."

Doug brushed past me and turned the handle of the bathroom door. I looked the other way as he went into the room, but he was out again in less than a minute.

"Empty," he said.

"What!"

I turned to my right and walked into Mark's room. His navy blue suit was laid out neatly on the bed with his white shirt and clean socks beside it and his dress shoes side by side on the floor beneath.

180

Doug and I looked at one another.

"Cheryl!" I called. "Come here please."

She had been in her room getting ready. She walked into Mark's room, her robe thrown hastily over her slip and her hair in curlers.

"Sorry," I said. "But your brother is missing. Do you have any idea where he went?"

She shrugged. "How would I know? He went into the shower after I was finished. I've been in my room trying to do something with my hair. It's so straight. I don't even know why I bother."

I could feel the blood throbbing in my temples, but I was still in enough control not to take it out on her. Doug and I did a quick search through the house and the backyard, but Mark was nowhere to be found.

"Now what?" Doug asked.

"You go back in and take your shower. I'm going to take the car and ride around the neighborhood. Maybe he was bored and took his bike out for a spin."

I ran around to the front of the house and had just opened the car door when my neighbor, Charlie, called me from his front yard.

"I'm in a bit of a rush, Charlie," I said, as I climbed into the front seat. "You didn't happen to see Mark this morning, did you?"

"Gone AWOL, has he?"

"I'm hoping he just decided to work off some energy riding his bike. But we have to be in church in less than an hour so I've got to find him."

"Tell you what," he said. "I'm not doing anything right now. Why don't you take from Clifton Ave. to the Styertowne Circle and I'll head up the other way."

"Thanks, Charlie. I'd really appreciate it. Let's check back here in twenty minutes. Of course, if you find him, bring him back right away. Please!"

"Sure thing. See you in twenty minutes and, Corraine, don't worry. He's sure to show up before the Confirmation."

As I pulled out, I noticed for the first time that it was a gorgeous spring day, warm and sunny with that wonderful clarity a cloudless day brings. Great day for a party, I thought. I wonder if there's going to be anything to celebrate. I could see all those people standing around in the spring sunshine, shaking their heads and shoveling down food. A Confirmation party for someone who probably wouldn't be confirmed. As I slowly cruised the streets, my head out the window, searching for a glimpse of a blond boy on a bike I was struck by the absurdity of the situation and began to laugh - at myself, at life, at my own foolishness in believing that I could get Mark to act the way I wanted him to. At every turn he thwarted my efforts. Part of me felt like throwing my hands up, turning around and going home. But my religion was my anchor and I wanted my son confirmed in my faith.

After twenty minutes of fruitless searching, I turned the car and headed home. My parents would probably be there by now since my Dad was standing as sponsor to Mark and he had wanted to talk to him for a few minutes before we left for the service. When I turned into the driveway, my parents, Doug, and Charlie were standing on the front porch. As if in a dream, I focused on how nice my folks looked, my mom in a white lace dress and white heels and my dad in his navy blue pinstripe suit. They came down the steps to meet me.

"Don't get out of the car," Charlie said. "Mark's in the park riding Cheryl's moped. I tried to get him to come with me, but he wouldn't. As soon as I got close to him, he'd take off. If Doug takes one car, you take another and I take my van, we can probably corral him between the three of us.

I looked down at my watch. Thirty minutes till church.

"Mount up and let's ride," I said.

The park was only five minutes away, but the meadow where he was riding was quite large and somewhat hilly. I parked on the east side, Doug on the west and Charlie to the north. The south side was bordered by apartment buildings. We got out of our cars and began to walk toward where we could hear the sound of the moped's engine. Mark saw us as we approached and he waved, but he did not stop. He raced up the nearest hill and disappeared on the other side where I knew he would run into Doug. I heard Doug shout for him to stop just as the moped appeared on the crest of the hill heading toward Mt. Prospect Ave. We should have walkie-talkies, I thought, as I walked forward, closing the gap. If Mark wanted, he could shoot right past me, but he knew that if he did I would knock him off the bike. With the mood Doug was in, I knew he would also grab him if he could. I spotted him again, wheeling across the flat part of the park and called for him to stop. His hair had blown back from his face and he was hunched over the handlebars, his expression one of wild excitement. I knew that he had forgotten about the confirmation and the party and was lost in the thrill of speed and defiance.

We narrowed the circle again and again with Mark riding madly between us. Now, he would have to break through one of us to escape. Charlie was his best bet because I was not sure he would grab Mark off the bike if need be. I signaled for him to do so if necessary. He gave me the thumbs up signal. Mark saw his gesture as he wheeled around and the fight went out of him. He pulled the moped up in front of me and killed the engine. I knew he was waiting for me to explode. I took him firmly by the arm and not saying a word, I marched him to the car. We drove home in silence. I did not trust myself to speak. I did not want to commit a sin on the day of my son's Confirmation.

At home, I pushed him ahead of me up the stairs and watched while he put on his shirt and suit and tied his shoes. I glanced at my watch. Ten minutes until the ceremony began. I left him in Doug's charge, ran into my room, ripped off my jeans and tee shirt and threw on my dress. I ran a brush through my hair while slipping on my shoes. I slicked on a little lip gloss, grabbed my purse and walked down the stairs, counting to ten so I wouldn't have a stroke. We made it to the church with one minute to spare.

I sat in the pew, watching Mark receive the holy sacrament of Confirmation, knowing that it meant nothing to him. I prayed fervently for the strength and the wisdom I would need in the coming years. With the sun shining through the stained glass window and the organ playing the hymns I had once found so comforting, I looked within and slowly, painfully, I accepted that there would be no miracle for me. Mark was my son and I loved him, but he was also a cross that would become heavier and heavier as the journey continued.

A month after his Confirmation, school ended. Doug and I both agreed that he needed a structured environment and that leaving him alone with Cheryl or my mom would be a big mistake. We talked about hiring a sitter for him, but dismissed that right away. If the school professionals couldn't handle him for more than a few hours, how could we expect an untrained, unsuspecting person to handle him? The principal suggested we send him to day camp for the summer months. The outside activities would be good for his overall co-ordination and the swimming, running and hiking would chip away at some of his high-voltage energy. Mark showed some enthusiasm for the project and to our surprise so did Cheryl. She did not want to stay home alone and since most of her friends were still from Nutley, she wouldn't see them much in the summer. We signed both the kids up for Camp Willow. I kept my fingers crossed.

After a week, the phone calls began. Mark was fighting with the other children. Mark wouldn't participate in Arts and Crafts. Mark ran away from the counselor in the woods. Mark wouldn't follow directions during swimming lessons. Mark was talking back to the counselor.

Doug and I tried to explain to Mark that he could not stay home alone during the day and that if he was thrown out of this camp, he would just have to go somewhere else that wasn't as much fun. Nothing we said made any difference. Punishing him, talking to him, yelling at him, using the behavior modification techniques failed to change a single thing. Mark continued his disruptive behavior and eventually was forbidden to return to camp, but by then it was almost September and school was about to begin.

This year, Mark would be attending P.S. 13, a new school where classes for the older emotionally disturbed children were held. I knew the change made him nervous and I dreaded starting the endless round of conferences and notes home and requests to pick him up halfway through the day. I had reduced his medication during the summer because I still feared the effects of long term use of a stimulant, but several weeks before school started I raised the dose to the amount recommended by Dr. Patterson. Mark became slightly more compliant, but I was no longer seeing the Jekyl and Hyde effect I had noticed when he'd first taken the medication.

When the Special Education bus arrived on the first day of school, I watched him climb aboard with mixed feelings. I held out little hope that this year would be better than the last, but I had liked Mark's new teacher, Mrs. Sorrington, whom I had met at a special conference for new students. She had a warmth I had not seen in Mark's other teachers and a genuine desire to reach her special students no matter what it took. I hoped that she and Mark would

184

click and he would like her enough to trust her a little. I hoped, but I no longer took it for granted that things would work out. And, as I watched him climb aboard the bus, I saw something that made my heart sink. In the defining outlines of his face and the broadening of his shoulders was the suggestion of the man he would soon become. Mark was no longer a little boy. He was quickly becoming an adolescent and somewhere in my heart, I sensed that with his approaching manhood, we were rapidly approaching a crisis.

Mark remained with Mrs. Sorrington for the next two years and, during that time, I communicated with her on a weekly basis. As I had thought, she was a deeply caring and dedicated educator and she tried every technique she knew to reach Mark. He, in turn, adored her, but he continued to slide backwards both behaviorally and academically. For each step forward, he took three steps backward. He was still reading on a second grade level although his age alone would have placed him in the sixth grade. His concentration was minimal and his behavior made it impossible for him to be mainstreamed into any of the other classes like music or art or physical education. His behavior deteriorated at the same rate as his academic progress.

I was just reading the latest note from Mrs. Sorrington during my lunch break when the phone rang. I no longer jumped when I heard the principal, Mr. Raynaldi's, voice on the phone though there were still times when I cried at work. I would just put my head down until it was over, then go into the ladies room and reapply my make-up. My co-worker, Rose, was wonderful. She would listen to my heartbreak, talk to me until I calmed down, and never complained when I had to go pick up Mark at school. She would even bring me articles about research on children with similar disabilities as Mark's.

"Mrs. Conaway, this is Mr. Raynaldi. Would you be available to come in for a conference after school today? A situation has developed on the school bus that needs our immediate attention."

I covered the receiver with my hand and mouthed his request to Rose. She nodded. Once again, I silently blessed my boss, Gene Jurewicz, who was the most understanding and sympathetic man I had ever known. He had never said no or made me feel guilty when I needed to take time off.

"Three thirty would be fine, Mr. Raynaldi," I said and hung up.

"What is it this time?" Rose asked.

"Something about the bus. Rose, I just don't know what to do. Every week I get a note home about something else Mark's done. Listen to these."

I took a thick folder from my desk and selected a few papers. "Are you ready for this?" I asked her.

"Shoot." She leaned back in her chair and closed her eyes.

"The first two are from Mr. Raynaldi, the principal." *Please be advised that during lunch activity on the playground Mark threw a rock striking another student in the head. This act was an unprovoked one. As a result of this, Mark has lost his privileges to eat and participate in our lunch program with the other students. Mark is also placed on in-school suspension. Another act of this nature will result in Mark's suspension from school.* And again, less than a month later...*Mark created a very serious problem during lunch with Mrs. Smith. He refused to listen to her and in fact pushed Mrs. Smith.* I looked up to see her regarding me sympathetically. I didn't want to cry again so I shuffled through the papers and pulled out two of the notes from Mrs. Sorrington and started to read. *Mark brought in a stapler today. He was shooting staples at another child. This is a hazard to other children in the class.*

"Rose, that wasn't the worst of it. Mark has developed an obsession with knives and toy guns. One day, he brought a penknife into class. He has never hurt anyone with the knives. It's almost as if he feels he needs protection and, if he shows the other kids the knives, they will leave him alone. Mark has been picked on a lot by the other kids, sometimes to the point of cruelty. Maybe he thinks they'll be scared of him now. Anyway, the knife incident seems to have set off something else in him. Let me read you the note about that." *Dear Mrs. Conaway, I regret to write to you with the news. Mark has been a very disruptive student in the last few weeks. Ever since the episode with the knife, he has refused to pay attention to anything. When told to take his book out for Math, he completely ignores the situation and carries on with whatever he wants to do. This has been going on every day during the past week. He brings in all kinds of toys and will play all day if I let him. Also, if I try to take them away, he begins to threaten me. I'm very much concerned about this...* "And that's only one of dozens of notes I've received.

I'm at my wit's end. I'm not making excuses for him. I'm not blaming Mr. Raynaldi or Mrs. Sorrington. I just don't know where to turn any longer."

"Have you ever thought about finding a residential treatment facility for him? Perhaps he needs more than public school is able to provide."

"What do you mean?" I asked.

"I was reading about special schools that deal with children who cannot be maintained at home. They provide twenty-four hour instruction and supervision as well as psychological counseling. Maybe Mark would benefit more from that sort of an environment."

I shook my head. "I can't send him away. Because of his background before he came to me, all those placements in foster homes, he would totally freak out if I sent him away. He'd think I was abandoning him. No, I've just got to find some other way, any other way of helping him."

I left work at three o'clock and arrived at Mr. Raynaldi's office just as school was letting out. I was surprised to find Mark waiting there as well.

"I thought it best not to have Mark ride the bus until we have worked out this problem. I have spoken to Mark and I think he understands what he has been doing wrong." I looked over to where Mark was fidgeting in the chair, swinging his legs and running a matchbox car over the arm of the chair. As far as I could tell he was completely oblivious to the conversation.

"What exactly did he do?" I asked.

"A number of things," Mr. Raynaldi said. "It started out with Mark refusing to close a window he had opened. When the aide and the driver asked him to close the window, he gave them an argument that included obscenities, an argument that went on for twenty minutes and resulted in the children arriving home late. Several parents were concerned and called to complain. The driver also told me several times that he has dropped Mark off at the Boys Club after school as per your directions and that he has seen Mark roaming the streets after that, smoking and bothering other children. During the last few weeks, he has been picking fights on the bus and the bus driver has requested that Mark be put in restraints while on the bus. He said he cannot drive and insure the safety of the other children at the same time. Mark has the right to ride the bus to school, but restraints are provided and used for those students who cannot restrain themselves. I'm sorry to be so blunt. We are concerned for Mark, but he cannot be allowed to jeopardize other children."

I looked over at Mark to see how the news affected him. He was still swinging around in his chair, playing with his car.

"No," I said. "I will not authorize the use of restraints of any kind on my son. If he continues to be disruptive, I will find some way of getting him to school myself."

"Mrs. Conaway, please understand. We are doing everything we can for Mark. I have released him from some classroom time so he can work with the janitor in the school. I also find jobs for him to do so he is not so restless in the classroom. Mrs. Sorrington has refused to give up on him. She works during her own time to research and create projects that might stimulate him."

"I have no complaints about Mrs. Sorrington or you. But you must look at this from a mother's point of view. I, too, have tried everything I know, psychological counseling, nutrition, medication, biofeedback, religion. I want to help my son. How? I just don't know how."

"Why don't you ask me?" Mark said.

Surprised, I swung around to look at him. He was glaring at me, nothing blank about his look now.

"I've tried to ask you, but you never answered me," I said.

"That's because you don't want to listen to me."

"I'm listening now."

"All right then. If you want to help me just leave me alone. No more testing, no more medicine, no more telling me what to do. You treat me like a little kid. I'm no little kid. You're always shoving me into classes with retards like George who can't even feed himself. He drools all over his face. It's disgusting. Everybody's always telling me what to do. Open the window, close the window, sit down, don't do this, don't do that. All day long. Here and at home. No pets, no fish, no birds. And no one cares when I get beat up. I take the blame for everything. Too bad, I'm not going to listen to any of you anymore. I'm going to do what I want to do and tough shit on what you want."

"I'm sorry you feel that way, Mark." I said. "But you are still a child under my roof. And so long as you remain under my roof, you do what I tell you to do. When you are an adult you may do as you wish. But not until then."

"That's what you think," Mark said.

I knew then that we had taken the first step into the crisis I had been dreading

PART THREE

❧

LEARNING

Chapter Eighteen

When the timer rang, I dropped my feet from the cocktail table and pushed myself from the soft comfort of the couch. All I really wanted to do was sit for an hour and stare at nothing, not even the television, just a mindless hour where I had to think about absolutely nothing. But I had a husband and two children to feed and the dinner was ready. I pulled the roast beef and baked potatoes from the oven and set them on the table. Cheryl laid out the dishes and silverware for me. I warmed up the rolls and green beans in the microwave and yelled up the stairs.

"Dinner's ready. Come and get it."

I could hear their footsteps on the stairs as I walked back into the kitchen. Doug was off from work tonight and he and Cheryl were talking as they came into the kitchen.

"Everything okay?" I asked as I looked from one to the other.

"Yes and no," Doug said. "Cheryl's still unhappy at Clifton High School. She wants to go back to Nutley High."

I decided not to get into the discussion tonight. This had been an on-going topic of conversation since Cheryl had started high school. She spent time on the phone with her Nutley friends and she did not participate in the activities or go around with any girls from Clifton. I knew she was unhappy. I just wasn't sure whether it was a passing phase. I wanted her to give it more time, to see if she couldn't adjust after she had been in the high school for a while. I had encouraged her to participate in some of the school clubs and organizations, but she had shown no interest in any of them.

"Cheryl, can we talk about this when I am in a better mood? Tonight, I'm really tired and I don't think I have the patience to listen properly to you," I said.

"You never have time to listen. You always come up with one excuse or another. You do have another child besides Mark. Or did you forget?"

"Bad timing, Cheryl. Did anyone tell Mark that dinner is ready?" I said.

Doug shook his head. Cheryl looked down at her plate and didn't say anything.

I walked to the bottom of the stairs and yelled up. "Mark. Come down. Dinner's ready."

No answer.

"Mark. Right now."

Still no answer. I was not about to climb the stairs after him. I had made it a rule that on the days when Doug was home from work, we would all eat together. Doug's schedule was so erratic that we didn't often see him for dinner and I wanted the children to have time with him when he was home. Tonight I was too tired to make the effort to drag Mark down the stairs for dinner.

I went back into the kitchen and listlessly played with my food.

"Isn't Mark coming?" Doug asked.

"Not unless you want to go up and get him.'

"Let him stay there then." Doug said. "He knows the rule. If he doesn't come down now, he doesn't eat. He's thirteen years old. He knows the ropes."

I wasn't sure I agreed. Doug still believed Mark could remember things if he wanted to, he just didn't want to. I still believed Mark's decisions were based on his impulse of the moment. He would eat when he was hungry and to Hell with any dinner time rules. I remembered the conference I'd had with Mr. Raynaldi and Mark's surprising awareness of his own impulsiveness. 'I'm going to do what I want to do and tough shit on what you want.'

Cheryl ate in silence and as soon as she was finished asked to be excused.

"I don't know why I bother," I said. I knew my voice sounded bitter, but I didn't care.

"She's a teenager. It goes with the territory," Doug said. He helped himself to another slice of meat and a baked potato. "How's Mark doing at the new sitter's after school?"

Mark was now in Woodrow Wilson Junior High School. Against the advice of Mark's teacher, Mrs. Sorrington, and the principal, Mr. Raynaldi, the Clifton Board of Education had insisted that Mark be promoted to junior high school. Doug and I had spoken to everyone who was anyone in education in Clifton trying to block this move, but once again we were unsuccessful. Mark's academic level still hovered around second grade and his emotional age was well below average. We knew with a surety born of long experience that Mark

194

would never make it in junior high school. We were, of course, correct. He had been suspended for fighting within two weeks.

Doug had been so furious he had gone straight to the principal and demanded that another placement be found for Mark. A few more serious disciplinary incidents had convinced the principal that Mark would not make a positive contribution to his school. He was able to convince the board that it was worth spending the money they had been trying to save to send Mark to an out- of- district school for the emotionally disturbed and neurologically impaired. We were still waiting for the results of their search.

The situation had also worsened at the Clifton Boys Club where Mark had been going after school. He rarely stayed at the Club, but wandered the streets instead, smoking and picking fights with other boys. He had also been found with penknives in his possession and a cigarette lighter that we later discovered he had stolen from one of the teachers at school. He now went to Mrs. Stone, a private sitter, who had agreed to take Mark for a few hours after school until either Doug or I could pick him up. Surprisingly, they had formed a bond of sorts and Mark enjoyed spending time with her. He had been going there for the last few weeks and, so far, there had been no trouble.

I held up my hand, fingers crossed. "So far, so good. He seems to like her and she said he's been no trouble to her. She's very warm and outgoing and she likes to feed him. He's enjoying the attention, but you know how it goes. Anything new grabs his interest for a few weeks and then we're back to the same old pattern."

Doug came around to rub my shoulders where I sat slumped at the table. "Come on, Corraine. This isn't like you. You're usually so filled with energy and enthusiasm. What's really bothering you?"

I reached up to pat his hand where it rested on my shoulder. "I know this is going to sound crazy, but I guess it's finally sinking in that Mark may not outgrow this handicap, that it's something we all are going to have to live with for the rest of our lives. When he was little I kept telling myself that when he got older, when he matured, things would change. He had such a rough start and I guess I blamed all of the problems on that. I honestly believed that with enough love and the proper guidance, he would overcome all his problems and grow up "normally" whatever that means. I'm having a hard time

195

accepting that our love isn't enough to help him. I'm frustrated and angry and sad and it's choking me."

Doug knew better than to argue with me or try to comfort me with meaningless words. He understood me enough to realize that I would never give up the struggle to find help for Mark, but that the struggle was emotionally draining and often exhausting. Tonight was just one of those nights when the exhaustion overwhelmed me and nothing anyone could say would help. We sat together in silence while the dinner congealed on the plates. After a while, I smiled at him.

"I suppose someone should go up and remind Mark to eat. If I don't remind him, I swear he wouldn't eat for days."

"Don't bother. I'll get him. I have to go upstairs anyway."

I smiled my thanks and got up to clear the table. Most of the food had gone untouched and I scraped my plate and Cheryl's into the garbage. I left the sliced meat on the table and put out some bread and mustard for Mark to make a sandwich. I was about to go into the living room when I heard Doug call me.

"What is it?" I yelled from the bottom of the stairs.

"Better come up." Doug's voice sounded odd and I couldn't tell if he was angry or concerned.

I plodded up the stairs and into Mark's room. One look and I knew it was empty. The bed was neatly made, my handiwork from this morning. Mark's school books were on the bed, but no clothes were strewn about. The lights were on and Doug was standing by the open window. We had replaced the old wooden windows last year because the sashes had warped and cold air had poured in through the gaps. The new windows could be locked but not nailed shut and Mark climbed out whenever he felt like it. He had used the windows to escape during the day, but he had never climbed out this late at night. I looked at my watch, the illuminated dial showing ten after eight.

"Don't panic," Doug said. "He's probably riding around the neighborhood somewhere on his bike and lost track of time. You stay here. I'll take the car and drive around the streets."

I nodded, not trusting myself to speak. I walked down to the kitchen with Doug and listened as his car engine faded away in the distance. Although I knew Cheryl was upstairs, the house seemed too quiet, as if it was listening with me. I turned the radio to a pop music station and picked up the telephone. Cheryl was talking to one of her Nutley girlfriends. I interrupted, asking her to hang up right away. She must have recognized something in the tone of my voice because she didn't protest and, a minute later, she came downstairs.

"What's the matter, Mom?" she asked.

"Hopefully nothing," I said. "Your brother's missing. Daddy's gone out in the car looking for him. I want Nana and Grandpa to come over and stay with you if Daddy can't find him. I know you're in high school now, but I would just feel better if someone was in the house with you in case I have to go out and search, too."

She looked like she was about to protest then thought better of it and shrugged. "If it makes you feel better, it's okay with me."

I kissed her quickly, then picked up the phone and called my folks. They promised to hurry right over and when they arrived twenty minutes later, Doug had still not returned.

"I wish he'd come back," I said for the twentieth time. The inactivity was starting to wear on me. I glanced at my watch, then back at the clock as if wishing would make the time go faster. My mom made me a cup of tea and insisted I sit down and drink it. An hour passed, then two. When I finally heard Doug's car pull into the driveway, I was up and out the door before he stepped foot on the ground. One glance through the passenger car window confirmed that he was alone.

"I covered everywhere I could think of that he usually goes. No sign of him."

We walked back into the house. I shook my head as my parents looked up from the table.

"What now?" Dad asked.

"Did you check near the power lines?" I asked Doug.

"I stopped there and called out the window, but I couldn't see anything."

"Do you think you should call the police?" My mother started clearing the table, her movements quick and nervous. Like me, she needed something to do when she was worried.

"Not yet. He might just be out roaming around and come home when he's tired. Doug, why don't you take the car and keep looking? Mom and I will search the land under the power lines and the laundromat in Richfield Village. Lately Mark's been hanging out there, talking to the customers. Dad, if you don't mind staying with Cheryl, I'd appreciate it. If Mark does come home, he's more likely to stay here with you and not run off again." Mark and my father had a good relationship. My dad always seemed to be able to reach him with humor while the rest of us were yelling our heads off.

An hour later, we all met back at the house. Mom and I had tromped through the wet strip of grass that ran beneath the power lines in the back of our house. The lines went on for a quarter mile and part way through our search, darkness had fallen. Flashlights had provided a little light, but we had both felt like ghost hunters, sneaking around beneath the spider legs of the looming electrical towers. We were damp and cold and I could feel the panic setting in. We hit all the laundromats we could find then headed home. I checked my watch. Ten o'clock.

I didn't have to ask my dad if Mark had returned or if there had been any phone calls. I could tell by his face that nothing good had happened. Cheryl had come down and was sitting with him at the table. I was glad she had someone to share her troubles with. One more problem with Mark had robbed me of the time and energy I needed to help her tonight. I made a resolution that as soon as this crisis was over, I would find the time to talk to her. Right now, I couldn't think about that, though. I had to decide what to do about finding Mark.

"Can anyone think of where he might have gone? Anywhere at all?" I asked.

"What about that new boy he's kind of friends with at school," Cheryl asked. "He's been here once or twice. What's his name?"

"Scott. I already tried calling his house. His grandmother said she'd call if Mark showed up there. I called the sitter, too. She hasn't seen Mark since I picked him up after work today."

The silence stretched out like an elastic about to snap. I waited for someone to say something, anything that would provide a solution. But I knew there was only one thing left to do. "All right, I'll call the police," I said.

I paced for the next fifteen minutes, rehearsing in my head what I would say to the police officers when they arrived. Doug and my parents had retreated into the den to watch television, but I couldn't sit for more than a few minutes. I tried not to think of Mark out there somewhere in the night, possibly hurt or beaten up and unable to get home. As soon as one terrifying picture pushed forward I pushed it back, disciplining myself to think of something else. I knew I wouldn't be able to keep it up long, but I didn't want to appear hysterical when the police came.

When the bell rang, I rushed to answer it. Doug followed and together we let the two officers in. They asked for a description and a picture of Mark and a list of places where he might have gone. I told them that his bike was missing. I debated about telling them that Mark was neurologically impaired. I knew they wouldn't understand. Instead, I told them he was a little slow and not to frighten him if they could help it. They promised to check back with us as soon as there was any word.

After they left, I wondered if I should have told them how clever he was at hiding and escaping. This wasn't the first time that Mark had gone out the window or the first time he had "disappeared" for a few hours, but it was the first time he had taken off at night. Before, when he had run off and I had asked him where he'd gone, he had been evasive. He loved to fish and more often than not, he would take a rod and some worms and go to a pond. I tried to emphasize to him that he needed to tell me where he was going, but that was another piece of information that went in one ear and out the other. If the impulse struck him to leave, he left with no thought of the consequences.

At midnight, we had still not heard from the police. My parents were exhausted and I told them to go home and sleep, that there was no sense in all of us staying awake. They were reluctant to leave, but I promised I would call as soon as I heard something. After they left, Doug and I settled down on the couch. My exhaustion had fled though I could feel the weakness in my arms and legs.

"Doug, what are we going to do? He's still just a little boy. I know he's thirteen but that's on the outside. Inside, he's really no more than eight or nine and he probably will never be more than that. I can't let him go off on his own, but he won't stay here. We both know this isn't the last time he's going to run off. He was never able to stay still, never able to settle in one place. He's always been running from something he can't understand or tell us about. How many of these kinds of nights can any of us stand?"

"I was reading something in the paper the other day and it hit home," Doug said. "I can't remember exactly what the story was about, but it involved a mother with a handicapped child. She said she had learned to live one day at a time, enjoying the good days with him and dealing with the problems as they arose. She said the worst thing she could do was anticipate the future because she would never get through the present if she did. Good advice, no?"

"Easier said than done. And in some way, Mark's problem is harder than more visible handicaps because people always seem to be blaming him for his problems and me for being a bad mother or disciplining my child incorrectly. I can't tell you how many times I've heard from friends and family that if I gave him a good beating, he would knuckle under. His brain doesn't function the same way as other people. But it doesn't show on the surface and so people forget. I'd like to take it one day at a time, but before I do that I have to find some way to help him so that he has a happier, more productive future."

"I know. I know. But right now, we need to deal with this. Do you want me to go back out and look for him?"

"No. Let's just wait until the police call. There's nothing you can do that they're not already doing."

The police called around two o'clock in the morning with no news. They would continue the search and if nothing was found, they wanted us to come into the station in the morning for a more complete report. They promised once more to check in soon.

Doug dozed fitfully on and off, but I couldn't sleep. As the night wore on, I paced and sat and drank tea and pictured my little boy lying somewhere in the dark all alone. I prayed frantically for him to be all right and promised God any number of sacrifices if he would just protect Mark through this night.

I was sitting in the kitchen watching the sun come up when the phone rang. The jangle of the bell flicked my raw nerves and I jumped, knocking over my tea cup and adding to my confusion. As I grabbed the phone, I noticed that my hand was trembling.

"Hello! Hello!" I shouted into the receiver praying madly as I did.

"Mrs. Conaway. This is Mrs. Stone." I heard Mark's sitter's voice, but at first it didn't register. I had to concentrate hard to pick up her next words. "I wanted to tell you that I found Mark and he is safe. He slept in the hallway of my apartment house last night. He stayed in the downstairs hall and he didn't ring my bell so I didn't know he was here until I went down for my paper just now. I woke him up and brought him upstairs with me."

"So he's with you now?" I said slowly. Her slightly accented voice and my sleep deprived confusion made comprehension slow in coming.

"Yes. He's here and he's safe," she repeated. "I know you must be so worried."

"Please keep him there," I said. "I'll be right over to pick him up."

I hung up the phone and burst into tears. Doug appeared in the doorway, rubbing his eyes. I leaned against him and cried while I told him what had happened. He touched my shoulder awkwardly and I could tell he was relieved by the deep sigh that rumbled through his chest.

"Let me just wash my face and brush my teeth, then we'll go pick him up. Call the police and tell them we found him," I said.

On the way to Mrs. Stone's house, we discussed how we were going to handle this. Grounding him was certainly not going to work. He would be out the window in no time. Even if we did discover some way of keeping his window shut, he would just find another way to escape. Depriving him of food was no punishment. Half the time Mark forgot to eat anyway. Smacking him taught him nothing. We had learned that from experience. We decided to take away his fishing equipment for a month. I wasn't sure that was such a great idea, but we had to do something.

When we rang the bell of Mrs. Stone's apartment house, I looked over at Doug. In the tightness of his face, I read the same anger that I felt rising in me. Now that I knew Mark was safe I wanted to beat him for all the anxiety he had put us all through. I took a couple of deep breaths and counted to ten. I had myself under somewhat better control when the buzzer rang and we walked in. Mrs. Stone's apartment was on the second floor in the rear. She opened the door on the first ring and smiled sympathetically. "He's having a little breakfast," she said. "Won't you come in?"

I was about to enter when Doug took me firmly by the elbow. "No thank you," he said. "Please send Mark out right away."

She nodded and in a few minutes, Mark appeared in the doorway alone. He didn't seem the least surprised to see us. Doug transferred his hand from my elbow to Mark's and we walked down the stairs in silence. Once in the car, I could wait no longer.

"Why, Mark?" I asked, the tears springing to my eyes. "Why did you do this? Didn't you think for one minute how worried we would be when you didn't come home? We had the police out looking for you we were so scared."

He looked up at me, a puzzled expression on his face. "But why were you so worried, Mom?" he asked. "I knew where I was all the time."

I shook my head, helpless tears darting to my eyes once more. I didn't know how to break through to my son, to make him understand that there were consequences for himself and for others, possibly devastating consequences, to his behavior. Tonight he had been lucky. But, next time, his heedless behavior might result in serious injury. In his neurologically impaired brain, no connection was ever made between cause and effect and no responsibility assigned to his actions. Nothing I had done so far, nothing anyone had done had succeeded in teaching Mark this vital piece of information necessary for his proper functioning in the world.

Chapter Nineteen

Doug and I searched frantically for a school that would accept Mark as a student. He stayed at Woodrow Wilson Junior High only long enough for the Board of Education to approve an out-of-district placement for him. Doug and I had gone to several schools for the disabled, but the attitude was always the same. If he acts out, we don't want him. They didn't want him at Woodrow Wilson either. The notes sent home reflected the growing difficulty they were having handling him even for a short time. Finally, they recommended the Calais School in Whippany, New Jersey. We were given a handbook to study and to read to Mark before we made our decision. What decision? If this school didn't accept Mark, what were our options? As far as I could see there were none.

The Calais School specialized in the neurologically impaired and emotionally disturbed. Their program was based on a strict token economy system in which the children earned tokens in all their classes by doing classwork, cooperating, behaving appropriately, paying attention and following rules. They could then exchange the tokens they earned for candy, gum and other small items from the school store. A token economy had not worked for Mark before, but I was willing to try it again. I was willing to try any reasonable approach to solving his difficulties. The Child Study Team and Mark's psychologists believed that he needed more structure and supervision in order to function. The Calais School was geared precisely to provide those services. Their program was quite strict, infractions of the rules were dealt with quickly by moving disruptive or non-compliant students to the Crisis Intervention Center where they would work one-on-one with the learning specialist and school psychologist. I kept my fingers crossed. Perhaps this was the place he needed to be now. Perhaps this was the method to help him develop some impulse control.

Almost immediately the notes home started. Mark refused to participate in group lessons, he was disruptive in the hallways and on stairs during class changes, he provoked the other students by making inappropriate comments and gestures. The time spent in the Crisis Center increased gradually from two days to five days to in-school suspensions of two weeks or more. Every Wednesday, Doug and I attended meetings with his teacher, learning how to reinforce at home what he was learning in school. We set up charts and posted them on the refrigerator, rewarding him for good behavior and punishing him for non-compliance. When he did not want to perform his chores or do his homework, he jumped out the window and ran away.

For a few months after his first overnight absence, Mark slept in his bedroom, but after school he was rarely at home. Doug and I were both working full time from necessity and, although we tried to make him stay with a responsible adult, twenty-four hour supervision was impossible. Whatever fears had chased him in his nightmares when he was little now remained hot on his trail at all times and he could never stay still. He wandered the streets, walked miles to my parents' house in Nutley, hung out at the local parks or got into trouble in the center of town. Soon the daytime wanderings carried into the night.

Several times a week, Doug and I would search the power lines or the apartments behind our house in hopes of finding him. Sometimes we found him. Sometimes he was gone all night. I never learned not to worry. Mark was still unable to discriminate between those who meant him good and those who meant him harm. Everyone was his friend until they stole from him or beat him up. Often, he would come home bruised or missing an article of clothing. And still he ran. When I asked him why, he had no answer. I don't think he knew. It was just something he had to do.

One night late, after I had returned from a fruitless search of the grounds of the Richfield apartments, I was surprised to find Cheryl curled up on the living room couch waiting for me. She had turned off all the lights and, at first, I thought she might have fallen asleep, but as I tiptoed into the room, she changed her position so she could look up at me.

"Did you find him?" she asked.

"No. I looked in all the usual places, but I didn't catch a glimpse of him. He's gotten more clever. If he doesn't want to be found, he won't be."

I plopped down on the couch beside her and closed my eyes. She usually didn't wait up for me and I didn't expect her to. Mark's episodes had been a part of her life since she was very young and I took it for granted that she could now just shrug them off and not be especially bothered by them. Like most teenagers, her friends were more important to her than her brother and she spent time with them after school and on week-ends.

"Mom, I need to talk to you." Cheryl's voice sounded strange in the darkness, sad and somehow disconnected from the person sitting beside me.

I sat up and switched on the lamp beside the couch. "I'm listening," I said softly.

She took a deep breath, struggling to keep her voice under control. "I know you have a lot of problems with Mark. I know he needs a lot of attention. But I have problems too and you don't ever have time to listen to mine. I've told you over and over again that I hate Clifton High School and that I'm very unhappy there. You keep putting me off and putting me off. Well, I just want you to know, you can't put me off any more. I'm not going back to Clifton High and you can't make me. If you try, I'll quit school. I'm old enough."

"Is that what you want to do? Do you want to quit school?" I asked.

She shook her head. We were both close to tears. I could feel the push of anger and guilt like a knife in my head and I needed every ounce of strength I had to keep it from cutting its way out and hurting her.

"I want to go to school in Nutley," she said. "I want to be with my friends. I didn't have any say in your decision to marry again or to buy this house. I was forced to go along with it regardless of how I felt. I want to be away from here and from Mark and all the problems. I want a normal life. You may not have noticed it, but I am really depressed and counseling isn't helping. I can't take it anymore. Mark's not the only child you have though sometimes it feels that way."

Please God, I prayed, don't let her blame me for all this, not now because if she does, it will be a bloodbath and neither of us will ever recover from it. I can't take any more.

"Cheryl, I can't give you an answer right this minute. I am not putting you off again, but I need to discuss this with Daddy and with Nana and Grandpa. If there is a way of working this out, I will do it. That's the best I can promise. Now, please go to bed before we both say things we'll regret later. I'm not mad at you. I'm just overwhelmed."

She got up and left the room, something in the tone of my voice warning her that one more word and I would erupt. I turned off the lamp and sat alone in the dark letting the anger break over me. I didn't expect life to be fair. I was no longer the romantic I had been when I married Dave. Life had taught me some difficult lessons and I had learned them well. But I had never expected the unrelenting onslaught of pain and frustration, hurt and blame. I felt I was being punished for something I didn't understand. I loved my children, raised them with a mixture of tenderness and discipline, taught them morals and religion, supported them with a strong nuclear and extended family. Surely, these were all the ingredients I had been taught gave children a firm foundation for happiness and success. What was it I had done wrong?

I asked Doug these questions when he came home from work at one thirty that morning and found me pacing the living room floor.

"You're forgetting, Corraine, that you didn't adopt the children until they were older. They both had a rough start in life and Mark has a neurological handicap besides."

"But what does that mean? Are you telling me that nothing we do will make any difference?" I asked,

"No. What I'm saying is that not everything is within our control. We can only do the best we can and hope that the love and security we've tried to give them all these years will outweigh the damage done before. There just aren't any guarantees."

"So what about Cheryl? Should we let her live with my parents in Nutley and finish school there? I can't see the point of keeping her in Clifton High when she's so unhappy," I said.

"This isn't the first time she's brought it up so it's not a passing phase or an overreaction to some party she wasn't invited to or whatever. Talk to your parents and see how they feel about it. If they agree we'll transfer her to Nutley High. Now can we go to bed? It's almost two in the morning. You have to get up and go to work."

"Mark's not home. I looked for him everywhere, but no luck. And that means I won't get any sleep tonight. But before you go I wanted to mention something my cousin Patty had suggested. I was complaining to her about how few schools will take someone with Mark's problems and if Calais hadn't accepted him, we didn't know what we were going to do. She suggested we contact the Division of

Youth and Family Services. They're the umbrella agency that deals with all types of family situations and their referrals are more extensive than anything we could discover on our own." I hesitated a moment, afraid to voice my next thought. I took a deep breath and plunged in. "She also said she thought they would help pay for a residential placement if that should become necessary."

"Let's face that when and if it comes," Doug said.

"Should I contact DYFS and see what programs they have? Maybe they know of something that deals directly with kids who have similar problems to Mark's. Doug, we've got to do something. Mark's behavior is worsening daily, both here and at school. We need some kind of intervention quickly."

Doug nodded. "Sure, call DYFS. What can it hurt?"

After work the next day, I went to my parents and asked them if Cheryl could live with them for the next year and a half. They had been more aware of her deep unhappiness than I had and they took little convincing. As much as I hated to admit it, Cheryl had probably come up with the best alternative for all of us. She would be happier in the stable environment my folks could provide, away from the constant pressures of Mark's problems and she would not have to compete for attention. She would receive as much as she needed from my parents. Doug and I could also concentrate on solving Mark's academic and emotional problems without feeling we were cheating Cheryl out of the time she needed from us.

We signed the legal guardianship papers the following week and Cheryl moved out over the week-end. She had made arrangements to meet with her friends on Saturday, so I dropped her off, had a cup of tea with my parents and left as if nothing unusual had happened. On the drive home, I fought with myself, my mind certain that Cheryl would be happier, my heart hurt by the loss of my child and my failure to give her what she needed.

When I returned home, the house was empty. Doug was working, Cheryl was at my parents and Mark was out wandering somewhere having once again escaped through a window. I had asked him to stay around to say good-by to his sister, but when it was time for her to go, he was nowhere to be found. The front and back doors were locked from the inside so he must have gone out a second story window again. For once, I didn't worry. I was grateful for the peace.

I took a long shower, fixed my hair and nails, read a few pages of a book I had been trying to get through for months and went out to dinner with a friend. Small things but nurturing, renewing things that made me feel like a woman in control.

Mark spun further out of control as the school year progressed. His behavior at home and at school veered now toward the belligerent and abusive. Doug and I were called to a conference because Mark had refused to hand in a workbook assignment. When the teacher reached for the book, he grabbed her arm and twisted it hard enough to cause her considerable pain. He was given a two week in-school suspension and placed on a thirty day probation. We were told that if he acted out physically toward a teacher again he would be expelled.

When Mark walked through the door that afternoon, Doug and I were waiting for him. Doug grabbed his arm and pushed him into the kitchen chair. Mark jumped up, but Doug forced him back down again. We had decided that Doug would handle this. He was usually calmer and more reasonable in confrontative situations. I blew up.

When Mark realized he was not going to be allowed to run, he slouched into the chair, his face distorted by an angry sneer.

"Sit up and look at me when I talk to you," Doug said.

Mark slouched lower in his seat, his hair fell over his eyes and he looked down, the sneer spreading from lips to eyes. Doug reached over and yanked him upright by his shirt collar. As soon as he let go, Mark slumped down again. I looked at Doug, wondering how he could keep his cool. I was already boiling.

"Mark, we were called to a conference today at your school. The principal informed us that you refused to hand in your book and when the teacher reached for it you twisted her arm. Is this true?"

"No."

"Why would they call us in and tell us you did this if you didn't. Obviously, the teacher reported the incident."

"Then she's a liar."

"Did you or didn't you twist her arm?"

"I don't know. Who cares? They'd say I did it even if I didn't. They hate me there and I hate them."

"They don't hate you Mark, but they can't let you do things that would put the teachers and students in danger. They also told us you are bringing cigarette lighters to school. Is this true?"

"Yeah!"

"Why?"

"So I can sneak a butt when I feel like it."

"You know it's against the rules to smoke in school. You can get thrown out for that."

"Good, because I don't want to be there. You put me there because you think I'm a retard, but I'm not."

"No. That's not why we sent you to Calais. We sent you there because no other school would put up with your behavior. If you blow it here, Mark, there may be no other schools in New Jersey that will take you."

"Good. Then I won't go to school."

"What will you do?"

"Hang out with my friends in the park. Play with my animals. Do whatever I want. I can take care of myself."

"Sorry, Mark. It's against the law for someone your age to be loitering about in public places. They'll pick you and put you in juvenile detention. You won't like it there any better than at school."

"Any place would be better than here. You treat me like a little kid. I'm not a kid. I keep telling you, I can take care of myself. You just don't listen."

"The bottom line, buddy, is that you'd better not touch another teacher or student at that school again." Doug said. I was glad he had not let Mark divert him from the true subject of the conversation.

"Or what?" Mark's face was now distorted with fury, his fists balled up and his eyes bulging. His voice had risen to a roar as he heaved himself from his chair.

Doug stood up, his six foot, two hundred pound frame dwarfing Mark's slight body. "Don't push it, Mark. You won't like the answer."

Mark bolted from the room, knocking over his chair. I heard the back door slam before I had gotten halfway across the kitchen.

"Let him go," Doug said. "Keeping him will only make things worse. One of these days, we will come to blows if he keeps pushing me. Did you have a chance to call the Division of Youth and Family

Services yet? We need to face facts. If he gets thrown out of Calais we might need to send him to a residential school. We've almost exhausted the possibilities here."

Part of me did not want to even think of sending him away, but Doug was right. If he kept running away and if he kept acting out in school, what else could we do?

"I'll call them tomorrow. Maybe we could get him involved in a vocational training program that could take the place of school. At least, he'd have a trade, a way of taking care of himself when he gets older.

The next morning, during a lull in the constant phone calls at work, I called DYFS and explained the situation. They promised to send a caseworker to the house within the next few days for an interview. The conversation had been short, pleasant and to the point. I didn't know why I felt such a sense of dread when I hung up the phone. I told myself I had not taken an irrevocable step, but I knew that if I had not been considering the possibility of a residential placement for Mark, I never would have called them. It was almost as if the die had been cast.

When the caseworker called back to set up an appointment, she asked that Mark and Doug be there as well. Doug rearranged his schedule and I managed somehow to get Mark to stay around for the interview. Doug had worked late the night before and I had stayed up to wait for him. As I sat at the table with my file of IEP's, psychiatric reports, school referral forms and letters from different teachers, I organized in my mind what I wanted to say to the caseworker. I wanted her to understand that I needed help in finding a program that would aid Mark in becoming a functioning adult.

It had become increasing clear to me and Doug that if Mark followed his present course something terrible, perhaps even life threatening, would happen. I loved my son, but I knew I could not handle him without help. He was out of control, not only my control, but that of his teachers, psychologists, learning specialists. Something had to be done and if it meant sending him to another special school, then I was willing to try it.

The social worker assigned to our case was Gail Everett, a warm, efficient, unpretentious woman who put us at our ease immediately. She explained that she was not here to judge or assign blame, but to help us work out the problem in the healthiest way possible. She had a ready smile and her easy manner quieted Mark enough so that he was able to answer some of her questions. I understood that she needed to discover if there was any history of abuse, but sitting there listening to Mark blame us was difficult to swallow. I only hoped that she had had enough experience with emotionally damaged adolescents to sort fact from exaggeration. When Mark showed signs of restlessness, she finished her questioning quickly.

"I'm out of here," Mark said. He jumped up and pounded up the stairs and, in a few minutes, we heard the front door slam.

"At least he didn't go out the window this time," I said.

Gail looked at me quizzically.

"Every window in this house has a history," I said. "Mark's been out each of them for some reason or other. Point to a window and I'll tell you an incident that led to Mark's running away."

She scribbled a few notes on a pad as she had been doing throughout the interview. "I will need copies of whatever records you can give me."

I handed her the file with copies I had made of all the pertinent information. She looked at me and smiled.

"We've been through all this before," I said. "You'll see that we have done everything we could think of to help Mark. Special education programs, summer camps, psychotherapy, biofeedback, nutrition, vitamin therapy, tutoring, counseling, socialization programs like the Friday Night Canteen for classified kids. You name it, we've done it. So far nothing positive has come of any of it. That's why we need your help. We were hoping you could involve Mark in some of your programs or recommend something other than what we've tried. We're really at the end of our rope."

"It's obvious you're concerned parents and I can see that you have Mark's interests at heart. Let me review the information you have given me and I'll get back to you with my recommendations. Are you satisfied with the school Mark is currently attending?"

I hesitated. "I don't know enough about special education from the teaching end to be able to make specific criticisms. Mark is still reading, writing and doing math on a second grade level. I can't see any improvement. I don't know if Mark's intellectual limitations are such that he will never get past that stage. No one will tell me if this is so. The general feeling I get is that his behavior is interfering with his academic performance. If that's true then shouldn't this school be able to change that? Isn't that what a school for the emotionally disturbed is supposed to do? On the other hand, Calais is the only school that would accept him so I don't want to cause problems."

She nodded. "I can't make any specific suggestions yet because you haven't been officially accepted as a client in need of the department's services. As soon as your case has been reviewed I will get back to you."

She stood up and extended her hand. There was so much more I wanted to say, but I knew we would have to wait once again to get help. It wasn't her fault. Government agencies worked slowly and in cases where there was no immediate need to remove the child from the household, the paperwork took time. We thanked her and, once again, she assured us she would be in touch as soon as possible.

When she left I looked at Doug, the feeling of helplessness almost swamping me.

"Did you hear what he told her," I said. "All he wants is for us to leave him alone and not tell him what to do all the time. Do you think she understood that he has no comprehension of right or wrong, that he's impulse-ridden and has no judgment about people? How can I let an emotionally disturbed thirteen year old go off on his own when he can't even function in a highly supervised environment? What am I supposed to do?"

Doug looked down at me, his face serious as he shook his head. "We can only do the best we can. The rest is out of our hands."

Chapter Twenty

Mark managed to stay in the Calais School by the skin of his teeth though the constant phone calls, notes home and conferences clearly showed that he had made no improvement there. I had signed him up for a special education summer camp and his adoptive father, Dave, had agreed to take him for a few weeks during August. Dave had stopped drinking and he had assured me that he was seriously involved in rehabilitation and in getting his life back under control. He wanted to reestablish a relationship with Cheryl and Mark and thought he could handle Mark for a little while as a starter. I explained to him how difficult Mark was to control now and I gave him some of his recent history. Dave still wanted to try. Between his three weeks at camp and his visit to his father, Mark would be gone for the entire month of August. I had to admit that I was looking forward to those weeks with profound relief.

The Saturday we were to leave for camp dawned golden and hot. The director of the Special Ed camp had sent a list to the parents of things the children should and should not bring. I had searched among the socks, underwear, shorts, T-shirts and bathing suits after Mark had gone to sleep and had removed two cigarette lighters, several penknives and at least ten packs of cigarettes. The instructions had clearly stated that the children would not be allowed to smoke on the camp grounds.

As we drove through the summer greens of the countryside my spirits started to climb. The winding road to Camp Bisler was heavily wooded, dark evergreens blending with the lighter shades of ash and oak. I pointed out to Mark the squirrels, chipmunks and raccoons that occasionally darted out from the underbrush. I had the windows rolled all the way down because he had been chain smoking since we'd left the house.

Mark, you know you can't smoke here," I said as we drew closer to the cut-off to the camp.

"Yeah, you've told me that a hundred times." He flicked a butt out the window and lit another one.

I went back to my contemplation of the woods. We drove on in silence for a few more miles. Nothing I said would help and anything I said would probably irritate him so silence was my best recourse. I didn't feel the least bit guilty about enrolling him in camp though he had tried to make me feel bad for sending him away. I needed a break and I hoped that being in the country where he could fish and wander around in the woods would do him some good. Besides, it was only for a short time.

We pulled into the dirt parking lot and walked to a lodge made of logs. Other families were arriving and we were all asked to go into a large meeting room. Mark sat next to us for a few minutes, fidgeting and swinging around to look at some of the fish posters and cases of Indian arrowheads mounted on the walls. After a short time, the director greeted us with an introductory talk about the camp, some of the rules and regulations and the activities the kids would be participating in. Mark was clearly not listening. I was glad to hear that there were plenty of hikes planned. I prayed that Mark would be interested enough in the nature hikes and the woodland animals to keep him from running off. We were then introduced to the counselors, each of whom had been trained or were in training for careers in special education. They called off the names of the boys who were in their bunks and asked them to say good-bye to their parents and to line up. I didn't kiss Mark good-bye because I didn't want to embarrass him. I gave him a quick hug instead. Doug shook hands with him and we left.

We backed out of the dirt lot and headed down the one lane road that led through the woods and back to the highway. For a few minutes, I felt strange, slightly bereft. Then Doug caught my glance and our smiles widened to open grins. Doug burst into a verse of "Happy Days Are Here Again." I joined in, our voices floating through the open windows. I straightened my permanently cramped shoulders and threw back my head, singing at the top of my lungs.

"Are we being awful?" I asked.

"No, just happy. I think we've forgotten what it feels like."

We stopped at a quiet country restaurant and I ordered a huge breakfast of pancakes, eggs, sausage and home fries. Doug ordered twice what I had and we took an hour to eat it, chatting and laughing and every once in a while looking at each other with a gleam in our eyes. I needed to get a few things for the house so we stopped off at a hardware store and browsed, making plans to fix the faucets and change some of the outdated light fixtures. We made plans as if everything we had ever wanted to do we would now be free to do. A wonderful interlude from reality.

Mark wrote us a few letters asking to come home. His writing skills had regressed to a first grade level with so many misspellings it was difficult for us to read them. I wrote to him every other day, simple letters about what Cheryl and Nana and Grandpa were doing.

Cheryl and I went shopping or to the movies. We were happy to have the time to spend together and I was more relaxed than I had been in years. Cheryl was almost a woman now, tall and attractive and mature. She would be graduating from high school next year and I spent the time getting reacquainted with my daughter who I hoped in time would also be my friend. She wasn't sure what she wanted to do when she graduated and I did not push her towards college. If she wanted to go, she knew we would support her. If she wanted to take some time off and get a job, she knew we would also support that decision. She did not ask about Mark and, for once, I did not push it. We both needed the time off.

I guess I knew that the truce with Mark was only a temporary one so when I opened the mailbox and saw the official looking envelope from the camp I wasn't surprised. My peaceful interlude was over. The letter detailed Mark's misdemeanors, an apology that they could no longer keep him there, and a request that I pick him up as soon as possible.

It was signed by the camp supervisor with the number of the director if I wanted to discuss the matter further. I folded the letter and stuffed it back in the envelope. I would call, but I knew it would make no difference. I would have to take another day off from work and my mom and I would make the trip to pick him up.

I called Dave and asked if he would take Mark a few days before we had planned. My voice was shaking and I told him honestly that I couldn't stand much more. I needed a break to put my thoughts in some logical order and to work through what would be best for all of us, including Cheryl. She had spent almost six months with my parents and, although she seemed happy, she would be going into her last year of high school and I wanted to be involved in helping her make her plans for the future. I wanted to spend more time with her, time that was galloping past and could never be halted or returned. I had devoted all of my time to Mark. Doug and Cheryl needed me, too. And I needed to get back in touch with myself. I didn't tell Dave all this over the phone, but I was sure he was able to tell much of what I was thinking by the sound of my voice. He agreed to meet me on Interstate 95 halfway between his house in Massachusetts and mine on Friday, three days earlier than we had planned.

I called my Mom.

"Feel like taking a ride?" I asked.

"Not Mark again," she asked.

"Mark again," I said. "I've got to pick him up after work tonight. Want to go?"

She agreed. I called the camp, told the director I would be there to pick him up this evening, and asked that he be packed and ready to go. I could tell he wanted to talk, but I cut him short. What could he tell me that I didn't already know, that I hadn't heard thirty times before? I didn't even ask what Mark had done.

On the way home from the camp my mother sat in the passenger's seat in the front and Mark climbed in back. I could tell by the tough guy walk and the smirk on his face that he was feeling defiant, even triumphant. Talking to him would make no difference. He kept up a non-stop stream of chatter about the animals he had taken care of at camp and smoked one cigarette after another. I didn't ask where he had gotten them. My mother shot me a few glances, but she did not speak and neither did I. Eventually Mark fell asleep.

"What are you going to do?" In the dark stillness of the car, my mother's voice sounded like an echo of my own thoughts.

"While he's up at Dave's I'll contact his caseworker from DYFS, Gail Everett, and ask her to find us a good child psychologist. Obviously, whatever they're doing at Clifton Mental Health isn't working. I also want to find out if there are any other types of medication that might be more effective for him. Things just can't continue this way. He needs help and somehow I'm going to find it."

Once again I felt a burden lifted from my shoulders when I saw Mark climb into Dave's car at the Howard Johnson's on I- 95. My mom had gone with me and we had met Dave there with no difficulty. He looked good, the puffiness I remembered missing from his face and, although the ravages of the alcoholism had carved a constant reminder into his features, he was definitely sober and aware. We had gotten a bite to eat at the roadside restaurant so that Dave and Mark could get reacquainted. Mark appeared to harbor no animosity toward Dave and chatted on about his animals and fishing. Dave had spoken to him on the phone a few times and had promised that they could cast their lines in a near-by stream.

When we had finished our meal, Mark climbed into Dave's Buick without so much as a good-bye even though he hadn't seen Dave since he was five.

"Call me if there's any problems," I said anxiously.

"I will," Dave promised. "But I'm going to try to handle them on my own. You need a break."

I turned the car around and headed back toward home. I couldn't help the slow smile that spread across my face as the miles started to accumulate.

"I hate to say it, but what a relief!" my mother said. "I only hope Dave can handle him for the next two weeks. I don't think he understands what's in store for him."

"You know, it was good to see Dave again. I felt no anger, no bitterness. I'm glad he's getting his life together and I'm glad he took Mark off my hands. He wants to be Mark's father again. Let him learn what that means. But, honestly, watching Mark climb into Dave's car without as much as a backward glance, really worried me. Do you think after all these years that he's formed no bond with any of us? Do you think that may be the root of all his problems, that he is not capable of really feeling anything for anyone?"

By the end of the week I had spoken to Gail Everett about the possibility of residential placement for Mark as one of the options I was considering. I had given her all the information and records on what had been done for Mark so far and also the latest update on the runaways and the camp. She suggested other options to explore before we got involved with placement hearings. She felt that forward movement depended on whether Mark made a good adjustment at the Calais School this year. I had told her about his difficulties last year and how I couldn't see any improvement in his academic progress. The few letters he had written from camp looked like they had been written by a first grader, the words misspelled and the printing large and crooked, strung across the page with little eye for placement or continuity. His verbal expression was that of a teenager, his writing that of a very young child. She said she would look into a tutoring program for Mark as well as a new psychologist. She explained to me that DYFS would not pay for these services. I asked her to please explore all options and we left it at that.

I was just starting to relax into my temporary reprieve when the inevitable phone call jarred me out of my illusion of a normal life. Dave and Mark had come to blows and Mark had run away. Dave had searched for him for several hours and could find no trace. He suspected that he had hitchhiked to I-95 and was heading home. Dave had stopped at a phone booth to call me. He was going to search the upper half of the route. Could I search between Clifton and the rest stop where we had met on the way up? I hung up the phone and called my mother since Doug was working late.

"Want to take a ride?" I asked.

"Again?" she asked.

"Again."

"Ready when you are," she said. Silently I blessed her for her help and understanding.

"Where to now?" she asked when I picked her up at home. I had hoped to see Cheryl and maybe convince her to take a ride with us, but she was off with her friends. Better than chasing her brother down some highway, I thought. My mother had told her where she would be and my dad would be home right after work.

"Mark ran away from Dave," I said over my shoulder as I backed out of the driveway. "I didn't get the full story. It sounded like they had a physical confrontation. Dave said something about Mark refusing to do any work. I'll talk to him later, once we find Mark. If we find Mark!"

"You don't think he'd run off and not come back, do you?"

I considered her question. It had never occurred to me that he would one day disappear for good. "I don't think so. I think he runs to escape. He never seems to have any particular destination in mind. He needed to escape from Dave so he's probably just running. When he calms down he'll try to make his way home. One thing about Mark, he can't remember anything long enough to hold a grudge. And it's not in his nature. He gets mad and then it's over and he forgets about it."

We had pulled onto Interstate 95 heading in the opposite direction from the way Mark would be coming. I pulled over and my Mom got into the back seat so she could search the shoulder on the opposite side of the road.

"It's going to be very difficult to find him this way," she said. "I can barely see and it's going to be full dark soon."

"I know, but we've found him before under some impossible conditions. Sometimes I think God leads us to one another. If this had happened a year ago, I would have been frantic. Now I know that somehow I will find him again."

We decided to drive for about twenty-five miles, then turn around and search the other side of the road. It was not quite dark, the twilight setting in late on a hot summer evening. I had opened all the windows in the car so we could stick our heads out if we thought we caught a glimpse of something. Between the road dust and my allergies, my eyes were stinging and I could hear my mother sneezing behind me.

"Over there!" My mother pointed across the road a little way ahead. A young man had just climbed out of a car that was turning off at the exit. I had to keep with the trend of traffic or risk an accident.

"Was it him? Should I get off at the exit and turn around?" I shouted against the roar of the wind through the windows.

"I don't know, but I think we should look. You don't see that many hitchhikers these days."

I swung off at the next exit and, after winding around several country roads, found myself back on the Interstate heading south. I prayed that if it was him, he hadn't been picked up by another car before I could get to him.

"Do you remember how far down the road he was?" My mom leaned on the back of my seat so she wouldn't have to talk above a normal tone.

"I landmarked it by a billboard for Marlboro cigarettes."

"Perfect for Mark," I said. "He's probably smoking under it right now."

I saw the billboard about a half mile down the road, but the traffic obscured the place right beneath it. "Please let him be there," I prayed. As angry as I was I could not bear the thought that someone

219

might pick him up and hurt or even kill him. He was only fourteen and very small. He would be no match against the strength of a full grown man.

He was there, thumb out, pale hair glinting against the last rays of the summer sun. When I pulled up, he ran to the car and jumped in. He smiled at me, waved to his grandmother in the back seat and settled down for the ride home.

"You're not surprised to see us?" I said.

"Nah! I knew you'd come and get me. And if you didn't, I'd just hitchhike the rest of the way home. I made it all the way down here, didn't I? I told you. I can take care of myself."

"Mark, doesn't it ever sink in that I worry about you when you run off? You can't keep doing this. One day you are going to get hurt besides the fact that it's wrong."

He turned away and looked out the window. I knew he wouldn't hear me no matter what I said so I saved my breath. I dropped my mother off and drove home with Mark. Doug had been home from work for a while. When we walked in, he looked murderous. I had left him a note explaining where I was.

"In your room, young man, and don't come out until I call you."

Mark swaggered slowly up the stairs, once more displaying that adolescent defiance that was becoming so much a part of his outward presentation. I wondered if my little boy was gone forever.

"He'll just climb out his window and slide down the chimney. If he does that I'm not sure what I'll do. I'm too tired tonight to go looking for him."

"He won't be going anywhere tonight," Doug said. "I figured out a way to keep the windows from opening enough for him to slip out. I'm going up now to lock his door. For once, you and I will get a good night sleep. I called Gail Everett at DYFS to report his absence in case we needed help. Corraine, we've got to start looking into a residential placement. I'm beginning to think Mark's not going to make it out of his teens at this rate. He needs protection from himself."

I bowed my head and asked that God's will be done.

Chapter Twenty-One

A few weeks before Christmas Mark was expelled from the Calais School. I was called to pick him up and told that he would not be allowed to return. An exit interview was scheduled for December 10th and, in the meanwhile, I would receive a letter detailing the reasons for his termination. I was informed that Mark would be waiting for me outside the school with a guard to watch him until I was able to come. Click! End of phone call.

I sat at my desk, wondering if the feeling of shock that accompanied these phone calls would ever go away. My mind immediately became a whirlpool of disjointed thoughts, what would we do, where would he go, what kind of help could I get for him, why was this happening again, what were Doug and I doing wrong? The questions were endless. I ran into the bathroom and leaned over the sink, letting myself sob in the privacy of the small space. A few minutes later, Rose came in.

"Time to fix your make-up again?" she asked.

I nodded and reached into my handbag for a tissue. "I don't know why I even bother. I should just paint mascara streaks down my cheeks and forget about it. They're there practically every day as it is."

Rose patted me on the back and waited for me to go on. I gulped some air and stared at myself in the mirror, waiting for the lump in my throat to shrink enough to let my words squeak past.

"Mark just got expelled from school again," I said. "Come pick him up, the principal said. He's probably waiting for me now."

"Go get him then," Rose said. "When you get back home, call DYFS and the director of the Department of Special Services for the Clifton School System. Find out if they can really do this."

I picked Mark up, told him to go to his room and called Gail Everett to inform her of this new development. She agreed to come with us to the exit interview and promised she would find out what she could before then. I asked her about the legality of Mark's termination and once again she promised to look into it for me. She also agreed to call and set up an appointment with the director of the Department of Special Services for the Clifton schools.

Several days later, I received a copy of a letter sent from the Director of the Calais School to the Clifton Department of Special Services.

Dear Sir,

I regret to inform you that we are no longer able to provide a program for [Mark Graham] at The Calais School. Termination of his program will begin effective today.

The decision for terminating this youngster's program was based on an incident which took place yesterday during the last period of school. During that time, [Mark] was taken out of the Crisis Center where he had spent part of the day and placed in isolation. This was done because [Mark] was unable to comply with the rules of the Crisis Center. It was during the time that [Mark] was in isolation that he attempted to set fire to one of the two chairs in that room. It is to everyone's good fortune that the material in the chair was fire retardant and did not burn.

With this kind of acting out behavior, I must consider the welfare of all the other students in this school. Therefore, it is imperative that [Mark's] enrollment at Calais be terminated.

Should you have any questions regarding this matter, please feel free to contact me.

Doug came home early that night and we sat down for another talk with Mark. As usual, Doug was the one to begin the discussion. He was still able to present things to Mark in a calm way, at least in the beginning. My patience had worn so thin that I was always on the offensive. Mark would retaliate and we would get into a screaming brawl which solved nothing.

We sat around the dining room table. Mark was fidgeting as usual, picking things up, putting them down again, swinging his legs, drumming his fingers, moving around in his seat. I wanted to scream for him to sit still, but I bit my lip and sat with my hands folded, waiting. I glanced over at the refrigerator papered with behavioral modification charts and winced. Our belief in so many things had led us once again to the same old place.

"You know that you've been expelled from school. That you can't return to Calais," Doug began. He waited for Mark to acknowledge his statement.

Mark stared down at the table where he was twirling a butter knife around in circles. I shot out my hand, grabbed the knife and put it on my lap.

Doug waited. Mark looked up at him, then me. "Yeah," he said.

"We have to go speak with the school's director tomorrow. He claims you tried to light a fire in a chair in the isolation room."

"I'm not that stupid," Mark said. "If I lit a fire in a locked room, I could have burned myself to death."

"So you're saying you didn't light the fire on purpose."

"That's what I'm saying." Mark looked up, his eyes defiant, his lips curled in a triumphant smirk. Suddenly, he looked much older than the child I knew he was inside. He looked like a fourteen year old punk.

This must be how they see him at school, I thought. But they should know better. They should know from his records and from his school work that he's still a very young boy. They should know how to deal with this. They should know how to help him.

"What were you doing that made them think you were lighting fires?" Doug asked.

"I didn't have nothing to do in there. I felt real antsy, like I was going to jump out of my skin. There were only two chairs in there. Nothing else. Nothing to do. All I had in my pocket was a cigarette lighter. They take away all the things I bring to do. They want me to sit all the time. Do their stupid work that they know I can't do. I hid the lighter so they couldn't get it. Then this chick, Evelyn, talks to me all the time. You know, the one who calls here. She annoys me and I get mad and I walk out of class to get away from her. She's okay, but she gets on my nerves.

So then I'm in the Crisis Center and they're at me about following the rules. Do this. Don't do that. I can't sit there anymore. The antsy feeling's real bad now. I got to get out of there or I'll explode. But they put me in this little room and lock the door. I don't know what to do. I walk around and around. I want to put my foot through the wall, kick it down so I do, kick it. But I just hurt my foot. Stupid, I think. Then I take the lighter out and start flicking it. I don't know how many times I flicked it, but I flicked it a lot before someone came and caught me. They said something about setting the chair on fire, but I don't know about that. I don't care if you believe me. But I'm glad I don't have to go back there. I bet nobody ever locked you in a little room with nothing to do."

Doug and I looked at one another. Mark jumped up and was gone in a heartbeat. Neither of us tried to pursue him. We just kept looking at one another, stunned by our realization of what the experience must have been like for Mark.

"He must have been desperate. A child like Mark who can't stand to be confined in any way. Can you imagine the panic he must have felt to know he couldn't leave, couldn't move, couldn't do anything? What they did was wrong! I'm not sure I would want to send him back there even if we could. Who the hell are these so called experts that would put a hyper-active, emotionally disturbed child in a situation like that?" I asked Doug.

My anger had not abated by the next day. As I dressed for the exit interview, I kept thinking about what Mark had said. I would confront them about their actions and explain to them the consequences of such actions on children like Mark. I didn't think it would change their minds, but maybe it would make them think twice before they did this to another child. If they were willing, maybe they could learn something from a parent this time, a parent who had dealt with the problems of this disability twenty-four hours a day, every day for twelve years.

The moment Doug, Gail Everett and I walked into the director's office I knew this interview would not go well. The faces confronting us looked hostile though partially masked by professional indifference. The director began with a recitation of the offense that necessitated the termination of Mark's program with their school.

From there he and the principal, working off one another like a tag team, launched into a recitation of Mark's emotional problems. He was disrespectful, willful, stubborn, unwilling to co-operate, disruptive in the halls and in the classroom. He refused to conform to the rules governing the Crisis Center, the lunchroom, the school bus, the gym and the classroom. He forgot his books, his homework papers. He even forgot what page he was supposed to be on during reading lessons. He rarely completed his assignments, never completed his modification goals and had not earned enough tokens in a half-year to shop once at the school store. In short, he had failed to show any progress either academically or behaviorally and now, his behavior in their opinion, constituted a menace to the students, the teachers and himself. The director finished his recitation with a flurry of unrelated complaints and the suggestion that Mark might be better off on a farm. Not a specific farm, but some farm, some place.

I waited quietly, listening to the fault being heaped on my son. I knew how upsetting, how frustrating he could be, but to listen to the complaints of professionals who were supposedly running a school for emotionally disturbed children unbottled the anger in me and I waited my turn to speak. When the intellectually disguised name calling came to a halt, I nodded to each of those assembled.

"It has been very enlightening listening to each of you explain the reasons why Mark was sent here in the first place. You knew his past history before you accepted him in your school and you assured me that you would be able to help Mark. I believed you and I put my faith in your skill and knowledge. A year and a half later, those same behaviors that you were supposed to address are now being used as an excuse for terminating his program here. As far as I can see you have done nothing to help my son and may actually have done him damage. Where does it say that the proper treatment for a neurologically impaired, emotionally disturbed child with attention deficit hyperactivity disorder is to lock him up in an isolation room? Is this how far our enlightened education has brought us? What you allegedly did was no different than the way they used to treat the emotionally disturbed a hundred years ago. Lock them in an attic room so they don't bother other people. If I had known this was your answer to my son's problems, I never would have let him come here.

Mark claims that he didn't set that chair on fire and I believe him. He is a difficult child, but not self-destructive, nor, as he said, stupid enough to light a fire in a locked room. I believe that charge was just an excuse to rid yourselves of a problem. Mark was an experiment that failed. Now it's time to dump him. Mark may have failed to conform to your rules, but you failed as educators. And now all you can suggest is that he be put on some farm somewhere. Well, that doesn't help me and it doesn't help my son."

I was trembling by the time I sat back down. The faces before me were now carved in stone. They had given their opinion. I had given mine. I wasn't sorry. My son was once again without a school, without a hope of gaining the skills he needed to live a productive life, and I was without a clue how to help him. I left the Calais School in pain, but with the uplifting feeling that I had spoken a truth that needed to be told.

My next meeting was with the director of the Department of Special Services for the Clifton School System. I had done a little research before the meeting and went equipped with the ammunition I needed to see to it that at least a reprimand be given to the Calais School. But more than that I needed to find out what our options were. Mark was fourteen, functionally illiterate, emotionally disturbed and he needed someplace to go where he could be educated and taught the skills he needed to make a life for himself. Doug and I would not always be here to take care of him and Cheryl, who had graduated from Nutley High School last year, had the right to her own life. I would not place the burden of responsibility on her.

Despite all Mark's problems, his I.Q of 75 was high enough so that he could learn. I had read that individuals with an IQ of 65 were considered educable. Somewhere there had to be someone who could teach my son as well as reach him before it was too late. He was already beginning to view school as a place, not to learn, but to be shamed, bullied and punished. If this continued, he would turn off to education completely and so end his chances for an independent life.

He listened to my complaints with patience. I presented the specific rights the Calais School had violated under the NJ Administrative Code and told him how angry I was at the way they had treated my son. I was asked if I wanted to try to have Mark reinstated. I didn't think it was a good idea, but I did want a letter sent stating the violations so that no other child and their parents would have to be subjected to the anguish that we had suffered. I was promised that the letter would be written and that the process of finding Mark a new school would begin immediately. I left Gail Everett's number and asked that the staff work with her to provide a comprehensive program for Mark.

A few days later, I received a copy of the letter sent to the Director of the Calais School.

Dear Sir;

I want you to know that we appreciate the fine help that you have given us during the past years. Our children have benefited greatly from the educational programs at the Calais School. However, your recent exclusion of [Mark Graham] leaves us in quite a predicament. His mother has declared that you have violated her rights under NJ Administrative Code 6:28-2.3 which speaks of adequate parental notice of change in educational programming. She also quotes NJ Administrative Code 6:28-7.5 which talks about termination of a pupil in an educational program. I believe during my last conference with her this anger had been diminished. However, I would like you to know in the future that we should be more careful when terminating a youngster from your educational program.

Not as strong an acknowledgment as I would have liked, but at least I felt that I had received a tacit agreement that things at Calais were not handled as they should have been. The haste with which they had terminated Mark's schooling in violation of the Administrative Code was a clear indication to me that, in Mark's case, they were unable to perform the job they had claimed they were expert at performing and did not want Mark as a constant reminder of this. I now needed to find another school for him.

The Christmas holidays crept up as I dealt with Mark's daily need for structure. I thought the cold weather would keep him closer to the house, but there were still nights when he stayed out so late I called the police to locate him. I had agreed to have him home schooled for a few hours a day until after the Christmas break because I understood that the search for schools was difficult during this time. I was delighted when I received a call that an interview had been set up for Mark at the Palisades Learning Center in Paramus. I ran to Special Services the same day to pick up the necessary paperwork and a student-parent handbook that I poured over later that night. Immediately I liked what I read.

The handbook began with a message to the parents detailing their rights and the rights of their handicapped children to a free and appropriate education under the Education for All Handicapped Children Act PL94-142. The writer of the handbook made a special point of the fact that the law held educators accountable for their deeds and that the child and parents were guaranteed their rights of due process.

Not only would Mark receive an appropriately geared academic program, he would also be taught socialization skills, vocational skills and would receive on the spot counseling if necessary. The curriculum was based on the development and mastery of four areas, the academic program, the behavior management program, the counseling program and the student enrichment activities. I especially approved of the student enrichment activities where the children volunteered their time to participate in such worthwhile community projects as the Salvation Army, the New Jersey Blood Bank and Project U.S.E. I hoped that when Mark saw how difficult the lives of others could be, he would learn to appreciate what he had.

On the morning of the interview, I made sure Mark was up early and that he showered and dressed neatly. If I did not remind him, Mark still did not remember to wash or to brush his teeth and often he left the house without eating. I wanted desperately to impress on him the necessity of making a good impression. During the ride to Paramus, I reminded him that he had been in seven schools already and that Palisades was one of the last schools willing to even grant us an interview.

"Get off my back, Mom. All you ever do is nag. I told you I'm sick of it. I don't give a shit about this school so just shut-up," he said, furious with me for making him go to yet another school.

I shut up. The last thing I wanted was for him to be in a towering rage when he walked into the principal's office. Who was I fooling anyway? All the talk in the world was not going to make Mark understand that he needed to have certain skills to make it in this world. His experiences running away had taught him only one thing. That he could survive as a homeless person, sleeping in basements, stealing food when he was hungry. It did not yet teach him that the world was cruel to those without money or power. I bombarded the heavens with prayers as I drove to the Palisades Learning Center.

The school was located in the roomy basement of a large synagogue. The walls were decorated with the children's artwork, some of it quite good I noticed, and there were many rooms opening off the central hall. I glimpsed through one of the windows a grassy courtyard where several of the students were smoking under the watchful eye of an adult. I didn't need to point this out to Mark. He had noticed it immediately and his sullen expression lightened a little.

We reported to the office and were greeted warmly by Mr. Felloes, the principal. When he shook hands with Mark, I noticed his manner was friendly and respectful, without the slightest hint of condescension. Over the years, I had become sensitized to the way people treated my son. Mark had no obvious handicap. He was an attractive boy, underweight, but well-built with sandy blond hair and bright blue eyes. He did not attract stares like children who were physically disabled, but those who knew him and his history treated him differently than they did other boys his age. Family and friends often felt they had the right to lecture him or reprimand him for his behavior; educators and professionals treated him like a troublesome client that needed to be dealt with; boys targeted him for bullying. Rarely was Mark treated with the respect he deserved on the basis of his humanity. I liked Mr. Felloes at once.

He and I spoke about Mark's past difficulties in school and at home, a conversation in which Mark did not participate, but looked off vaguely into space or fidgeted in his chair. I caught Mr. Felloes watching him now and then as he explained clearly his approach to education, the philosophy of his school and what I could expect from the program. I liked everything I heard, especially the student discipline policies. Distressed students had immediate access to counseling and, if the problem could not be solved in that way, the student might be suspended, but only after an investigation had taken place and the student given the opportunity to respond to the allegations.

"Do you understand what is expected of you, Mark?" Mr. Felloes asked, addressing Mark directly.

"Yeah. Can I smoke here?" he asked.

"With written permission from your parents, you will be allowed to smoke at certain times and only in the areas approved for smoking.

You can't smoke in the classrooms. Do you smoke when you're out fishing? I bet you love to fish."

Mark stopped fidgeting and looked at Mr. Felloes for this first time since we had arrived. A smile caught his mouth unawares and he leaned forward in his seat. "How'd you know that?" he said.

"I could tell just from looking at you. I bet you love animals, too."

I sat back and said nothing, watching with wonder the instant bond that formed between my son and the principal of his new school. Mr. Felloes had unerringly found the way to Mark's healthy side and, for the next fifteen minutes, I listened to my son speak knowledgeably about a subject he loved. When Mr. Felloes skillfully brought the conversation to a close, Mark was still smiling. He talked about animals all the way home and how great it was that Mr. Felloes liked fishing as much as he did. I was not surprised when a few days later, I received notification that Mark would begin at the Palisades Learning Center at the start of the spring semester

.

Chapter Twenty-Two

Doug and I attended parent support group conferences at Palisades Learning Center every other week. We discussed strategies for problem solving and I learned I was not alone in my fears and frustrations over my son. So many of the other parents experienced similar difficulties and feelings. Sharing ideas and working towards solutions fired my flagging hopes and I believed once again that we could bring Mark through the worst of his troubles.

Doug and I had worked together with the teachers and staff and had developed an Individual Educational Plan geared specifically towards Mark's academic and behavioral problems. He was placed in a highly structured environment in which he was given one-on-one instruction as often as possible. His IEP made it clear that he needed structure and close supervision as well as a task orientation that would give him the chance to earn rewards and privileges on a regular basis. His first quarterly report was the best he had yet attained throughout his years of schooling. His teachers were pleased with his progress and reported that his behavior in class and on the school grounds was fine. His progress report actually stated that "Mark has made extremely positive gains, especially in the affective domain. His behavior is much improved. He has shown an ability to stay on task."

I read the report twice just to make sure I wasn't dreaming, then hugged the paper to my chest and danced around the kitchen. When Mark came in, I hugged him and showed him the report. He smiled at my enthusiasm and sat down at the table, watching as I prepared dinner. I felt as if I was living in an old fantasy, the one where we were a "Leave It To Beaver" family and life followed some ordered plan orchestrated to make everything work out fine in the end. Here I was chatting with my son while preparing meat loaf, the kitchen cheery with spring sunlight and the birds chirping outdoors. Please God, let it remain this way forever, I prayed. Let this school be the answer to our troubles. I know Mark will never be a scholar, but please allow the teachers in this school to give him the skills he needs to live a good life.

My prayers were immediately answered when, at supper, Mark announced that he had found a job. Doug and I looked at one another and I knew he was thinking that this was too good to be true. I jumped in before he said something that Mark might take wrong.

"Where's your job?" I asked.

"Franklin Pizza in Nutley. I used to hang out there sometimes and the guy who owns it asked me if I wanted to clean up. You know, wash the floors and wipe up the counters and stuff. He's going to pay me, too. I got to be there after school and on week-ends."

I kicked Doug under the table. He threw me an ouch look, but he did congratulate Mark and so did Cheryl. I felt like jumping up and hugging him again. I reached out to pat his hand when I noticed he was wearing a heavy silver chain bracelet on his wrist.

"Where did you get the bracelet?" I asked.

"All the guys at school wear them. You should see some of them. They've got so many chains you wouldn't believe it."

"But where did you get the one you're wearing?"

"I bought it off one of the kids at school. I can buy more when I get paid from my job."

"Where did you get the money to pay for it?"

A defiant look crept across his features. "I borrowed it from one of the kids. All right?"

I didn't want to question him further and spoil the good mood we were all in so I filed it in the back of my mind to bring up at the next support group session.

From the group sessions I had learned that many of the students at Palisades Learning Center were street-wise, an adaptation to the poverty of their living conditions. Mark was beginning to emulate their speech patterns and personal presentation. The way he held himself, his gestures and the swaggering way he walked reflected this influence. Since his grades were still improving and his behavior holding steady I did not want to make an issue of it, but I was uncomfortable with the changes.

Over the next few weeks these changes became more noticeable. Mark now wore a denim jacket with the sleeves ripped out and a Native American design on the back. He refused to cut his hair and it hung in dirty strings from beneath a backwards baseball cap. A collection of heavy chains, sometimes as many as eight, hung from around his neck and he talked about having his ear pierced so he could wear studs. His language was tough, peppered with street talk, but he wasn't acting out in the old ways and he hadn't run away since he started Palisades.

When I brought up the street swagger in the parenting group, we agreed that, although we did not approve of our sons acting like this, it was better than having them engaging in destructive behaviors. I knew Mark was trying to belong, to be one of the guys. He would do anything to make friends. So far that did not include anything criminal, but I was concerned.

One night when Doug came home late from work, I was waiting for him in the family room. When I got up to greet him he gave me one of those "oh, no what now" looks. I smiled.

"I have a great idea," I said.

He groaned in mock protest and I playfully hit him on the arm. He took off his jacket, poured himself a cup of coffee and sat down next to me on the sofa. I reached over and, with the remote, shut off the television.

"So what's the great idea?" he asked.

"Let's go away together. Just the two of us. Mark's holding his own for now and Cheryl's old enough to take care of herself. My Mom could stay here for a few days and we could get away. What do you think? We've certainly earned a vacation."

"You're really excited about this, aren't you?" he said.

"I am. We haven't had this chance for a long time and who knows if we will have another one soon. Let's take it while we can."

I looked up at him, unable to contain my excitement. He laughed. "You look like a kid at an amusement park. And it's good to see you like that. I'll do what I can about work. Any place special you want to go?"

"No, just anywhere we can be alone together and have some fun. I'll get travel brochures and when the kids are asleep we can go over them."

By the end of April, we had decided to go to Mexico. Doug was only able to take a week off from work so we booked a six day tour at the travel agency for the last week in April. My mom agreed to stay at our house and look after things. I had assured her, truthfully, that Mark was doing well both in school and at the pizzeria. I left her his schedule and a list of numbers including our hotel room if there was an emergency. Try not to call, I shouted out the open window as we pulled away from the house.

She didn't call, but I did. After five wonderful days away I phoned home to let them know our arrival time. My mother's voice was strained. I asked her what was wrong, but she wouldn't tell me. Just that we'd discuss it when we got home.

"Is Mark all right?" I asked.

"He's fine and so is Cheryl. Enjoy the rest of your vacation. There's nothing you can do now, anyway."

It didn't sound good, but as long as the kids were healthy I wasn't going to let whatever it was ruin the wonderful time I was having. Doug loved touring and we visited many attractions and discovered Mexico's historical treasures. The beautiful hotels and sight-seeing trips refreshed my tired spirit and the fun of eating delicious foods in four star restaurants lulled me into a sense of well-being I felt reluctant to give up.

"Be prepared," I told Doug as we wandered for a stroll. "Something happened at home. My mother won't speak about it on the phone, but it doesn't sound good."

"Why don't we stay here?" Doug said. "No more work, no more kids. I'll buy a boat and we can cruise around for a while."

"I wish, but think of my poor Mom. We'd be cutting her life short by twenty years."

We flew home the following day. Doug had parked the car in Newark Airport's long term parking so we didn't have to bother anyone to pick us up. We had bought souvenirs for everyone and, despite a slightly uneasy feeling about what awaited us, we were both in a relaxed mood.

"We're home," I called as I pushed open the side door. Mom and Dad came from the kitchen to help us with our bags. I gave them both a hug and a kiss.

"So how's everything?" I asked. "The house looks wonderful. It's so nice not to come home to a mess. Where are the kids?"

"Mark's out wandering the neighborhood as usual and Cheryl went to pick up some groceries. She should be back soon and Mark..." She shrugged her shoulders.

Doug and my Dad brought the suitcases upstairs. My Mom made a fresh pot of coffee and after she had poured Doug and Dad a cup and given me my hot tea, she gestured us all to the table. "Bad news is best gotten over," she said, "so I'll just get it over with. We had an incident with the police while you were gone and, of course, it involved Mark. You know my habit of always making sure everything is locked up and the kids are in their rooms before I go to sleep. Mark was in his room and so was Cheryl when I finished watching the late movie. I checked all the windows and doors. This was Thursday night and I set the alarm to make sure Mark had plenty of time to get ready before the school bus came.

When I woke up the next morning I had a feeling something was wrong. The alarm had not gone off and the clock read 5:30, but it didn't feel like five thirty. The sun was up and the birds were singing outside the window. I stayed in bed until six, then got up to put on the coffee and call the kids. Mark was not in his room although his bed was made. My first thought was how nice it was of him to do that and that he was really improving. I knocked on the bathroom door and Cheryl answered. I called Mark again. No answer. A thorough search of the house did not turn him up, but the strange thing was that all the doors and the windows were still locked. How could he have gotten out?

Cheryl came downstairs dressed and ready for work. I told her Mark was missing and she offered to go look for him before she had to leave. It's only seven o'clock, I told her. You don't have to leave for another hour. She looked at her watch. "No, it's almost eight," she said. "I'll ride around for fifteen minutes, then I have to go." The school bus came and went. No Mark. I had called your father and asked him to look in Nutley in case Mark went there, but he didn't see him either. Dad went to work and I paced the floor, wondering where Mark was and how long he had been gone. Obviously, he had turned back my clock some time during the night or early morning so I wouldn't wake up too soon and discover him missing.

Shortly after noon, I looked out the door and saw a police car pull up. The officer told me Mark had been found in Belleville, a neighboring town, racing a motorbike against cars on the highway and having himself a heck of a good time.

"But Nana," he said to me. "I obeyed all the rules." I took the officer aside and explained Mark's condition to him and how he didn't understand that he was doing anything wrong. He let Mark off with a stern warning but, Corraine, I didn't know he had lied to the police officer. He told him he was sixteen and that the bike was his when really he had taken it without permission from your neighbor, Mr. DeVito, four doors down. They were very understanding. I guess they know about Mark and they didn't want to press charges. They talked to Mark. I talked to Mark. But we couldn't make him see that he had done something wrong. He says he only borrowed the bike and that he obeyed all the traffic laws. Maybe you'll have better luck getting through to him."

"We'll both talk to him for all the good it will do. If we hammer it into him enough, he'll eventually get the message. But will he be able to apply it to the next situation that comes up. No! If he wants to do something, he'll do it the minute the impulse strikes him."

"But he's older now," my Dad said. "The impulses are more dangerous. What if he decides to steal a car and hurts someone with it or he hurts himself?"

Doug looked puzzled. "I know this is off the point, but how did he get out of the house if all the windows and doors were still locked?"

"I couldn't figure that out at first either," my mother said. "Then I remembered you left your house keys on the dresser in case I needed them. When he turned the alarm clock back, he picked up the keys and relocked the doors after he left. They were in his pants pockets when he came home with the police."

Mark came back around dinner time. Doug and I took turns telling him that taking someone else's property was a crime and that he could go to juvenile detention if he ever did it again. After a half hour of repeating the same thing over and over, he stopped saying that he had just borrowed it, but I still wasn't satisfied that he understood that he had done something wrong and that he would not do it again. I made him apologize to Mr. DeVito and the next day I set up an appointment with Jed Cruise, a psychologist the school had recommended as having been successful in helping some of their other students recognize the difference between right and wrong. Mark had been in counseling almost his entire life and no one yet had succeeded in this task, but I was willing to give it another try. Jed Cruise had a proven track record with adolescents. Maybe he could succeed where others had failed.

As the late May days eased into the warmth of summer, Mark's running became chronic. Doug, Cheryl and I would go looking for him, but he was older and more adept at hiding from us. The police were no more successful than we were at finding him until the morning Mark was once again brought home in a squad car. A complaint had been sworn out against him for criminal trespass and intent to commit bodily harm.

When the police officer left, I grabbed Mark by the front of his shirt and threw him onto the couch. The adrenaline pumped and I knew that if I wasn't careful I could hurt him this time. As I tried to calm down, my thoughts ran back to my childhood. Never in all the time I was growing up had I or any member of my family been involved with the police and the courts. The thought of being drawn into the whole sordid business frightened me and I didn't want to think of the implications for Mark if he continued in this way. I looked down at him in his black leather vest and his unwashed hair and his load of silver chains, a dog collar around his neck and I wanted to shake him until his teeth rattled. Instead, I paced the floor until I was able to think rationally. When I had calmed down enough to speak I said with what I thought was admirable calm, "Please tell me what happened."

"Why should I?" Mark asked, his voice a mixture of defiance and defeat. "You won't believe me so why waste my breath."

"I'll believe you if you tell the truth. I can usually tell when you're lying."

"Yeah, how?"

"Never mind. Just tell me what happened."

"He threw me out," Mark said. "That made me mad. I wanted to get back at him for throwing me out."

I shook my head. "I have no idea what you are talking about. Please start from the beginning."

"That guy, Mr. F, let me come over sometimes. He was pretty cool. I guess he thought I was homeless or something. I never told him about you. He had all this neat stuff in the backyard he let me play with. But then, all of a sudden, I didn't do nothing, he threw me out and said I couldn't come no more. I didn't think he meant it so I stood there. I didn't do nothing bad. I just stood there. He said if I didn't go he would call the police. I asked him why, but he kept yelling. I went back the next day. I threw some stones and some sticks from on top of the hill. He came out again when I was throwing the sticks, but I wasn't throwing them at him. He said I was, but I wasn't. Honest."

I held on to the edge of the couch and swallowed hard. "Go up to your room and don't come down until I call you. And God help you if you run away, Mark, because I won't. You leave this house tonight, you leave for good."

My hands shook so badly I could barely dial Doug's number at work. When I heard his voice, I managed to sputter out what had happened. Doug promised he would call the police station and find out what happens when a complaint is sworn out and call me back.

The phone rang ten minutes later. The complaint would be taken up by the Family Part of the Passaic County Court system if the plaintiff decided to press charges. An intake hearing would take place first, then a court date established. If Mark was found guilty of the charges, he would be considered a juvenile delinquent and could be remanded into the custody of the Juvenile Detention Shelter.

"When will we know all this?" I asked.

"We should receive a written copy of the complaint and an appointment for the intake interview within a month."

It was not until July 16th that the notification actually came. Mark was scheduled to appear for a pre-judicial conference in August. He never made it to the conference because by then he was confined to the locked ward of the adolescent psychiatric unit at St. Clare's Hospital.

Chapter Twenty-Three

Without the constant structure of the school environment and immediate access to counselors whenever he felt distressed and uncertain of the appropriateness of his actions, Mark's behavior continued to deteriorate throughout the summer. The fear that had troubled him all his life was now submerged beneath a street punk attitude. He dressed and talked like a juvenile gang member though he did not belong to any gang. The years of having been picked on and sometimes physically assaulted by other boys had made him verbally aggressive and he often talked about beating people up or cutting them with knives if they bothered him. He needed constant supervision. I applied to as many of the special education camps that had programs applicable to Mark's disabilities, but none would accept him. Some camps did not allow smoking, others would not accept children with police involvement, and still others were only for children below the age of thirteen.

"Doug, what are we going to do?" I asked late one July night when we had come back from looking for Mark. He had run away again and a search of the parks, Richfield Apartments and twenty-four hour Laundromats had failed to yield a clue. "I could quit my job and stay home, but if I did how would we pay for Mark's psychologist, the lawyer, the doctors, the medication and everything else."

"If you quit your job and stay home, would it make any difference? Do you honestly think you can handle him the way he is now?" Doug asked. "Right at this minute, he's just talking tough, but what if he decides to go after you physically?"

I shook my head. "I don't think he'd do that."

"We've had some physical confrontations in the past," Doug said.

"But you're a man. Not that I'm saying it's right, but it's not unknown for teenage boys to test their fathers that way."

Doug stood up. "I don't want to argue about this again, Corraine. He's out of control and getting worse. I want you to contact DYFS and have them look into residential placement. He needs twenty-four hour structure before he hurts someone or himself. Do you really want to wait until that happens?"

I was so confused and the constant arguments with Doug over what we should do were wearing me down so I could barely think. "I'm so afraid that sending him away will ruin him for good. I know how afraid he is of being abandoned. I don't think the terror of all those placements when he was young ever left him. If I leave him somewhere I'm afraid that will be the trigger for him to go over the edge and never recover. I don't know what to do."

"Corraine, he's not getting better only older and his behavior is becoming more dangerous. We certainly aren't helping him by allowing him to run around the streets and get into trouble. If you have a better solution, I'd like to hear it."

Mark had an appointment with Jed Cruise, his psychologist, at the end of the week. We decided that I should talk to Jed and see if he felt he was making any progress with Mark. If we could manage him through the summer, the structure provided by his school might give him a foundation to make up for his downward slide over the summer.

My interview with Jed Cruise was not encouraging.

"I'm glad you came in," he said, gesturing me to a chair in his spacious office. "I was just on the verge of calling you myself."

"That doesn't sound like good news."

"No. I wanted to give you a progress report on Mark. We have established a good rapport and I know Mark has been as honest in expressing his feeling as well as he is able to. As you know, Mark's judgment is very poor and his need to belong very strong. Coupled with his extreme impulsivity, this puts him at risk to be influenced by anyone who claims, even momentarily, to be his friend. He is also highly sensitive to anyone who he imagines is threatening him. His talk has become quite aggressive and there is a possibility that the talk may evolve into action because of his impaired judgment. As you are aware, he doesn't understand the consequences of his actions. He just acts. And even if he doesn't resort to violence himself, he may become part of a gang that does, putting him at risk for arrest and prosecution."

"Jed, I've heard all this before, many times. What I need to know is what can be done about it. Can you help him? If you can't, who can? I refuse to give up on my son. I refuse to believe there is nothing that can be done for Mark."

"I'd like to suggest something that I know may be difficult at first, but I want you to consider it. St. Clare's Hospital in Denville has an excellent adolescent psychiatric ward. I'd like Mark to go in for a thirty day stay. I think he could benefit from the therapy he would receive there, but they could also prescribe and monitor medication that might help him with his aggression. I think it's worth considering before Mark gets into serious trouble."

I walked around in a fog for the next few days, unable to reconcile my memories of the beautiful little boy I had fallen in love with at the park and the young man I was being asked to consider committing to a psychiatric ward because he might assault someone. I couldn't make the pieces fit. Mark was neither mean nor malicious. He was often generous and affectionate and always forgiving. He loved and cared for his animals with a gentle understanding I had rarely seen in others. But when he was frightened, which I now believed he was most of the time, he responded with fear tactics of his own. So far he had never really hurt anyone, but was he capable of doing so on the most primitive level. I didn't know. I only knew that I loved him. I had always loved him and had tried to do everything I could to make him feel physically safe and emotionally secure. I did my best for him and would continue to do so. I just didn't know how any more. I went to St. Andrew's church every day and lit a candle, hoping the light would illuminate the darkness of confusion I was now suffering.

Mark himself provided the answer one afternoon in late July. He walked through the door, the side of his face bruised, and his eye blackened. He was wearing his denim jacket with the sleeves ripped out and I noticed an ink tattoo colored on one arm. Around his neck he had fastened a studded dog collar and several silver chains hung onto his bare chest. His eyes were blood-shot, a large welt forming beneath the right one.

"Do you need any help cleaning up?" I asked. I had learned not to rush at him when he came home like this. It would only drive him back out of the house without the medical attention he needed.

He swaggered over to the sink, ripped off a paper towel and dabbed his face with cold water.

"Don't worry about me," he said. "I scared him good. He'll never mess with me again."

My heart leaped into my throat and I had trouble getting the words out.

"Who did you scare and how did you scare him?"

"I found this big old knife in the grass at the park. It was bitching. I sliced it right under the kids' nose and told him that if he wanted to fight, I was ready. You should have seen him run. Ha! Want to bet that kid never bothers me again."

"Did you hurt him?"

"Nah, just scared him. He's okay."

"Did anybody call the police?" I asked.

"Nah, there were no cops. I told the other kids there that if anybody said anything they'd have to deal with me. What did you think, I was going to let them run home to their mommies and tell on me? I'm not as stupid as you think I am so quit asking me questions, okay?"

"No, Mark, it's not okay. You can't go around threatening people with knives. It's wrong and you can hurt somebody that way. Or someone can hurt you. Can't you see that this is not good? You could go to jail for what you did."

He pushed his battered face a few inches from mine. "Is it right what they did to me? How come you're never on my side? Huh! Why is it you always think I'm the one who's wrong? Answer me. I want to know. Why am I always wrong?"

He was screaming in my face, his own contorted with rage. My heart hammered in my chest and I felt the sweat, hot and sticky on my forehead. I was alone in the house. If the impulse hit him to hurt me, would he? I was the closest person on earth to him, but rage could be blind and Mark had very little impulse control. I tried to calm him down.

"Mark, you know I am and always have been on your side. I want to help you, but I don't know how. Tell me what I can do to help you and I will."

He had swung away from me and I saw him grab something from the kitchen counter. Images passed through my mind with split second accuracy, the pictures vivid and clear as they flashed in my brain. Yes, I had left a small paring knife on the counter after peeling potatoes for dinner. He turned around at the same time as I jumped up from the chair.

242

"Help me!" he cried. "You don't want to help me. You just want to get rid of me. I know about the plans you and Dad have to send me away. I hear you talking. I'll hurt you before I let you do that."

I stood behind the kitchen chair, trembling, but outwardly calm. Some instinct told me not to move or to say anything. I knew from past experience that Mark's rages did not last long. He watched me, his eyes narrowed, his hand behind his back. It struck me then that he looked more like he was being attacked than that he was ready to attack. My breathing slowed a little, but I was still tensed and ready for flight. Suddenly, he wheeled around and bolted through the door. He was gone for two days before the police brought him home. Doug and I had called Jed Cruise and had him make the arrangements for Mark to be admitted to St. Clare's Hospital.

As I had predicted, Mark seemed to have forgotten about the incident with the knife and I did not mention it to him until Doug, Mark, Jed Cruise and I met at Jed's office. Jed spoke to Mark about the incident and how he needed more help than any of us were able to give him right now. I kept watching Mark's face for signs of rage, but I could see only anxiety and confusion there. Jed told him that at the hospital they would be able to discover new ways to help him. As Jed talked, I prayed silently that Mark would accept this and go to the hospital peacefully.

"How long do I have to stay there?" Mark asked.

"Only a month. For them to help you they need that long," Jed said.

"And you really think I should go? You really think they can help me stay out of trouble?" Mark looked at Jed. Doug and I kept silent, knowing that our interference would make Mark rebel.

"I really believe they can help you, Mark."

"Okay, I'll go then," he said.

I breathed a sigh of relief. I still did not know if this was the right thing to do, but if Mark was willing to try it, I would keep my reservations to myself and pray that we were being guided in the right direction. I had packed Mark's suitcase the night before and put it in the trunk ready to go. Jed Cruise called St. Clare's to alert them that we were on our way.

Doug drove. I sat in the front seat and stared out the window, concentrating on keeping myself from falling apart. For once I was thankful that Mark did not have the ability to anticipate a situation. He had never been confined before and my mind was filled with fears of what he would do once he learned he could not leave the ward for thirty days. I knew he did not fully comprehend this. He was incapable of understanding anything he did not experience and even then, he did not internalize the knowledge gained from experience.

I went through the process of filling out the admission papers in a daze, like an accident victim in mild shock. An aide took us to the adolescent unit where we had to be buzzed in through the locked door. I had a quick impression of a long corridor lined with rooms at the beginning of which was a sunny open meeting space. I caught a glimpse of several young people sitting at tables smoking and talking softly.

At the nurses' station, a small room shielded by a plastic window, we surrendered Mark's suitcase. He had to give the nurse his belt, the content of his pockets including his cigarettes and lighter and his shoes. I knew Mark was surprised and, for the first time, I saw anger flash into his face. The nurse explained that if the doctor allowed it, Mark could smoke in the public room. She signaled us to follow her and we walked down the corridor to his room. Some attempts had been made to cheer up the institutional look of the room, but because of those patients with suicidal tendencies, not many extras were allowed.

"Now what?" Mark asked the nurse.

"The doctor will be by to see you soon. He will probably want to talk to your parents first, then he will come to see you. He's with another patient now, so why don't you put your things away?" she said. "Is there anything more I can do for you?" She looked at us kindly, but with professional detachment. I wondered how many other heartbroken families she had led through the same routine.

"Do you know how long the doctor will be?" I asked. "I'd like to go down to the chapel for a few minutes if I have time."

"He should be by in less than a half hour," she said. She smiled and left us alone in a silence that grew as loud as nails scraped on a blackboard. When I could stand it no longer I said much louder than I had meant to,

"Doug, stay here with Mark. I'll be back in fifteen minutes."

I ran out of the room and called for the nurse to buzz me out. It took me a few minutes to find the hospital chapel. Mercifully, it was empty. I slid into one of the pews and covered my face with my hands. I cried aloud, the sobs shaking my body till I thought they would tear me apart. After all the hope, the hard work, the love, all the years of searching for answers and trying the solutions, here I was leaving my son in a psychiatric ward. It had actually come to this.

"Dear Mary," I prayed. "As a mother who has suffered for her son, have mercy on Mark and me. Please make this the answer to my prayers. Please give the doctors the power to heal my son."

Calmer now after my tears and my prayers, I reentered the ward just as the doctor was about to visit with Mark. He had a kindly face and his manner was natural and friendly. He shook hands with Mark and explained to him that he was one of several doctors who would be working with him, then asked Mark how he was doing.

"I changed my mind. I don't want to be here. I want to go home." Mark's hands were moving quickly, jerkily as he talked and I knew he would soon become agitated.

"Everyone feels that way when they first come. Give us a few days to see if we can't make you feel more comfortable about a lot of things. Now, if you'll excuse us, I'd like to talk to your parents for a few minutes. I'll be back in to see you as soon as we're finished."

Dr. Lowenthal led us into a small office around the corner from Mark's room. Once more we sat on the hard leather of office chairs and faced another expert who would tell us how he would try to help Mark. My mind filled with questions, but I sat quietly on the edge of my chair, my hands sweating and my heart pounding.

Dr. Lowenthal must have noticed my tense posture because he nodded sympathetically. "I can't tell you very much until I've had a chance to go over Mark's records and to talk with the boy. Usually the first few days are rather difficult and then we can begin to work with him. He will be given medication that will help with the agitation. I suggest that you wait for a day or two before you come visit. I or one of my colleagues will be better able to answer your questions then. If that's all right with you, I need to ask you some questions now."

Doug and I answered the usual questions about Mark's medical history, what medications he took, his school problems, neurological evaluations, psychiatric evaluations, previous psychological sessions and our own problems dealing with him at home. Dr. Lowenthal wrote down all the information and occasionally asked us to clarify some of the statements we made. I could have answered his questions in my sleep I had heard them so many times. I felt that some part of me had actually gone to sleep, the hopeful part, the part that had held on to the belief that Mark was going to be fine. What small measure of youthful innocence I had held to so dearly had been rendered unconscious by this last proof of life's harsh realities.

He walked us to the door of Mark's room, then went back to the nurse's station while we said our good-byes. Mark paced the room and barely answered when we told him we would see him soon. I raced down the corridor, afraid that if I did not leave immediately, I would go back and sign Mark out. Once outside, I leaned over to catch my breath, the pain in my chest so intense I thought I might faint. Doug stood beside me and patted my back. There was nothing he could say that would make me feel any better. I turned to look at the lighted windows of Mark's hospital ward and there, at one of the windows, I saw him, his arms outspread against the glass, his face twisted in an expression of anguish. Weeping, I walked away.

Three days later, we returned to St. Clare's Hospital. In the meantime, I had called DYFS and they had agreed to evaluate our request for residential placement. Doug and I had spent many hours discussing Mark's need for structure and supervision and, although our talks had been like pouring salt into an open wound, I had to acknowledge that we could no longer manage him at home.

I was anxious to see Mark. I wanted to reassure him that Doug and I would always be there for him no matter what and that if ever he needed us we would never abandon him. I brought him some cake, which was permitted so long as the pieces were cut up at home. We were not allowed to bring anything that might possibly be used as a weapon or a means of suicide. I also brought him fresh socks and underwear though I had packed plenty in his suitcase. I wanted to do something small and homey for him so that he wouldn't feel that I had left him without family or support. Cheryl wanted to come, but I asked her to wait until next time because I didn't know how Mark would react to our visit. I was afraid that he might be angry and rejecting and I did not want her to be hurt by his lashing out.

When the door to the adolescent unit buzzed open, I felt my heart begin to pound. Doug and I checked in at the nurse's station and were told that Mark was in his room. I asked if I could bring the cake and other things to him. She asked me to leave them with her for the time being. I knew she had to check through them to make sure no forbidden material was included. I appreciated her delicacy in not searching them in front of us. As she led us down the hall, she informed us that Mark's behavior had been quite aggressive and that he might become agitated if we stayed too long. I looked at Doug. His face was grim, but determined. He took my arm and we entered the room.

Mark was lying on the bed, but he jumped up when we entered. The harsh light of the barred window detailed the sunken hollow of his cheeks and reflected the mirrored blankness of his eyes. But there was nothing ephemeral about the fury that twisted his voice into a snarl.

"I want to get out of here. Right now!" he said.

I didn't know what to say. I didn't want to upset him, but I didn't want to lie to him either.

"We have to talk to the doctor first, Mark. He will know whether you are ready to come home yet."

"When you talk to him, tell him I hate it here. He can't make me stay. Only you can make me stay here and if you do I'll..."

"We have to talk to the doctor now, Mark," Doug said firmly. "We'll be back to see you later."

We waited for Dr. Lowenthal in the small office around the corner from Mark's room. I was determined this time to get answers. Mark obviously was not feeling better and I wanted to know what they planned to do to help him. We had been waiting nearly ten minutes before Dr. Lowenthal entered. He shook hands with us and took his seat behind the desk.

"I know you've already seen Mark and that you must be upset by what you've seen. Mark has been exhibiting aggressive, uncontrollable behavior. He is angry because he has to stay here and unresponsive to our attempts to help him. I have increased his Ritalin dosage and started him on medication to balance his mood and help with the agitation and aggression. But it takes time to find the proper dosage and even the best medication for his problem. Once we are able to calm him down and he becomes more cooperative, we can use therapeutic techniques to teach him to control himself."

"How long will all this take?" I asked.

"I can't give you an exact date, but he should show improvement after two weeks. A lot depends on finding the proper combination of medication and dosage."

"Does this mean he'll have to stay on some kind of drug for the rest of his life?"

"I can't answer that with any certainty. Mark has been diagnosed with Organic Personality Disorder and Atypical Impulse Control Disorder, both of which can be caused by a chemical imbalance. If we can adjust this imbalance, Mark will stabilize and his behavior improve. As I said, if we can calm him down, we can work on the other problems that are treatable by therapy like low self-esteem and low tolerance levels."

"Do you think we will be able to keep Mark at home if the medication works?" I asked.

Dr. Lowenthal shifted in his chair so that he was facing me directly. I could see the sympathy in his eyes. "I can't tell you that now. I wish I could say that everything will be solved and that the medication is a miracle, but it's not. Right now, Mark is preoccupied with a need for power and strength and sees himself as capable of doing anything in order to achieve these goals. However, although he talks like someone who is extremely aggressive, underneath it all there is a strong wish to please others and a desire to be liked and accepted. That can be something that can work in his favor as long as he wishes to please those who have his best interests at heart. In two weeks I should know more about his prognosis."

It was not until the third week of Mark's hospital stay that we began to see a marked improvement. The increase in Ritalin had had no effect on his behavior, but the withdrawal had caused severe stomach distress and an inability to sleep at night. He was now taking a new combination of medications for anxiety, aggression and insomnia.

On this visit Mark met us in the sunny public room we had glimpsed when we had brought him in that first night. He was now permitted to smoke and after he had greeted us calmly, he lit up a cigarette. We sat at a table near one of the windows and he told us how he had been out on a pass with one of the attendants and how well it had gone. His speech was slightly slurred and his eyes looked glassier than usual, but other than that, I could see little visual effect from the medication. He asked about Cheryl and about what was happening at home. His usual demands and threats were absent from the conversation and, although he was certainly more compliant, he did not seem like himself. I didn't know whether to be encouraged by that or concerned.

We met with Dr. Lowenthal because Mark was scheduled to be released August twenty first, which was only a week away. He stressed the need for strict adherence to the medication schedule and behavioral modification techniques they had been using to control Mark's impulsivity. Dr. Lowenthal had been in contact with DYFS. The director in charge of residential placements had agreed to schedule a placement review. Because of summer vacations, the review could not be held before September fourth, two weeks after Mark's release from the hospital.

"Do you think you can manage him at home for a while until a placement is found?" Dr. Lowenthal asked. I looked at Doug.

"Are you saying that even with the medication, he should still be in a school where he'll be away from home?" I asked.

He handed me a copy of a letter he had sent to DYFS. "Please read my recommendations at the bottom of the letter," he said.

Since Doug did not have a copy I read mine aloud to him.

"I have recommended continuation of psychotherapy, continuation of medication, and feel that the prognosis is still quite poor. Primarily I would recommend a highly structured, supportive residential placement. It is my concern and fear that this young man who feels it is okay to throw stones and sticks at others, and who talks about liking to beat up others, as he continues to get older and stronger may very well hurt someone if they do not understand him and in any way threaten him. He apparently does somewhat better with people who are stronger than him than those who are not. The residential setting should be set up so that he does not feel more powerful than the other people there."

All of my mothering instincts arose in protest at the tone of the letter. "No, I can't agree with this. This isn't Mark," I said. "Maybe he has verbally threatened people. Maybe he has talked tough and frightened people, but he's never hurt anyone. He's the one who gets picked on. He's the one who gets beat up. I've never seen any arrest reports on the kids who have beaten him up. I don't deny that Mark has problems, but I don't want him characterized as a potentially violent offender."

"Mark has very poor impulse control," Dr. Lowenthal said. "If he decides to act out on one of his threats, he could hurt someone. Do you want to take that chance?"

"I understand that Mark needs a kind of structure that we cannot give him at home. I have to work. So does Doug. We both know that Mark cannot be left alone, but that's because his judgment is poor and he is easily led by others into behaviors that will lead to trouble."

I let the matter drop and we went on to discuss Mark's discharge. When we went to pick Mark up a week later, he was much calmer, his judgment clearer and his talk contained none of the threats that had peppered it when we had brought him in. He was happy to see us and for a brief shining moment I dared to believe that the combination of medication and therapy might make life more manageable for us all. I no longer looked for miracles. I no longer lived in a fairy tale with a happily-ever-after ending. I had learned to live one day at a time, even one hour at a time when things were at their worst, but I still hoped for more good days, good hours, than bad.

Chapter Twenty-Four

"Did you switch my orange juice again?" Mark asked, swiveling his gaze from my mother's face to mine.

"You were sitting here watching us the whole time. How could we?" I didn't dare look at my mother.

We had played this game ever since Mark had come home from the hospital. He had been on good behavior for the past two weeks, but had balked at the medication. It made him feel strange, not like himself, he said. I was tempted to say good, but I held my tongue and developed devious ways of getting the medication into him without his knowledge. One was a version of the old shell game. I would pour the orange juice at the counter, then slip the medication into one glass and place that glass in front of someone else. Mark would sip his juice to make sure it didn't taste funny. When he was satisfied that there was nothing but orange juice in the glass I would distract him while the other person quickly switched glasses. Mark grew suspicious, but he never caught me in the act.

Mark returned to Palisades Learning Center in September, but the honeymoon period was over. Within a week, Mark was talking tough and looking like a street freak. The school had expanded and the new class to which Mark had been assigned had a higher percentage of city bred street kids. They were tough and Mark easily fell under their influence, attracted by their machismo and independence from parental supervision. Many of these kids were truly "on their own" and reacted violently to any attempts to curb their impulsivity. Mark now sported a sharply studded dog collar and a chain with a large collection of keys dangling from it. He clanked when he walked.

I decided to ignore the dog collar, but I had to know where he had gotten the keys and what they were for. One evening, after I had slipped his medication into his drink and he had swallowed it, I asked.

"Mark. Where did all those keys come from?"

"Around."

"Where around?"

"Places."

I took a deep breath and cleared some of the dishes from the table. He wasn't going to tell me. Sometimes he wouldn't tell me because he thought I was meddling in his business. Sometimes he wouldn't tell me because he knew I wouldn't like what he had done. Questions of right or wrong never entered his mind, but he did know that there would be an episode of some kind if I didn't like what he did.

"What are the keys for?" I thought a different approach might elicit more of a response.

"Nuthin'. They're just cool. That's all." He was getting restless. I knew he would bolt in a few minutes, but I had to know who the keys belonged to.

"Did you steal them?"

He jumped up and raced for the door. "Yeah! I stole them," he shouted. "You happy now."

He didn't come home that night or the next. I called his school and Mr. Felloes, the principal, promised he would ask Mark's classmates, but no one knew where he was. Doug and I searched the parks and the apartments and the all night Laundromats with their odd collection of night owls, but no Mark.

"I wish I could just give up," I said when we parked the car for the last time that night and made our weary way up the walk to the side door. "There are parents who let their teenage sons roam around all night and think nothing of it. So what if they get beat up, so what if they're on drugs, so what if they get some girl pregnant and abandon her. I bet those parents don't lose sleep. Why do we care so much?"

"Because if we all felt the way those parents did, we'd have a society of sociopaths. Morals and values are not just for good times when it takes no effort to practice them, but for the times when they become the foundation that keeps us from sinking into despair and degradation. We have to keep caring."

I looked at Doug, surprised. "Have I told you recently how much I appreciate and rely on your support?" I said.

"You don't have to though it's nice to hear once in a while," he said. Arm in arm, we walked into the quiet house. I thought about Dave and our many discussions about wanting a family, but it was always Doug who was there for me and the children when we needed him.

Doug was at work when the police car pulled up to the house the next day. I had left work an hour early and had just changed into an old T-shirt, shorts and sneakers. I planned to get in a few hours searching before I started dinner. I heard the police radio blaring and I ran to the front door in time to see Mark step out from the back of the vehicle. He was filthy, his hair a stringy mess and his clothes covered with dirt to which bits of twigs and leaves were stuck. My first thought was that he looked like one of the homeless people you see sleeping on park benches. I kept a spotless, beautiful home and my son chose to sleep on the ground. I didn't know a heart could break so many times and in so many different ways.

"What did he do now?" I asked. I tried to smile, to show the officer that he was a kid not a criminal, but my face was stiff and my voice had the texture of sandpaper.

"Is this young man your son?" the officer asked. He was middle-aged, paunchy, with a complexion that was ruddy and a nose that was decidedly red. I wondered if his red nose came from being out in the sun too long or from drinking too much. I knew I had never seen him before.

"Yes Officer, he certainly is."

"Identification, please."

I showed him my driver's license, Mark's social security card, and several pictures of Mark and me together. He seemed satisfied.

"Did you file a missing person's report on Mark Graham?"

"I did. Can you tell me where he was found?"

He gave me a hard stare. For a moment, I wanted to defend myself, to tell him I was a caring mother, that I hadn't abandoned my child to the streets. I reined myself in. I had committed no crime. I had no need to tell this stranger anything.

"Do you know anything about this?" He reached into a bag he was carrying and pulled out a medium sized metal object.

My heart went into overdrive, the blood surging through my head so fast I couldn't think above the roar. I managed to force a few words through my frozen lips.

"Did he ...did he...?"

"It's a toy gun, ma'am," the officer said. "Your son was waving it around, threatening other youths with it. We could arrest him for disturbing the peace, but I'll let him off with a warning if you can guarantee he'll stay at home under your supervision. He's been sleeping in an equipment bin in the park where we picked him up."

"Has a complaint been filed?" I asked.

"Not at the present time."

"Is there anything else I need to do, Officer?"

He gave me a sour look. "Just keep the kid off the streets," he said. I stood on the front stoop and watched as he stepped into the police car and drove away. Front doors were open up and down the block and I could see the shadows of my neighbors as they watched the patrol car turn the corner. I was past being embarrassed and well into not caring what anyone thought. My childhood had been so quiet, so sheltered. My Uncle Joe was a Newark police officer and I remembered the stories he told of high speed chases and shoot-outs in dark alleys. That's what police did. They didn't come to good people's homes. They didn't come to my home. Not once in all the time I was growing up. I felt like Alice after she had fallen down the rabbit hole. Whose life was I living now? Whose reality had I bumped into? Certainly not my own. I closed my front door and called Jed Cruise. We set up an emergency appointment for the next day.

Mark was readmitted to St. Claire's Hospital on September thirtieth, a little over a month after he had been discharged. Never in my wildest dreams had I imagined we would have to return there. When we had left the locked doors of 1B, I'd been ready to put this experience behind us forever. Now, after a month, we were back, but with a difference. Last time Mark had been cooperative. This time he was angry. He blamed Doug and me for being too strict with him. He had no remorse and refused to take any responsibility for running away or for frightening his parents or the children he'd threatened with the gun. He said it was "no big deal." He did not want to stay and had to be restrained when it was time for us to go. We learned that on several occasions during the course of his stay he punched the walls so hard it was necessary to X-ray his hands. No fractures, but he had to be sent to a "quiet room" to calm down until his behavior was back under control.

"I'm not doing this again," I said to Doug one evening when we were returning to the hospital. "You know and I know that Mark needs twenty-four hour supervision. Temporary stays in the hospital are fine for the short term, but it's clear that as soon as he gets out, medication or no medication, he's going to go right back to his old ways. He can't help himself. He's handicapped and he needs help. I'm going to make sure he gets it this time. I don't care what it takes."

Doug looked at me, alerted by a new tone in my voice. "Isn't that what we've been trying to do all this time?"

"Yes and No," I said. "All this time we've been relying on experts to help us - psychologists, social workers, educators, doctors, and nothing's come of any of it. I'm not blaming anyone. Some of them have been good people, others clearly incompetent, others just over burdened by the bureaucracy of the system. Now I'm going to do what I need to do for my son. This experience has taught me that nothing is going to get done for Mark unless I make sure it's done."

Over the next few weeks I demanded that a residential placement hearing be held for Mark at DYFS and called everyone who needed to send in reports or who needed to testify that Mark required residential placement. I argued against placing Mark in an after school day program with the same street wise clientele with whom he was associating in school. I knew this was not the answer to his problems but another "finger in the dike" method of refusing residential placement. The cost to the school district and to DYFS for placing a child in residential treatment was high. I understood that and I knew there would be resistance, but I no longer cared. I didn't need to please anyone in a position of authority any longer. I had been raised to be a lady, polite, cooperative, unassertive, people pleasing. But none of that mattered any longer. They could say what they wanted about me, they could fight with every weapon they had. I would fight back. Mark was going to get the help he needed at last.

The Division of Youth and Family Services Residential Review Committee met in September. Dr. Lowenthal, Jed Cruise and Louise Rosenberg from St. Clare's Hospital and Gail Everett, the Director of Residential Placement, and several others from DYFS attended. I was not permitted to sit in on the committee, but was guaranteed a copy of the minutes which I awaited eagerly and had to call several times to obtain. As I had suspected, DYFS was resistant to the idea

255

of residential placement, but had agreed to investigate possibilities on the recommendation of Dr. Lowenthal, and Jed Cruise.

I handed Doug a copy of the minutes the same evening I received them. "Guess who's the bad guy in all this according to our friends at DYFS," I said. I poured him a cup of coffee and he sat at the table, the five page document spread out before him. He perused the pages, his frown deepening with each paragraph. "I'm not even mentioned. This report makes it appear as if Mark has no father."

"And I'm presented as the one who is obstructing Mark's chances of improvement." I snatched away the minutes and searched for the paragraphs I wanted. "Did you read this one? *Ms. Everett stated that she attempted to get Mark involved with the Barnert Day School, but Mark's mother did not like the clientele. Ms. Everett stated that she feels that the mother will request a service, but once the service is found, the mother will often reject it for various reasons. Usually the service does not meet up to her expectations.* Because I do not want my son in an environment that had already proven detrimental to him, I'm being labeled as uncooperative. They fail to mention altogether that Barnert refused to accept him. You know damn well I never refused any services offered, if any were offered. And listen to this one." I ruffled through the pages again. *The administrator who is in charge of residential placements states, that since the mother did not want the Barnert Program, she might not want the residential placement for the same reason. It was a concern that after work is done to try and place the child in a residential facility, Mark's mother might say she does not want this assignment.* Isn't that a hoot? Who's been requesting this placement?"

"I don't blame you for being angry, Corraine, but Dr. Lowenthal and Jed Cruise certainly made it clear that residential placement was needed and their testimony prevailed over the financial concerns of the Division of Youth and Family Services." Doug took back the minutes and flipped to the last page. "It says here, it will take approximately 3 months to find a residential placement for Mark. He can only stay in St. Clare's for a month. What do we do in the meantime? I don't think Mark will stay here now. He's angry with us. I can almost guarantee he'll run away as soon as he's discharged."

Mark ran away, but he did not wait until he was discharged from St. Clare's Hospital. He had been in the hospital several weeks and with the help of medication he had calmed down to the point where he was able to participate in group discussions and walk on the grounds with attendants. DYFS had set up an interview with The Burlington Children's Home in Mt. Holly, a town in southern New Jersey. The staff at St. Clare's felt that he was ready to handle the interview. I had brought him fresh clothes the previous day and he was washed, dressed and ready to go. I signed him out with permission and Doug and I started the drive to South Jersey.

As we neared the exit for Mt. Holly, I felt my heart start its nervous fluttering. I was certain that residential placement was right for Mark. He needed the supervision and the security of knowing that someone was always there when he became confused or frightened. I still wished I could be the one to provide that for him, but I was no longer so idealistic. I needed to work to provide the extra income for Mark's medical, psychiatric, educational and court costs. But leaving him somewhere he did not want to be with people he did not know still made my hands sweat and my heart pound.

As we pulled up to the building, my first impression was not reassuring. "Looks like something out of Oliver Twist," I said to Doug under my breath. The large building stood square and aloof, dreary even in the bright light of the warm October afternoon. Fall's bright bouquet of yellow, orange and red that we had seen lining the roads on the way down was absent here, the trees surrounding the structure tall and dark. The Burlington Children's Home looked to me like an old-fashioned orphanage.

I glanced at Mark as we stepped from the car. He was smoking a cigarette and looking up at the blank windows. I didn't know what to say to him. His expression was closed and for once, he looked much older than his fifteen years. He ground out his cigarette on the gravel of the driveway and for the first time he looked at me.

"Ready?" I asked. I did not bother to smile.

"Does it matter?" Without waiting for my answer he walked toward the front door. I grabbed Doug's arm and we followed him into the building. Inside, some attempt had been made to brighten up the place, but the patterned curtains and the few paintings on the walls could not disguise that this was an institution, not a home. An aide brought us to the office of the director, who then showed us around the building from the dormitory rooms where the boys slept to the classrooms, large recreation area, bathrooms and outside to the playing fields. Everything was neat and tidy and the children were quiet and well behaved. Discipline was certainly maintained. It had been arranged that Mark would stay there overnight so he could get a feel for the place. I was struggling to reserve judgment though all I could think about was an old black and white movie I had seen of Dickens' Oliver Twist, especially the scene where he asks if he might have some more food.

"Do they get plenty to eat?" I blurted out.

The director looked at me oddly. "We've never had any complaints," he said.

I nodded, my face aflame. He then explained, a little slower than usual, I'm sure, about the educational and behavioral programs they maintained there. Same old stuff. After nine schools, I had become quite an expert in educational methodology and behavior modification techniques. I hid my skepticism. I was less concerned with Mark's reading and math skills than I was with his adjustment to a full-time institutional atmosphere. When there was no more left to say, we were shown the room where Mark would be sleeping that night.

"If there are any further questions, please call us," the director offered. "We'll be happy to answer any concerns you might have. Now I think we'll settle Mark in for the evening."

We were clearly, but politely, being asked to leave. Mark had said very little during the tour of the place and he did not look at us now. I knew he was angry, but I hoped that in time he would understand that Doug and I were doing what we thought best for him. I hoped, but I didn't believe he would actually see it that way. We said our good-byes and arranged to pick Mark up at 5:00 the following afternoon. According to the rules at St. Clare's, Mark had to be back in the ward by midnight the following night or he would be considered checked out and not be allowed back in the program.

All night I walked the floor, battling with myself. I don't know what I had expected, but Burlington Children's Home wasn't it. I hadn't formed an exact picture in my mind of what I thought the residence would look like, but now I realized that I had imagined it more like an estate with a large home, some outbuildings and plenty of lawn for the children to play on and perhaps, gardens to care for.

The dreary brick building with the dark woods running up to the back fence didn't match the picture in my mind. I turned on all the lights in my home and walked around the rooms. I looked at the mementos I had collected over the years, the patterned curtains I had selected with such care, the thick muted carpets, the comforting tweed and leather furniture in the family room. Why couldn't my son be happy here? Why did he have to be sent to some institution miles away? If they accepted him, what would I do? If I refused, DYFS would say I was uncooperative and refuse to help me. If I accepted, Mark would be sent to an institution where I was convinced he would never be happy.

Once again, Mark solved the problem his own way. I had gone to work in the morning, but had left early to prepare for the long drive to Mt. Holly. My mother and I were going to pick him up and take him back to St. Claire's. Doug was working and we decided that it wasn't worth it for him to take the day off. As I was changing into more casual clothes, the phone rang. I picked it up, ready to tell whoever it was to call back when an unfamiliar male voice asked, "Mrs. Conaway?"

"Speaking," I said, already feeling my heart start to race.

"Mrs. Conaway. This is the director of the Burlington Children's Home. I'm afraid Mark has run off and we are unable to locate him. I have called the police and they've begun a search. We're doing all that we can, but I suggest you and your husband come down right away. He may be frightened of the police and not willing to cooperate with them."

"What happened?" I asked.

"He was sitting in on one of the classes. The teacher asked him to read aloud in front of the class. He refused and bolted out the door. The teacher alerted my office immediately and we searched the building, but he could not be located, neither inside nor on the grounds."

"I'm on my way," I said. I dropped the receiver, then picked it up again, and called Doug. He was home in less than a half hour. My mother wanted to help so we picked her up and started the two hour drive.

"I guess it's safe to say that Mark didn't like it there," my mother said. The hint of laughter in her voice caught my attention and I relaxed slightly.

"You think they'll accept him after this?" I asked, pretending innocence.

Doug turned slightly in his seat, keeping one eye on the road and one on me. He saw that I was teasing and he laughed. My mother and I joined in.

"Anyone listening to us would think we'd lost our minds," I said.

"Anyone living with Mark as long as we have would have lost their minds if they didn't have a sense of humor," Mom said. "I'm glad we've all been able to keep ours."

The scene that greeted us at the Burlington Children's Home was anything but humorous. Three police cars were lined up at the door and the director was standing in the driveway peering anxiously down the road. When we pulled up, he ran toward our car and helped me out.

"I'm sorry. There's been no word so far. The police have searched the main roads and the surrounding neighborhood. It's been several hours. He could be anywhere by now. The police are searching the woods behind the back fence again."

"We'll start there," Doug said.

I glanced at my mother. "Do you want to wait here?"

She had dressed in slacks and a sweater and I noticed she was wearing sturdy shoes. "Let's go," she said.

The director led us to a gate that was chained closed with a padlock. He fitted the key in the lock, opened the gate and let us through.

"I have to relock this," he said, sounding apologetic. "But I'll have someone check every half hour in case you want to come through."

"Is there another way out? " Doug asked.

He nodded. "The fence is only around our property. The forest is open on the other three sides but it's a long way through."

There was nothing more to say. From the gate a path led into the woods and we started down it in silence, but after a few hundred yards we began calling his name, our voices quickly swallowed by the spongy darkness beneath the pines.

"Talk about finding a needle in a haystack," Mom whispered to me as we peered into the cool shadows. "If he doesn't want to be found, we'll never find him in there."

"But we always do," I said. "Somehow we always find him."

When we came to a fork in the road, we decided to split up. Mom and I stayed on the old path, Doug took the new.

"Have you got your flashlights?" Doug asked.

We switched them on, the beam weak in the fading twilight. We had had the foresight to fill them with new batteries a few days before, expecting to use them when the inevitable midnight searches became necessary.

"If you see him, give a shout and shine your beam into the air. I'll see it on the tops of the trees and head in that direction. Do you want to set a time to meet again?" Doug looked tired already and I was feeling weary, but I shook my head.

"We search until we find him," I said.

Doug trotted off down the path, his voice becoming more distant by the moment. As soon as he was out of earshot, I yelled, "Mark, if you can hear me, please come out. I'm not going to make you go back to that place. Just come out so I know you're okay."

My words disappeared beneath the pines and a deep silence settled in around us. The shrill warning of a bird and an occasional rustling beneath our feet let us know we were not alone, but the deeper we went into the woods and the darker it became, the more isolated from humankind we felt.

"Where are the police?" I had not seen a single flash or heard the shout of another person since we had left Doug on the trail.

"Maybe they caught him. Maybe we should go back and check. We might be doing this for nothing." I could barely see my mother. Night had fallen and although there was a moon, the shadows of the trees made it seem like midnight.

"Lord, this is spooky. I wish he'd answer and we could get this over with. You know me, I do get a bit scared," she said,

We walked on, calling his name. I had no idea how long we had been in the woods, but the darkness and the chill were slowly creeping into my bones and I found myself shivering uncontrollably. My voice was hoarse from shouting. I gave it one last try,

"MARK.   FOR GOD'S SAKE, IF YOU CAN HEAR ME, COME OUT NOW."

We held our breath. Nothing. Not even the startled cry of a bird nesting nearby or the flicker of a field mouse running for its hole.

"Let's go back. Hopefully, they'll have found him and if not, at least we can get a cup of tea before we go back out again," my mom said. With our flashlight beams pointed to the ground, we hurried as fast as we could back the way we had come. I wondered how Doug had made out alone. I had not heard his voice nor seen the wavering of a light in the tree tops so I assumed he had not found him either. Our last hope was the police. If they had not found him, then I knew we would never make the two hour trip back to St. Clare's on time. If he was in a wild and threatening mood or if he tried to run away from us again, I didn't know what I was going to do. Cross that bridge when you come to it, I told myself.

Doug was waiting at the gate, staring anxiously down the path. He ran to us when he saw the beam from our lights. We didn't need to say anything. Mark was not with either of us. That was answer enough.

"Have you seen the police?" I asked, my voice a raspy croak.

"Not yet. I just got here myself."

Luckily, we didn't have to wait long. Searchlights were playing across the fields and into the woods near the gate. We stood in their glare and waved and soon the director came out to open the lock. I had a feeling he had been watching for us, but he didn't ask any questions. He quickly agreed to our suggestion of a cup of tea and he had someone bring it to us in his office. We asked if he had heard from the police and he informed us that they had checked in with him less than an hour ago but there was no news.

"He could be home by now for all we know." I glanced up at the clock. Nine-thirty. To amuse myself I calculated how long it would take us to get to St. Clare's if we drove all the way at eighty miles per hour.

"Should we go out again?" I asked after I had finished my cup of tea. My knees were weak and my arms felt like dead weights, but I couldn't sit still. Doug was on his feet pacing, but my mom looked like she was about to fall asleep.

262

"Mom, you stay here. Doug and I will take the car and cruise some of the back roads. Who knows, he may not have been able to hitch a ride and fallen asleep by the side of the road. He's done stranger things, Heaven knows." I glanced up at the clock once more and said a quick prayer that if he was going to be found tonight, he'd be found in the next ten minutes or we'd never make it back to St. Clare's.

Doug pulled open the door. I brushed past him and stopped dead. We both backed into the office. Two police officers entered and between them marched Mark, his face muddied and scratched, twigs and leaves sticking to his clothes, a bandanna around his head, looking like a blond Rambo.

"Oh, thank God," I said, clinging to Doug for support.

"I'm not staying here," Mark shouted. "You can't make me. I'll run again. I swear to God, I will."

"You don't have to stay," Doug said. "As a matter of fact, you have to go. Right now if we're going to make it back on time."

Mark looked at him suspiciously, but didn't say anything. I quickly explained to the officers and the director that we had to get Mark back to St. Clare's by midnight or he would not be allowed to return. I'm sure they wanted to see the last of us so they did not try to detain us. I gave my promise that if there were any papers to sign or court appearances to make, I would return, then hustled Mark out of there as quickly as possible.

We had exactly one hour and forty minutes to make the two hour journey to St. Clare's. There was little traffic on the road, but Doug still needed to drive well over the speed limit all the way home. I sat in the back with Mark because I did not want my mother to be there if he was going to be nasty.

"What happened, Mark?" I asked as soon as I could settle myself down. The speed made me nervous and I was keyed up from the search, but sitting there in tense silence made every movement feel like the searing pain of a toothache.

"Nothin'."

"Then why'd you run? Something must have happened."

"They wanted me to read out loud in front of all those kids. I said "no thanks" as polite as could be, but the teacher kept it up and kept it up. You know I can't read. Why should I let all those kids make fun of me, huh? And there was this other kid there. I knew him and we didn't get along. There would have been a fight sooner or later. I didn't want no fight so I left."

I hung onto the edge of my seat, staring into the darkness of the window as Doug barreled down the highway. The minutes were ticking and I felt each one of them in the constant throbbing of my head. The smoke from Mark's endless chain of cigarettes made me nauseous.

"Does anybody know what time it is?" I asked after what seemed like hours had gone by.

"Eleven forty. I just passed the sign for Denville. We should be at the hospital in ten minutes. That gives us ten minutes to spare."

We turned off the exit a few minutes later. Doug had to reduce speed on the town roads and once he had to stop for a red light. Go through it, I urged, but Doug pointed out that if we were stopped by the police we would never make it. I saw the lights of the hospital loom up before us.

"Eleven fifty five," Doug said before I asked.

I pulled Mark from the backseat and ran with him to the emergency room door. We pounded through the corridor and reached IB, the adolescent psychiatric ward with two minutes to spare. They checked him in at 11:58 and he was in his room by midnight. I signed him in and left. Tomorrow was another day and I would deal with the fall out then. Right now, all I wanted to do was to go home and sleep.

Chapter Twenty-Five

"I'd like to suggest a different program than any we'd discussed before." Gail Everett, Dr. Lowenthal, Doug and I sat in the office on Ward IB discussing Mark's discharge. He was due to be released in two days and so far no residential placement had been found. Gail had reported that he had been rejected from four facilities DYFS had contacted. The residences felt they could not handle someone with Mark's history. Doug and I still did not feel we could manage him at home and he could not stay at St. Clare's. He had been stabilized on medication again, but he still would not speak in group therapy sessions and, although he was no longer aggressive with the other patients, he clearly did not feel he could benefit from interaction with them.

I leaned forward, eager to hear what Gail Everett had in mind. "Sometimes we assign children to what is called a "teaching family." These are couples who have been trained to manage difficult children through behavioral modification techniques. Mark would live with the family so it would be a residential placement, but not in a large group setting. The family I have in mind for Mark would have three other children in placement. He would be within a family environment and he would have round the clock supervision."

I looked at Doug. This was definitely not something we had considered. I felt again the familiar clench in my chest. Mark had been in foster placements often when he was a toddler and, somewhere in the back of my mind, I had always held the numerous placements responsible for his inability to lead a normal life. What if this "teaching family" believed in physically disciplining children or worse? What if they locked him up in isolation for long periods of time? Certainly they wouldn't tell a social worker from DYFS about that. But on the other hand, DYFS couldn't afford the scandal of placing children under their jurisdiction in abusive households. Pros and cons bumped one another off like hit men in a mad Mafia movie.

"I'm sure you must have some questions," Gail suggested as Doug and I continued to look at one another dumbly.

"Are you suggesting foster placement," I asked.

"In a way, but we would not be taking Mark from you. You wouldn't have to go to court or anything like that. He'd stay with the teaching family and you could visit him whenever you wished."

"What about school?" Doug asked.

"He would have to go to a local school. One with a special education program would be researched for him and a decision made. He will not be allowed out except with supervision and they would make sure he did his homework, school projects, etc."

"How about therapy and medication?"

"Taking him to therapy would be your responsibility, but they would administer his medication in the morning and at night." Gail looked at me kindly, but after having read the residential placement report in which she had stated I was uncooperative, I did not trust her as I had before. "I know you are concerned about what kind of home Mark will be going to," she said. "I assure you that these people are kind and caring and well trained in handling young people with problems similar to Mark's."

"What about his running away? We all know that if Mark doesn't like it there, he'll take off," I asked.

"I can't promise you he won't find a way to run off if he really wants to. This is the best we can do. As you know we've sent to a number of places and we have inquiries out on quite a few more. So far, no luck. This family is willing to try with him. Since they are not attached to him as you are, they may be better able to see his problems objectively and handle them more easily. I'd say it's worth a try. At least interview them and then make your decision."

I turned to Dr. Lowenthal. "We'd like to hear what you think. Since this is a new one on us, Doug and I don't quite know what to say. Mark had all those foster placements in the past. Do you think this will freak him out?"

Dr. Lowenthal steepled his fingers and rested his chin on the tips. He seemed to choose his words carefully. "Mark shows no signs of psychosis which would require long term psychiatric hospitalization. However, he has very little insight into his own emotional and behavioral problems and he blames others for provoking him into behaving improperly. His judgment is extremely poor and where he might not get into trouble on his own, he can be easily led into it by others who do have criminal or psychotic disorders. As I have said before, he needs constant supervision as well as immediate and very concrete feedback regarding his behavior. I'm not sure a teaching family home will be enough for him, but it is the only alternative besides returning home with you."

Doug and I finally agreed to visit the teaching family home the next afternoon. We knew if we brought him home he would continue to behave as he always had. We, also, knew we were unable to change that. So that alternative was out and no other option presented itself at the moment.

Mark was discharged from St. Clare's Hospital in late October and went to live at the teaching family home in November. He'd had a private tutor when he had been in the hospital and he went back to school as soon as he had settled himself with the new family. The reports from school were not encouraging. Mark had obviously given up on learning. Although he attended classes it was clear that he had no interest and no hope that he would learn anything. He put in his time because he was required to do so and because he had nothing else to do. His classmates were tough and Mark gained a reputation as a "guy who would do anything."

During my visits with him, I tried to encourage him to talk about his experiences at the teaching home, but he was uncommunicative. In answer to my questions about whether he liked it there, what they did, how he got along with the other people, whether he was getting his medication, he would grunt unintelligibly and walk out of the room.

Mark stayed with the teaching family one month before he ran away. The call came just after I had gone to bed. I picked up the phone knowing by the late hour who it would be. Mark had run off with another boy who had been assigned to the home. The police had been notified and I should expect them shortly. I woke up Doug and, by the time we had finished dressing, the police were at our door. Once they were satisfied that we were not harboring the boys they left. I asked them if they were going to the home of the other boy who had run away, but he lived in Essex County and as they were Passaic County Police, they had no jurisdiction there.

"But what if he's found at this young man's house?" I persisted.

"Then I suggest you go pick him up yourselves and bring him home."

An hour later we received a call from the Essex Office of DYFS that they had picked up the other boy at his home and taken him back to the teaching family, but that we had better come get Mark because they had no jurisdiction over him. He had committed no crime because he had not been assigned to the teaching family by the courts. We were given the Newark address and left to fend for ourselves.

I woke Cheryl up, told her where we were going and took off for the Newark Projects somewhere in the heart of the city. I had lived in Essex County all my life, but had never ventured into the crumbling, crime-ridden inner city. The burned out tenements and blank staring windows of the abandoned factories, the homeless men along McCarter Highway and the filthy vacant lots between over-crowded apartments might have been no different than could be seen in any other American inner city, but tonight they were personal, a face to the fear I held for Mark's life. Would he be one of these men whose glassy eyes were sightless to the future, who lived from one bottle to another, from one shot of heroin to the next? If something happened to me or Doug, would he be living in one of these rat infested holes in some fog of hopelessness and despair? My fear for him was reflected in my fear of the night city and I could hardly breathe for the lump in my throat.

We rode around the streets searching for the cut off to the projects. We heard cries and the crashing of bottles, but we did not stop to look. We had to find Mark and bring him home. When at last we did locate the address neither Doug nor I wanted to get out. I prayed as I rang the doorbell that Mark would be waiting for us and we could leave a minute after we had come. I didn't think the woman who had been kind enough to keep Mark there would be in the mood for polite small talk. I know I wasn't. We rang the bell again. Please God, let him be here, I prayed. Please don't let him have run off again. On the third ring, a woman answered the door. She was younger than I had expected, the expression on her dark, high cheek-boned face contemptuous.

"Didn't think you'd come here at night," she said.

"Could you send Mark out to us now?" I was in no mood to exchange insults or racial slurs.

Mark appeared in the doorway behind her.

"Let's go," Doug said.

Mark eased past the woman, who rested against the door jam, one long, slim arm arched to support herself. Mark slipped underneath and stood waiting while I tried to thank the woman for keeping Mark with her. She merely raised one eyebrow. Doug gestured impatiently and we left.

Mark sat in the back, smoking, while I clung to the dashboard in an effort to steady myself while Doug sped along the dark and silent streets. "Do we bring him back to the teaching home or to our house?" Doug asked. His voice was controlled, but I could sense the effort this was costing him.

"If you take me back to that place I'll just run away again. I don't belong there. There're not my kind of people if you get my drift." Mark's voice floated up from the backseat between the curling puffs of smoke that were making me choke. I didn't dare open the windows because we were driving through one of the more crime ridden areas of the city.

"I suggest you keep your mouth shut," Doug's teeth were clenched. I was afraid of what he would do if Mark kept it up.

Mark had never been able to pick up social cues and his judgment was impaired by his disability. He kept on as if Doug had never spoken "Where are you going to dump me next, huh? Why don't you take me to some open field and leave me there like you would a stray cat? You could forget about me and go on with your own lives. That's what you want, isn't it?"

"Right, that's why we're here in the middle of Newark at one o'clock in the morning. Because we don't care! That's why we chased around the woods in the dark for hours when you ran off from the Children's Home. That's why we've practically bankrupted ourselves with therapy, hospitals, tutors, you name it. Because we don't care! As nuts as you are, you've got to know better. You just have to."

"Screw you,"

I saw Doug jerk forward and I leaned a restraining hand on his arm. I didn't want him to pull over. I wanted to get out of the city. I wanted to open the window and breathe in some fresh air so I could clear my head.

"Let's just go home," I said to Doug. "We can call the teaching family and tell them Mark will be staying with us. At least for tonight. We can figure out what to do long term after we get home."

"We should have left him there," Doug mumbled, but I knew he didn't mean it.

Mark remained with us a few days before it became necessary for him to reenter St. Clare's Hospital for the third time. The episode in Newark had so agitated him that he was totally out of control and I felt petrified whenever he was in the house and worried when he was not. I don't know why he agreed to return to the hospital this time. Maybe some still healthy part of him was frightened too by the way he was feeling or acting. He reentered Ward IB on December 12th. It broke my heart to know that he would be there during Christmas. Dr. Lowenthal took him off his current medications because it was apparent that they had no effect on his acting out. Mark's behavior remained the same with or without medication.

Dr. Lowenthal reported that the entire time Mark was on the ward, he talked of nothing but going home and he showed no capacity to understand that he could not have everything the way he wanted. DYFS still could not find a placement for him. Dr. Lowenthal consulted with the Adolescent Unit at Trenton State Psychiatric Hospital to see if a placement could be made there, but the Hospital Board strongly opposed the placement as completely inappropriate because of a lack of psychosis and because Mark was not tough enough for their conduct disorder unit. Mark told Dr. Lowenthal that he had had enough and that he would not willingly go to any other hospitals or homes. He refused to participate in group therapy sessions. He didn't care about the other teenagers' problems. He just wanted to go home. And he got his wish. In January with nowhere else to go and no facility willing to help him or us, he came home.

Doug and I walked around for the next few weeks feeling that we were living on the slopes of a smoking volcano. Mark returned to Palisades Learning Center, but we all knew that he was just doing time. He had lost all interest in academics if he'd ever had any. The only interest he had remained his animals and he continued to bring strays home, a source of ongoing tension and argument since his "strays" often had owners who came looking for their animals. Strays weren't the only thing that Mark stole.

He had been home less than a month when we discovered Cheryl's gold hoop earrings were missing. She had graduated from high school and was working full time at Northwest Finance. Mark related to Cheryl better than he did to the rest of us. When she was home, he would wander up to her room to talk with her and she would listen for a time. None of us wanted to believe that he would deliberately take her earrings. He had pierced his own ear and wore studs or small hoops in the several holes he had made. The earrings that were missing were slightly larger than the ones he usually wore.

When Cheryl came down to breakfast that morning, she asked if I had seen her hoops. "I left them on the dresser. I think I was in a rush and didn't put them back in my jewelry box, but I remember taking them off and putting them on top."

I went upstairs with her. We searched the floor, looked behind the furniture, hunted through her jewelry box and the top drawers of the dresser. She didn't want to say anything and neither did I, but we were both thinking the same thing. When there was no other option, I called the school and asked Mr. Felloes if he could see what kind of earrings Mark was wearing. I did not say why I wanted to know, but Mr. Felloes and I had established a relationship where such explanations were no longer necessary. He returned to the phone and told me Mark was wearing several plain gold studs and a pair of medium-sized gold hoops.

"He's got them all right." I said. "Please have him take them off and I'll run up on my lunch hour and pick them up."

After that, we often found some item missing, sometimes it was jewelry, but more often, money disappeared from my purse, Doug's wallet or Cheryl's room. Whenever he was home, we were always on guard, hiding things or locking them up, switching hiding places or checking Mark's pockets when he wasn't watching.

One morning, after the school bus had picked up Mark and I was putting the finishing touches on my outfit for work, I realized that I had forgotten to replace my diamond engagement ring. I had taken it off last night when I was doing some heavy cleaning. I walked back into my bedroom and reached up to grab it from the top of the dresser. There was nothing there. The dresser top was empty.

I had always made it a habit to put everything away in its proper place each night so I wouldn't have extra work in the morning before I had to leave. My family teased me about being a neat freak but it made life easier, especially when Mark was home and things were so emotionally chaotic. I made a thorough search of the floor. On hands and knees, I searched under the dresser. Nothing. Okay, I told myself, I'll give Mark the benefit of the doubt though I already had that sinking feeling. I called Doug at work. He had seen the ring last night, but couldn't remember if he had seen it this morning. "Call the school," he said. "If you wait any longer, you may never see it again."

I called and told the principal, Mr. Felloes, that I was missing my ring and that I was afraid Mark had it and meant to sell it. Mr. Felloes sent someone for Mark pronto while I waited on the phone. Mark arrived in the office some minutes later and, in the course of the conversation, Mark admitted to taking the ring because one of the guys in his class had offered him one hundred dollars for it. By some miracle Mark still had the ring. He gave it to Mr. Felloes and he was dismissed back to his regular classroom.

"Do you want to press charges?" Mr. Felloes asked.

I dreaded the idea of getting involved with the courts and police again so I declined. "Doug and I will take care of it at home," I said. I told him I would be up to get the ring immediately and that I would consider the matter dropped if he would.

A week later, we were in court with Mark. My hope of avoiding the judicial system had been nothing but a hope. I must have known Mark would run afoul of the law sometime. I was just putting off the inevitable both for him and for me. We had run through every other social institution in our efforts to raise Mark so why not the institution of last resort.

Mark's behavior had once again become threatening and his absences from home longer. Because the weather had dropped to the teens, he was not staying out in the parks, but he had begun to stay overnight with "friends" he had met either in school or on the streets. I tried to get names and addresses so I could find him and make sure he was all right, but more often than not, I didn't know where he was.

He had been gone for a day before Valentine's Day. I had called several places because I wanted Mark to come with us to a family Valentine's Day party. I finally located him at a friend's house and I asked Cheryl if she would please pick him up. Cheryl had her own car and she was not busy at the moment so she agreed. The friend lived only a short distance away and when Cheryl pulled up in front of the house, Mark and a few other young men were standing on the front lawn. Cheryl tooted the horn and waved to Mark to get into the car. Mark pretended to ignore her. Cheryl beeped again. This time Mark looked up at her, but he still did not move. Uncertain what to do, Cheryl stepped out of the car and called to him.

"Come on, Mark. Mom and Dad are waiting. We have to be at the party in a few minutes."

Mark's face took on a nasty sneer. "Here's a message for Mom and Dad, Cheryl. Tell them I can do whatever I damn please. They can't tell me what to do. I'm not going to any damn party so get back in your car and leave."

"Mark, come on. Everyone will be there. Can't you just do this for them? Just this once."

Mark walked over to where Cheryl stood beside the car. He was wearing his dog collar and chains and his hand was thrust deep in the slash pocket of his vest. A few inches away he stopped, his face contorted with rage. From his vest pocket, he slowly pulled a pocket knife and held it close to her face.

"Get away from here, Cheryl. Get away before I have to cut you. And tell Mom and Dad they better stay away from me, too. Get it. Stay away." Mark flicked the knife closer then away again.

Her hands shaking, Cheryl slid behind the wheel of her car, but before she could drive off, the loud wail of a police siren sliced through the shocked silence. Two patrol cars pulled up in front of the house. Too surprised to run, Mark was thrown across the front of one of the patrol cars, handcuffed and searched. The knife was removed from his pocket and he was taken to the Passaic County Juvenile Detention Shelter in Haledon.

Cheryl did not know where he had been taken, of course. When she told us what had happened, I called the Clifton Police Department and spoke to an officer who told me where he was. Mark was well known to the Clifton Police because he had been picked up so many times for running away. I learned that the arresting officer was Detective Reilly and that he was willing to talk to us if we came down to the police department immediately. Cheryl was terribly upset, but I convinced her to go to the party where she could be with other members of the family.

"If we need you, we'll call you," I promised. "Hopefully, we can clear this all up now and bring Mark home tonight."

At the front desk of the Clifton Police Department, we asked for Detective Reilly. After a few uncomfortable moments in the fake leather chairs of the waiting room, staring at the concerned faces of other supplicants, we were shown into a crowded office. Detective Reilly was seated behind his desk, but he came around to draw up two more fake leather chairs for us. We shook hands, tensely proper and polite. The detective then reseated himself behind the desk.

"Mr. and Mrs. Conaway. I know you must be upset by what happened, but your son had a knife in plain view. This is a lot more serious than his previous problems. He posed a threat to ..." he consulted his notes, then went on, "...Cheryl, your daughter. For this offense, we could not just release him with a warning."

"But Cheryl told us he didn't use it. He was just trying to scare her away. She doesn't think he would have hurt her. He was just doing his "tough guy" routine."

"I'm sorry, Mrs. Conaway. What Mark did was against the law. We have to detain him until a hearing can be scheduled. And, may I speak frankly..."

Doug and I nodded.

"I think Mark would be better off having this hearing. The court system has a wide variety of resources that Mark wouldn't have available to him if he didn't go through the system. A judge could order that Mark be placed in a hospital or rehabilitation center for a prescribed period of time and have the full force of the law behind him. DYFS is limited because they cannot order a placement. The court can. With a judge and DYFS working for him he will have twice the chance of finding help. Think about it. In the meantime, Mark is in the Juvenile Shelter in Haledon. I'll call for you and arrange visitation privileges."

What Detective Reilly didn't tell us, and probably didn't know, was that even if placement was court ordered, a private institution was not required to accept Mark. Had we known this, we would not have been so quick to enter the judicial system.

We were able to visit Mark that day and bring him a change of clothes, underwear and a few approved items from home. The large building where he was confined looked and felt like a prison, with barred doors, wired windows and uniformed guards patrolling the corridors. The items we had brought from home were searched before we were able to give them to Mark. Our visit was supervised. While I waited for them to bring him, I wondered whether he would be in handcuffs. I wasn't sure I could handle that without breaking down. Thank God he wasn't, but he looked so slight, so small and so bewildered that I had a hard time keeping myself together.

"Can I go home now?" Mark asked.

"No, not yet. That's why we brought you some things. You have to stay here until we have a hearing. Then the judge will decide when and if you can come home."

Mark looked scared and I wondered if Detective Reilly might not be right. Maybe a trip through the court system would be the experience he needed to reinforce what we had been telling him for years. Maybe fear would teach him what loving kindness could not. I wanted to shout at him, "This is the consequence of your impulsive behavior. This is what happens when you don't think before you act." But I didn't. Yelling at him only made him more defiant, it never taught him anything he would remember for more than the time it took me to shout it at him.

The court date was set for the end of February. The complaint had been sworn out by Detective Reilly. The lawyer we contacted and Detective Reilly advised us to have Mark plead guilty to the case. There were enough witnesses willing to testify against him. Cheryl had been subpoenaed to appear as a witness and she was upset about having to speak against her brother, but the incident had scared her and she did not want to have to live in the same house with him. I wanted Mark to get a court appointed placement. After several sleepless nights, Doug and I decided we would tell Mark to plead guilty. We believed that the courts could help Mark by providing him access to facilities we could not.

I had never been through a court appearance and had no idea what to expect. Mercifully, the hearing was not long. Our lawyer entered a plea of guilty on Mark's behalf. The Judge asked Mark if he understood what he had done and if his lawyer had explained what a guilty plea meant. Mark answered yes. I wanted to jump up and shout that he did not understand, that he acted on impulse and not only did he not know the difference between guilty and not guilty, he didn't know the difference between right and wrong, but I held tightly to the arms of the chair and listened.

Detective Reilly testified to Mark's actions with the knife. Gail Everett explained the nature of Mark's disabilities and the history of his involvement with the Division of Youth and Family Services. The Judge asked her if she had been able to find a placement for Mark. My breath caught in my throat. Had she come through with something last minute? The blood drummed in my ears so hard I could hardly hear.

"Not a permanent placement, your honor, but the Mapleton Psychiatric Unit at Deveraux in Pennsylvania has agreed to take Mark for a thirty day evaluation. Deveraux has a wide range of facilities and programs, none of which Mark has qualified for in the past. However, given his hospitalizations for psychiatric problems, they feel that he may fit into their juvenile psychiatric unit."

We had been rejected by Deveraux in the past. His borderline IQ and lack of psychosis did not qualify him for either the developmentally disabled unit or the psychiatric unit. He still did not qualify under their guidelines but, obviously, they were willing to cooperate with the court and DYFS in permitting him an evaluation. Questions rose to mind immediately. What if Deveraux rejected him after the evaluation? What happened then? Would the court order another placement or would Mark wander through the maze of the system once more and be released without resources? I wanted the lawyer to ask the Judge that, but he refused. We had pleaded guilty. We had no say in the judge's adjudication. Mark was ordered to remain at Deveroux for the period of thirty days to complete an evaluation. Pending the outcome of the evaluation, a new hearing would be set at the end of the thirty days. Tomorrow, the police would take Mark from the shelter to the Pennsylvania border where he would be picked up and brought to Deveroux. Hearing over, the police took Mark back to the shelter and Doug and I were left feeling as if we no longer had any involvement in Mark's life. We had been shut out and the judicial system had taken over.

Chapter Twenty-Six

One month later, Mark was driven in an ambulance from the Devereux Foundation to the New Jersey border where he was picked up, handcuffed and driven back to the Juvenile Shelter in Haledon. I was furious. When I had gone for the original interview at Deveroux I had begged the Administrator, not to keep Mark here for an evaluation if they did not feel he would be appropriate for a longer residential placement. I wanted to spare Mark the disappointment of being rejected from yet another program after I had convinced him to cooperate with the staff.

The Devereux Foundation had over 2,000 residents and had developed specialized programs for emotionally disturbed children and adolescents, learning disabled children and adolescents, developmentally disabled and autistic children and adolescents, developmentally disabled adults, head trauma survivors, deaf emotionally disturbed adolescents, a psychiatric hospital and a nursing home for handicapped adults. I could not understand why Mark was so unique that he could not fit into a single one of these programs, but I was determined to find out. I wrote first to the presiding Judge.

Superior Court, Family Division
Court House Annex
Paterson, NJ 07110

Your Honor,
My son, [Mark Graham], appeared in court before you on February 23. [Mark] is a multiply handicapped adolescent. He is classified with a primary diagnosis of emotionally disturbed, neurologically impaired, perceptually impaired, borderline developmentally disabled (IQ of 70 -75) and, he has a learning deficiency. Mark has been in many different schools. We have moved only once necessitating a change of schools. Most of the other changes have been because Mark could not be handled or educated in any school environment. He also spent three months last year in St. Clare's Hospital in Denville in the psychiatric unit. We have been

working with DYFS to find a proper placement for him. He has always been a hyperkenetic child.

Since this was [Mark's] first offense and you understood his handicap, your instructions were for [Mark] to successfully complete a stay at Devereux Foundation Psychiatric Unit in Devon, Pennsylvania. According to your court order, he was admitted there on February 25. I am enclosing copies of his academic reports. He did achieve success in this area as you can see by his marks. This is the first time [Mark] ever received A's. I am also enclosing copies of three letters. The first exhibits his loneliness and depression, the second is still desperate with another plea for help as well as a statement that he wants to kill himself, the third is a happier letter reflecting his adjustment to the unit and a feeling of personal progress.

On March 24th, the social worker from Deveroux, or the Administrator, informed DYFS and my husband that they wanted to discharge [Mark]. I spoke to the social worker twice on Friday, March 27th to try to understand why he was to be discharged. Not more than two weeks earlier I had spoken to [Mark's] psychologist, and she explained that she felt [Mark] was just beginning to adjust to the unit and that he still posed a danger to himself and others. She recommended that [Mark] be in a long term psychiatric setting for a neurologically impaired person. She stated Devereux completed their agreement with DYFS to keep [Mark] on a thirty day provisional basis and that within their foundation which had locations in nine states; they do not have an appropriate setting for him. They have given DYFS and [Mark] a ten day extension and plan to discharge him on April 3.

What do I tell my son? They cannot help you here at Devereux and we must find another placement yet again? I am frustrated and find it very difficult to believe that in our great country we do not have the resources to help my son. Is [Mark Graham] so unique he fits in nowhere? My goals for [Mark] are twofold: that he become a good Christian and citizen and that he learns to become self-reliant and productive so he can earn a living and support himself. How can this goal be achieved if he cannot get the help he needs now? [Mark] is sixteen years old and time is running out. I will do whatever is in my power to help him but I cannot and do not have the authority as you do. Please advise what can be done as far as his legal charges and future placement are concerned.

Thank you in advance for the time you have taken to read this letter. I know it is lengthy, but my concerns are great. Please call me if you have any questions or would like to set up another meeting.

Sincerely,
Mrs. Corraine Conaway

I also requested Mark's psychiatric and educational evaluations and copies of his discharge report. I read the Psychiatric Summary twice before I realized that it told me nothing of what I needed to know:

Psychiatric Summary

[Mark Graham's] adjustment to Mapleton Psychiatric Institute has been quite poor. He is impulse-ridden. He runs away, steals, gets into a lot of trouble and has no apparent remorse. His intellectual functioning is very limited. He has marked impairment of memory and conceptual thinking. He can be very pleasant and get into some antisocial behavior the next minute. He requires a lot of supervision and structure. At present he is fairly comfortable and seems to be trying to comply… Because of the neurological and developmental disorders, it is my opinion that it is unreasonable to expect him to improve in a short time to a level where he could move to an open unit. He will need a long term facility that is able to provide close supervision and a lot of structure. The prognosis for improvement is poor.

The summary by the Clinical Psychologist, proved no better in providing concrete answers as to why Mark was so different than the thousands of other developmentally and/or emotionally disturbed residents of Devereux.

Clinical Summary

Upon admission, [Mark] was programmed for individual therapy, community meeting, recreational therapy, the level system and special education. However, it was evident during the first few days that [Mark] was unable to handle full program expectations. He required a highly specialized program based on concrete goals and incentives in addition to a reduction in environmental stimulation. [Mark] stole property from peers and continually denied his behavior; he was impulsive, lacked judgment and required the Observation/Stabilization Room when he became threatening to others and was agitated. One-to-One supervision was necessary when [Mark] was out of his room to monitor stealing and interpersonal relationships.

[Mark] appears to be a neurologically impaired, impulsive youth who requires long term treatment in a highly structured environment. Unfortunately, MPI is short-term and [Mark] would be inappropriate for an open residential unit within the Foundation due to being a high risk for dangerous behavior and an inability to learn from experience and process information.

I poured over the reports searching for clues that would tell me exactly why Mark was rejected from a foundation that specialized in exactly the type of educational and social adjustment problems Mark had always suffered from. I needed to know why my son was the one who could not be helped anywhere. I would not let it go. I didn't care if they thought I was a nut or a crank. I would keep calling and writing until I received answers that satisfied me. I decided to devote myself to this full time.

Manhattan Maintenance, the company where I had worked for ten years had been bought out. I left my job in March, a few weeks before Mark's discharge from Deveroux. I had already been informed that Deveroux would not accept him, so when the letter came informing me that he would be discharged to the Juvenile Shelter I went into immediate action. Gail Everett had asked me if I still wished to pursue residential placement. There was no doubt in my mind that Mark needed long term supervision and I made sure there was not a doubt in hers either. I demanded residential admission packets sent to as many facilities as DYFS had access to.

I also began to research on my own and discovered SCRIPT, an organization which provided me with a computer print-out of schools and foundations for special needs children and their phone numbers. I began weeding through the list, eliminating schools that were inappropriate or too far away. I wanted Mark to know that I could come to him whenever he needed me. I could not afford to hop on a plane to California whenever he felt panicked, but I could drive all day if necessary. But before then I needed to know why Mark was being rejected and my best source of that information was the Devereux Foundation. I called daily, refusing to be put off by the stalls and the call backs that never came. I persisted until I spoke with everyone on my list.

Mark's psychologist told me that Mark had just begun to adjust to the unit and that he still posed a danger to himself or others. When I explained that was the reason he was sent to Deveroux by the court and to discharge him while he still constituted this danger made no sense, she abruptly ended the conversation. She did not return my next two calls, but she instructed the social worker to call me. I was informed that the original determination stood intact - that there is no facility within Deveroux in the nine states in which there were foundation campuses that would suit Mark's needs. She told me that the board did not feel that Mark could function in an open unit, but recommended that he be placed in a long term psychiatric setting for neurologically impaired individuals. I asked where I could find such a facility. No answer. She did agree to send me a breakdown on all the problems Mark had experienced that made him ineligible for residential placement there.

The phone calls clearly showed the frustration of the staff in dealing with Mark as did the case reports. When I read the comments of the team assigned to work with Mark, they reminded me of so many similar comments from so many professionals who had been unable to help him. I read some of them aloud to Doug one night after work. With Mark still in the Juvenile Shelter, our tension did not run to screaming or fighting, but to talking in quiet, urgent tones.

"Listen to this!" I read him a few of the comments. *Patient is unable to attend group therapy due to provoking peers and distractibility.* Or how about this one. *Patient talks back to staff, verbally threatens physical harm and has difficulty responding to feedback. Patient is unable to comply with program expectations and requires a partial isolation program due to threats of violence and disruption.* And here's a gem for you. *Patient refused to shower during the first week of admission.* Doug shook his head, his expression as bewildered as I was feeling. "Let me read you the summary," I rushed on. "Patient has been unable to maintain minimal progress noted at variable intervals. He is highly explosive, demanding and challenging of authority. He has difficulty processing feedback and behavior patterns are highly repetitive. He presents a danger to others and is unaware of the seriousness of his ideas and actions. Judgment is impaired. It is recommended that he be discharged to DYFS and that DYFS seek placement in a long term facility which manages neurologically impaired, potentially violent patients."

"So what's your impression of that?" I asked.

"If I didn't know better, I'd say he scared the daylights out of them"

"Exactly. Which leaves me with my usual question. What separates these qualified, credentialed, highly paid professionals from us? They are supposed to know how to deal with these problems, but all we ever hear from them is their own fear and frustration and another rejection without even the admission that they can't help. It's always Mark's fault that he can't fit in. For God's sake, he's handicapped, not them. Isn't there anyone qualified to help him? Isn't there anyone talented enough in their field to realize that he never hurt anyone, that his threats are because he's scared and trying to defend himself against his own fear. Does it take a genius to figure that out? I know what's wrong. I just don't know how to help him. It seems no one else does either with all their M.D's and Ph.Ds."

"What a speech, Corraine. Maybe you should give a speech like that where it counts. Maybe there are other parents who have faced the same frustrations and are looking for the same kind of help we are." I looked up to see if Doug was teasing me and saw the genuine admiration in his face. Doug's suggestion stayed with me for the next few weeks as I struggled to find help for Mark. He was scheduled for a hearing with the Passaic County Child Placement Review Board in April. The Review Board decided that it was in Mark's best interest to remain in the Juvenile Shelter until his court date, May 5th, when an initial disposition would be made.

DYFS had not had any success in finding a residential placement for Mark. It was during this time that I discovered the Juvenile Court had no authority in placing children in a residential program. If the individual school or facility did not feel the child met their standards for treatment, they could refuse and the court could do nothing about it. The only placements the courts could make were to Juvenile Detention Centers. Mark's "crime" did not merit such a placement. Another dead end, another hard lesson for Doug and me and an expensive one at that. Our legal costs were mounting with each hearing. So was my anger.

I kept thinking about what Doug had said. Maybe if I told my story to the public, someone might know something I didn't and could help me. Or if not, I might save someone else the suffering our family had undergone. I did not know how to get my story to the public, but my conviction that I needed to grew as I sat in the courtroom on that afternoon in May.

The judge listened patiently and our lawyer argued persuasively and Mark was returned to our custody. No school. No residential placement. No program. No hospital. Just right back where we had started. But not exactly. Mark was to be on what was termed home detention, a condition of release that required him to call in to a home detention officer every day. He was also placed on probation which necessitated a weekly visit to the probation officer. Only Doug's restraining hand on my arm kept me from jumping out of my seat.

"How can they do this?" I whispered. "How can they not understand that Mark runs away every chance he gets. If he runs, he won't call in and we'll have to go through all this again. Do you know what this means? It means I'll have to be with him every minute of every day. I can't. If I even stop to go to the bathroom, he'll be gone. Doug, it's impossible! It's wrong! They're putting me on home detention, not Mark."

The judge advised DYFS to continue their search for residential placement and ordered them to keep the court informed on the results of their search. A final disposition hearing was scheduled for June. I walked out of there beside myself with anger, vowing never to set foot in another courtroom.

I barely had time to exhale before I was back in court again. Sister Ellen, the principal of St. Andrew's School, had lodged a complaint of criminal trespass against Mark when he refused to obey her command to leave the school grounds. She agreed to drop the charge if I could guarantee that Mark would not trespass again. I gave my guarantee. I would have agreed to anything to keep Mark from violating his probation before I could find a permanent place for him.

I stepped up my investigation of the schools on the list SCRIPT had given me. After dozens of phone calls I narrowed the possibilities to three or four. Some of the schools on the list were not New Jersey approved schools. I decided to find out what I had to do to get the schools approved. If they accepted Mark, I wanted to make sure he could go there. So far DYFS had been unsuccessful in finding a residential placement for Mark. Thirty schools on their list had rejected him so far. I told them to keep trying.

Keeping tabs on Mark was a minute by minute task. If I so much as turned around, he was gone. I had impressed on him the importance of calling in to his detention officer by telling him that if he didn't, they would take him back to the Juvenile Shelter. He wanted what comparative freedom he had with me more than he wanted to run away. But even that threat was not enough to keep him close to home when the carnival came to town.

Chapter Twenty-Seven

I was in a hurry as usual. Earlier in the morning, I had taken Mark for his probation appointment and then to Mountainside Hospital for a hearing evaluation. I wanted all the paperwork ready to send to a residential facility in Virginia that I was hopeful would take Mark. I had spoken to Dr. Moss, the Director of Timber Ridge School, a week earlier and had explained to him the difficulties I was having placing Mark. To my relief, he listened. Instead of the immediate but polite, we're not interested speech, he asked me to send him the paperwork with the assurance that he would speak to me again when he had reviewed it all.

Placing Mark in Timber Ridge would be a problem because the school was not certified by the state of New Jersey. Without that certification, neither DYFS nor the Clifton Board of Education would allot tuition money or any payment for the placement. I decided to tackle the problem one step at a time. If Timber Ridge would accept Mark, I would find a way of getting him there. As I drove up Allwood Road, I reviewed in my mind the forms I needed to send to Dr. Hall. It was only after Mark repeated something several times that I realized he was talking to me.

"I bet I could get a job there! I bet they need someone like me there!"

"What?" I was still in a daze, trying to sort out what forms I had and what I needed to get.

"At the carnival, Ma."

A spot of color by the side of the road grew into a sign announcing this year's carnival and I suddenly realized he was talking about getting work there. Clifton hosted a summer carnival nearly every year. I had taken the kids to it when they were little and they had gone with their friends when they had grown past the age where they wanted to be seen with their parents. Honky-tonk music, food stands, rides and games of chance - a touch of country small town in a Metropolitan suburb, a remnant of a less complicated time when summer meant swimming holes and stick ball and pie-eating contests at county fairs.

"I don't know about that, Mark," I said. "Its rough work and you have to know what you're doing. They probably don't hire local people. Insurance and all that."

Mark gave me his "you know nothing" look, lit a cigarette and stared out the window. I went back to composing my mental lists.

July ran into early August while I ran around to the Clifton Board of Education, Jed Cruise, St. Claire's Hospital, DYFS and Family Court gathering a complete packet of documents detailing the essentials of our struggle to find help for Mark. Somehow, I found the time to watch him carefully and make sure he called in to his probation officer every day although I was still angry that I was being forced to monitor him for home detention.

By early August, we were both feeling the strain. Mark still chain smoked and his requests for cigarettes irritated me beyond my ability to cope. One morning while I was scrambling eggs for breakfast, Mark sat down at the kitchen table, twisting and snapping the package from an empty pack.

"Ma, when are you going to go to the store for cigarettes?" he asked.

"Mark, do you know how many times you asked me that this morning?"

"Dunno, but when are you going?"

"When I finish breakfast. I have a few chores to do and I'll pick them up when I go out."

"When will that be?"

"After breakfast, Mark. Do you want some scrambled eggs?"

"No. I want cigarettes."

"After breakfast, Mark."

My hands shook. I scrambled the eggs faster hoping to work off the tension. I had just slipped the spatula under the eggs to lift them out when he asked,

"Are you ready yet? I really need a pack of cigarettes."

I threw the eggs back in the pan, grabbed my purse and handed him a ten dollar bill. "Get the cigarettes and come right back. If you're not back in fifteen minutes, I'll take the damn cigarettes and throw them out."

Mark picked the bill from my trembling fingers, gave me a bright smile and disappeared through the door. At that moment, I didn't care whether he ever came back. I had not a single moment's peace all summer and the bang of the screen door slamming sounded like a celestial choir to me.

I took my cold eggs, toast and tea outside and relaxed, letting the warm sun bake away some of the tension from my shoulders. Before I knew it, a half hour had passed and Mark had not appeared. After an hour I knew he wasn't coming back. I called my mother on the odd chance that he might have walked to her house. Mark was still a great walker and thought nothing of taking a little stroll for a couple of miles. He wasn't there.

I showered, dressed in what I called "hunting for Mark" clothes, a tee shirt, jeans and sneakers and drove around to the parks and Laundromats where he had hidden before. Since he had been home, he had not been "hanging out" though he still received phone calls from people he identified only as friends. If I questioned him about these friends, he turned nasty and told me to mind my own business. Confrontations never yielded information and as long as he was conforming to the rules of home detention I tried to keep the arguments at a minimum.

By late afternoon, I was tired and I returned home to an empty house. The doors were locked just as I had left them. No sign that Mark had returned. I paced the kitchen floor, watching the clock. Mark had to call in to his detention officer or he would violate the conditions of his probation. Where the hell was he?

A small blob of color grew in my mind, though at first I couldn't recognize what it was. I concentrated and the blob grew into a sign. Clifton Carnival! I raced to the car and drove down Allwood Road to the island where the sign had been posted. I pulled over and studied the garishly painted announcement. I skipped over the attractions and focused on the dates. August 10 - August 16. Today was the 16th. The carnival ended at sundown today. I glanced at my watch. I was hoping I could grab Mark and get him home before eight o'clock. I knew his probation officer had evening hours and maybe, just maybe, he would accept Mark's late call if I thought of some clever excuse for the tardiness. It was now seven thirty. The park where the carnival was being held was only ten minutes away. There was still a chance. I raced through town, praying no cops would stop me and parked as close to the entrance as I could. People were still milling around though the crowd was clearly heading for the exit. Some of the food stands were closed and men were scraping the leftovers into huge garbage bags. The last group of thrill seekers spilled from the great Ferris Wheel and the gay music carried a more wistful sound, lingering on the wind like funeral flowers. I circled the arcade and searched the back fields where cables lay in twisted loops on the grass. A man jumped down from the open doors of an eighteen wheeler,

"Can I help you?" he asked.

"I'm looking for my son, Mark Graham. I think he's working here. Just today. I need to find him right away."

"Don't know all the locals by name, but you'll probably find him tearing down one of the rides. We use the local kids for that. The regulars like to pack up their own stands."

I rushed past him with a muttered thanks and ran to where the Ferris Wheel still split the sky with its lacy spokes. A crew was at work disassembling some of the smaller amusements. I approached cautiously. I didn't want him to see me and run before I had a chance to talk to him. In what I hoped was a calm tone, I asked one of the young men nearest me if he knew Mark Graham. He was bare-chested and he scratched his belly lazily as he thought. I felt my nerves pull to the breaking point.

"He's the kid who dislocated his shoulder this morning. I know because I pulled it back into line for him. Brave kid, that one. You looking for him?"

I nodded. I couldn't trust myself to speak.

He pointed a finger in the general direction of another crew of workers near the next ride. "Probably with that group," he said.

The gray haze of late twilight had fallen, making it difficult to see at any distance. I walked carefully over to the crew hoping to sneak up on Mark before he knew I was there. Too late. He had turned and spotted me and in an instant was off and running.

"Mark! Wait! Don't run! I need to talk to you."

He ducked around the back and took off across the field. I lost sight of him for a moment as he skirted one of the concession stands, then saw the streak of his shirt as he dashed away. There were few people in the park, but everywhere there were cables and planks and equipment scattered about. I ran down the aisle, crossed into the open space behind, jumping cables and shouting,

"Mark! Stop! You have to call in to your probation officer."

Mark slowed down, peering over his shoulder at me while he ran. I wasn't sure if he had heard me or if he realized that he had nowhere to go. We had reached the edge of the carnival and the thin line of trees ahead marked the end of the park. The carnival was over. Only the silence of the empty street awaited him. He stopped and turned, watching me like a cornered animal. Breathing heavily, I slowed my pace and approached him cautiously. I couldn't take the risk that he would turn and run again.

"If we leave now, we might be able to make it back in time to call in. I don't know what time the probation office closes. I can't promise we'll make it but it's worth a try. Want to try it?"

"And if I don't?"

"Then you have to take your chances with the court, Mark. I'll help you like I always have, but I can't do it for you. Calling in is your responsibility."

"Let me get my pay."

I walked with him back to the eighteen wheeler. The sky was black and, although the lights provided some illumination, I could not see my watch. I watched the men break down the carnival with a sense of loss. I knew in my heart I had lost and that, once more, I would be facing the carnival of the courts and the social system that had broken down where my son was concerned. I wondered if there were other parents out there looking at the night sky and wishing there was someone who could help them.

By the time we reached home it was after nine o'clock. Mark tried calling in, but he received no answer. When I woke up the next morning, he was gone. I spoke with his probation officer and learned that Mark had indeed violated his probation. The report had already been sent in and Mark would have to be returned to the Passaic Juvenile Shelter. I told him I did not know where Mark was and that I would not be responsible for incarcerating him there.

Mark was picked up the next day, but not before another complaint was filed against him, this time for sexual misconduct. The complaint stated that Mark "within the jurisdiction of this court committed an act of Criminal Sexual Contact upon C. T., age 18, by intentionally touching the intimate parts, vaginal area and breasts with his hands upon said victim with intent to humiliate said victim. A court date was set for September 14th".

"This is absolutely ridiculous," I said. Doug had just walked in the door when I handed him the complaint. "I'm not condoning what Mark did nor do I doubt he did it, but do you know how many thousands of kids are engaging in the same conduct. They're not getting arrested for ... for... doing that and more. And the girl is eighteen. Mark's only sixteen. Shouldn't the criminal charges be reversed? She's the adult, not him."

Doug laid the complaint form on the table and shook his head. "He's got a reputation now, Corraine. If he sneezes too loud they're going to pick him up. Maybe we should talk to the parents of this girl and see if we can figure out what's going on."

That night I sat down with my phone book and made a list of the calls for the following day. I had started a notebook of calls and appointments and, as I looked back, I realized that every day for the last year, I had been involved in some way in seeking help for Mark. If I had kept notebooks for the last twelve years, they would have revealed the same thing, that caring for a child with a disability takes all the strength and love one has to give all day, every day. My notebook was a reflection of how I had grown and matured, the internal obstacles I had overcome, the well-spring of love that had never run dry. Instead of feeling discouraged as I had so often in the past, I congratulated myself. I had climbed the mountain before and I would continue to do so until my son could reach the pinnacle with me.

The next morning I called the Passaic Juvenile Shelter and learned that Mark was having a difficult time adjusting. I decided to visit that afternoon though I hadn't planned on going until Doug's next day off. I also called Dr. Hall at the Timber Ridge Residential Facility. He had received the information packet I had sent him and, although he hadn't finished reviewing it, he did not immediately reject the application. I told him Mark was in the Shelter and I would call him back to set up an appointment after I knew what the court decision would be. Finally, I called C.T's mother to discuss the sexual misconduct complaint. She was perfectly willing to speak with me. I learned that her daughter was developmentally disabled and that they were also going through the same trials trying to find a school that would accept her for residential placement. She did not want her daughter to have to go through the anxiety of a hearing and agreed to write a letter explaining the circumstances of the situation. The family was moving soon and a hearing would prove to be an inconvenience.

The sexual misconduct charges were dropped and the circumstances surrounding the probation violation explained, but the time spent in the Juvenile Shelter took its toll and Mark was once again a patient at St. Clare's Hospital. I no longer believed that his hospital stays would affect any lasting change in him, but the medication he received there and the therapy did calm him for short periods.

Dr. Lowenthal wrote a letter to the courts stressing the need for residential placement. DYFS replied with a list of over fifty facilities that had refused Mark admission. Dr. Lowenthal suggested I contact Judy Horner, the executive director of a group of private, non-profit treatment centers called the New Jersey Association of Children's Residential Facilities. He did not know if she could help me, but it was a lead if Timber Ridge did not take Mark.

Mark's behavior continued to deteriorate and by the time he was discharged at the end of September, a change had occurred in him that frightened me more than anything that had come before.

From St. Clare's, he had been allowed to come home with the same conditions of home detention and probation. I had told Mark very clearly that it was his responsibility to call in and that if he did not, he would be returned to the Juvenile Shelter as he had been before. He acted as if he did not hear me, but for two days he called in without my prompting.

He also started again at Palisades Learning Center and had been up and on time for the bus. I did not bother him about the chains and the keys and the jackets with the arms ripped off though he had acquired a tattoo with a strange symbol that disturbed me. When I pointed it out, he shrugged and gave me a glassy-eyed smile that made me shiver. He began receiving phone calls late at night and afterwards, I'd hear him muttering and moving things in his room. In the morning, though, I found nothing changed.

I made an appointment with Judy Horner, the woman Dr. Lowenthal had recommended I speak with about residential placement. Still actively pursuing the Timber Ridge placement, I wanted to keep all doors open. Whatever information she could give me I would be grateful for. I walked into her home loaded with questions. She received me warmly and, in a few minutes, we were comfortable with one another. I learned from her that the number of people waiting for placements in New Jersey numbered in the hundreds.

"It's such a shame, Corraine," she said. "So many of the cases that come to me are like your own. Parents and children who are in desperate need of help and who are turned away because there are no facilities for them. Either they don't match what is available or nothing is available. There aren't enough resources in the community to handle them there and there aren't enough residential facilities to accommodate them outside of the community. What happens to them is the same as what's happening to Mark. These kids get lost in the maze of social services and never receive the kind of help they need. They are thrown away by the system. We need a good strong lobbying group to go to Trenton and work to get these facilities built."

"What would it take to get a group together to send down to Trenton?" I asked.

She looked at me sharply, assessing me. "Is this something you would be interested in organizing?" she asked.

"Actually, Judy, it is. I've been mulling over the idea of getting involved on more than just a personal level. My concern is my son, of course, but I'm not getting very far on my own. If you are willing to help me, I'm willing to try. I just don't know how to get started."

Although I spoke confidently, I was more than a little surprised by my response. Ever since Doug had mentioned the idea, I had considered it now and then, but I hadn't known I was this close to taking action. Judy took for granted that my confidence was grounded in a long standing commitment.

"The first step would be to test out the level of involvement in the community," she said. "Call a meeting, advertise in the paper that such a group will be forming and see what kind of response you get. If there's a big enough response, we'll go from there."

We ironed out a few of the details and when I left, I knew I would follow through on it. Perhaps with enough numbers we could get our cases heard and together learn what we needed to help our children. One more piece of the giant jigsaw puzzle that needed to fall into place before the system recognized the picture we were presenting. I had a feeling that when all the pieces were assembled the picture would reveal the word HELP!

When I reached home, it was a little after three. Feeling energetic, I ran up the stairs to Mark's room to tell him about the group I would be forming. The door was partly ajar. I peeked in. Mark was sitting on the floor, cross-legged, a black candle lit before him and he was chanting, strange syllables I could not make out. Unaware of my presence, he continued his ritual and in the half-light of the darkened room, I saw the crucifix above his bed was turned upside down.

I walked into the room calmly ignoring the rage and fear that threatened to paralyze me. At the head of the bed, I righted the crucifix and snapped open the shades. Sunlight flooded the room like a benediction. I knocked the candle over with my foot, stamping out the flame, then kicked it under the bed. Mark looked at me, his eyes furious and filled with a malevolence that started me shivering again.

He jumped to his feet and rushed towards me. I was nearest the door. I ran out, slamming and locking it behind me. I couldn't remember if his bedroom window was bolted. If he climbed out of it, he could reenter the house by the door. I ran downstairs and locked all the doors from the inside, then sat down on the couch and tried to regain my breath. I was shaking so hard I could not sit. I couldn't think what to do. Should I call the police? Should I call an ambulance and have them take him to a hospital? Sweat dripped into my eyes mixing with my tears. I wrung my hands until they were raw and cracked. When I could trust myself to speak, I called Doug at work and told him what had happened. From his silence, I could tell he was stunned. He promised to leave work immediately. I told him I did not know where Mark was and that I was afraid to look. I was afraid he would come back and try to hurt me. Doug told me to stay in the house until he came home.

I did not see Mark again for two days though I lived in constant fear of his return. Sunday morning I left the house for the first time.

I wanted to go to church and Cheryl had agreed to accompany me. Glancing in my rear view mirror while backing out, I saw him turn up the driveway to the house. He was filthy, his hair in strings around his face, his clothes stained and torn. He looked gaunt, as if he hadn't eaten for days and his eyes were blood-rimmed and rolling slightly. My first thought was that no one but God could help him now. I jumped out of the car, grabbed him by the arm and hauled him into the front seat. Cheryl jumped into the back.

"What're you doing?" he said. "I want to go home."

"After church."

"I'm not going to church. I can't go to church. I'll die if I go there. The Master will punish me. He'll torture me if I go there." Mark's voice rose on a high pitched wail.

"What Master, Mark ? Who are you talking about?"

"The Master of the Gates of Hell. Satan." He was screaming now, his eyes wild and his hands clutching at the door handle. I parked the car, jumped out and ran around to the passenger door. I had no idea what I was dealing with. All I knew was that I needed a miracle to free my son from whatever torment he was writhing in. I grabbed him by one arm and signaled Cheryl to hold on to the other. In his weakened state, he struggled, but we were able to overpower him and drag him into St. Andrew's. I chose the last pew, afraid that Mark would make a scene before I could get him to the communion rail. He sat next to me and I could feel him twitching uncontrollably. His eyes were rolled back and his breathing turned hoarse and shallow. I held him in my arms as long as I could, but when he began to wretch, his body heaving convulsively, I ran him out the door. He became violently sick on the lawn. Alone with my son in the shadow of the cross, I prayed to Mary to give me the strength to accept what my child was suffering just as she had accepted the suffering of her own son. With Cheryl's help I carried Mark's frail, convulsive body to the car and drove home.

When we returned to the house, Mark ran for the phone and I ran for the backyard where Doug was reading the Sunday newspaper. I told him what had happened at church. He laid aside his newspaper and walked into the house. I could hear Mark talking in an excited voice, describing what I had forced him to do and occasionally saying, "Yes, Black Priest," as if receiving instructions. Doug asked him who he was talking to. Mark turned his back. I heard him tell the black priest that he would take care of his father and not to worry. Doug's face turned livid, the skin mottling with red. He grabbed the phone from Mark's hand. Mark swung at him twice then fell back as Doug hit him in the stomach.

"If the black priest tells me to, I'll stab you in the back and drink your blood. My voices tell me not to be afraid. The voices of Satan tell me it's all right to kill. We kill all the time, mice and raccoons and we drink their blood. We do what the high priest tells us to do. If he tells me to go home one night and kill you, I'll do it. I will. I swear it." Mark broke from Doug's grasp, reeled across the room and ran through the door. We searched all night, but this time we could not find him.

Two nights later, on September 30th, the phone rang shortly after 10:30 pm. The Clifton police informed me that Mark was in the emergency room at St. Mary's Hospital. He had frightened an elderly woman by knocking on her door and asking to use the phone. He was wearing a death's head mask and was highly agitated.

Doug and I left for the hospital immediately. My mom, dad and Mark's DYFS caseworker met us there. When we arrived we were met by a member of the Crisis Intervention Team who told us that Mark was with another member of the team and that it might be best if we did not attempt to see him at the time. Mark had again spoken about killing us at the bidding of the black priest and the devil's voice he had been hearing in his head for almost a month. We learned that the black priest was someone he had met at St. Clare's on his last hospitalization there. He had described to the Crisis Team the ritual sacrifices they practiced in a tunnel under the highway. I asked for the location of the tunnel and the name of the black priest, but they would not tell me.

Mark also threatened the crisis counselor.

"What did he say?" I asked her, fearful that Mark had committed another illegal act that would lead to his being incarcerated at a long term juvenile jail.

He said, "I can't stay here with all these crosses. I'll go crazy, use my black magic to kill you. I don't think you want that."

I sagged down in my chair, all hope lost as I looked at her, strangely detached from what she had said. I felt as if my body was there, but all that I had held on to, all that I had believed possible fled with her words. I had no idea what we were going to do and I had no will to do anything. She was talking again, but I only caught snatches of her conversation. "Do you understand?" she asked me at last.

"What?" I said.

Doug explained. "Dr. Kim has advised the Crisis Intervention Team to call for an adolescent bed at Trenton State Psychiatric Hospital. They will accept him in the morning, but they need a judge's signature for the commitment. Mark will stay here in the Emergency Quiet Room overnight and he'll be transferred in the morning. He will be in restraints so he doesn't hurt anyone or himself. He is very agitated and the medication they gave him doesn't seem to help. They called St. Claire's but Dr. Lowenthal couldn't accept him back. He says there's nothing more they can do for him. They called St. Michael's, Beth Israel, Union Hospital. No beds are available. They'll tell us when he's going to be transferred to Trenton so we can follow him down in the morning."

Because Mark was still threatening to kill us, the Crisis Team advised us to go home without seeing him. I sat by the phone all night, shaking and drinking tea, waiting for someone to tell me if my son had made it through the night without killing himself or someone else. When the phone rang, I slipped to the floor, hugging my knees to my chest in an effort to keep myself together. Somehow I managed to pick up the receiver.

"Mrs. Conaway. It's Detective Reilly, Clifton Police. I talked to Mark about the Hell's Gate Cult this morning. He was much better than when we brought him in last night. A crisis counselor from Juvenile Justice also spoke to him and Mark was polite and cooperative. Dr. Kim advised commitment to Trenton Psychiatric, but the judge wants him back in the Juvenile Shelter. He just signed the warrant for his return there. He'll be transferred later today. You can see him there if you like."

I whispered my thanks for his phone call. I had barely the strength to lift myself from the floor. Doug was still sleeping and like a ghost from the grave I sought the warmth of the living, curling up against him and, at last, closed my eyes. I did not hear him get up for work and I was grateful that he did not wake me. I woke again more than twenty-four hours later.

Chapter Twenty-Eight

Determined that my son would not spend what was left of his childhood in the Passaic County Juvenile Detention Center, I redoubled my efforts to send him to Timber Ridge. I needed to get the school licensed by The New Jersey Department of Education and the Division of Youth and Family Services. Without the license, the state would pay neither tuition nor room and board. No in-state facility would accept him and the state would not accept Timber Ridge. Like Sisyphus, I knew I was pushing a boulder up a mountain, but my shoulder was already pressed against the rock. One inch at a time, I told myself.

I called Dr. Moss at Timber Ridge. I promised him that if he flew up to interview Mark I would meet him at the airport, bring him to the shelter, cook him dinner and let him sleep at our house so he wouldn't have to pay hotel accommodations. Talk about desperation. I didn't care. I was so grateful when he agreed. I would have done anything within reason.

In the two weeks before Dr. Moss's visit, I met with Judy Horner and Peggy Brower from the New Jersey Mental Health Association. Together we threshed out the details for a support group we would call Children in Crisis Advocates. We designed ads for the local papers. Peggy suggested I contact the Bergen Record to see if they would be interested in running an article on Mark. Parents who needed help might miss the ad, but not a full length article. I called the next day and, although they did not promise coverage, they did not reject the idea outright. They told me to speak with Mark Magyar, the reporter who covered our beat. He agreed to interview me in October.

Time was the enemy I now engaged. I could not afford to waste a minute. Mark was miserable in the Juvenile Shelter and I needed to get him released to a facility where he would have twenty-four hour supervision. I had spoken to him earlier in the week and he said he wanted to kill himself. I called the crisis counselor immediately. There was little they could do but watch him carefully. I needed to get him out of there, but I could not help him at home.

I contacted the Clifton Board of Education for the proper person to speak with at the New Jersey Division of Education. My first few calls were not successful, but I finally reached someone who told me of the mountains of paperwork I would need completed before they could consider my request. Luckily, I had gathered many of the medical and psychological evaluations for Mark's application for Timber Ridge and DYFS had most of the others including the refusals for in-state residential placement. What I really needed though was Mark's acceptance to Timber Ridge. No action would be taken before that crucial Yes was delivered. I couldn't wait until Dr. Moss arrived.

The morning I was to pick him up at the airport I woke at dawn, rushed through breakfast, called the Juvenile Shelter to see how Mark had made it through the night and spoke to his counselor informing him that I would be bringing Dr. Moss to interview Mark later this afternoon. I wanted Mark showered, decently dressed and awake for the interview. Some of the guards had befriended Mark and I wanted the word passed down that he should be helped through this.

At the airport, my nerves were screaming as loud as the approaching jets. I pushed through the crowds to the gate where Dr. Moss would be arriving though I knew I was a half hour early. I was taking no chances on missing him. I sat in the lobby watching the planes arriving and departing. So much depended on the outcome of Dr. Moss's visit. I needed him to understand that Mark was not a juvenile delinquent, but a child so bedeviled by fear that he would do anything to escape it; a child who did not have the intellectual capability of sorting out the fear from the behavior prompted by it. How could I get that across to him when I had been unsuccessful in making anyone else understand what I had come to understand so well? While I waited, I prayed for the right words to reach this man whose judgment was so important to Mark's future.

When the plane landed, I peered at each of the disembarking passengers intently. I had forgotten to ask Dr. Moss for a description so I narrowed my scrutiny to business men traveling alone. There were several men dressed in conservative suits, carrying brief cases, but only one who stopped near the door and looked around expectantly.

I approached him boldly if uncertainly. "Dr. Moss?"

He looked down at me in relief. He was tall, casually dressed with a broad open face and alert, intelligent eyes. "I remembered on the plane that I had not given you a description to identify me nor had you told me about yourself," he said, shaking my hand. "I assume you're Corraine."

"That's me," I said with a smile. My first impression of him was positive. Warm, personable, but not overly ingratiating. I felt he could be strong when needed, but not rigid or unfair.

"I hope you had a pleasant flight." I guided him in the direction of the exit and out to the parking lot keeping up a rush of small talk that allowed me to collect myself before launching into a discussion about Mark. Once we were on Route 21, I relaxed a bit, comforted by the growing belief that he would give Mark a fair hearing.

"Do you have any questions you'd like to ask me about Mark or would you prefer to meet him first and talk about him later?" I asked.

"I'd rather interview him now, then you and I and, hopefully, your husband can sit down and talk about whether Mark and Timber Ridge would make a good match. If I don't feel we can help him there, I'll tell you honestly."

I prayed silently all the way to the Juvenile Detention Center in Haledon. I must have said, "Please, God! Please!" at least one hundred times before we arrived. Dr. Moss requested the opportunity to interview Mark alone. He felt he could get a better picture of Mark's personality and more honest responses to his questions that way. I sat on the cheap vinyl seats in the waiting room and watched the clock, adding another hundred "Please Gods" to the hundred I had said on the way here. Forty-five minutes passed before the door opened and Dr. Moss stepped in. I could read little from his expression except that he appeared more thoughtful than he had before. He fumbled with the clasp on his briefcase, securing it more carefully.

He asked me if I wanted to visit Mark. I stood up and walked towards him still trying to read his reaction.

"Is he expecting me?"

"I don't think so."

"Then I'll wait. I had planned to visit him tomorrow and tell him your decision, one way or the other."

We drove back to the house in silence. Dr. Moss offered no information and I was too afraid to ask. If we were to be refused again, I wanted Doug there for support. Doug had arranged to leave work early and I hoped he was at the house already. I had run out of my store of small talk and I couldn't wait to hear Dr. Moss's decision.

My prayer was answered. Doug met us at the door. After Dr. Moss entered, Doug raised an inquiring eyebrow at me. I shrugged.

"I know what a long and difficult process this has been for you," Dr. Moss began. "I want to assure you right away that my decision has been based on a careful evaluation of the written material you have sent me and my interview with Mark. I have worked with many boys over the years, most of whom have gone on to find themselves and live law-abiding and productive lives. Some have not. I cannot give you a guarantee that Mark will choose the straight and narrow, but I believe we can help point him in that direction. I'd like to try. In other words, my answer to your application is Yes."

Tears flowed down my face. I made no effort to wipe them away. A river of relief poured through me and I let it sweep me away. Doug patted my hand and Dr. Moss looked slightly embarrassed.

"Sorry," I said. "You have to understand what I've been through. Since March I've spoken to everyone from Clifton's Mayor to the New Jersey Governor's Office and all the political appointees in between trying to get help for my son. Everyone promises and no one delivers. It's such a relief to finally get a yes. To hear someone say Yes, I am willing to help Mark. I'm just so grateful."

Dr. Moss smiled. "We still have a long way to go. As you know, an examination and approval of Timber Ridge by the appropriate agencies from New Jersey will be necessary before Mark can be placed at our school. I am more than willing to submit to as thorough an examination as is needed for their approval, but arranging this often takes time. Not on my part, they can come whenever they like, but I've dealt with state agencies and they tend to drag their heels. I'll write the necessary letters and send for the application right away, but I would suggest you also stay on their trail. If you could get letters from members of Congress requesting that they expedite the process, it couldn't hurt."

"No problem. I'll just keep making those calls. I've nothing to lose and everything to gain."

Dr. Moss nodded. "I'm sure you must have many questions you want to ask me about Timber Ridge. We didn't cover many of the specifics over the phone and I want you to be sure that our school is the kind of environment you want your son to be in."

I stared at him blankly. The relief in hearing that Mark was accepted had washed away any reservations I may have had. I looked at Doug helplessly.

"Why don't you tell us about it?" Doug said. "If we have any questions, we'll ask them as they come up."

"Well, let's see. We've been in operation for twenty-five years. Our school is licensed and we are accredited as a long term residential treatment center for young men with serious educational, emotional and adjustment problems. Our program is highly structured and stringent, the boys don't get the opportunity to get into trouble. And eight out of ten boys who complete the program remain trouble free for at least two years following discharge.

The boys are not confined. Life at Timber Ridge is modeled after a traditional boarding school. Our students are assigned to dormitories and assume responsibility for maintaining their living quarters. They are taught good management and personal hygiene skills. There is also training in leisure skills and constructive ways to use leisure time. We do engage in competitive inter-scholastic athletics including football, wrestling, basketball, baseball, soccer and track. Our older kids, like Mark, learn independent living skills that prepare the boys for life on their own. These skills would include getting and holding a job, either on campus or in the community, and moving off campus to supervised apartment living on a trial or permanent basis."

Dr. Moss waited politely for us to ask any questions. I wanted to hear about the educational aspects of the program, but assumed he would go on with that. Everything he had said so far met with my approval and when I looked at Doug, he nodded his agreement as well.

"On to education and treatment then," he said. "Realistically, not all of our boys will be able to earn a high school diploma. Although our school does not accept boys below a low normal IQ, so many of the children that come to us have a history similar to Mark's. They are so far behind it is impossible for them to earn a regular degree. Many do receive a high school diploma, others take the test for a GED and others are enrolled in vocational programs that offer them the chance to learn the skills and attitudes needed to enter the work world. Some of our students are so far behind that we begin their studies with basic reading and mathematics survival skills. Students, of course, can move up as their skill level or interest improves. Each child's program is individually developed with input from the child himself, the family and the placing agency. We will send you regular progress reports so you'll know how Mark is growing. Our class sizes are small and every child receives one-on-one instruction when he needs it.

Finally, there are our treatment services. They take many forms at Timber Ridge. We have individual sessions with a licensed professional counselor as well as group counseling on a regular basis. If necessary, we take the boys to AA and NA meetings. In addition, the boys attend class sessions on social skills, such as peer relations, conflict resolution. and anger management. We are very proud of our program and of the success we've had in helping these boys live decent and productive lives."

The next day, when I drove Dr. Moss to the airport, we reviewed the steps I needed to take and the people I needed to contact in order to get Timber Ridge approved. Dr. Moss would send for the application and write the necessary letters to the New Jersey Department of Education and the Division of Youth and Family Services. I would get letters from the appropriate members of Congress, and keep in constant contact with DYFS. I also arranged to visit Timber Ridge on the weekend of October 13th. Mark was due in court on October 27. I hoped he could be released right to Timber Ridge. That is if all went as I was determined it would.

That same day, I called Gail Everett at DYFS and told her the outcome of my visit with Dr. Moss. She told me they were still pursuing a placement for Mark at Willow Glen in Wisconsin, but she did tell me to contact the Exceptional Funding Coordinator for DYFS in Trenton. I called and spoke to him about Timber Ridge. He made it clear that DYFS was pushing for a quick placement at Willow Glen, but that he would also look into Timber Ridge. He did not feel that I would have a choice if Willow Glen was approved first although I had registered an objection to the place. I wanted Mark closer to home in a facility where Doug and I could visit him regularly. An interview had been set up with a representative from

Willow Glen. Mark would be ordered by the court to go there if approval came through before Timber Ridge.

If I had been smoldering before, I was now on fire. Every day I made several phone calls, pleading my case. Senator Roe and Senator Lautenberg's offices promised to send letters to DYFS and the New Jersey Department of Education requesting timely approval of Timber Ridge. I followed up on the promises until I received confirmation that the letters had been received. I wrote a letter to the director of DYFS in Trenton informing him of the situation and requesting he give it his personal attention and I flooded DYFS with letters from State Senators, Congressmen and social service agencies.

Dr. Moss had done his part and sent in the application as well as a letter to DYFS requesting the necessary inspection of Timber Ridge for their official approval. Still the wheels of the bureaucracy turned slowly. The best I could get was a confirmation that DYFS would send a representative to Timber Ridge prior to Mark's court date. If DYFS okayed the school, then one of the three parts needed for approval would be complete. For Mark to be sent there I needed Licensing Approval, Contract Approval and Educational Approval. DYFS would check with the state of Virginia for Licensing Approval as well as a review of the school's financial records. The New Jersey Department of Education would have to approve the educational portion. They would send their own representative and so far I had heard nothing from them.

I contacted Mark Magyar, the reporter from The Record, and received a commitment from him for an interview on October 16th. I wanted the article to come out before our first meeting of Children in Crisis Advocates. We had made our plans for the first meeting. Now we needed to find and encourage parents who were suffering alone to come join us.

The interview was long and painful; the results well worth the suffering. The article by Mark J. Magyar appeared on the front page of The Sunday Record. I scanned the article, then sat down to read it thoroughly.

Mr. Magyar had done an excellent job chronicling the long journey we had taken to find help for Mark, beginning with his adoption at 3 years old and the difficulties his hyperactivity had presented from the start. His school years, his classifications as neurologically impaired, emotionally disturbed, learning disabled, developmentally disabled all leading to the admission by school officials that they could not help him were starkly presented and brought tears to my eyes. But I was happy to see that the article was not just about Mark, but also about the other children and their anguished parents who, like us, were wandering the maze of schools, courts, mental health and social service agencies desperately seeking help.

The inadequacy of the social service system in providing treatment, and the insufficient number of beds, only 600 in 14 residential settings, resulting in hundreds of out-of-state placements, was made painfully clear as was the need for change in the way troubled children were treated throughout the state. Mark's path through the maze had ended in his incarceration at a Youth Detention Center, a fate shared by so many disabled youths with nowhere else to go. The article ended with an admission by the Deputy Human Services Commissioner that New Jersey's troubled youngsters were not getting the treatment they needed.

That afternoon and for the following week, calls poured in from parents who had tried unsuccessfully to have their severely emotionally or physically disabled children placed in residences in New Jersey. Their stories horrified, then angered me, strengthening me in my conviction that something had to be done. The suffering was appalling. Many of the parents agreed to come to the first meeting of Children in Crisis Advocates, not only to gain emotional support, but to discuss strategies for getting the state to listen to our need and act on it. I grew more impassioned by each phone call I received. Something had to be done and I was going to do it.

The days flew by, lost in a barrage of phone calls to DYFS and the State Department of Education as well as the calls from people interested in Children in Crisis Advocates. I made a quick driving trip to Timber Ridge and returned more convinced than ever that this was the place for Mark. The rural setting, the rustic grounds, the beautiful green of the surrounding hills and the tasteful architecture of the buildings was everything I had pictured for Mark's home away from home. I was given the freedom to enter the dormitories, sit in on classes, inspect every aspect of the residences and I was impressed with everything I saw. Classroom management was excellent, learning enhanced by a fair and consistent reward system and creative approaches to learning.

Disruptive behavior was dealt with immediately either by the teacher or by the arrival of a counselor who took the child away for a therapy session. I was impressed and more determined than before that Mark go to Timber Ridge. DYFS pushed Willow Glen and we were beginning to go head to head on that. I had spoken to the Public Advocates office and had been informed that I would have to go along with that placement if it was approved before Timber Ridge, especially if it was supported by a court order.

On October 27, the presiding judge ordered that Mark be placed immediately in either Timber Ridge or Willow Glen and that the order stand as a mandate to whatever agencies were involved in the placement procedure. Mark was to remain in the Juvenile Detention Center until he was released to one or the other facility. The judge was beginning to lose patience with the repeated delays and his courtroom demeanor reflected his annoyance. I hoped his sternness would have some effect on DYFS's decision to get Timber Ridge certified as soon as possible.

Chapter Twenty-Nine

I paced to the door and peered into the darkness. I had come to the Clifton Recreation Building where we were holding our first meeting of Children in Crisis Advocates a half hour early to set up refreshments and to practice the talk I was giving. So many parents had responded to our advertisement and to the newspaper article that I had great hopes for a good turn-out tonight. The meeting was scheduled for 7:30 pm. It was now 7:20 and no one had yet opened the door.

I checked the refreshment table again. Judy caught me rearranging the cake plates and laughed. "Don't worry. They'll be here. Take it from me. No one wants to be first at meetings like this. Everyone will show up a few minutes past 7:30."

She was right. By a quarter to eight the room filled up. Judy and I greeted each parent individually and introduced ourselves. I wanted to create an atmosphere in which people felt comfortable talking about their children and the problems they had encountered getting help for them. I wanted them to know they were not alone and that they no longer needed to be alone. As the trickle of people increased to a steady stream I realized that we had attracted parents not only from Passaic County, but from Bergen, Essex and Hudson counties as well. I wondered if many of these parents had fought as I had fought and had come here because they believed that this was their last chance to get someone to listen to their plight.   When I studied their careworn faces and knew, as only another parent of a disabled child could know, how much suffering they had endured and how much love they had for their troubled children, my determination to help them grew.

At eight o'clock, I walked through the scattered knots of people clustered around the room, stood alone at the front and called the first meeting of Children in Crisis Advocates to order. Chairs scuffled across the floor as people took their seats. As soon as it was quiet, I took a deep breath.

"I'm Corraine Conaway and I'd like to welcome you to Children in Crisis Advocates. I have spoken to many of you on the phone, but for the others, I'd like to tell you a little about myself and why I decided to start this advocacy group. For years I have tried to place my son, Mark, who is neurologically impaired and emotionally disturbed, in a treatment program. After years of switching schools, repeated visits to hospital crisis intervention units and rejections from nearly sixty schools and treatment programs, I am still trying to place my son. Right now, he's in the Passaic County Detention Center where he has been warehoused for six weeks.

I'm here today because I don't want any other child to go through what Mark's been through before he or she can get help. Waiting years for treatment because of the inadequacies of our social service system can destroy a child as well as the family. We don't want our children to fall through the cracks in the system, squeezed between DYFS, the family court, mental health facilities, schools, and jails, none of whom know what to do for them.

I'm not saying we can perform miracles, but if we get hooked up together as a group, we can create a center for processing and dispensing the vital information we all need to find the appropriate services for our children. And equally important, we can give each other support as well as information. My short term goal is to help us live with the day to day difficulties of raising a handicapped child. Long term, I'd like to see our group become a major voice in the lobbying process and to make our legislators realize the need for more residential facilities in New Jersey, especially state funded programs for our kids. Now I'd like to introduce Judy Horner, executive director of the New Jersey Association of Residential Health Care Facilities."

I took a vacant seat in the back row where I could watch the faces of the parents as Judy began to speak. The applause when I had left the podium had been rich and warm and the expressions hopeful. Judy and I had agreed to keep our remarks brief. We wanted to hear from those who had come out tonight, their hopes and fears and the struggles they had experienced which would create a bond between us. I tuned into Judy's speech. She was talking about the need for space in current facilities and the creation of new residential treatment centers

"In order to even make a dent in the waiting list we need 500 to 1000 beds in a wide range of programs. But those are only the numbers. What this group can do is force state officials to look into the faces of the parents and children who aren't getting help. We need them to understand the pain, fear and frustration of loving families torn apart because of the inadequacies of the current social service providers. No one has ever tried anything like this. There are special interest groups that focus on specific problems of the developmentally disabled or the learning disabled, but none that are as broadly focused as this group. Aside from giving one another support and sharing knowledge, you can make real for legislators the human stories behind the numbers. Now we'd like to throw the meeting open to you. We want to hear those stories."

I walked back to the front of the room amidst a field of waving hands. Great! I wouldn't have to pull people's stories from them. They wanted to speak and I wanted to listen. I made a mental note to rearrange the chairs in a circle for the next meeting so members wouldn't need to raise their hands.

A woman in the second row was waving papers trying to get my attention. I asked her to stand up and speak loudly so we could all hear.

"These are my son's court papers. The judge sentenced him to six months in Jamesburg for attempting to commit suicide while he was on parole. My son doesn't belong in prison. He needs help, not punishment. When I tried to introduce his school records that clearly show he had been classified as multiply handicapped, emotionally disturbed and neurologically impaired, the Judge refused to look at them. I'm here because what the court did was wrong. I asked for help for my poor child and they put him in prison. Is that where they put children they don't know what else to do with?"

Hands flew up all over the room. Everyone wanted to speak so I randomly chose a woman from the back of the room.

"I just want to tell you that I have been through Hell. The agency, DYFS, just hasn't been there for me. I'm the mother of eight children and I have spent the last seven weeks living on the streets and in my car. I was evicted because welfare checks did not cover the rent and utility bills. I had a heart attack and couldn't work. I needed help for my children and DYFS dragged their heels. I didn't know how I was going to feed them. We now have a place to stay and I thank God for that. But I still need help for my children, especially one of my girls. DYFS expects you to be drunk or slovenly or a bad mother before they'll help you. In my opinion, the agency has a "don't call us, we'll call you" attitude. I hope this group works because it feels like an open door when so many have been shut in my face."

One story after another erupted from the floor. One man spoke of how his son had been discharged from a program for emotionally disturbed children and had been waiting two months for a school to accept him. The child had written to the White House for help when no other help was available to him. He ended the letter with the line, "If you're too busy, I understand."

Another woman told how her fourteen year old son had been expelled from school nine months ago, but state officials have refused to provide a tutor, as state law required. I sat through the meeting with tears in my eyes. I understood the anguish of parents who loved their troubled children and could find no help for them.

When the meeting broke up three hours later, I propped my weary feet on the table and turned to Judy. "I don't know whether to laugh or cry. Hearing those parents speak nearly tore me apart. But I'm exhilarated because I feel we have a solid group who have been pushed to their limit and are ready to speak up for themselves. Next stop - Trenton. What do you think?"

Judy stopped collecting the used cake plates and cups long enough to smile at me. "I think you've really got something going here, Corraine. But it's going to take a tremendous amount of work to keep it going. You have to research your issues, get your numbers, fight City Hall or in this case, the State Hall and give it the human touch we heard tonight. Are you up to all that?"

I gave her a cheeky grin. "What have I got to lose? I'm bugging everybody and their uncle in Trenton as it is. What's a few more phone calls?"

I continued my barrage of phone calls to DYFS and the New Jersey Department of Education. Mark was becoming more desperate by the day. I had to get him out of there. I checked daily the progress of the three part evaluations on Timber Ridge, hoping to convince the DYFS director or the director of field operations to push forward the evaluation. The answers I received were often curt, but I was beyond the point of caring. My feelings were a low second to my son's life.

On the morning of November 16th, I received the call. DYFS and the New Jersey Division of Education approved Timber Ridge and agreed to pay Mark's tuition. I hugged myself and spun around in circles. YES! YES! YES! I could hardly believe it. I picked up the phone and called Doug, then my parents, then the Shelter to tell Mark. He didn't care about Timber Ridge. All he wanted was to get out of there.

I called Family Court and set a date for Mark's release hearing. They were able to accommodate us the next morning at 9:00 am, but the clerk informed me that they would need to confirm the approval. I gave her Dr. Moss's number at Timber Ridge as well as the Trenton numbers for DYFS and the New Jersey Department of Education.

I couldn't sit still. I called Dr. Moss's office and asked when Mark was expected and what he would need to bring. A list of clothes and personal items would be sent to me, but for the meantime, the secretary dictated a partial list to bring with me on November 20th. Only three days from today! I hung up the phone and with list in hand, started packing. I was so overjoyed by the opportunity given to Mark that it hardly struck me I was packing to send my son away. That Mark might not welcome this chance as much as I did never occurred to me.

I picked Mark up at the Juvenile Shelter the next morning. His clothes hung on him and the bones of his face stuck out sharply against the gray-white of his stretched skin. His hair hung limp and lifeless and the blank look I had so dreaded was back in his eyes. He looked in my direction and for a moment I wondered if he recognized me. I thanked God for the hundredth time that Timber Ridge had accepted him.

After a stern admonishment, the Court released Mark on the condition that he report to Timber Ridge on the morning of November 20th.

"So, what about this place you're sending me to? Bet it's another juvenile shelter with a fancy name," Mark asked as soon as we started driving. Before I had a chance to answer he said, "Stop at the store. I need another pack of cigarettes."

I went with him to buy his cigarettes, afraid that if he left the car I might not see him again for another week or two. I planned to watch him like a hawk for the next day and a half. I would not breath easily again until he was safely settled into Timber Ridge. He smoked two cigarettes, one after the other, during the ten minute drive from

Paterson to Clifton. I started to tell him about Timber Ridge and my hopes for him there, but he shut me off with a "Not now. I'm tired and hungry and I can't listen to you going on about this stupid school."

After a shower and a change of fresh clothing, he looked more like himself though his skin was pasty from being inside so long and he was so thin it was frightening. To reassure myself, I cooked him a big breakfast. I described to him the green grass, rolling hills, and beautiful trees surrounding Timber Ridge and how the program there included plenty of time for outdoor activities. He shoveled in the food and looked up at me once in a while. Was he listening? I couldn't tell.

When he put his fork down, I moved in. I didn't want him to bolt. With a firm hand under his elbow, I guided him upstairs, explaining on the way that I needed his help sorting out clothes to pack. He sat on the edge of his bed, head down, hands between his knees, while I held up shirts and sweaters for his approval. I managed to get two suitcases packed before he became restless, jumping up to look out the window and walk around the room.

"We can do the rest of this tomorrow. I planned a nice dinner for your Bon Voyage tomorrow night. Come on. We'll do some shopping. You can pick out the cake and whatever other food you especially want. Then, Nana and Grandpa want to see you. They're coming over as soon as Grandpa comes home from work. And, of course, Cheryl wants to see you then, too."

He had been cooped up so long, even shopping, which he never liked before, now had a certain novelty to it and he did want to see his grandparents and his sister. Cheryl had come with me a few times to visit him in the shelter and, although their relationship was slightly strained, Mark always talked to her more than he talked to me or Doug. Besides, I wanted as many people around as I could muster. The more people, the less chance Mark could escape without one of us seeing him.

That night I checked on Mark five times. I'd fall asleep, only to wake up with a start, jump out of bed and run to Mark's room. I'd listen to his steady even breathing and, reassured, tiptoe back to my bedroom, only to wake up again an hour later and start all over.

I awoke, showered and dressed at dawn. Over morning coffee, I confided to Doug my fears that I wouldn't be able to keep Mark from running away. He had been in the Juvenile Detention Center for months and he was leaving again tomorrow for several more months. I had the strongest feeling he'd want to roam the neighborhood, visit familiar places, say good-bye to people he'd known who he considered friends.

"It's a perfectly normal thing to want to do. My fear is that old places will trigger old patterns and he'll take off. If he lets me, I'll drive him around, but I don't think he'll want me tailing along after him."

Doug finished the last of his breakfast and stood up. "Tell him you need his help setting up for the party, then take him to your parent's house on some excuse. Take your mother with you on your errands so one of you can watch him at all times. He'll need some new clothes and things for Timber Ridge so keep him focused on that. If there's any real trouble, call."

I wanted everything to go smoothly. I wanted Mark's transition to Timber Ridge to be a positive one, not one fraught with anxiety for him or for us. Except for that first question when I had picked him up at the shelter, he still hadn't said a word about Timber Ridge. I didn't think it was good for him not to be the least bit curious so when he came downstairs around noon, I made him lunch, poured myself a cup of tea and sat at the table with him.

"Are there any questions you'd like to ask me about our trip tomorrow? You know, I visited your school while you were away. I don't know everything about it, but I can tell you a little bit."

"Nah."

"Aren't you the least bit curious?"

"Nah."

"Mark, it is so important that you go to this school and learn the things you'll need to get a job and make a living. You can't run away from your problems forever. No matter how far you run, you'll still be carrying your difficulties with you. You need to face them and work to overcome them. Mark, do you understand this?"

"I understand plenty. I understand that I don't have any choice. The cops'll bust me if I don't go. Right? Isn't that the deal you made with them so you can send me away?"

I didn't answer. I knew that if I tried to make him see the truth he'd get mad and storm out of the house. Just what I didn't want. All afternoon, we sorted clothes and personal items he wanted to bring with him. As we worked, I watched him out of the corner of my eye. He paced the room, looked out the window, sat on the bed, jumped off the bed, but this was normal for Mark. His actions showed no particular nervousness, no restlessness above his usual hyperactivity. Sometimes, he'd turn and stare at me, but I couldn't tell what he was thinking. It wasn't the blank stare but a waiting look, like a cat considering just the right moment to pounce.

He stayed with me during our shopping expeditions and, later, he carried the laden bowls and food dishes to the table for me. He asked me who was coming to his good-bye party. I peeked at him to see if I could surprise some expression that would clue me in to how he was feeling, but no luck.

"Nana and Grandpa are coming. Aunt Sis, Aunt Patty, Uncle Mike, Uncle Joe, Aunt Ann, your cousins Little Patty, Joanne and Paula and Cheryl and Karen, of course." I listed the names of a few more close relatives and friends. I expected close to twenty-five people. "They all want to wish you the best, Mark. They are all delighted by your acceptance by Timber Ridge."

"I'm going outside for a smoke, Ma."

I bit my tongue and watched out the back door, praying each time he inhaled that he wouldn't take off. He put out the cigarette and stared off into the backyard for a few seconds. When he turned back to the house, I scooted behind the curtain. I didn't want him to think I was spying on him, even though I was. It's with the best intention, I told myself. After all I had gone through to get this chance for him, I'd be damned if he'd blow it.

People began to arrive at 7:30. Mark greeted them at the door, showered and shaved and, although still dressed in his leather and chains, he looked more like himself than he had since he'd left the shelter. Between kisses and handshakes, he talked to his step-sister Karen and Cheryl and his cousins. I relaxed my guard slightly when Doug came home. Between us, we managed to keep him in sight most of the time. I noticed that Mark still refused to talk about Timber Ridge. His uncle, Joe, a Newark Police Officer, joked with him about the time spent in the shelter. Mark took the teasing without flying off

313

the handle for once. This is going to work, I thought. Mark is finally going to be okay.

We had a long trip ahead of us and the court had ordered us to be there as early as possible tomorrow, so close to nine o'clock, I went into the kitchen to cut the cake and pour the coffee, signaling the near end of the evening. Everyone had eaten. The men were patting their stomachs and complaining about how much they had consumed. The women cleared the table and came in to the kitchen to distribute the pieces of cake and fix coffee for themselves and their husbands. I let them know we needed to get up early. Enough of a hint. The house began to empty out and by ten o'clock only a few people remained.

Cheryl wandered into the kitchen, a stack of paper desert plates and cups piled in her arms.

"Tell your brother it's bedtime. I don't want him dawdling for an hour in the morning because he's too tired to focus."

Cheryl dumped the used plates and cups in a large garbage bag and walked back into the living room. In a minute she was back.

"He's not there," she said.

"What do you mean he's not there? He's sitting on the coach talking to Uncle Mike and eating a piece of cake. I just gave it to him." My voice had risen so loudly on the last few words that Doug and my parents came in from the porch where they'd been saying good-bye.

"What's wrong?" Doug asked, glancing from me to Cheryl and back.

"Hopefully nothing," I fought to remain calm. "Mark isn't where I thought he was, that's all. He's probably in the bathroom. But, Doug, please look outside. He might have wandered into the backyard for a smoke."

A thorough search of the house and yard yielded no trace of him. I didn't bother to fight the tears that hammered like the retort of a gun behind my eyes. With arms folded, I laid my head on the kitchen table and sobbed. All my hard work, all those hundreds of phone calls, all the hope I had put into this chance for Mark flooded away in the tears I could not control.

"We'll find him, Corraine. We've found him before, we'll find him again." Doug patted my shoulder awkwardly. He had often seen me in tears, but not the hopeless sobbing that swept me away now.

He knew about all the work I had done to get Timber Ridge approved, but he had not done it himself, had not lived with it for months, and aware of this, he did not know how to comfort me. I was inconsolable.

When I was spent and exhausted, he brought me my coat. Cheryl had already gone out in her car, looking for Mark. My Mom and Dad agreed to wait at the house in case he came home.

Doug helped me into our car where I huddled against the cold window and stared out miserably into the dark night. We drove past all the familiar haunts and around the edges of the parks, flashing our lights into the empty fields in the hope of seeing someone running or ducking behind a tree trunk. The night stared back empty and undisturbed, the stars pitiless and cold in their brilliance.

I sent my parents home and tried to get some sleep. Doug dozed on the bed, but I couldn't relax enough to lay still. I tossed around for a while then got up and went downstairs. Too numb to cry, I sat alone in the dark of the living room and asked God to please let me know what I had done to deserve such suffering as this. I prayed until the glow of the street lights faded and first light appeared in the sky. I decided not to wake Doug. My mom came back and together, paper cups of tea in hand, we began slowly driving around town again. I stopped at all the early morning coffee shops and all-night Laundromats, searched the parks in the pale morning light and drove past the houses of his friends.

Discouraged after a few hours, we started home.

"I'm going to check the Laundromat in Richfield Village one last time," I said. "Mark hangs out there a lot and I just have one of my hunches he might be there."

I parked in the back lot, and telling my mom I'd be right back, dragged myself out of the car. My legs felt hollow and my head swam from lack of sleep. The few steps to the front of the Laundromat felt like a mile. It was no longer early morning and there were people about though the Laundromat seemed deserted. I opened the front door, adjusting my eyes to the dim interior. The machines were silent, their doors open in a gauntlet down either side. I scanned the lines and was about to turn away, when from the side of one of the washers a black shadow leapt at me, snarling and barking. I flew backwards as the huge black dog lunged forward, lips drawn back in a snarl, saliva dripping from its jaws. My hollowed out legs collapsed and I fell back against one of the machines, but before he could reach me, he was hauled back by his chain. I let myself sink to the floor.

"Where'd you get the dog, Mark?" I asked.

"Around."

"Did you steal him?"

"I didn't," he mumbled.

"Who does he belong to?"

"Some guy."

"It's time to leave for Virginia, Mark. You've got to give him back to whoever you got him from. You can't bring pets with you."

"I'm not going to this place you've found to dump me."

"The name of the place is Timber Ridge. It's a school and, yes, you are going."

"You can't make me."

I fought to keep my temper. "That's right, I can't," I said calmly. "But if you don't come with me now, I'll call the police and they'll take you back to the Juvenile Shelter. That's where you'll stay because I've gone as far as I'm willing to go for you. Blow it this time, Mark, and there are no more chances. Think about it."

We tied the dog back up to the fence where Mark claimed he had borrowed him and drove home. I blasted the horn in the driveway and when Doug came out, I asked him to load the suitcases and boxes in the trunk and to finish what he needed to do so we could leave. We dropped my mom at home. I stayed in the car with Mark. We left for Virginia at 11 a.m. on a cold, grey November morning.

Chapter Thirty

I slept most of the journey to Virginia. Occasionally, I woke to hear Mark and Doug arguing, but I was too worn out to care what they said. Doug and I had agreed that we would make one stop for lunch on the six hour journey. If Mark had to use the restroom, Doug would go with him. Then, if I was in shape, I would take over the driving since Doug had slept only a few more hours than I had.

By the time we pulled into the parking lot of a roadside restaurant I felt like my head was stuck to my neck by a single strand of muscle. Every nerve ending fired at once and I groaned aloud as I peeled myself from the front seat. With Mark firmly wedged between us, we hobbled into the restaurant. I sat on one side of the booth, Doug and Mark on the other with Mark pressed against the inside wall. As I looked at their grim faces, gray skin and bloodshot eyes, I wondered for the hundredth time why life was so unfair. Images of the little boy I had seen and fallen in love with in Verona Park flashed before my weary eyes. It wasn't supposed to have turned out this way. I loved my son, but instead of the wonderful life filled with sunny memories I had planned, I had an album of gray days and dark hours searching sleazy hang-outs and all-night Laundromats.

"No!" I told myself so violently I was afraid I had shouted it out loud. No, I would not think that way. Timber Ridge was another chance for Mark and I would muster all my determination and energy to help him take advantage of the positive possibilities this chance offered. So what if my energy was at an all-time low? I would recover. I would go on doing what was right for Mark because I would never give up on him.

I drove the rest of the way to Timber Ridge. Doug sat in the back with Mark for the last half of the ride. We had agreed to this because neither of us trusted him to stay in the car once we turned off the highway. If Mark felt frantic enough, he would jump out of the moving car and take off into the wooded areas beside the country roads.

The blue-green Virginia countryside rolled past us. I looked in the rear view mirror when we passed the horse farms to see if Mark noticed the sleek and beautiful animals frisking in the fields or nudging up against the fences, but I couldn't catch his expression. I felt it wisest to refrain from talking about the beauty of the countryside because Mark would certainly say something to the contrary. If I said it was spectacular, he'd say it was nothing special. I decided to let him form his own opinion. I found a country music station and turned up the volume. The blues guitars and the sad "somebody done somebody wrong songs" did nothing to lighten my mood, but the music kept Doug from falling asleep.

Close to seven o'clock, we pulled into the long driveway leading to the Timber Ridge Administrative Building. I had planned to leave Clifton around six that morning so we could spend the afternoon at Timber Ridge with Mark helping him adjust. Doug and I had reservations at a local motel, but Dr. Moss had suggested that we not return the next morning for a visit. The sooner Mark realized that he could not go home with us the better. He had suggested we spend the first afternoon with Mark to help him get settled and then firmly say good-bye. That afternoon had been wasted.

I took Mark's arm as we entered the building. I could feel the tension buzzing through his muscles. He was on the verge of flight, his face set in rigid lines, his eyes darting here and there like bees in a jar. The secretary sent for Dr. Moss who met us a few minutes later. He shook hands with Mark and Doug and smiled at me sympathetically, a look flashing between us that conveyed his awareness of the situation.

"I do have a few papers you need to sign, but first I'd like to show you where Mark will be staying for the first sixty to ninety days he's here." As we walked across the campus, Dr. Moss explained, "All our students begin in the intake unit. We limit this unit to ten students so each student can receive the individual attention they need to begin the adjustment process. We also observe the students and conduct additional tests if they are necessary for evaluation, then we make an assessment of the student's needs and design an individualized program to address those needs."

As we entered the intake unit, which looked more like a country house, Dr. Moss showed us first the small, but comfortably furnished lounge, the bathrooms and the educational spaces contained right in the unit. Then, with a quick glance at Mark, he led us to the room where Mark would be staying while in the intake unit. It was warmly decorated with two beds covered with colorful blankets, two desks and dressers and an extra chair for reading. Light spilled in through the windows which I noticed were sealed and the glass was thick.

"Our intake unit is more self-contained than the open units to enhance the assessment of our new students. If all goes well, which I'm sure it will, Mark should be in an open unit in a few months."

On our way back to his office, Dr. Moss showed us the common areas as well as some of the beautiful grounds that stretched to over 126 acres. When Mark was on an open unit he would be able to participate in activities in the educational resource room, recreation hall, arts and crafts room, the gym, weight lifting room, outdoor recreational areas, the canteen and the laundry facilities.

After we signed the necessary papers, he invited us to dinner in the dining room. He explained that the students ate in shifts so the dining room was never over-crowded or noisy. Students who had difficulties with over-stimulation were not as disturbed as they would be in a regular school cafeteria where the noise and activity levels were often unmanageable for children with attention deficit hyperactivity disorders. I was glad to see that Mark ate some of the mashed potatoes, chicken and corn. I watched as he ate. His expression of mingled fear and defiance had not changed. I caught Dr. Moss watching him, too. Once again our eyes met and I read reassurance in his. He had seen hundreds of children in his tenure at Timber Ridge. I had to trust that he would know what to do.

I slept poorly that night and on the ride home the next morning I did not feel like singing "Happy Days Are Here Again" as I had previously when I'd dropped Mark off at camp or at Dave's house in Massachusetts.

"Do you think he's going to stick it out there," I asked Doug when we stopped at a roadside cafe for breakfast. I had wanted to get on the road as soon as possible so we would be home early and I could catch some extra sleep.

Doug shrugged. "I was impressed. I'll admit that. The program looks well thought out and the staff dedicated to helping these kids function in the outside world. But whether Mark will give them a chance to help him, I don't know. We'll have to wait and see."

"But what if he doesn't?"

"We'll deal with it then. All we can do is hope he'll wise up and see we're doing this for his own good and not to punish or get rid of him. Stranger things have happened."

"Well, he certainly wasn't aware of it when we left last night. Did you see how defiant he looked?"

"He was probably scared. Mark doesn't adjust to change well and being left in a new place upsets him. Once he gets used to it, he'll do better."

I wanted to believe that Mark would succeed at Timber Ridge, but the expression on his face when we said good-bye stayed with me all the way home. I had seen his eyes, untamed and staring out at me with a fire in their depths. I knew he blamed me for sending him away. He blamed me for everything. It hurt, but I didn't care for myself. I cared because he interpreted my actions, not as those of a loving mother who wanted her son to have the skills needed to survive in the world, but as someone who wanted to hurt and push him away. Once again I had to remind myself that what I had done in sending Mark to Timber Ridge was to give him the chance to acquire those skills. I had long accepted that I could not do so. I needed to give someone else the chance to teach him socially and educationally, someone who had been trained to work with people who had problems like Mark's.

I slept that night and most of the following day. I needed to get back to my work with the Children in Crisis Advocates. I was looking forward to it, but the work I had done getting Mark into Timber Ridge and the emotions of the trip caught up with me and I found myself unable to hold my head up. I made dinner for Doug around eight o'clock, then went back to bed.

The next day I received a letter from Mark's Intake Case Supervisor, Joshua Bonnett, detailing what the rules were for the intake unit. Mark could receive only two calls a week although he encouraged us to write daily if possible and to ask him to write to us as often as he could. Any packages, money, or food had to be cleared through him first. He wrote that the program operated with very strict rules which must be consistently maintained to have the desired effect. I wondered if one of the punishments evoked for non-compliance with the rules was isolation. I hoped not. Mark did not respond well to that kind of discipline as I had learned to everyone's discomfort. Mr. Bonnett closed his letter with the intention of calling or writing once a month to inform us of Mark's progress and leaving his own number in case we had any questions. I considered calling to tell him about Mark's reaction to isolation, but decided against it. Let them observe and discover what they felt worked and did not work for Mark. Perhaps what had not worked in one setting would work in another. I would wait and see.

Mark's successful placement in Timber Ridge spurred my efforts on behalf of the other children and parents involved in Children in Crisis Advocates. Shortly before my trip to Virginia I had received a letter from United States Congressman Torricelli "commending my concern for others and the leadership role I had assumed" on behalf of the families of emotionally disturbed children. I was encouraged by his offer of support and decided to initiate a letter writing campaign to flood our federal and state senate members with letters detailing our concerns. Newspapers could be our allies, too. I was sure Senator Torricelli had learned of our organization through the newspaper account in the Bergen Record. But my first concern was organizing a lobbying effort and a platform upon which to balance this effort.

At our next CICA meeting we started to hammer out our program. Our immediate needs were to provide guidance and referral services for all parents who came to our group seeking help. We planned to do this through discovering and contacting the agencies responsible for dealing with the types of problems our children had. Our discussions made it clear to all of us that there were services available that few of us had heard of. A top priority was to establish a central information service with a directory of the agencies and services available to us. Once we had that information, we would set up and man a telephone hotline to distribute the information.

Although satisfied with the goals we had developed, I pushed the group for a list of long range objectives. I kept my fingers crossed that things would work well for Mark in Timber Ridge, but from the letters he sent begging me to take him home, I knew he was having a hard time adjusting. I wanted to get things rolling on the state level while I had the time and energy to devote to it. If Mark needed my help I would have to drop everything and run. I was free for the moment. I wanted to accomplish as much as I could while I could.

I didn't have as much time as I thought. On the morning of November 29th at 8:00 am, the phone rang. I was up early, drinking my morning cup of tea and looking over my notes from the last CICA meeting. Since I began Children in Crisis Advocates, my phone rang non-stop throughout the day though usually not that early. I didn't think much of it when I answered the phone, my mind still focused on what I had been reading.

"Mrs. Conaway?" I recognized the voice as Joshua Bonnett, Mark's Intake Case Supervisor. I had spoken to him only once in the two weeks Mark had been at Timber Ridge. He had followed up his letter with a reassuring call that Mark was fine and making some small strides in his struggle to adjust to the rules of the intake unit.

"Mr. Bonnett. How are you?" I asked pleasantly, assuming that he was calling to discuss Mark's progress which I hoped was better than his letters seemed to indicate.

"Mrs. Conaway. When Mark didn't appear for roll call this morning, I checked his room. His bed had been slept in, but he is not in the intake unit now. We searched the grounds to no avail. I'm afraid he's run away. We have our people out searching for him, but we want your permission to bring in the local police."

I took two deep breaths to steady the rapid pounding of my heart. "Of course," I said. "Do whatever you need to do." For some absurd reason I felt like apologizing, as if somehow this too was my fault, not theirs. Truly, no one was to blame, but I felt that someone should take some responsibility for this. I just didn't know who.

Mr. Bonnett promised to keep me posted on the results of their search. He reassured me that there was no need for me to come down right away. He was certain they would find him. I wanted to warn him that Mark could be very clever. He'd had enough practice in eluding his pursuers, but again, I said nothing. I didn't want to believe any of this was happening.

After that, it was impossible to focus on anything. I tried to get back to organizing my notes, but the words swam on the page and I found myself reading the same thing over and over again. By ten o'clock the walls of the house closed in on me. I had to get out. I didn't know where I wanted to go. I didn't know who to talk to. I had told my story to so many people in so many agencies, I was all talked out. But as I walked the streets, bundled into my winter coat, chilled by my own sense of frustration, it came to me that perhaps I hadn't talked enough about what kids like Mark really needed. I hadn't talked enough about it because I hadn't been sure what it was he did need. I turned around and practically ran back home.

At the kitchen table I began to draft a list of demands to present, not to those who already knew and had lived with the problems every day of their lives, but to those who didn't know or understand the problems, but were in positions to make the changes we needed. In less than an hour I had listed seven long term goals.

The next problem was to get those demands into the hands of the legislators and agency heads who could benefit from them most. I started making phone calls. When I got nowhere with the State Department or the Governor's Office, I called the contacts I had made at the newspapers. One of the reporters suggested I call a press conference and invite reporters from the various newspapers statewide. This I needed to think about. I still had not heard from Timber Ridge. I didn't want to tie up the phone but I knew if I didn't do something, I'd pace myself into a state of nervous exhaustion waiting. I called Timber Ridge. No word.

By the end of the day, I had commitments from a dozen families to accompany me to Trenton if I was able to arrange a press conference there. I set up my schedule of calls for the next day, then waited for Doug to come home. Too tired to cook and unwilling to leave the phone to go to a restaurant, I called my parents and asked them if they wanted to pick up a pizza and come over for dinner. I had phoned my mother earlier to let her know about Mark. They had gone on so many of my "hunting trips" searching for Mark so they knew how I would be. They understood how difficult it was to sit around alone, staring at the clock, half mad with anxiety and half angry at being put through the same anxiety again and again.

"Think of the bright side," my father said, laying the warm, fragrant pizza on the kitchen table. "It's cold out there and we could be cruising around in the car looking for him till past midnight instead of eating pizza in here. The worry is the same, but the physical discomfort isn't." He smiled, taking the sting out of the words.

Doug had just walked through the door when the phone rang. I glanced quickly at the clock. Seven-thirty. The police had found

Mark on some back road miles from the school. He hadn't said where he was going or why he had left. They brought him back to Timber Ridge. For disciplinary action he had received demerits and would not be permitted to leave the intake unit without supervision for several weeks. I had doubts that I did not voice. Mark hadn't been there long enough to get used to their form of behavioral modification. Maybe once he "got with the program" he would work to earn the rewards and privileges, but I had my doubts. The honeymoon period had lasted two weeks.

Mark ran away twice more in the following week. Each time he was apprehended and brought back within a twenty-four hour period. Each time the restrictions were increased. They did not have locked units, but Mark was kept under heavy surveillance and his shoes were taken away from him, making it more difficult for him to run. It was now the first week in December. Although the weather was not as icy as in New Jersey, it was cold enough that having to walk barefoot through the fields might be a deterrent. His behavior also prevented him from earning the privilege of a Christmas home visit.

Mark's failure to adjust was, in part, counterbalanced by my success in arranging a press conference at the Statehouse Annex in Trenton. Judy Horner and I drafted a letter which I intended to present to the Governor which included the list of long range goals Children in Crisis Advocates intended to work towards. I chartered a bus and, with a dozen families from our group, made the trip to Trenton. On the bus, I distributed the letter and read over it with them to make sure we all knew and agreed with our lobbying platform. Balancing between the two front seats and shouting above the protesting creaks and groans of the bus I read to my faithful followers:

We are the parents of emotionally disturbed, troubled children who are being denied necessary services and treatment by the State of New Jersey. Our children are described as "falling between the cracks" or "being in the gray area." They and we are bounced from one agency to the next. They wait months, even years, for evaluations, services, and placement in treatment facilities. They are sent to jails because there is no other place for them. Hundreds of children are sent out of state, far from home and family. In one

DYFS region, placements are frozen and children languish in psychiatric wards, shelters and are denied services. Numbers are not provided to agencies and these needy children become the hidden children. Budgets are balanced by denying services to the most needy and troubled children. New Jersey compares poorly to other states in serving its children. We parents love and care for our children. They and we need your help.

We ask you, as governor of this wealthy state, to provide the leadership to insure that children - our most precious resource - are no longer denied treatment and services. We ask you to invest in New Jersey's children - its future.

On behalf of our children, we ask the following:

1. Within one month, obtain from each DYFS office the number of children waiting for residential placement; obtain from DDD the number of children waiting for placement and the number waiting for evaluations; obtain from DOC, detention centers and shelters the number of children waiting for placement; obtain from DMHH the number of children in psychiatric hospitals waiting for placement. Provide this information to the legislature and child advocate organizations so that these children will no longer be "hidden children."

2. Determine what services are needed for these children. How many additional community services, group homes, and residential treatment centers are needed? What kinds of programs are needed?

3. Convene a cabinet level working group to develop a plan to create and fund the needed services.

4. Insist on and provide the resources for quality programs for our children.

5. Do not permit emotionally disturbed or developmentally delayed children to be jailed because of lack of alternative services.

6. In your budget this year, demand sufficient funds to provide quality treatment for New Jersey's most troubled and needy children.

7. Bring our children back from out - of - state; bring our children home!

You said in establishing the Governor's Committee on Children's Services Planning, "New Jersey's children should be afforded the opportunity to develop to their fullest potential and, in order to further this development, problems confronting children and their individual needs should be effectively addressed by state and local government." Many of the committee's recommendations have not been implemented. We ask you to make the rhetoric a reality. We ask you to provide the leadership to insure that New Jersey meets its children's needs now!

Children in Crisis Advocates

My shaky reading was greeted with applause. If the mood of the members was tentative before, they were fired up now. We did not have unrealistic expectations, but we meant to make a difference and we all had our children's welfare at stake. We were determined to be listened to. I had invited representatives from all the major newspapers throughout the state. Someone had to listen to us.

As the bus pulled up in front of the Statehouse I felt the familiar flutters in my stomach. I believed in everything we had written in the letter to the Governor, but I had never given a press conference before. It was so important that we came across as well informed, concerned parents who were serious about getting help for our children. I did not want us to be dismissed as troublemakers with "bad" kids. Or worse still, what if we walked into an empty room, no press, no government, no agency representatives who felt our cause was worth taking the time to investigate.

I squared my shoulders. I was used to setbacks. If no one cared, then I would find a way to make them care. If not this time, then next time. I marshaled my milling troop and led them into the imposing building, inquiring of an aide where Room 410, Statehouse Annex might be located.

When we arrived we were a few minutes late, enough time for those invited to the press conference to have arrived. To my relief there were many faces I didn't recognize, most of whom quickly identified themselves as reporters from half a dozen newspapers as well as representatives from the Governor's Office. The room was open and airy, with plenty of seating and large windows that let in the watery winter light. A large American flag stood sentinel in the corner of the room.

Once everyone was seated, I introduced myself and began my carefully prepared set of opening remarks:

"Thank you all for coming. Today, we are here not only to present a petition to the Governor but, equally as important, to talk about our special children, to put a human face on a problem that is so often presented in terms like "beds available" or "evaluations necessary". We are concerned about those issues as well, deeply concerned, but each of those beds and each of those evaluations represent the lives of real children in need. No, our children are not in wheelchairs. They have invisible handicaps that put them on the bottom of the visibility list. Our children are hyperkenetic, impulsive, emotionally disturbed, mentally ill, developmentally disabled and neurologically impaired. And they need help. But instead of getting that help, they are left to languish at home or in juvenile detention centers and psychiatric hospitals because there is nowhere else for them to go. We need residential facilities geared towards our children's special needs and we just don't have them. I was lucky enough, after receiving 55 rejections, to place my sixteen year old son in a school in Virginia. Why isn't he in a New Jersey facility? Because there aren't enough facilities in New Jersey to accommodate all the children who need placements. We are here today to try to do something about that. Now I'd like to turn the floor over to other members of Children in Crisis Advocates so they can begin to put faces to the statistics for you."

We spoke for over two hours, each family telling about their special nightmares in getting help for their children. I watched the faces of the reporters and representatives and wondered if they were touched by the real life drama enacted for them by each of these suffering parents and their children. After everyone had spoken, we handed the petition to the Governor's representative and, emotionally spent, walked silently from the building and back into the bus. Despite my exhaustion, I was elated. My instinct told me we had made an impression. How that impression would impact on those legislators in a position to help us was yet to be seen. We had spoken and our anguished voices had been heard.

The next day I bought up all the papers I could find at my local newsstand. We hadn't made front page, but our story was carried in all the major newspapers, some even with pictures. I looked at myself critically and decided that I had presented a decent image, one that other mothers could identify with. I hoped it would bring more members into our organization. I also read in the paper that the director of the State Division of Youth and Family Services, when contacted by the newspapers, agreed to address our group next month. I had been in contact with his office, but had received no confirmation of the date he would speak with us. Now it seemed he would be coming in January. I immediately contacted his office for confirmation and to inform him of the date of our January meeting. I wanted to steamroll into the next year, flattening the opposition and building roads that would eventually lead home for our troubled kids.

Chapter Thirty-One

Early on the morning of December 20th, the doorbell rang. Groggy from a heavy sleep, I stumbled to the door in my terry robe and slippers. It was a chilly, rainy morning and I peered blearily through the rivulets of rain running down my window before recognizing the blue uniforms of the Clifton Police. Sleep-slurred thoughts chased each other through my mind. Mark was in Virginia! They couldn't want him! Why were they here? Had there been an accident?

Quickly I unlatched the door. The officers politely scraped their feet on the welcome mat before entering. The next person to enter was not so polite. He clomped in, tracking rain and mud across my carpet and shaking out the blanket wrapped around his skinny frame.

"Hi, Mom. Thought I'd come home for Christmas," he said.

"Does anyone know you're here, Mark?" I asked. I fought for control, not wanting to blow up in front of the police. I was afraid they would take him into custody if I did.

"They do." He flicked a careless finger at the officers, then pointed at me. "Now you do, too."

I had seen the "tough guy" act so often it didn't faze me, but I could see by the officers' expressions that it was not making the best impression on them

"Go upstairs. Dry off and get into some clean clothes," I said.

I was grateful that for once he didn't argue. He threw me what passed for a conspiratorial look and I realized he was terrified I'd turn him in. I was tempted, but I didn't want them to take him to the Juvenile Detention Center. As calmly as I could, I explained the situation to the officers and guaranteed them he would be back in school in two days. He was not officially under arrest since no complaint had been lodged against him. The police reluctantly left him to me.

I locked all the doors, then sat down to wait until Mark had finished changing his clothes. What could I say? Words had never broken through to him. After years of therapy and all the special education techniques we had tried, his response was still as primitive as any creature in the wild. If something upset or frightened him, he ran. If he was trapped and could not run, he fought. At Timber

Ridge, he felt trapped by the demands made on him to learn and to conform to a strict set of rules. Home was safer so he ran home. But as soon as I began to expect a certain standard of behavior from him, he would run from me as well, seeking a safer place. Always seeking a safer place and never finding it. He did not understand that for someone with no skills, education or social savvy, society provided no safe place. All the words in the world would never make him understand this. I knew that now, but still I could not manage him at home.

After a while, he came downstairs, flung himself into a kitchen chair and lit a cigarette. I sat across from him and waited.

"I ain't going back," he said at last.

"Where will you go? You can't stay here."

"Why not? I'll be better this time."

"You don't know how to "be better". That's why you're at Timber Ridge, to learn how to behave and until you do, you can't stay here."

"I'll go to my father's house in Massachusetts. He'll let me stay."

"No he won't."

He laughed. "A lot you know."

"I do know," I said. "I talked with Dave and he wants you to stay at Timber Ridge. He won't keep you at his house, either."

"Then I'll just go somewhere else. I'm not going back. Do you know what they made me do last time I ran away. Huh! I bet you don't. They made me stand against the wall with no shoes on. So what do you think of that?"

"I think you failed to learn anything from it because here you are again."

The next day it snowed making the roads a slippery mess. The storm tracked down the coast as far as Virginia so I postponed the return trip until the following day. I called Dr. Moss to inform him Mark had been brought home by the police. I asked him about Mark's statement that he'd been forced to stand barefoot against the wall. Dr. Moss confirmed that Mark's shoes had been taken from him and that he had been made to stand against the wall to try to get him to think twice about running again since he did not respond to lack of privileges as a deterrent. While he continued to run away and be disruptive in class, he would have to remain in the intake unit where the punishments were stricter than they would be in the open units.

My mom and I drove Mark back to Virginia on December 22nd, three days before Christmas. I had been of half a mind to keep him with us for the holidays, but Doug and Dr. Moss both felt that would be rewarding him for running away so I packed up his Christmas gifts, put them in the trunk of the car and drove through the snowy landscape to Timber Ridge. Carols played softly on the car radio, but I didn't make any attempt to catch the spirit of the season. Impotent anger burned through me as I sat bundled in my winter coat, alternately sweating and freezing according to the whims of the car heater. I would cheerfully have laid waste to whoever came in my path if I thought it would do any good. I had spoken to Dr. Moss. There was nothing more to discuss. They would do everything they could to keep him there short of locking him up. Timber Ridge was a school, not a prison or juvenile detention facility. Their job was to help Mark take responsibility for his own life and eventually come to understand that he needed to learn basic life skills. Great, I fumed to myself, and just how are you going to do that if you can't keep him in one place long enough to teach him this.

We dropped Mark off and started the long ride home the same day. The weather had taken a warmer turn rolling fog across the highway. As night approached, visibility decreased to nothing. I nearly rode up the rear end of an eighteen wheeler, the red tail lights saving me at the last minute.

"Hang on, Mom," I warned her. "I'm going to drive in the glare of this guy's tail lights. It's the only thing I can see for guidance. Just pray he doesn't have to stop short for any reason."

The fog lifted as the snowy hills rolled into the suburbs of Harrisburg, Pennsylvania. I chanced a quick glance at my mom. Her face was white as the snow, her hands laced so tightly in her lap the fingers looked ready to snap. I laughed shakily.

"Want to do this again next week," I said, hoping to break the tension. Silently I promised that I would never subject any of my family to this shattering stress again. Christmas was only three days away. I would make a Merry Christmas for Doug and Cheryl and my parents if I had to kill myself to do it. I wanted to make up to them for the years of attention I had taken from them and given to Mark.

I threw myself into the project enlisting Cheryl and my mother to help. We decorated the house with wreaths and garlands, baked cookies, twisted silver bows around brightly wrapped gifts, hung the tinsel on the tree and cooked the traditional meal. If my smile looked a bit tarnished, nobody said a word. They knew I needed to do this.

Christmas Eve was my parents' special time and their house overflowed with cousins, aunts and uncles, friends and family. For days, I worried that Mark would show up there, an unexpected Christmas present. As the evening approached, tension snaked its way up my spine into my head, squeezing it like a vise. By the time Cheryl called me to put my coat on, the pounding was almost unbearable. Even from hundreds of miles away, Mark could cause me pain.

"Before we go to Nana's, why don't we call Mark and wish him a Merry Christmas," Cheryl suggested.

Doug and Cheryl looked at me, waiting for my answer. I didn't know what to say. If he was there, I would be able to relax. If not, I'd know what to expect. But I didn't want my Christmas ruined knowing he was somewhere out there in the dark and the cold trying to get home. I froze. Doug took over.

"Good idea!" he said heartily. "The devil you know is better than the one you don't."

"Not a very Christmasy sentiment," I said, trying to smile.

Doug phoned Timber Ridge while I waited tensely beside him, strung tighter than a violin string. Anyone who tried to play a carol on me would certainly have bowed a sour note or two. Doug was silent waiting for Mark to come to the phone. As the time lengthened I tensed till I thought I would break at any minute.

"Hi Mark! Merry Christmas. Did you open your presents yet?" Doug's voice held a note of false gaiety, but I was grateful to him for not turning the phone over to me right away. The relief I felt struck me like a rock and I swayed with the impact. By the time, Doug and Cheryl had finished wishing him a happy holiday I was composed enough to keep my voice steady. Of course, he wanted to come home for Christmas, but he knew he couldn't. He was angry because they had punished him for running away, but they were allowing him to join in the Christmas festivities and he was looking forward to that. We spoke for a few minutes longer. I promised I would call Christmas Day.

Mark ran away again a week after New Year's Day, but was picked up before he left Virginia. During that week I had sent letters to State Senators Bubba, Orechio, Codey, Brown and Graves as well as a number of Assemblymen and Directors of State Agencies urging them to support budgetary measures for the construction of new facilities for emotionally disturbed and neurologically impaired children. My press conference had led to a spot on WOR-TV's Viewpoint and I was looking forward to Mr. Caswell's meeting with CICA on January 13th. I felt that the right people were beginning to listen to us. My hope that I could help parents avoid the catastrophe of seeing their children jailed when they might have been helped kept me going.

Despite a bitterly cold night, our members turned out in force for Mr. Caswell's presentation. I had cast a doubtful eye at the icy roads more than once during the day, wondering if Mr. Caswell would brave the treacherous highways to be accosted by a group of angry parents. I only had a few miles to drive. The ice on the trees sparkled as my headlights cast a false flash of daytime illumination. Needle-nosed icicles hung from electrical wires and decorated porch roofs. At any other time I would have parked the car and jumped out, amazed at nature's majesty. Tonight I drove steadily on, cursing the weather that I was sure would put a halt to my crusade's forward momentum.

Surprised by the number of cars already parked at the Clifton Recreation Center, I eased my way into a space and cautiously crossed the lot. I had spoken to my parents before I left. They were determined to make the meeting, ice storm be damned. I grinned as I thought of my father grumbling about not being an old man yet. I silently blessed them for the support they had given me through the years, the support that had gotten me through so many of the hard times beginning with Dave and ending only God knew where.

Mr. Caswell stood among a small group of people, chatting comfortably, but when he caught my eye, he excused himself and walked over to me.

"Mrs. Conaway," he asked.

I smiled. "I know we've talked on the phone a number of times, but how on earth did you know who I was?"

He turned to point to one of the women in the group behind him. "I asked her to tip me off when you entered the room." We shook hands. He then introduced me to the field director of DYFS. "You've certainly caught the ear of the state officials in Trenton," he said with a smile.

"That's welcome news. I hope we can convince them to do more than listen though. Our kids need action, not kind attention alone. We want to save them, not see them become a danger to themselves and others. But be forewarned. You'll hear plenty of statements like that tonight."

"Hopefully I can answer some of them," he said.

I looked around the room, hoping some of our more vocal members were in attendance. The large meeting room had filled up and there were many new and familiar faces. I saw my parents slip in behind me and take seats near the podium. In a few minutes, Mr. Caswell signaled he was ready to begin. I asked everyone to be seated, then introduced our guest speakers. The room quieted quickly.

"I'd like to congratulate you for forming this advocacy group," he began. "It is very important that you are providing a constituency for children. I need to have feedback from you as parents. That's why I'm here tonight, not to talk, but to listen."

Hands flew up all over the room. One of our regulars spoke up . "Excuse me, Mr. Caswell, but we want answers not excuses or promises. I know. I've heard them all. I finally had to sue the State of New Jersey to get my ten year old emotionally disturbed son into a treatment program in Arizona. Maybe the beds aren't there for all the children who need them, but don't tell me the money isn't available. New Jersey is one of the richest states in the country, but our money isn't going to my children and your children. We are here to tell state officials that the days of drugging these kids and locking them in their rooms at home are over. I want help for my son right here in New Jersey." Approving applause erupted as she took her seat.

A mother from a near-by town stood up immediately. Still seeking help for her 20 year old developmentally disabled son, she called for a mass protest. "When New York tried to cut special education programs, 250 parents blocked the Board of Education building. They wouldn't let anyone out until we got forty-three teachers' jobs back in Queens alone. If everyone of us went down to Trenton and said. "We're going to leave our emotionally disturbed kids in your office until you solve the problem, we'd get action pretty quickly."

Several other parents spoke about their difficulties in getting services for their handicapped children. I noticed that my dad had his hand raised and I tried to catch Mr. Caswell's eye. He noticed my head jerk towards my father and called on him next.

"We need a 911 approach to this situation. These children are often in crisis and the parents can't find immediate help. They don't want to call the police whose solution is to take the children to the juvenile shelter where they are warehoused with burglars, rapists and the like. They come out of there worse than when they went in. Give people an 800 number to call where they can get up to the minute help. These people are in a crisis situation." Once again applause erupted from the floor. Mr. Caswell held up his hand.

"DYFS does have an action line. But one of the problems in keeping pace with a youth in trouble is that so many institutions, including schools, courts, county and state agencies, are often involved with so little coordination among them. We need to make better use of the resources that are already in place, but coordinating them is an intractable problem. Clearly this needs to be a top priority."

I raised my hand. "I'd like to clarify a few things, if I may. Every one of us here tonight would love to be able to keep our children home and provide for them from the resources available in the community. But we can't. The system of community care is not working because the resources are unavailable or so wrapped up in red tape or so overburdened, they are useless to us. Too often, it's jail the kid or send him home. Both ways the children lose. Or, God forbid, if an incident occurs in which an emotionally disturbed child hurts himself or someone else, then right away it's the kid's fault and the parent's fault, even though we all have begged for help from a system which has failed us again and again. You've heard tonight what we've been through. It's only a matter of time until an innocent child is hurt or worse. We want to prevent that. And, for some of us, the only way to do that is to put our children in a safe, secure, supervised facility for the emotionally disturbed. We need those facilities."

"Mrs. Conaway, I can only say that I agree with you about the need for additional programs in New Jersey for youths who need supervised, 24 hour care. I assure you that it is a top priority, if not the top priority, to seek additional funding for expansion of residential services. I will take your concerns back to Trenton and make sure they are heard."

After the meeting, we served hot coffee, tea and refreshments. I had expected people to grab their drinks, a cookie or two and rush out before the streets turned into a skating pond, but I was wrong. People lingered, eager to speak to Mr. Caswell about their personal concerns. Some of the comments seemed to especially disturb him.

"Good," I thought. "Maybe what we're saying is coming home to them on a personal level. Maybe the anguish in these parent's eyes can reach them on a deeper level than petitions and words ever could."

A month after the meeting I visited Mark at Timber Ridge. He had not made any runaway attempts since the beginning of January and his teachers and counselors were encouraged. He was still housed in the intake unit under strict supervision, but he had made some gains in his academics. I wanted to see Mark, but I was a little leery that a visit from his family might disrupt his adjustment and make him want to come home again. I spoke to Josh Bonnett about that possibility, but he felt that Mark really needed to see us and that we needed to see the progress he had made. We would be able to speak with Mark's teachers.

The Blue Ridge Mountains were snow-capped, the trees and meadows lacy with frost. I had brought a heavier winter coat for Mark and a few of the personal things he had requested in his letters and in our phone conversations. I was anxious to see him, hopeful that our meeting would be warmer, more loving than our parting had been. I tried not to set myself up by being too optimistic that Mark had finally settled down and found a place where he could grow and learn. But my head and my heart were not communicating. Deep down inside I wanted this to work more than I had wanted anything in my life.

We arrived shortly before dinner. Since Mark had not yet earned an off-campus pass, we had been given permission to eat with him in the school dining room. We were escorted to the intake unit. Strangely I felt nervous, uncertain what I would say. I didn't want to say the wrong thing. When we walked into Mark's room, he was sitting on his bed. My first thought was, Oh, how thin and pale he looks. I was glad when he walked over and gave me a hug, then shook Doug's hand.

"Are you hungry?" I asked. "We didn't stop for lunch and I'm famished."

He shrugged. "You know me, I'm never hungry, but they said I could eat with you. We can go now if you want. I just need to tell Mr. Bonnett where I'm going and when we'll be back."

Over dinner, Mark asked about Cheryl and Karen and when we thought he could go home. My heart sank a bit, but I explained to him that he couldn't come home for a visit until his teachers and counselors felt he had earned the privilege.

"Not a visit. I want to go home. I'll be much better now. You'll see. I won't run away or anything."

"You know that's impossible so let's not spoil our visit by talking about it. Daddy and I are proud of the way you have been behaving the last month. And your report card was great. All seventies and a ninety-two in Math. You should be proud of yourself, Mark."

"I want to go home."

The following day we met with Mark's teachers and counselor. He was still having problems adjusting to the classroom because he was so easily distracted and because he demanded so much attention. His social skills were poor so he ended up alienating the other boys, but he showed a definite improvement over the last month. He was certainly capable of learning and with extra help he was handling his academic subjects. We were told that if his progress improved at a steady pace, he would be moved from the intake unit to a regular open unit where he would have more freedom and less constant supervision. His case manager felt he would be more comfortable there since he chaffed so under the restrictions of the intake unit. I wasn't so sure that was a good idea.

Mark begged us to take him back when we left that afternoon. He said he hated it there and that they punished him every time he did something they didn't like. I left with tears in my eyes. I knew it was normal for him to rebel against a strict authority, but I had wanted him to reassure me that he was feeling better. Silly for setting myself up that way, but I didn't want my child to suffer any more tan he already had. I wanted him to be happy.

By April Mark had not only earned a place in the open unit called Oz, but he was allowed his first visit home. My parents had visited Mark earlier in April for Easter and, although my Dad broke his finger playing football, the visit had been an encouraging one. In an awards ceremony, Mark had been given certificates for Most Improved Academic Student - Woodstock Unit and Most Improved Residential Student - Woodstock Unit. My parents were thrilled and so was I.

Shortly afterwards, I received a letter informing me that Mark's first home visit had been arranged for April 28th. We were to pick him up on that Thursday and return him no later than 6:00 pm the following Monday. It was only a three day visit excluding traveling days. Doug and I discussed it and we felt we would be able to handle Mark at home for that amount of time. I arranged several activities for us to do as a family so that Mark would not be on his own much of the time. Timber Ridge had also sent us a list of objectives for this visit that they felt Mark could handle and that they had been practicing with him. I read them over several times committing the phrases to memory- Mark will follow all directions immediately and without questions; will interact with others appropriately without interrupting; will be accompanied by an adult when out in the community; will help with chores. All right, I thought, we'll give it a shot.

Mark was as sunny as the Virginia spring when we picked him up. I had rarely seen him so happy and I dared to hope that it had more to do with his accomplishments at Timber Ridge than it did the chance to go home. During the six hour drive he chatted almost non-stop about the school and his unit, the teachers and the fields and animals he was allowed to visit now. He asked questions about Dave, Cheryl, Karen, his cousins and his grandparents. He was anxious to see them all. I had arranged for a spring get-together which would include aunts, uncles, cousins and friends. He was happy to know they wanted to see him. I reminded him of the objectives of the visit and he seemed determined to comply.

Friday went off without a hitch. He slept late in the morning, then went with me to visit my mother. We took him out to eat and to visit his cousins, Patty, Joanne and Paula. We shopped for food for the party on Saturday, some new clothes for him to take back to Virginia. He wanted to spend time with Cheryl so we went home early and I fixed dinner while they talked. He was still restless, running up and down the stairs, popping up from his seat in the middle of a conversation, but he made no attempt to leave the house on his own. I was grateful not to have to police him and happy for the chance to mother him. He got along well with Doug, helping with the chores and barbecuing at the party. I noticed that he was better able to converse with people, making eye contact and listening to what they were saying without fidgeting too much.

On Sunday, he wanted to visit a few of his old friends from the neighborhood. I refused to drive him around because I did not think the old associations would be good for him. He was disappointed and sulky, but he did not react in his usual demanding way. He did ask a few times if he had to go back to Virginia. Doug and I were friendly, but very firm in our replies. Yes, he had to go back.

Mark had to be back at Timber Ridge by 6:00 pm the following day. We wanted to make an early start so we could have a leisurely trip, enjoying cherry blossom season down south. Mark slept late the past few mornings so I suggested he go to bed early. Doug and I got into bed around eleven. Mark had been asleep for almost an hour.

When the alarm sounded its 7:00 am wake up call, I turned over, flipped it off and got up to take my shower. I wanted to be washed and dressed before anyone else made demands on the bathroom. In a half hour I was ready. Cheryl was next in the bathroom because she had to be at work by 8:30. Mark took longer than Doug, so I decided to wake him first. I wanted to be on the road by nine at the latest.

Mark's bedroom door was shut, so I knocked softly. No answer. I knocked again, more loudly this time and, when I didn't hear him stir, pushed open the door. I took a deep breath, fighting the dizziness that came so quickly. Mark's bed had not been slept in.

"Doug! Wake up!" I ran for the bedroom. Doug sat up, looking dazed. "Mark's gone."

"Since when?"

"Don't know. His bed hasn't been slept in which gives him a good head start. I'm going to call my parents and, if he's not there, I'm going to call the police. Maybe he went to Massachusetts to see Dave. I'll have him call the Massachusetts police. And Timber Ridge. I have to call Timber Ridge because we'll never make it back there by 6:00 now."

The police found Mark on the Massachusetts Turnpike and returned him to us that evening. He had stolen Doug's old army uniform and was wearing it to make hitch-hiking easier.

I didn't notice the cherry blossoms blooming along the roads on the way back to Timber Ridge. I was tearful, Doug silent and Mark defiant during that long drive to Virginia. I was fighting furiously what my instinct was telling me so painfully. I refused to accept that we had fallen back into a nightmare I thought had faded. I should have listened. I might have been better prepared if I had.

During the next two months, Mark ran away seven times, once for as long as four days. He had hitched a ride with a trucker out West where he had been found wandering in the desert near Kingman, Arizona. The trucker had molested him and Mark had run away, but without money, food or water, he had nowhere but the highway to go. When the sheriff picked him up he didn't tell him about Timber Ridge or about his family. It was days before we knew where he was or whether he was safe. Faced with prosecution, Mark admitted his age and told the sheriff who to contact. I wired the money to Kingman and the sheriff permitted him to fly back to Timber Ridge. There, they took his clothes and his shoes away from him and made him stand against the wall, but a week later, he ran away again. Dr. Moss asked Doug and me to drive down to talk with Mark.

We were allowed to take him for a walk in the fields to discuss the situation with him in private. Doug and I decided what we would say on the long drive down. We both agreed that threatening, yelling or cajoling him would make no difference. On that trip we finally accepted that Mark was going to run and keep running whenever he was faced with his own fears. I needed to hear him say it, though.

We sat down on a felled log near the edge of a meadow dotted with wild flowers. I looked at him, open now to the misery he was feeling.

"Why, Mark? Please help me understand," I said.

He looked away over the meadow to a distance I couldn't follow. "You know, the last time I hid out in the woods," he said, "there was this beat-up old pick-up truck parked in a yard near this house. I didn't think anybody would see me so I crawled into the truck. The guy, you know, the one who owned it, had a loaded gun in there and I picked it up. I just put it to my head, right above my ear, and I thought, "Pow! It'll be all over." I was really going to do it that time. But the guy must have seen me 'cause he comes up and says real calm, "Not in my truck, you ain't." He kicks me out, but he talks to me and gives me some food."

On June 19th, the Timber Ridge Administration and DYFS terminated Mark's acceptance at the school. The discharge papers read Discharged to Unknown-Runaway Status. The papers stated that Mark made no progress while at Timber Ridge. His constant running away made attempts to implement our behavior modification program impossible. When he was here, he displayed excessive defiance toward authority demands and limit setting and in general was non-compliant and demonstrated no commitment to the need for placement in our program... Mark earned many restrictions for rather serious offenses. The most often committed offenses were running away and stealing. The report went on to state that he had improved for a period, but his constant running away made it necessary for them to discharge him. Recommendations included that he be placed in a structured, therapeutic secure setting, where running away could not be used to avoid necessity for change. The report concluded with the necessity of demonstrating to Mark that repeated confrontations with authority would inevitably result in disappointment and failure.

Disappointment and failure. I was ready to accept them, but before I did I needed to find my son. He was still missing.

Chapter Thirty-Two

When I answered the summons of the doorbell eleven days later, I knew it was Mark. Although I still worried when he was AWOL, I no longer feared I would never find him. Somehow either I found him or he found me. This time, he returned with a broken nose and eyes blackened from the result of a fight. He had hooked up with a carnival in Virginia and had worked his way up to Dave's house in Massachusetts. Dave had sent him right back to me.

During the days Mark was missing, I had spoken several times with Dr. Moss. Our discussions simply confirmed what I had known all along, that Mark's inability to relate cause and effect made it nearly impossible for him to anticipate the consequences of his behavior. Without that ability, each event that occurred in his life was singular and isolated. Learning could not be transferred from one consequence to the next. Rewards did not entice him to behave well and punishments did not deter him. If he was punished it was because authority figures were mean and arbitrary and had nothing to do with his behavior. He acted out because the impulse moved him to act out. Dr. Moss did not feel they could do anything to help him at Timber Ridge. They had tried their best within the confines of the program with little or no result, not even in training him to follow a routine. Dr. Moss repeated his recommendation that Mark be placed in a secured setting until he learned the skills necessary to function in society.

For his part, Mark never asked about Timber Ridge. It was summer, he was home and life went on as it always had. He started hanging out again in the parks and with "friends". I heard him on the phone speaking with a girl, but when I asked him who it was he told me "some girl I lived with for a while in Virginia." My phone bill confirmed a Virginia number.

Through Children in Crisis Advocates, I started once again my painstaking search for a secure environment for Mark. I had been able to hook CICA up with other organizations dedicated to the goal of creating space for handicapped children in New Jersey facilities. This umbrella organization, Statewide Parents Association for the Children's Effort, S.P.A.C.E., included the Mental Health Association of New Jersey, Bergen County Division of Family

Guidance, Union County PUSH, New Jersey Self Help Clearing House and Concerned Families of Essex County. I had helped other parents find help through the services of our member associations throughout the state. Now I needed help for myself, but before I had progressed very far, Mark was arrested again.

I had just returned from food shopping and balancing one bag on my knee and the other in the crook of my arm, I managed somehow to open the side door. I called Mark to help me when I heard him shouting at someone. At first, I thought maybe Doug or Cheryl had come home from work early, but as I pushed my way into the kitchen, juggling my bags, I realized he was on the phone. A few minutes later, he slammed past me, his face purple with rage. He did not return for three days. On July 9th, I received a phone call from the Kearny police, advising me that they were holding Mark at the police station there. Kearny is a neighboring town, about twenty minutes from Clifton. I drove slowly, taking the time to calm myself down. "You've been through so much of this already," I told myself sternly, "Settle down and think straight." But I couldn't. Each time it happened felt like the first time. I arrived at the Kearny Police Station with my jaw clenched and my stomach shredded to tissue paper.

Mark had received three auto citations and a juvenile summons for drinking because the police had found an open beer can in the car although Mark had told them that there were other kids in the car and they had been drinking, not him. A hearing was set for early August. One of the police officers called me aside as they were processing Mark's papers and told me that Mark had a cut across his wrist that looked to him like a possible suicide attempt. I called St. Mary's Crisis Team from the police station. They agreed to send someone out to meet us at the house.

"Aren't you going to say anything," Mark demanded when we got into the car to drive home.

"What is there to say? If I ask you why you were driving a car when you haven't got a license, what are you going to say to me, Mark? The same old garbage about how all this is my fault. I'm sorry you feel that way, but I just don't want to hear it again."

From St. Mary's Hospital, Mark was transferred to St. Clare's Psychiatric Unit where he had been several times in the past. I arranged with Dr. Schaeffer, the doctor who would be examining Mark, to come in for a consultation on July 15th.

I went alone, remembering the first time I had left Mark there and how I had looked back to see him spread-armed at the window, the light behind him forming his body into a cross. I thought then my heart would break, but hope had held it together. Hope that the professionals there could cure my son. I no longer had that hope. My heart was held together with spider webs.

Dr. Schaeffer led me to the usual corner office. She looked through the papers on her desk, then glanced up at me with a sympathetic smile.

"I can see you've been through this before. First, I want to assure you that the cut on Mark's wrist is superficial. He told me that he had an argument with his girlfriend and that he cut his left wrist with a broken bottle because he wanted to commit suicide. Did he mention this wound to you?"

She looked at me over the top of her glasses. I shook my head. He had not been bleeding when he had stormed out of the house the afternoon of July 6th.

Dr. Schaeffer looked down at her papers. " He also tells me that he smokes marijuana almost daily, abuses speed around three times a week, drinks 12 cans of beer daily, a bottle of scotch and sometimes champagne."

I laughed out loud. Dr. Schaeffer looked startled, her eyebrows arching above her serious eyes. "Dr. Schaeffer, can't you see how ridiculous that is? Mark has been in a closely supervised school for the last seven months with no alcohol on the premises. He's only been home for two weeks and except for this last episode I have seen him every day and every evening. He has not been drunk or high once in that time. He has never had a drug or alcohol problem. I clean his room and I assure you there are no empty bottles or bags of marijuana anywhere. And you must admit that anyone who is smoking marijuana, using speed, drinking twelve cans of beer, a bottle of Scotch and champagne every day, wouldn't be around long to tell about it. Am I right?"

Dr. Schaeffer's expression lightened as she tried to keep a smile from creeping onto her face. "His lab work shows his urine drug screen to be completely negative. We've started him on medication every six hours to calm his agitation, but that's the only drug in his system at the moment. Now tell me, is it true that he was picked up by the Kearny police for driving a vehicle without a license to drive, without insurance and with leaving the scene of an accident he caused?"

I nodded, the light moment over. "It wasn't really an accident, though. He backed into a parked car."

"And the status of that?" she asked.

"He has a hearing in August, but if he is in permanent placement, they will suspend that, I hope. I don't know if you have read all the past history on Mark's case, but he has had many hospitalizations and court dates for minor offenses. My husband and I cannot control Mark at home. Before this, he has threatened suicide and he had threatened others although he's never hurt anyone. Now, we're into something more serious. He's actually cut himself and he could have hurt the other kids when he backed into the parked car. Now he is a danger to himself and others. Let him out and I can't answer for what is going to happen next."

On the recommendation of Dr. Louise Schaeffer, Mark was transferred to the Psychiatric Adolescent Unit of Trenton State Hospital. The medication they had given him at St. Clare's had calmed him enough so that he did not react wildly to what was called "the Welcome Spot" at the Lincoln Complex. During intake, I was told that he would be placed on a stronger drug for agitation for seven days and that assault and escape precautions would be taken. While he was in "The Welcome Spot" he would also be reevaluated. I wondered how Mark would respond to that. He had been evaluated and reevaluated so often that he knew some of the sections of the standard tests by heart even with variations. I mentioned this to the intake counselor, but I could tell by his expression he did not believe me.

I had been chosen to attend a Training Institute in Boulder, Colorado sponsored by the Children and Adolescent Service System Program. I was scheduled to leave two days after Mark was transferred to Trenton State Hospital. I didn't know what to do. I had been looking forward to this conference for so long, but I didn't want to leave Mark alone in a new place. I tried to find someone to take my place, but no one could make it on such short notice.

Doug and Cheryl both urged me to go. "We can hold down the fort. If he really needs you, planes fly out of Denver Airport all the time. You could be back here in five or six hours. He's in a secure environment. What could happen?"

What could happen? With Mark, if it could happen, it would. But I went anyway. I called him before I left to reassure us both that I would be there if he needed me, then flew out of Newark Airport.

I had never seen the Rocky Mountains and the sight of them, rising misty purple, over the city of Boulder took my breath away. As they soared above me, I felt as if I was standing in the presence of something far greater than myself and immediately I felt better, more able to put things in perspective. I hadn't realized how much I needed to get away, to escape for a few days the constant tension and turmoil my life had become. Somehow I had come to accept the perpetual upheaval as normal and the sight of the majestic and ancient mountains reminded me that peace and tranquility are also a normal part of life. I promised myself I would remember that and try to give myself a few minutes of the Rocky Mountains every day at home.

I kept in constant phone contact with Doug. Mark was adjusting to the hospital better than we had expected. Of course, he wasn't happy to be there, but he wasn't fighting it either. The doctor in charge of Mark's case assured Doug that Mark was behaving in a friendly, co-operative manner. I kept my fingers crossed. I no longer hoped for miracles, minor improvements in maturity were enough. One day at a time had become my motto.

I was anxious to learn as much as I could at the training institute. I kept notes, read the books we were given and took from the seminars what I hoped would be helpful information for our members, although Mark was always on my mind, making it more difficult to focus solely on the training sessions. Alone in my hotel room, I organized my notes into a short paper which I planned to present to S.P.A.C.E. at the August 9th meeting back home. I wanted to share with them the new knowledge I had gained at the conference.

I had learned that placement in a residential school or institution was not the only recourse for a child experiencing a severe emotional disturbance. I, also, learned that the lack of services and programs for emotionally ill children in New Jersey is common to the nation as a whole. This was evident in the representation of professionals and parents from twenty-nine states. The purpose of the Training Institute was not to gain funding to build new facilities, but to deinstitutionalize seriously emotionally ill children to the least restrictive environment, preferably at home and in their own communities. The overall emphasis was on keeping the family together.

Although I agreed in principle, the major criticism I had with the home-based programs were that they seemed to be geared to a single treatment option. Most disabled children experience crisis situations frequently and need help whenever they occur as well as needing help through different developmental stages of their lives. If a home-based service was to be truly successful, it must include a variety of treatment options appropriate to the need and level of crisis. The knowledge of having a back-up program in times of need would lessen the intensity of isolation these families feel and as a result of providing a complete range of services, the need for out-of-home placements would diminish.

I wanted to emphasize that even with home-based programs many children would still need to be hospitalized or would need placement in residential facilities for extended periods of time. By reducing the number of beds in hospitals and emphasizing the home-based programs, the cliché "putting all your eggs in one basket" seemed appropriate. The transition of treatment must take place over extended periods of time with close and ongoing monitoring as to the actual success rate of home-based services. Hundreds of children were still attending schools out of state. A combination of new facilities for those who needed supervised care and new programs for community based intervention seemed the best hope for our disabled children.

Shortly after returning home, I visited Mark for the first time since he had been admitted to Trenton Psychiatric Hospital. He told me they were doing the same old tests and he was tired of them. He knew the answers they wanted. If he felt like giving them the right answers he would; if he didn't he'd talk about something else and ignore the tests completely. He also told me he wasn't getting along with the other adolescents on the ward. Some of them were tough and since he was skinny and wouldn't back down, they picked on him. He was being scapegoated, but he said he was working on this in therapy and could he please go home now. I told him no, that he probably wouldn't be able to go home for quite a while. I did not tell him that an involuntary commitment hearing was scheduled for August 3rd.

When I had received notification of the commitment hearing, I had called Mark's social worker, and told him that scheduling problems made it impossible for me to arrive in Trenton before 10:00. I requested that he either reschedule for another day or push Mark's hearing back until after ten on that date. No problem, he told me. He could schedule the hearings so Mark's would be the last one heard.

Doug and I arrived at exactly ten that morning. We hurried to the meeting room and stopped dead in the doorway. The room was empty. I looked at Doug, then reached in my purse and rechecked the notice. Yes, we had the right date. We waited for a few minutes, but when it became obvious that no one was going to be arriving, we went in search of Mark's social worker. We tracked him down after a brief search. The hearing had been held early because there had been only a few commitment cases to be heard. The judge couldn't wait around for us to arrive.

"What was the judgment?" I asked.

"Discharged pending placement," he said.

"But that can't be. The recommendation from Timber Ridge and St. Clare's clearly says he needs a twenty-four hour secure environment. Isn't that why he's here now? And where are you going to place him? I've searched years for a residential placement for him and, when I finally did find one, he wouldn't stay. You know all this. You've read his papers."

"All I can do is suggest you write to Judge Farkas and request another hearing," he said. "In the meantime, I'll be working on finding Mark a placement in a residential program."

"Good luck," I said as I slammed out of the office.

"What is it going to take to make people understand that Mark doesn't have the ability to make it on his own in the world?" I asked Doug as we drove home in the heat of late summer. "Does he have to be badly hurt, beaten up, or involve other people in a car accident for someone to listen to me. Do they think I'm lying? Even when I show them the evidence I've collected over the years, they still don't listen. I don't want to lock my son up, but there are just too many pitfalls for him to stumble into that could make his life a living hell. I want to prevent that from happening. But every time I think I'm making progress, some well-intentioned, but misguided person sends us back to the start. Another unsecured program and another twenty runaways and another twenty chances for him to get molested, hurt or even killed. What is so difficult to understand? Mark isn't vicious, but he can't think before he acts. He doesn't understand consequences. He could hurt someone. Why won't they help us? What am I going to do?"

I wrote numerous letters requesting that I be allowed to attend the next hearing. In the meanwhile, Mark was having problems with some of the other patients on the ward. Toward the end of August, he fought with another young man and sustained a "boxer's injury", fractures to the fourth and fifth fingers on his right hand. His social worker told me that since Mark had shown no signs of escape behavior they had lifted the escape precautions and that his evaluation was scheduled for completion on the last day of August. Depending on the results and the success of finding a placement for him, he could be discharged within a month. Two months later Mark was still awaiting placement in a residential facility willing to have him.

Chapter Thirty-Three

Another meeting! Another program! We were shown into the usual small conference room and seated around a table with a few other parents of adolescent patients. A burly man was setting up a slide projector near the front. His skin was weathered and his eyes were creased at the corners as if he squinted a lot.

Great, I thought, now we have Buffalo Bill taming wild kids. I swallowed my bitterness and prepared to listen with a cynical ear. He threw up a slide of a wagon train and turned to address us.

"Among the Plains Indians, the rite of passage into adulthood was marked by a solitary wilderness experience, a quest for a vision that would guide a young boy into manhood," he began. "Alone in the wilderness, the youth learned to rely on the skills taught to him by his elders, took responsibility for his life, and accepted his adult status and responsibility for his tribe. Since 1973, Vision Quest National LTD. has been re-creating that experience for troubled, hostile youths who would otherwise be in hospitals or juvenile correctional institutions. Most of our kids have been in several institutions, have ten to fifteen arrests on their records and have been diagnosed as having behavior disorders. What we do here is give kids a rigorous experience in nature that lets them know they can complete what they start and make successful decisions."

He changed the slide, flipping onto the screen what looked like a tipi village. "The kids start out at Impact Camp where they have a chance to adjust to the requirements of the program. For some of our urban kids, this is quite a shock. They are required to be responsible for their living quarters, food and the tasks they will be assigned. Nature teaches them to accept the consequences of their own actions. If they set up their tipi improperly and it rains, they have to get up in the middle of the night and fix it. Blaming the problem on someone else doesn't give them a warm, dry place to sleep. Fixing the tipi does. At Impact Camp, the kids receive schooling and counseling as well as instruction in the survival skills needed for the second phase of our program, the Quests.

Each youngster is required to participate in Quests which might be a three week tour through a national forest, or a cross-country horseback expedition or participation in our Buffalo Soldier program which fosters pride and community involvement. Youngsters who participate in our program know they are not allowed to take drugs, drink alcohol, have sexual relations or run away. If the kids do not perform up to expectation or begin to "act out" they are confronted by one or more senior staff members in an attempt to get them to deal with their behavior. We've been criticized for our confrontational style, but this is a tough program dealing with tough kids who have to learn to respect themselves and others. We use no locked doors, physical restraints or medication to control our kids.

Youths who have been institutionalized learn to use hysteria, anger and suicide gestures as emotional releases and may welcome medication or being strapped to a bed because it eliminates the need to make choices and face up to the consequences of those choices. We don't allow that. We confront them and make them understand that they are making choices all the time. Wrong choices bring consequences for them just like for everyone else in life. And no, we don't beat the kids up, but if they come at us physically, we will physically restrain them."

He had been showing us slides of the various activities the kids would participate in while he talked. Now he threw up the original picture of a wagon train winding its way through green hills with snow covered mountains in the background.

"During the course of their stay with us which usually lasts for 12 to 18 months they will take authentic Wagon Train journeys. Our trains usually have ten to twelve mule-drawn wagons and our trips last months. The kids learn a new sense of time and distance, experience the beauty and the demands of living in the wild. Here again, kids learn to take responsibility for their lives because their actions have consequences. If you don't care for your mule properly, he's going to balk at pulling your wagon. The wagon train program mixes pioneering with survival skills as well as their regular schooling and counseling. Youngsters graduate from our program by completing a three week quest which includes a three day stress hike and a three day solo - the vision quest- which provides a chance for the kids to think about their lives, past, present and future. We are committed to turning these boys around and we are available to them twenty-four hours a day, seven days a week. Thank you for your attention. If you have questions, which I'm sure you do, please ask."

Mark was discharged from Trenton Psychiatric to Vision Quest. The program was expensive, but DYFS and the Clifton Board of Education agreed to pay their share, this time without the same difficulty as before since Vision Quest was already treating 66 other New Jersey kids. Mark would be staying at the Lodge Impact Camp in Franklin, Pennsylvania, near Pittsburgh for orientation. He was excited about the program and looked forward to leaving, his attitude better than I had ever seen it on the eve of a change. He talked incessantly about the animals and the freedom he would have there. I told him he couldn't run away. He wouldn't need to run away, he told me, because he'd be on the move, traveling all the time. Maybe that's the trick, I thought, my fingers crossed.

Our first set of reports were hopeful and his letters home filled with what he was doing, not the usual promises of better behavior if he could come home. His first quarter report card showed C's in his academic courses. His teachers commented that he showed no enthusiasm for schoolwork, but that when he applied himself he was successful. When it came to his outdoor tasks, he approached them with a willingness to learn that was wholly lacking in his academics. He spent as much time as he could outside. He was still having trouble getting along with others, either withdrawing from the group to be alone, or acting aggressively to put them off, but no real confrontations occurred. Doug and I both knew not to be overly enthusiastic. Mark always had a honeymoon period when he first started his programs. When he tired of the novelty, which he usually did quite rapidly, he reverted back to his old habits and ways of handling problems.

Mark didn't run away although he complained about the hardships of living outdoors when winter set in. He had been on several quests into the forests when temperatures had fallen below freezing and had been forced both to toughen up and to co-operate in the survival of the group. His problems with attention span made it difficult for him to complete tasks, but he was not being allowed to drift off. Staff members stayed with him making sure he did what he had been assigned to do. Mark had occasionally become belligerent with them, but the counselors had helped him work it out.

During the months while Mark was in the Lodge Impact Program in Franklin, Pennsylvania, I visited him every month. Mark was having trouble performing simple acts of personal hygiene. After fifteen years of daily reminders, he still did not remember to shower or wash his hair. When his counselors reminded him to shave or shower or brush his teeth, he complied willingly enough, but the next day they had to remind him again. He showed no signs of initiating any of the actions himself. But in other areas, he showed improvement and he had displayed no desire to run away. I kept my fingers crossed, but I did not exhale the long breath I had been holding ever since he had started Vision Quest. I knew it wasn't the program itself or the work of the teachers or counselors that was holding him there; it was the animals and the opportunity to join the wagon train. He wanted to take care of the horses and mules on the journey and, within limits, he was willing to do what he had to do to get that chance. The mule dangled the carrot in front of Mark and not the other way around.

He had been approved for the East Coast Wagon Train which was currently traveling through the state of Tennessee. He would pick it up there and stay with it for several months. On my last visit to Pennsylvania I promised him that Nana and I would visit him as soon as the Wagon Train moved closer north.

I remained in contact with the Wagon Train as it slowly traveled the East Coast. Mark's short letters still took me a long time to decipher, the words almost impossible to read even phonetically. His report cards showed a C average but I wondered just what he had to do to attain a C. Individual Educational Programs were mailed to me periodically showing what goals Mark had accomplished and the new goals that had been set for him. I knew that these goals would not be long-term habits, but would disappear as soon as he left the therapeutic setting where the goals were daily, even hourly, reinforced. After fifteen years' experience with Mark, I knew his patterns intimately. I could only hope that some of the learning would accidentally land in a quadrant of the brain where, below the level of consciousness, it would take hold and become habit. I hoped for little else.

It was not until that summer that my mother and I were able to arrange a visit to the Wagon Train. We would fly out to Michigan, rent a car and hook up with Mark and the wagon train in a small town not far from Holland, Michigan.

I wasn't certain where the Wagon Train was encamped so after we had gone through several small towns, we stopped at one to ask directions. The main street consisted of a few clapboard houses, painted white, a luncheonette, a laundromat, one or two bars and the usual country store where you could buy anything from Pepto Bismal to cattle feed. I parked in front of the Laundromat so we could stretch our legs. My mother laughed.

"As long as there's one of these around, Mark should feel right at home," she said.

I crossed myself. "God, don't listen to that."

"Should we ask one of the local folks in the luncheonette where the Wagon Train is camped," she asked.

"Just so long as we don't have to eat there."

When I pulled open the chrome door, the local lunch crowd looked up. I could tell by their startled expressions that they didn't get much out-of-town company there. Everyone looked at us expectantly. Nobody said anything. I walked up to the waitress behind the counter and asked, "Would you happen to know where the Vision Quest Wagon Train is camped?"

She stared at me blankly. Just when I had begun wondering if she had heard the question, she shrugged. "Any of you boys know anything about a wagon train?" she said.

More shrugs, then someone from a table near the back pointed toward the door. I looked over my shoulder. A police car had pulled up beside our rental.

"I'm sure he would know," I said to no one in particular. It was my excuse to leave the restaurant without buying something. When we left I could see the disappointment settling into their faces. We had provided them with some amusement, but not enough to give them something to talk about for days.

The town's single law enforcement officer knew nothing about the Wagon Train, but he volunteered to help us find it. We followed him to the one room police department at the end of the block where he made a few phone calls. Finally he pinpointed the location which he marked for us on our map. We still had a ride of about ten miles through open country.

As we neared the camp, I understood better the definition of wilderness. We had driven miles without seeing another living soul, not even a house or a barn. I thought of my home, with its neat 140x50 foot lot, and houses so close you could reach out your window and practically touch the window of your next door neighbor.

"You know, Mom, maybe this is where Mark belongs. Maybe the constant stimulation of the metropolitan area, the fast pace and constant change is bad for him. Somewhere like this, he might fit in better. He can spend most of his time outdoors with his animals and have plenty of room to wander without running away."

"Do you remember what the neurologist told you?" she asked.

"Which one?" Mark had been evaluated by so many doctors over the years that it was beginning to be difficult to remember who had said what.

"The one who told you that if Mark was his son, he would buy him a couple of acres and some animals, leave him there and let him make his own way."

I did remember and, at the time, I thought it was a harsh judgment, but that was before we had been through all the programs that had promised to help him adjust to society. Now I wondered if it wouldn't be kinder to let him take his chances in a survival situation.

We located the Wagon Train in a large clearing at the end of a dirt road. Covered wagons with billowing white canvas tops stood in a circle unhitched, the mules and horses in a quickly constructed corral. Several young men briskly went about their cooking chores while others were seated on stumps listening to an older man, obviously a counselor or teacher. We stood watching them for a while. I did not spot Mark among those closest to us.

"We're supposed to check in with the Wagon Master," I said. "He knows we're coming, but I couldn't give him an exact time. He could probably tell us where to find Mark."

Mom and I picked our way carefully over the rutted ground. Neither of us was exactly the outdoor type, but we were game. When we neared the circle of wagons, a man approached us politely, then brought us to Gil Spikes, the Wagon Master. I was anxious to find Mark, but Mr. Spikes hesitated and asked us to be seated. The wagon was not exactly spacious and the interior had a filtered twilight look. I sat down on a small bench and folded my hands. With all my heart

355

I hoped he wasn't going to tell me that Mark had run away and we had traveled all this way for nothing. I steeled myself. Instead he talked about Mark's love for the mules and his pride in taking care of them, but I knew he was leading up to something.

"Has something happened?" I asked.

He told us that Mark had been trying to force one of the mules to move by slapping him on the rump. The mule had lashed out and kicked Mark in the knee. Mark had told no one of the incident, but when he'd started limping badly, his treatment counselor had noticed. Mark had a painful bruise which was being treated. Nothing to be concerned about, he said. He just mentioned it because he didn't want us to be surprised by the way Mark was walking. When he'd finished talking, he pointed us toward the corral.

I caught a fleeting glimpse of Mark, a moment's impression, before he caught sight of us and came limping over. I looked over at my mother and saw the bewilderment on her face. Mark looked like a poster boy for poor hygiene. He had not remembered to shave and his acne burned his face red and raw. His T-shirt was stained under the arms and the front had a smear I could swear was manure. His face was drawn with the pain of walking, but he was obviously proud of the huge cowboy hat he was wearing. He shook hands in a manly way with my mother and me and led us slowly over to the wagon he shared with several other young men. I reminded myself of my vow not to over-react.

"How's your leg?" I asked, attempting to sound casual.

Mark looked down, his expression conflicted. He almost never cried and rarely admitted to pain of any kind, physically or emotionally. He rolled up his too large pant leg to show me a huge purple and blue bruise.

"It's getting better," he said at last. "It was really bad at first, but it's getting better. I can do my chores now and they didn't stop letting me take care of the mules."

For the rest of the afternoon, Mark showed us around camp. He was perfectly willing to talk about the tasks each of the boys had to perform to keep things running smoothly though often he drifted back to what he had learned about mules. He was not interested in his academic subjects, but he had a wide knowledge of animal lore. He knew everything from the feeding to the mating habits of horses and mules. Why could he remember all that and not how to spell simple words or read simple sentences?

I spoke with his treatment director, counselors and teachers. Mark was still having problems getting along with others, problems he wouldn't admit or discuss in group counseling sessions or individually. He showed little interest in school and in improving his hygiene habits. Same problems, no solutions, but they all felt that Mark was happy at Vision Quest and that the life skills he was learning would help him in the long run.

We ate with the wagon train that evening. I noticed that Mark still hoarded his food, eating rapidly the first few bites, then quickly losing interest. I resisted the temptation to urge him to swallow a few more bites. I thought of all the years, all the hundreds of meals that had turned dinner into a constantly recurring nightmare for all of us. All the coaxing and yelling and instructions on table manners and he ate the way he had when he was three years old. He was painfully thin, burned to a match by the hyper-activity that kept him constantly on the move and he still had no table manners. I was the one who had learned, not Mark. I had learned that criticizing him would do nothing but bring on sulks and cause him to run. When dinner ended and he showed signs of restlessness, we said good-bye and left for the small motel where we had previously called for reservations. Our visit had been more successful than I had hoped and except for the bruised knee, Mark looked content. He had found a place with the Wagon Train and I hoped it was a place he'd be content to stay.

Mark traveled with the train for the remainder of his eighteen month stay at Vision Quest, returning home only once to attend Cheryl's wedding. Mark successfully completed all the phases of the program, but he was still not ready to return to a less heavily supervised environment. He was scheduled to be discharged from Vision Quest National into their New Jersey Transitional Living Program. At the Transitional Living Program he would enroll in community based special education classes for reading and they would help him find manual labor employment. He would be supervised while learning real life skills based on the skills he had learned during his wilderness living phase. Skills like completing tasks, being responsible, getting along with co-workers, accepting team goals, handling money appropriately and others.

Mark ran away from the Supervised Transitional Living Program. The next day he called the Resources Coordinator and told him that he was in Virginia with a friend and that he would not go back to the group home. He returned to Clifton the following week and nothing I said would convince him to go back. He threatened to run away if he was forced to return to the Transitional Learning Center. He would not explain why. DYFS discharged him into my care. I called Vision Quest to ask if they would employ Mark to work in their program teaching other kids to care for the mules. Although he was very good with the animals and he could be trusted with their welfare, he had not advanced enough in other areas for such a responsible position. He was now nineteen, uneducated, unemployed and past the age for residential juvenile placement. This time, we were further back than when we started.

Chapter Thirty-Four

For a few weeks, Mark made an effort to settle down. He found work mowing lawns for neighbors on our street and my Dad got him a job cleaning beach umbrellas at the local swim club. My father still had a way with Mark. He was able to turn Mark's anger aside with a joke or to explain what was required of him over and over again without losing patience. But my Dad had been diagnosed with melanoma and his battle with the disease had left him weak. Mark began to take more than he had left to give.

Without my Dad to give him guidance, Mark lost his job at the swim club and took off again, this time with a carnival he had picked up at the Meadowlands Sports Complex. He had been missing a few days when he called to tell me that he had a job with the carnival and that he had his own place there.

"You've got to come see where I live. It's great." he said.

I went, not because I believed him, but to make sure he was all right. He met me near where the trucks were parked and showed me into one of them. The interior of the truck was divided into sections and each section had a little cot for sleeping. Mark pointed to his section, his eyes alight in the semi-dark of the windowless compartment. I was appalled, but I kept my opinion to myself. We had always lived a decent lifestyle in a home that was clean and well cared for. Even when we had rented the apartment in Nutley, I had made sure it was as homey and comfortable as I could make it. What Mark saw in this dump of a truck to get so excited about, I couldn't understand. Maybe he felt a part of the carnival family, accepted there when he was so often rejected elsewhere. I tried to be as encouraging as I could even though I still wanted to wipe the ketchup from the corner of his mouth and run a comb through his tangled hair. I kept my napkin, comb and comments to myself.

He traveled as a Carney for a while, calling me from the road now and then to check in. He had been gone a month when my Dad took a serious turn for the worse. We knew by now his cancer was terminal. The doctors couldn't tell us how long he had, but we all knew that it wasn't long. The next time Mark called in I told him about Grandpa and asked him to please come home. He said he would have the carnival caravan drop him as close to home as they could and he would call us from wherever he was.

Three days later he called me from a rest stop on the New York Thruway near Nyack, New York. My dad was in the hospital and I knew my Mom needed a break. I phoned the hospital and asked her if she wanted to take a short ride with me. I could hear her talking to my dad. She had been with him since he had been admitted and she didn't want to leave him. But she was exhausted and we both knew she needed to get away for a little while. Finally, my Dad was able to argue her into it.

I picked her up at Veteran's Hospital and together we went to meet Mark. I had no trouble finding the restaurant and just prayed that Mark hadn't become restless during the hour drive and decided to hitchhike home. My mom and I entered the crowded restaurant and tried to spot Mark at one of the tables. The rest stop was crowded and, at first, it was hard to distinguish faces.

Suddenly, my mother grabbed my arm and pointed to the back of the large dining area. Mark was making his way toward us down the aisle. His T-shirt was ripped, his pants baggy and frayed at both knees and his long hair was covered with a coonskin cap complete with hanging tail.

Convulsed with laughter, my mother pointed to his hat. "Something's moving in there," she gasped. "If I didn't know better, I'd swear it was chickens."

The straight face I was trying to keep dissolved and the laughter bubbled up and escaped in helpless giggles. Sure enough, Mark had four baby chicks tucked into the fold in his coonskin cap and one fully grown chicken perched on his shoulder. All over the restaurant, people were pointing and laughing. The closer he got the harder we laughed.

Before he could say hello, we had him out of the restaurant and into the car. "What am I going to do with my chickens?" he asked. "I can't leave them here. They're just babies."

I took a good look at him then and noticed for the first time that he had nothing with him except what he was wearing. His clothes, his Walkman and tapes and everything else he had taken from home to put in his sleeping section were gone, but he had his chickens and that was all he cared about.

We took the chickens home with us in the car and built a coop for them in the backyard. When my Dad died, the chickens were a better comfort for Mark than Doug and I could ever be.

Mark was heartbroken over my father's death. Of all the members of our family, Mark had had the warmest, most trusting relationship with my father. With his loss, Mark began drifting further away, lost in his private world of grief and confusion. He spent his time wandering aimlessly, staying out all night with friends who expected nothing from him and who cared nothing about him.

In January of the following year, he was accepted for vocational training at the West Essex Vocational/Rehabilitation Center. The Clifton Board of Education accepted the responsibility for tuition and for transportation. The night before Mark was to begin this new program, I sat with him at the kitchen table.

"Mark, what do you want to do with your life? Have you ever thought about what kind of life you want?"

"Yeah, I just want people to leave me alone."

"But how will you support yourself? How will you live if you can't learn a skill or hold a job? Every job you've ever had you lost because you get into trouble or can't pay attention to what you're doing."

"Don't worry about it. I've lived all right so far." He lit another cigarette from the one he had been smoking.

"That's because Daddy and I have supported you and bailed you out of trouble. We can't and won't keep doing this."

"I'll make out. Don't worry."

"Will you at least try to learn the jobs they'll be teaching you at this new school? If you do, you might be able to find work and have your own money for an apartment or whatever else you want."

He jumped up and started for the door. I didn't stop him. I'd said all I meant to say. Whether he heard it or not, I couldn't tell. I didn't know how far his thought processes went. My dad had once said that in order to understand Mark you had to try to imagine what it was like to be trapped inside the confusion of his mind, constantly battling to understand things most of us took for granted. Mark worked harder than all of us with far less result. I knew his frustration was terrible. More than that I could only imagine.

Mark remained at West Essex Vocational Center until March when he was asked to leave. His discharge report stated that,

[Mark] has evidenced an extreme amount of difficulty adhering to the structure of this work setting. Based on our observation of [Mark's] behavior in this setting, we conclude that he is unable to meet the demands of working at this time. Behaviorally, [Mark] does not possess the control to work successfully within the setting that sets boundaries or limitations for him. He is extremely defiant and resistant to authority and/or supervision.

[Mark] is very immature emotionally and acts very impulsively with no concern or forethought as to the possible consequences of his behavior. He lacks good judgment and has very weak decision making skills. As well, [Mark] has evidenced a very low frustration tolerance and limited coping skills. When he has becomes angry or frustrated within this setting,[Mark] has responded by becoming verbally aggressive and abusive as well as by threatening staff members and co-workers. Although the issue of whether [Mark] would carry out any of his threats is questionable, he was quite intimidating to his fellow program participants. [Mark] seemed to enjoy intimidating others and to thrive on the negative attention he received as a result of doing so.

When [Mark] has been confronted about his inappropriate and unacceptable behaviors, he became very angry and defensive. It had been apparent that [Mark] lacks insight and has no real awareness of the negative impact his behavior will have on his ability to succeed vocationally. Examples of some of the inappropriate behaviors that have been exhibited by Mark include: bringing beer to work; carrying a knife at work and boasting about using it to harm someone after work; threatening co-workers with bodily harm because he assumed they had "told on him"; using abusive language toward staff and co-workers; refusing to work in certain work areas; playing his radio extremely loud in the building despite having been told repeatedly not to; speaking defiantly and disrespectfully toward staff members; shouting out in his work area and disrupting others, etc.

It is felt that [Mark] has quite severe emotional problems that must be addressed before he could ever again pursue vocational training or job placement.

Unemployed and unemployable, uneducated and uneducable, Mark took to the streets again. By April he had moved out completely, coming home occasionally to visit or for a meal. When I asked him where he was sleeping, he said he had moved in with a friend and his mother in a neighboring town. His friend was also developmentally disabled and his mother thought it might be good for the boys to pal around together since she was working and her son was alone much of the time.

There was no point saying that Mark couldn't stay there. I had no jurisdiction over him because he was nearly twenty though I was still pursuing the possibility of a supervised residential facility for adults. The cost of residential care was enormous, far more than Doug and I could ever pay. I had applied for help from the Department of Developmental Disabilities. I was in the process of having Mark reevaluated again, but that involved getting new medical, academic and psychological tests done and that took time.

He had also started going to Social Connections, a drop in center in Clifton for people with mental health problems. Mark enjoyed going because there was no pressure there to conform to anyone else's expectations, no lessons to learn, no tasks to perform. People could socialize on their own level, play pool, get together with friends, play games and have fun. Mark went a few times a week when he felt like it. Sometimes he dropped by the house on his way there for a short visit. Since he was unable to read or write, he was unable to obtain a driver's license, but as in the past, that did not stop Mark from traveling. He walked wherever he could and if the distance was too great, he found a bicycle to ride.

Spring was late that year, the cold weather lasting until well after Easter, but finally, by the end of May, the weather had turned and we had a string of beautiful clear days. Doug was working evenings and Cheryl had called to see if I wanted to have a barbeque. She would bring her sons down and we could spend some quiet family time together. We arranged to get together on Wednesday of that week. I marked the calendar for May 29th. I thought about calling Mark, then decided against it. Cheryl and her husband and children had moved about forty minutes away and, although we tried to get together as often as possible, I didn't spend much alone time with her any more.

Wednesday evening was beautiful, mild and fragrant with the smells of spring. While the boys played in the backyard, Cheryl and I made some quick salads and grilled a steak. I had gone inside to put the coffee on when I heard the boys shouting and laughing. Cheryl signaled me from the window.

"Guess who's here?" She gestured with her thumb, but I had already seen Mark roughhousing with the boys.

"Hey, stranger. You want to eat. We've got steak," I called out the window.

He was still so thin and slight he didn't look much older than my grandsons and it occurred to me that developmentally, he really wasn't that much older. He bolted down a few bites of food and jumped up from the table.

"Well, I'm off. Just wanted to say hello."

"Where you going in such a hurry?" I asked out of habit. Mark had been living on his own for months and I didn't call every night to find out where he was, but for once, he didn't act as if I was meddling.

"Social Connections. I want to check out the girls there."

He jumped on his bike, his smile both sweet and mischievous and he was gone.

"He still blows in and out like a hurricane and he still makes me restless. Do you want to take the boys for a walk around the neighborhood before I take them home? Maybe they'll sleep in the car and give me some peace." Cheryl collected the plates and utensils we had used and I started washing them.

I had just slipped into a light sweater when the side doorbell rang. When I answered the summons, two men who were obviously plainclothes police asked to speak with Mark. The familiar clenching feeling near my heart took hold and I couldn't breathe easily. Cheryl came to stand by my side and together we tried to discover what Mark had done. They wouldn't tell us. We only want to talk with him was the response we received to every question. I saw two other plain clothes men standing near the back of the house.

Dear God, what has he done that they need to surround my house, I prayed. I didn't know what to do. If I refused to tell them where he was, would I be arrested for obstructing justice? I felt paralyzed. I stood in the doorway with my mouth open, but no words found their way out. I looked at Cheryl and slowly she nodded. I knew what she was thinking-that they would find him eventually and if he was aware of their search, he might try to run. I still didn't know why they were looking for him, but if it was serious, I didn't want him to be hurt for resisting arrest.

After they left, I couldn't settle down. I paced the floor, watching the clock tick by minute after minute. Why didn't Mark come back? Why didn't someone call?

"Should we go down to the Clifton police station?" I asked.

Cheryl shook her head. "He might not even be there. And the officer that came to the door was from the Belleville Police so if they take him anywhere, it would be there."

I called around and spoke with his friends. No one knew where he was and no one had seen him after he had stopped by my house.

"Cheryl, I've got to do something. If I don't, I'll go crazy. Maybe we should take a ride to Social Connections. I can see if he's still there or if he's not, maybe someone will know where he is."

She shrugged. "I'll take a ride with you if you want. I'll stay in the car with the boys while you run in and see if he's there." I could tell from the tone of her voice that she was trying to control her anger and I remembered my promise that I would not drag any of my family members into my never ending nightmare with Mark. Cheryl had lived through so much of it with me. She deserved a break.

"Let me call the Belleville Police first. Maybe they can save us a useless trip."

After a long stall, they informed me that a Mark Graham had been picked up for questioning in connection with a sexual assault complaint.

"Cheryl," I said very calmly after I hung up the phone. "I think you should take the boys home now. I'm going to call your father and we'll handle it from here."

"Mom, if you need me…"

"Thanks, honey, but…"

The first calm that comes after a shock was beginning to wear off and I did not want to frighten her and the boys with the fury and panic that was beginning to crawl up my spine into my brain. I rushed her out the door and called Doug. He promised to come home right away.

I met him at the door, dressed to go. "If I allow myself to even think about this, no less discuss it, I'll be completely useless. I want to go to the Belleville Police Department and see if Mark's there and what we have to do to get him out if he is. I can't believe this is serious."

When we arrived at the Belleville Police station, Mark had already been arrested and was being taken to the Essex County Jail in Newark pending arraignment. We rushed home and called a friend who specialized in criminal law to visit Mark at the jail. I still didn't know what had happened.

"How bad is it?" I asked the lawyer when we met for the first time. For the last few days, I had suffered all a mother could when faced with the blackest nightmare of her life. I had cried and prayed and made bargains with God. Now I needed to know what I had to do to help my son.

"The prosecutor has what amounts to a confession," he said. "When the police picked up Mark they told him they only wanted to ask him some questions. They asked. Mark answered. Did he understand what he was doing? I don't think so, but there's no way of proving that. Mark is slow, but not to the point where we can argue that he is incapable of understanding the situation. The police did read him his Miranda Rights but, once again, did he understand that he could have an attorney present before answering any questions." He shrugged. "Anyway, the story in a nutshell is that Mark met a girl through a friend. It seems this friend was dating another girl and the four of them went out on a couple of dates. Mark now considered the young lady his girlfriend. According to Mark, the girl asked him if he wanted to "make it" with her. Mark didn't say no, even when the girl asked if her friend could come along and watch. The friend said she would pay a dollar if she could watch.

They went to an abandoned building and one thing led to another. When they started having intercourse, the girl told Mark he was hurting her. Mark claims that he immediately withdrew and they all went home. But the girl who had been watching was frightened by what happened. She waited a few weeks then told her teacher who called the police."

He hesitated as if thinking about his words, then shook his head slightly. "The girl that Mark had intercourse with was only twelve years old. Mark claims he didn't know that. I believe him. I'm just not sure it's going to make any difference whether he knew it or not. He's already admitted to having sex with her."

"So what are our options?" I asked.

"First, we need to bail Mark out. Once that's taken care of..."

I raised my hand to stop him. "This may sound harsh to you, but my husband and I have discussed this and we both agree that bailing Mark out would only add to his troubles. He cannot understand the difference between right and wrong as you can see from your discussion with him. He could get out tomorrow and do the same thing the next day, not maliciously, but because he doesn't understand that what he did was wrong. He was having sex just like thousands of twenty-year olds do every night in some motel, park or the back seat of a car. It doesn't matter to him if the girl is twelve or twenty-five. He doesn't know the difference and he'd never think to ask. I want Mark released to a residential facility not back out on the streets."

Our lawyer promised to do his best, but Mark was not released, nor was he scheduled for a hearing. I could not understand the reason for the delay. On August 29th after making many phone calls to officials in the criminal justice system, I wrote the following letter to Warden James Turing.

Dear Warden,

First of all, I'd like to thank you in advance for taking time to read this letter. The following is a brief synopsis of my son, [Mark Graham], age 20 and the ordeal of the last three months. Mark was arrested on May 29th at the Passaic County Mental Health Building by Belleville and Clifton Police. He was charged with aggravated sexual assault and within a short time, he was transferred to Essex County Jail. Within a week, he was again transferred to protective custody after I advised the county office of his altercation with other inmates in the form of them throwing a blanket over him and punching him around as well as threatening him with rape. For nearly two months, for his own protection/safety, he has been locked up nearly twenty three hours a day. No fresh air, no exercise, no diversion. He smokes and traps mice and roaches for pets. It certainly is a good thing for him that he loves animals and insects. These conditions are inhumane and deplorable.

Your question may be - why didn't I bail him out? Simply because [Mark] cannot be trusted with any responsibility and cannot be relied upon to appear in court. He is impossible to handle at home, is completely idle and is unable to work due to his attention deficit disorder and emotional disabilities. In the last five years, he has had eight psychiatric inpatient hospitalizations in several hospitals. He has a personality disorder, conduct disorder, extremely impaired judgment, borderline IQ, developmental disorder, no understanding or reasoning of cause and effect, poor impulse control and an academic level of education of approximately 2nd grade. Does he need long term, therapeutic residential care? Absolutely! He should qualify under the Division of Developmental Disabilities. Should he be punished for a crime which he hasn't even been indicted for yet? No! I have requested several times for an in-depth hospital evaluation through my calls as well as calls from the lawyer representing Mark. All to no avail. I have even had to call the prison to intercede for him to get aspirins for flu-like symptoms. He had already asked to see the nurse or doctor three times.

We have struggled with many systems over the years to find a proper placement for [Mark]. He's had several with no lasting effect or learning taking place. I have dealt with many bureaucracies in the past, but never with a system so backlogged and inefficient as the correctional system. The correctional officers are helpful and polite, for the most part, but they can only do so much. I realize that in this time of budget cuts and layoffs it only serves to make this system more dysfunctional, but isn't this one of the biggest crimes to do such an injustice to a human being by incarcerating those with severe problems and handicaps present since birth? We don't even treat prisoners of war with such disregard.

[Mark] requires a permanent placement in a therapeutic environment. He does not need more punishment. What a sad comment this is on such a great nation. It seems that no system can provide Mark with what he needs nor will any system take responsibility or initiative in this matter.

Sincerely,
Corraine Conaway

The struggle to get Mark released into a residential or treatment facility while trying to maintain him safely in prison began to take its toll on me. Gradually over the summer, I had started to feel that anything I needed to do was an effort. I blamed it on depression and exhaustion, but towards the beginning of September, I found it hard to even get out of bed. The exhaustion showed in my face. My skin was gray and I had black circles under my eyes. I continued to write letters and make phone calls on Mark's behalf, but I curtailed my activities for CICA and I napped whenever I could. I was working four days a week at a doctor's office, but I could barely drag myself through the day. One morning, so weak I had to fight myself to get up and take a shower, I stumbled into the bathroom. My legs were covered with blood just as they had been many years ago before I'd had the partial hysterectomy. I made an appointment with my gynecologist immediately.

He scheduled the usual tests. When he called a few days later and asked me to come in for a visit, I began to suspect it might be a cyst. I remembered the pain and recovery of the last operation. I didn't have time for that now. Like last time, it would have to wait until I had straightened out the situation with Mark. I continued to blame the unusual exhaustion on anxiety and depression, but my doctor didn't agree.

He referred me to a specialist in gynecology/oncology at St. Barnabas Hospital in Livingston, New Jersey. After two weeks of testing and a biopsy, the results confirmed a very rare form of cancer in the vaginal wall. At the time, only about 100 cases of this type of cancer had been reported and here I was one of the lucky ones.

Doug drove me home from the hospital. I could not have driven, blinded as I was, not by tears, but by rage. How dare such a thing happen to me? Hadn't I suffered enough? What more could I give to life? How much more could I endure?

For days I refused to speak about it, unwilling to accept the truth. If I pretended it wasn't true, I could make it go away. But my family wouldn't allow me to disappear into a haze of denial and depression. My oncologist wanted to begin treatment as soon as possible. He recommended several weeks of radiation to reduce the tumor. The sooner we begin the sooner it will be over, he told me.

Would it *all* be over soon? I wondered. Both my grandparents and my father had died of cancer. I walked around the house in a panic, exhausted but barely able to rest for fear that I would never wake up. As difficult as life had been, I had never thought of death. Now all I could think of was dying.

To divert myself from my fears while I was undergoing the radiation, I continued to try to interest someone in Mark's case. In October, he was finally indicted on two counts of aggravated sexual assault and two charges of endangering a minor. A plea of not guilty was entered at the time. Mark went back to jail and I continued with the radiation treatment for several more weeks, then entered the hospital for an implant. Another month revealed that the radiation had not worked. My only option was surgery.

Beside myself with fear, I entered the hospital in May for preliminary tests before surgery. When the surgeon came to my room, I prayed that the serious expression on his face was unrelated to the test results. When he sat down on the side of the bed and I looked into his eyes, I knew that those prayers had been in vain.

"I'm sorry but it looks like the cancer may have spread to the colon and bladder as well as the vaginal wall. I want you to be prepared for the worst. I'm not saying that all of this will happen, just that it might. If we find that the cancer has imbedded itself in these other organs, we will have to remove all or part of them. We may have to remove the colon, the bladder, the vaginal wall as well as your ovaries and whatever other tissues are involved. I know it's tough to face, but you may have to wear two bags, one for liquid and one for solid waste removal. Do you understand what I am telling you?"

I understood the words, but not the meaning. Some things you can deal with; others you can't. I didn't have time to go through stages of acceptance or to make my peace with God or myself or anyone. Either I was going to die or I wasn't and I had the faith to believe that it wasn't in my hands. My thoughts were no longer for myself, but for those I might be leaving behind.

The day before my surgery, I spoke with Doug and my mother and explained my wishes should anything happen to me. Their pain and fear were now greater than my own, but if I should die, I needed to know that Mark would be taken care of for the rest of his life. He could not take care of himself. He needed to be looked after. I kissed Cheryl and told her I loved her and asked her to tell the boys I loved them too. We prayed together and they left.

I was home from the hospital in less than two weeks. I still had my life. And on top of that, a life without an ileostomy or colostomy bag. The cancer, though extensive, had not intruded into the organs necessitating their removal. I was whole and intact, though so fragile I was afraid I would break if anyone so much as spoke a harsh word to me.

For several weeks I drifted through a haze of hurt, anger and exhaustion, leaving the business of life to Doug. I hadn't had the time to go through the stages of grieving before the surgery, but now that I knew I was going to live, the unfairness of it all threatened to overwhelm me. I was grateful for my life, grateful for the support of family and friends, but I didn't understand why my life held so much suffering. Maybe God had a reason, but believing that didn't help. I wanted an answer, any answer, though I knew there was none, or at least not one whose magnitude I could grasp. Painkillers and prayers got me through the days and slowly, I began to recover though I remained fragile for a long time.

Our finances became increasingly fragile as well. We had to terminate the services of Mark's private attorney and we applied for the Public Defender to represent Mark. In January, the attorney assigned to Mark's case recommended that I make a personal appeal to the Judge for action. A pre-trail disposition hearing was scheduled, but had to be postponed three times because of the heavy case load of the Public Defender's office.

Finally, in July, after Mark had been incarcerated for fourteen months, he was transferred to the Forensic Hospital in Trenton for a complete evaluation. No movement had been made toward finding him a residential placement. The hospital evaluation was to determine whether he was competent to stand trial. I was slowly and painfully regaining my strength, but I was still not strong enough to visit him there. I spoke to him often on the phone. He told me he had been assaulted twice by fellow inmates. Once a man had tried to gouge his eye out and another time he had been cut so badly he required stitches. Both my son and I were now in a desperate struggle for survival.

Mark was found competent to stand trial. His attorney immediately recommended that he plead guilty to one offense of first degree sexual assault. If he did, he would work out a plea with the prosecutor and Mark would probably not have to do any more jail time. The time he already had in would be used against the sentence and if they could get the judge to agree, he would be sentenced to five years with parole granted after two and time off for good behavior.

On November 25th, Mark was convicted of one count of aggravated sexual assault, a sentence that would stay with him for the rest of his life. Because of the mitigating circumstances of the case and the determination that Mark did not constitute a danger to the community, he was released on his own recognizance and into our custody for the Thanksgiving holidays with the stipulation that he return to Avenel Diagnostic Treatment Center. At Avenel he would be tested to determine whether his actions in committing the offense were characterized by a pattern of repetitive and compulsive behavior. If the examination revealed that this was so, the court would sentence him to Avenel for a program of specialized treatment. If not, he would be sentenced under normal procedures. The Judge asked Mark often whether he understood what was being said. Mark answered yes to every question, but I knew that he did not understand. He only wanted to be out of jail. Nothing that came before or after made any sense to him.

Everyone in the family was nervous about Mark coming home for Thanksgiving. Doug and I went to pick him up after making an appointment to have him tested at Avenel. The Judge had warned us that it might be months before Avenel would be able to take him because the backlog there was so great. He would remain in our custody until his appointment because sentencing could not take place until the Judge received the information from Avenel. I had warned the family that Mark was coming to dinner. No one knew how to act. No one knew how Mark would act. I was just as nervous as the rest. My recovery was progressing slowly, but I was still frail and in frequent discomfort. I knew that if Mark really acted up I could not cope with it. I didn't want to have to cope with it. I wanted a warm and comfortable holiday season to help me heal. Mark was always testing the limits and, because of my surgery, my limits were very narrow.

Mark was subdued during the holidays. His experiences in jail had frightened him enough to keep him from wanting to repeat them any time soon. He missed his grandfather as we all did, but most especially during the holiday season.

"Things just aren't the same without him to talk to." His eyes filled with tears and, for the first time in a long, long while, I saw again my little boy for whom I had so much hope. And once again, I wondered what it was like inside his jumbled up mind. Could he ever understand why he had been in prison? Would he ever learn that there were consequences to the impulsive actions he took?

Mark was examined at Avenel and sentenced on May 21st, two years after he had been arrested. In the interim months while we were waiting for sentencing, I had re-enrolled Mark in Social Connections and in the CrossOver program run by the Mental Health Association in Passaic County. CrossOver was an intensive case management program to support young people who were psychiatrically impaired. I had also petitioned the Division of Developmental Disabilities to re-open his case in the hope that they would be able to provide residential placement for Mark.

According to the law, Mark was sentenced to five years with a court recommendation of immediate parole. He had already served 546 days in jail which the Judge indicated was probably more time than most people would serve on an assault conviction on a five year sentence. But in order for Mark to be considered for parole, he had to return to custody for review by the parole board. The Judge recommended that he be placed in protective custody and transferred to the Garden State Youth Correctional Facility at Yardville and that his parole hearing be expedited. Despite that recommendation, Mark remained in Yardville until the beginning of September when he was finally paroled. Nearly three years and a conviction that would stay on his record for a lifetime because of a sexual seduction by a precocious child. I did not exonerate him nor make excuses for his action, but I was furious. Of all the systems that had failed Mark before, the Correctional System was the worst. I would not have believed the inefficiency and inhumanity I had encountered there if I had not lived it through my son.

Chapter Thirty-Five

Despite my best efforts, I could not keep Mark out of jail. Less than a year after his release from Yardville, he was arrested and charged with attempted aggravated sexual assault and supplying alcohol to minors. He was held in the West Milford Jail and bail was set at $100,000.

When I went to West Milford to discover what had happened, I was told that Mark had said something dirty. No touching, no sexual contact or physical involvement of any sort. I was dumbfounded. $100,000 bond for talking dirty? How was that possible? I could get no further information from the arresting officer and drove home in the soothing greyness of shock, detached from all feeling though my mind kept repeating the same question over and over. Why? Why? Why?

That night I lay awake, nestled in my numbing cocoon, my mind churning with scenes, both fantastical and factual. Maybe someone was out to ruin Mark. He had made some serious enemies in prison. Could they have set him up for a fall? Or maybe it was the manager of the trailer park where Mark was living. He had called several times to complain about the stray animals and excessive garbage around Mark's camper. Or perhaps the owner of the Rottweiler who had torn Mark's leg to ribbons last month and been arrested for the incident. Maybe it was his former girlfriend looking for revenge after he had trashed her apartment and left her for another woman. The list went on and on making less and less sense the more tired I became. I dozed around dawn, but was up a few hours later to begin researching lawyers who might be willing to take Mark's case.

I had just finished organizing the papers I thought would be needed when the phone rang. I had already spoken to my close friends and relatives to let them know what had happened just so I wouldn't be disturbed. I had also spoken to Mark on the phone that morning. He was distraught. He could not understand why he was back in jail. Over and over, he told me that he had never touched any girl. He had invited some kids over to the trailer park where he was living after they had asked him to buy them some beer at the local liquor store. Did he buy it? Maybe yes; maybe no. But even if he had, once again he had no idea how old the kids were. They looked about his age, he thought. I promised him I would visit him in the jail as soon as I could.

"Did you see the Herald and News this morning?" my neighbor asked, his voice thin and distant through the fog I still kept wrapped around me. He had just had his paper delivered.

"I think you'd better get a copy right away. Mark's on the front page and the article makes him sound like another Jesse Timmendequas. You know, the man who killed that poor little girl, Megan Kanka. They even mention Timmendequas in the article about Mark."

Before I had a chance to sit down and catch my breath, my neighbor brought over his copy of the paper. He did not stay long, seeing how distressed I was, but he squeezed my hand in sympathy as he was leaving. When I was alone again, I opened the folded paper to the front page. Mark's picture hit me square in the face along with an inflammatory headline labeling him as a sex offender accused of attacking a girl. But it was the second article, also on the front page, that filled my eyes with tears and bit into my chest like a knife. With no attempt to ascertain the facts, the reporter had branded Mark a habitual sexual offender who had been returned to society only to repeat the same heinous crime of sexual assault again.

Mark's arrest was detailed in the following paragraph followed by a review of unrelated sexual assaults, leading to the death of innocent children, including those of Megan Kanka, Amy Wengart and Divina Genao, who was kidnapped, raped and strangled by a man who allegedly lured the child from her home with a quarter. The article closed with a call for the legislature to enact new laws designed to stiffen penalties on previously convicted sex offenders so criminals would have less opportunity to continue their predatory behavior.

Slowly, the heat of my rage burned through the haze I had cloaked myself in since Mark's arrest bringing with it a painful clarity. I understood now why bail had been set so high. Mark had already been tried, convicted and sentenced by anticipated public outrage. He had been linked with rapists and murderers. He had been named a habitual sex offender when nothing about the circumstances of the first offense and nothing at all about the nature of the second offense had been investigated. He had not even been indicted and from what he had been telling me, there might not have been any offense at all beside the misdemeanor of obtaining alcohol for minors. I was determined that this twisting of the truth would not go unchallenged.

That afternoon, an equally damning article appeared in The Record. At least in this account, the reporter had made some attempt to gather facts though the implication was the same. Mark was labeled an unemployed drifter on parole who bought alcohol for minors and enticed them to parties at his trailer with the intent of sexually assaulting young girls.

I read the articles over twice, forming a plan of attack. My anger had turned cold, my mind sharp and clear as an icicle. I called Doug and asked him if he was aware that Mark had been tried and convicted in the local newspapers and that he was being written about in the same paragraph as Jesse Temmendequas and other rapists and murderers. He had not yet read the papers, but promised to send someone out for them right away. He called me back an hour later.

"Do we have grounds for a lawsuit?" I asked.

He wasn't very hopeful that such a suit would be successful since the reporters had said the magic word "alleged" when referring to the offenses Mark supposedly was involved in. No one said outright that he was a rapist or a murderer and, although linking him with convicted rapists and murderers implied that he was in the same category, there were no clear libelous statements to hang a case on.

"That's what I thought. Second question. Would you be willing to back me up if I asked a reporter to come and hear our side of the story?"

When he agreed, I called the North Jersey Herald and News. I knew they would send a reporter because Mark was front page news and because I offered them an exclusive. They agreed immediately and we set up a meeting at an attorney's office for the following afternoon. I spent the rest of that day and the following morning collecting the files I needed for documentation. At 1:30 Doug and I picked up my mother. As we drove through the tree lined streets and turned into the parking lot of our lawyer's office, I thought about how I wanted to present our story. I wanted to reach the hearts and minds of the readers. I wanted to put a human face to the man the papers had convicted without the knowledge of what he had suffered. What we all had suffered.

Joe Orlando, the Herald and News reporter, showed up exactly at the appointed time. I was still cold, almost numb with anger, but my thoughts were clear and organized. I wasn't looking to accuse or blame anyone, but I was determined that my voice be heard and that this distortion of the truth and apparent headline seeking by members of the West Milford Police Department not go unremarked.

We settled in a semi-circle around the desk, piles of folders containing evidence stacked next to my chair, a tape recorder on the desk. When Mr. Orlando nodded, I took a deep breath and began,

"I want to start on the evening Mark was arrested for aggravated sexual assault. Not this arrest, but the prior one. I want to start at the end because I want your readers to know that this is not a necessary nor inevitable conclusion to not only our life story, but their own. There are so many parents suffering and striving to get help for their disabled children who are falling through the cracks of our social service system. Perhaps if they read this story, it will give them the strength and motivation to say No to those who claim there is no help for their children. Change comes from those who will fight against the indifference of an overburdened, underfunded system. This story is for them not for Mark nor for me."

Slowly, painfully, I walked him through the evening Mark was arrested for aggravated sexual assault, how Cheryl and I had just finished dinner and were preparing to take a walk. I tried to make him see the two men standing on my doorstep, casual and cold, the flash of light on the badge and my sudden look of terror, a lifetime of pain communicated in a single second.

I told him how Doug and I watched the darkness deepen, waiting for the phone call that would surely come and how while I waited, I thought about how often I had feared this exact event, and how many times I had tried to get help for my troubled son. I spoke about the private learning specialists and the therapists, the hospitalizations and court hearings, the state agencies and special schools, the doctors and nutritionists, the police and the courts and how one by one they had failed to make any difference in Mark's life. I wondered aloud if there was anyone out there who could have made a difference, who might have prevented Mark from falling into the nightmare I had worked so hard to keep him from. I wondered...

He asked about Mark's history. I showed him the papers, one after another after another, fifteen years of varying diagnoses from developmentally disabled, learning disabled, intellectually impaired, emotionally disturbed, neurologically impaired to attention deficit hyperactivity disorder, paranoia, schizoid and anti-social personality disorders. I explained how his thought processes were characterized as random and that he was unaware of the consequences of his actions; that he was remorseless, wild, uncontrollable, untrainable.

When he questioned what solutions had been presented to address Mark's problems, I pulled from piles of paper and aging files, the same set of excuses couched in different language. Yes, he is developmentally disabled, but his IQ is not low enough to qualify him for the programs run by the Department of Developmental Disabilities. Yes, he is learning disabled, but he acts out and that disqualifies him for entrance into special schools that deal only with the well-behaved learning disabled student. Yes, he is emotionally disturbed, but he must attend the public junior high school, where he lasted less than one marking period. All the difficult positives in Mark's life translated into even more difficult negatives. No, we can't help you. No, we can't help you. No, we can't help you.

"And the worst of this is that Mark has been blamed for his inability to function in a society that does not understand his difficulties and has proven incapable of treating them. You see, Mark does not have the kind of dramatic disabilities that a physical problem thrusts on the public. He is not missing his arms or legs. He is not spastic or convulsive, nor does he have a facial abnormality. When he takes care of himself, he is a nice looking young man. But he can barely read or write or sit still for two minutes at any one time. He cannot make value or moral judgments, does not understand cause and effect, has no concept of right or wrong and therefore, cannot feel remorse for his actions. His behavior is directed by the impulse of the moment, not because he is defiant or mean. Just the opposite. Mark is a warm, affectionate, constantly forgiving young man, but one whose disabilities makes it impossible for him to anticipate the consequences of his behavior. He does not seek to hurt anyone, but he does not know before he acts that his behavior can and will be hurtful. He simply does not know because he is disabled.

Mark's disabilities have been diagnosed, tested, quantified and documented. But have they been effectively treated. No! And Mark is not alone in suffering a life where he has been forced to wander through the maze of bureaucratic dead-ends, crawling from one social institution to another because no one knows where he belongs. In my journey to find help for my son, I have met many other anguished parents who are stumbling along the same path, watching their children grow into dysfunctional adults, many of whom end up in state psychiatric hospitals or county prisons, not because they need hospitalization or imprisonment, but because there is no other place for them. These are not abusive or neglectful parents, but mothers and fathers with the same bright hopes for their sons and daughters that all loving parents cherish.

For me those bright hopes died when the phone call I had been waiting for finally came. Totally unaware of having done anything wrong, Mark was arrested and charged with the felony of aggravated sexual assault because he never thought, would never have thought, to ask the age of the girl who had asked him if he wanted to have sex with her…"

The next day an article, which would eventually win a major journalism award, appeared on the front page of the Herald and News. I read it carefully, studying the summary of my life as it appeared in print. I felt gratified, not healed, but gratified. Mr. Orlando had done an eloquent job of getting my point across and when, on January 27th, the grand jury failed to indict Mark on the sexual assault charge because of lack of evidence, a small part of my belief in the judicial system was returned to me. Mark remained in the Passaic County Jail in Paterson on the charge of supplying alcohol to minors. He was doubly anxious to leave the jail because his girlfriend, Wendy, was pregnant with his child. The baby was due the end of May and he wanted to be there for the birth.

The trial was postponed several times, the last time on the grounds that a private hearing was needed to protect the 12 juveniles subpoenaed to testify against Mark. By April, Mark had been in jail almost six months and the baby's due date was approaching. He was becoming frantic, unable to cope with the continued confinement and the memories of the horrors he had suffered during his previous sentence. He worried constantly about Wendy and the health of the baby and wanted desperately to be there to participate in the birth. Although it had been a mistake to plead guilty to his previous indictment, for the sake of Mark's mental and physical health, we agreed to a plea bargain and, on May 3rd, Mark pleaded guilty to the misdemeanor of possession of an open alcoholic beverage in a public place. He was given 18 months' probation, counseling and mandatory attendance at AA meetings.

On May 21st, after a difficult three day labor, Mark Graham, Jr. was born. He was a beautiful, healthy boy, perfectly formed and showing all signs of normal intelligence. In October, Mark and Wendy married. Since that time, Mark has had no involvement with the law. His love for and pride in his son is apparent, though he and Wendy are now divorced. He still cannot hold a job and his devotion to animals keeps him one step ahead of the health department, but he is participating in a new program and has not missed meetings with his probation officer or counselor. How long this will last no one can say. Perhaps it is love after all, a mother's love for her son and that son's love for his little boy, that can work the miracle that modern, multi-million dollar supported, highly credentialed educational and government agencies could or would not.

Made in the USA
Middletown, DE
11 May 2020

94558006R00227